Large–Scale Distributed Computing and Applications:

Models and Trends

Valentin Cristea
Politehnica University of Bucharest, Romania

Ciprian Dobre
Politehnica University of Bucharest, Romania

Corina Stratan
Politehnica University of Bucharest, Romania

Florin Pop
Politehnica University of Bucharest, Romania

Alexandru Costan
Politehnica University of Bucharest, Romania

T0338744

A volume in the Advances in Systems Analysis, Software Engineering, and High Performance Computing (ASASEHPC) Book Series

Information Science
REFERENCE
An Imprint of IGI Global

Director of Editorial Content:	Kristin Klinger
Director of Book Publications:	Julia Mosemann
Acquisitions Editor:	Lindsay Johnston
Development Editor:	Julia Mosemann
Publishing Assistant:	Sean Woznicki
Typesetter:	Tom Foley
Production Editor:	Jamie Snavely
Cover Design:	Lisa Tosheff

Published in the United States of America by
Information Science Reference (an imprint of IGI Global)
701 E. Chocolate Avenue
Hershey PA 17033
Tel: 717-533-8845
Fax: 717-533-8661
E-mail: cust@igi-global.com
Web site: http://www.igi-global.com

Library of Congress Cataloging-in-Publication Data

Large-scale distributed computing and applications: models and trends / by Valentin Cristea ... [et al.].
   p. cm.
  Includes bibliographical references and index.
  Summary: "The book has three overall objectives: offer a coherent and realistic image of today's research results in large scale distributed systems; explain state-of-the-art technological solutions for the main issues regarding large scale distributed systems; and presents the benefits of using large scale distributed systems and the development process of scientific and commercial distributed applications"--Provided by publisher.
   ISBN 978-1-61520-703-9 (hardcover) -- ISBN 978-1-61520-704-6 (ebook) 1. Electronic data processing--Distributed processing. 2. Large scale systems. 3. Computer networks. I. Cristea, Valentin.
  QA76.9.D5L37 2010
  004.6--dc22
                            2009040555

This book is published in the IGI Global book series Advances in Systems Analysis, Software Engineering, and High Performance Computing (ASASEHPC) Book Series (ISSN: 2327-3453; eISSN: 2327-3461)

British Cataloguing in Publication Data
A Cataloguing in Publication record for this book is available from the British Library.

Advances in Systems Analysis, Software Engineering, and High Performance Computing (ASASEHPC) Book Series

Vijayan Sugumaran
Oakland University, USA

ISSN: 2327-3453
EISSN: 2327-3461

MISSION

The theory and practice of computing applications and distributed systems has emerged as one of the key areas of research driving innovations in business, engineering, and science. The fields of software engineering, systems analysis, and high performance computing offer a wide range of applications and solutions in solving computational problems for any modern organization.

The **Advances in Systems Analysis, Software Engineering, and High Performance Computing (ASASEHPC) Book Series** brings together research in the areas of distributed computing, systems and software engineering, high performance computing, and service science. This collection of publications is useful for academics, researchers, and practitioners seeking the latest practices and knowledge in this field.

COVERAGE

- Computer Graphics
- Computer Networking
- Computer System Analysis
- Distributed Cloud Computing
- Enterprise Information Systems
- Metadata and Semantic Web
- Parallel Architectures
- Performance Modeling
- Software Engineering
- Virtual Data Systems

IGI Global is currently accepting manuscripts for publication within this series. To submit a proposal for a volume in this series, please contact our Acquisition Editors at Acquisitions@igi-global.com or visit: http://www.igi-global.com/publish/.

Titles in this Series

For a list of additional titles in this series, please visit: www.igi-global.com

Service-Driven Approaches to Architecture and Enterprise Integration
Raja Ramanathan (Independent Researcher, USA) and Kirtana Raja (Independent Researcher, USA)
Information Science Reference • copyright 2013 • 367pp • H/C (ISBN: 9781466641938) • US $195.00 (our price)

Progressions and Innovations in Model-Driven Software Engineering
Vicente García Díaz (Universidad de Oviedo, Spain) Juan Manuel Cueva Lovelle (University of Oviedo, Spain) B.
Cristina Pelayo García-Bustelo (University of Oviedo, Spain) and Oscar Sanjuan Martinez (University of Oviedo,
Spain)
Engineering Science Reference • copyright 2013 • 352pp • H/C (ISBN: 9781466642171) • US $195.00 (our price)

Knowledge-Based Processes in Software Development
Saqib Saeed (Bahria University Islamabad, Pakistan) and Izzat Alsmadi (Yarmouk University, Jordan)
Information Science Reference • copyright 2013 • 318pp • H/C (ISBN: 9781466642294) • US $195.00 (our price)

Distributed Computing Innovations for Business, Engineering, and Science
Alfred Waising Loo (Lingnan University, Hong Kong)
Information Science Reference • copyright 2013 • 369pp • H/C (ISBN: 9781466625334) • US $195.00 (our price)

Data Intensive Distributed Computing Challenges and Solutions for Large-scale Information Management
Tevfik Kosar (University at Buffalo, USA)
Information Science Reference • copyright 2012 • 352pp • H/C (ISBN: 9781615209712) • US $180.00 (our price)

Achieving Real-Time in Distributed Computing From Grids to Clouds
Dimosthenis Kyriazis (National Technical University of Athens, Greece) Theodora Varvarigou (National Technical
University of Athens, Greece) and Kleopatra G. Konstanteli (National Technical University of Athens, Greece)
Information Science Reference • copyright 2012 • 330pp • H/C (ISBN: 9781609608279) • US $195.00 (our price)

Principles and Applications of Distributed Event-Based Systems
Annika M. Hinze (University of Waikato, New Zealand) and Alejandro Buchmann (University of Waikato, New
Zealand)
Information Science Reference • copyright 2010 • 538pp • H/C (ISBN: 9781605666976) • US $180.00 (our price)

www.igi-global.com

701 E. Chocolate Ave., Hershey, PA 17033
Order online at www.igi-global.com or call 717-533-8845 x100
To place a standing order for titles released in this series, contact: cust@igi-global.com
Mon-Fri 8:00 am - 5:00 pm (est) or fax 24 hours a day 717-533-8661

Table of Contents

Preface

Many today's applications follow the distributed computing paradigm in which parts of the application are executed on different network-interconnected computers. Examples include Web browsing and searching, Internet banking, enterprise applications (for accounting, production scheduling, customer information management), and grid applications (for data intensive or compute intensive processing). The extension of these applications in terms of number of users or size led to the unprecedented increase of the scale of the infrastructure that supports them in terms of number and geographic dispersion of resources, number of services supported, number of administrative organizations involved, etc. The large scale distributed computing, which encompasses the concepts, models, patterns, technologies, systems, platforms, and applications, is the subject of this book.

Several motivations for using distributed systems exist: reducing the program execution time, increasing systems' reliability and fault tolerance, realizing the functional specialization, and exploiting the inherent parallelism of applications. There are some other advantages of using distributed systems such as price/performance ratio (it is cheaper to share common resources than buy equipment and software for exclusive use), easier user access to remote resources (the network supports the interconnection of users and resources), incremental growth (permits adding to existing infrastructure rather than completely replacing the existing resources with more powerful ones).

Designers face several challenges when conceiving and developing distributed systems. Most of them are related to what is called **transparency**, which means "make the distributed system appear as a single computer" (Tanenbaum & van Steen, 2007) to the user or to the application developer. Transparency has several facets that have been approached by specialists, and solutions have been proposed for hiding the resource replication and location, concurrent access to resources by several users, resource failure, resource migration, and others. Another challenge is the **openness**, which means the interoperation of components and systems by respecting the same set of rules. This allows easily extending the system with new services or moving the applications from one system to another without major modifications. Security is another important issue, which is related to the preservation of confidentiality, integrity and availability of the distributed systems and of their components. Finally, the **scalability** is the ability of the system to extend itself without dramatic performance penalties. This is the most problematic issue. The difficulties are due to the explosive growth of the number of users, the geographic dispersion of users, and the size of the applications. It's enough to look at distributed applications like searching the Web with Google, e-commerce applications on Amazon and eBay or the photo sharing application with Flickr to get an idea of this phenomenon. The solutions are based on extending the capacity and / or the number of resources to respond to the new higher requirements. In order to keep the performance unchanged, scaling is associated with new models and techniques such as: data replication, partitioning and distribution to support parallel transactions, caching to reduce the communication time required in data access, fast parallel transfer for file distribution, load balancing, code migration, and service replication for reducing the response time, etc. While several issues related to scalability are still waiting for adequate solutions, some of successful large scale distributed systems and platforms incorporate stable, proved, innovative concepts and implementations which might constitute the subject of a book on this domain.

Performance improvement is just one subject of the actual research in large scale distributed systems. Another important one refers to extending the functionality. Web 2.0, the second generation of web-based communities and hosted services (such as social-networking sites, wikis, blogs, etc.) aims to facilitate creativity, collaboration and knowledge sharing between users and opens up an incredible number of options for flexible web design, creative reuse and easier updates. Applications such as those found on Google, Amazon, and eBay are driving Web 2.0 processing to the end users computer, leveraging the idle distributed computing capability of web clients. We are entering the era of Distributed Internet Applications, which have all the benefits of desktop applications yet leverage the Internet while remaining easily deployable to a mass market.

Web 3.0 makes steps ahead towards the Semantic Web (W3C, 2009), which uses technologies like Resource Description Framework (RDF), The Extensible Markup Language (XML), and Web Ontology Language (OWL) to make the Web content more meaningful to programs (machines) not only to people. Another dimension is offered by the Internet of Things (Dodson, 2003), which aims at extending the action of the Internet from people to any thing. This is based on the micro-miniaturization of Radio-Frequency Identification (RFID) tags that are able to associate Ids with the Things they are attached to, and of sensors that are able to detect changes in the physical status of those Things.

Many applications that support scientific research in astronomy, biology, medicine, engineering, high-energy physics, environment and other fields are also data- and compute-intensive (Foster and Kesselman, 2004) at large scale. To respond to their requirements, which overpass the capabilities of single high performance computers, **Grid** infrastructures have been conceived and developed. A Grid encompasses resources of various kinds and sizes that are linked together in a large area network and are used collaboratively by people working on common projects. The policy is to use the resources on demand, with some restrictions related to resources' availability and applications' QoS (quality of service) requirements. Since this might claim for moving large volume of data over the network and running long jobs on Grid resources, the good operation of the Grid is achieved by the use of complex coordinated resource sharing strategies, very fast data transfers, very efficient error recovery procedures, and very easy user access to storage and computing facilities or services. Finding new, efficient solutions for these complicated problems has been and still is a challenge for the specialists in the domain of large scale distributed systems.

As an alternative to sharing their own resources, users can pay for and use resources offered by a provider. This is the idea behind the **cloud computing** concept. The cloud encompasses hardware and software computer resources in data centers, which are accessible remotely through the Internet. For example, Amazon (2009) sells different services such as storage, databases, queue, Web applications, and others. Support for Amazon Web Services development is also provided. Cloud computing faces problems that are similar to Grid computing. The difference is that resources in a cloud belong to a single authority, which makes simpler the administration of resources and services. On the other hand, companies can collaborate to offer services in a cloud. For example, Amazon has partners that build solutions using Amazon Web Services (Amazon, 2009).

Other large scale distributed applications are developed on **peer-to-peer** infrastructures that include nodes with similar capabilities that communicate directly to each other for exchanging information (data) and performing collaborative tasks. Examples include Gnutella (2009), Kazaa (2009), BitTorrent (2009), and Skype. Peers voluntary join specific system to offer some service or resources and look for the services and resources offered by other peers. Consequently, important issues of peer-to-peer systems relate to searching for specific resources or services, information monitoring, security, and reliability.

OBJECTIVES

The book has three overall objectives: offer a coherent and realistic image of today's research results in large scale distributed systems; explain state-of-the-art technological solutions for the main issues regarding large scale distributed systems, such as resource and data management, fault tolerance, security, monitoring, and controlling; and present the benefits of using large scale distributed systems and the development process of scientific and commercial distributed applications.

The book will also make readers familiar with new concepts and technologies that are successfully used in the implementation of today's large scale distributed systems or have a good chance to be used in future developments. The approach is to not separate the theoretical concepts concerning the design of large scale distributed systems from their impact in real-world environment. For each important topic that one should master, the book plays the roles of bridge between theory and practice and of instrument needed by professionals in their activity. To this aim, the topics are presented in a logical sequence, and the introduction of each topic is motivated by the need to respond to the claims of new distributed applications. The advantages and limitations of each model or technology in terms of capabilities and areas of applicability are presented as well. The case studies included in each chapter offer models of how to use these instruments in solving the problems of some large scale distributed systems.

CHAPTER BY CHAPTER PRESENTATION

Chapter 1, Introduction, addresses the definition, goals, and fundamental issues related to large scale distributed computing. The presentation takes a pragmatic approach. It starts from typical examples of actual large scale distributed systems, which cover the well known categories, such as Enterprise Information Systems, Peer-to-Peer Systems, Grids, Utility and Volunteer Computer Systems. For each category, the motivation of use, the requirements and the problems raised by their implementation are taken as a base for introducing specific concepts, models, paradigms, and technologies. The presentation, which follows a historical perspective on large scale distributed computing, creates the framework for introducing future trends in the domain and paves the way to approach the convergence issues toward the future Cyberinfrastructure. In the same time, the chapter introduces a comprehensive set of concepts that are developed in the next chapters.

Chapter 2, Architectures for Large Scale Distributed Systems, introduces the macroscopic views on the components and their inter-relations in distributed systems. The importance of the architecture for understanding, designing, implementing, and maintaining distributed systems is presented first. Then the currently used architectures and their derivatives are analyzed. The presentation refers to the client-server (with details about Multi-tiered, REST, Remote Evaluation, and Code-on-Demand architectures), hierarchical (with insights in the protocol oriented Grid architecture), peer-to-peer (with its versions: hierarchical, decentralized, distributed, and event-based integration architectures), and service-oriented architectures including OGSA (Open Grid Service Architecture). For each category, the chapter describes the model, presents the main issues and the actual research trends. Also it provides concrete cases of use in the actual distributed systems and platforms and clarifies the relation between the architecture and the enabling technology used in its instantiation. In addition, Chapter 2 frames the discussion in Chapters 3 to 10, which refer to specific components and services for large scale distributed systems.

In Chapter 3 we analyze current existing work in enabling high-performance communications in large scale distributed systems, presenting specific problems and existing solutions, as well as several future trends. By their nature, communication is an inherent aspect of every distributed application. Applications running in Grids, P2Ps and other types of large scale distributed systems have several specific communication requirements. For this reason we present the problem of delivering efficient communication in the case of P2P and Grid systems. The chapter starts with the review of high performance networks and technologies, where we analyze existing state-of-the-art solutions to enabling high quality communication over high speed networks. We present next peer-to-peer communication issues and solutions, moving on next to the specific requirements of the communication technologies in Grid systems. Also several patterns are analyzed from the point of view of semantics, methods and technologies. The chapter concludes with a presentation of the challenges in developing multicast and very high-speed communication software components.

Resource management is a central component in large scale systems. It can be implemented for a variety of architectures and services. Chapter 4 considers the management of distributed physical and virtual resources, and provides the requirements that are specific to large scale distributed system. Taxonomy of resource management methods is used to identify approaches followed in the implementation of actual systems, including Grids, and to discuss the solutions adopted in research and commercial platforms. The resource management system can support different users and resource owners' constraints, according to different policies. Obeying to one policy could ask the resource allocation mechanisms to solve a multi-criteria optimization problem. An important subject is related to agent frameworks for resource management, which offer mechanisms for distributes resources management. An important subject presented in this chapter is Agents Frameworks for resource management that offers a mechanism for distributed resources management. The chapter ends with presentation of WSRF (Web Services Resource Framework) that is the new solution for resources management based on SOA (OGSA – Open Grid Service Architecture).

Chapter 5 presents the task scheduling problem in large scale systems (with examples from Grid and Web- based systems). The scheduling models are analyzed based on systems architecture described in chapter 2. The chapter presents scheduling algorithms for independent and dependent tasks, and provides a critical analysis of the most important algorithms. The workflow scheduling algorithms are presented for complex application management in large scale systems. The new scheduling mechanisms, like resources co-allocation and advance reservation, multi-criteria optimization mechanisms for user and system constraints (e.g. load-balancing, minimization of execution time) are described and analyzed in this chapter. The Implementation issues for scheduler tools are also presented.

Chapter 6, Data Storage, Retrieval and Management, introduces specific issues related to data handling in distributed systems. The chapter approaches topics related to the challenging problem of storing large amounts of data in distributed environments and of retrieving them for further analysis. In this context, the problem of ensuring a fast and reliable data transfer becomes crucial and is extensively explored. The chapter further discusses key features for an efficient transfer solution to be used in large scale distributed systems and matches them with existing protocols and tools. The main problems of replication and consistency (that are related to issues like performance and fault tolerance) are discussed in the specific context of large scale distributed systems, highlighting particular models and solutions used there.

Chapter 7, Monitoring and Controlling Large Scale Systems, approaches the role, models, technologies and structure of a distributed monitoring platform. Monitoring is effectively used in many systems but has specific roles in Grids and other large scale distributed platforms. Monitoring data is used not only for services related to the past activity in these systems but also for prediction and learning purposes (e.g. scheduling further jobs according to a registered execution profile, avoiding bad schedules, and so on). The chapter discusses the challenges and requirements, the models used, the current architectures and specific solutions for all phases of the monitoring process: data production, data dissemination, data collection and presentation.

Chapter 8, Fault Tolerance, approaches the fault tolerance and other techniques used in the design of dependable distributed systems, a crucial characteristic for deploying highly-available, life-critical applications in modern large scale distributed systems. The chapter presents the special requirements for fault tolerance in large scale distributed systems, analyses the models used in representing the failures at different levels, and continues with the presentation of the most important strategies used in designing fault tolerance large scale distributed systems and applications. Emphasis is put on the special case of reliable communication in such systems. The chapter concludes with the techniques used to enable recovery from failures in large scale distributed systems.

Chapter 9, Security, starts by presenting the threats and vulnerabilities in large scale systems, and the difficulties encountered in preserving their confidentiality, integrity and availability. The Chapter is organized around the concept of security architecture and addresses three important problems: secure communication (with emphasis on the secure group communication), access control (more specific the access control in distributed multi-organizational platforms), and security management (especially key distribution management and trust management). For each problem, specific security models, mechanisms and protocols are described. The case studies used in this chapter refer to the security in Web, Grid, and peer-to-peer systems.

Chapter 10, Application development tools and frameworks, presents the engineering aspects of the distributed software development, from requirements to deployment and use. Specific tools, frameworks and portals for different development phases are introduced. The first section discusses the evolution of web applications and makes an overview of the current development platforms, especially Java EE and .NET. The chapter continues by presenting programming tools for Grid environments (such as Cog Kit and Grid MPI), which are mainly targeted at scientific applications. Clouds and peer-to-peer systems are addressed in the following sections, while the last part of the chapter is dedicated to distributed workflows – as the usage of workflow management platforms has been constantly increasing during the last years.

Chapter 11, Applications, start with a description of current projects and applications in large scale distributed systems, like those from OSG projects in USA, EGEE applications in Europe and Asia, and DEISA (Distributed European Infrastructure for Supercomputing Applications DEISA) initiative. We present the requirements for application development in Grids and P2P systems. Grid applications and Web-Based applications offer a reference for application development and related issues presented in the book such as application scheduling, application monitoring, data management, and application security.

TARGET AUDIENCE

The work is a scholarly book addressed mainly to researchers, professors, and teaching assistants who can find here a quick reference to the actual issues and research results in the domain of large scale distributed systems. The book could also represent an important help for PhD Students when documenting their research and looking for appropriate references to specific problems in this field.

This book is also well-suited for non-IT researchers and specialists from other data and intensive processing fields (physics, biology, etc.) who use large scale systems to run their applications and need a better understanding of the technologies involved. In this respect, the presentation of the specific concepts, research subjects, case studies, and distributes systems applications and application development tools is beneficial.

Individuals outside universities wishing to learn more about this important topic might also find this book useful. It targets software architects and developers, solution designers, IT specialists from professional environments interested in distributed systems for seeking appropriate solutions to their specific problems. For them, the book includes an informative introduction to the domain with emphasis on the design and implementation solutions of the large scale distributed systems and their applications.

After reading the book, the reader will be able to identify and use the concepts and technologies related to large scale distributed systems, from models to the implementation of technological solutions addressing the scheduling, monitoring, dependability, security, and other issues. The book introduces the reader to the high-level architectural view of large scale distributed systems and then to the technological solutions of the real-world implementation. The book facilitates the understanding of the new concepts used in a comprehensive set of real-world case studies. The reader will be able to easily recognize the concepts and structure of large scale distributed systems and will master the up-to-date technological solutions supporting the implementations of such systems.

CONCLUSION

The book presents the actual large scale distributed systems that are becoming more and more attractive in academia and industry as preferred computing infrastructures to be used for a wide-range of actual and next-generation applications. Most IT vendors and enterprise solutions adopters view distributed systems and their characteristics (such as virtualization, resource reallocation, automation and self-management) as foundation of the technology of the future, involving new kinds of IT procurement, delivery and usage models such as service oriented and utility models. Large scale distributed systems are presently helping many organizations to dynamically integrate their disparate, heterogeneous compute and storage resources. For these reasons the book presents the advantages of using large scale distributed systems and the development process of scientific and commercial distributed applications for the benefit of academic and business professionals as well.

The book also presents up-to-date technological solutions to the main aspects regarding large scale distributed systems, a highly dynamic scientific domain that gained much interest in the world of IT in the last decade. Distributed systems have matured from the large scale distributed computing science projects of the '90s to commercially viable business computing and network infrastructures. The book discusses nowadays computational large scale distributed systems that are used in solving some of the thorniest business problems affecting today's networked economy: supply chain integration, virtual organizations, collaboration, and more. Along with covering the architecture and components behind the large scale distributed computing paradigm, the book introduces readers to the technologies that make up today's large scale distributed platforms.

REFERENCES

Amazon. (2009). *AMAZON Web Services*. Retrieved August 21, 2009, from http://aws.amazon.com/

BitTorrent. (2009). *BitTorrent*. Retrieved April 11, 2009 from http://www.bittorrent.com/

Dodson, S. (2003, October 9). The Internet of Things. *The Guardia3*. Retrieved August 21, 2009, from http://www.guardian.co.uk/technology/2003/oct/09/shopping.newmedia

Foster, I., & Kesselman, C. (Eds.). (2004) *The Grid: Blueprint for a New Computing Infrastructure*, San Francisco: Morgan Kaufmann Publishers, Elsevier.

Gnutella2. (2009). *Gnutella2*. Retrieved April 10, 2009, from http://www.gnutella2.co.

Kazaa. (2009). *Kazaa*. Retrieved April 10, 2009 from http://www.kazaa.co.

Tanenbaum, A.S., & van Steen, M. (2007). *Distributed Systems. Principles and paradigms*, 2nd Ed.). Upper Saddle River, NJ: Prentice Hall

W3C. (2009). *OWL Web Ontology Language Overview*. Retrieved August 21, 2009 from http://www.w3.org/TR/owl-features/

Acknowledgment

The authors would like to acknowledge the feedback of anonymous reviewers, who made very useful suggestions and helped us to discover where the improvement of the book and clarification were needed.

Special thanks also go to the publishing team at IGI Global, whose contributions throughout the whole process from inception of the initial idea to final publication have been invaluable. In particular we thank Julia Mosemann, who continuously offered the best support for keeping the project on schedule, and provided quick answers and advice.

The Authors
September 15, 2009

Chapter 1
Introduction

INTRODUCTION

The general presentation of Large Scale Distributed Computing and Applications can be done from different perspectives: historical, conceptual, architectural, technological, social, and others. This Introduction takes a pragmatic approach. It starts with a short presentation of definitions, goals, and fundamental concepts that frame the subjects targeted in the book: the Internet, the Web, Enterprise Information Systems, Peer-to-Peer Systems, Grids, Utility Computer Systems, and others. Then, each of these actual large scale distributed system categories is characterized in terms of typical applications, motivation of use, requirements and problems posed by their development: specific concepts, models, paradigms, and technologies. The focus is on describing the Large Scale Distributed Computing such as it appears today. Nevertheless, presenting actually used solutions will offer the opportunity to found that older theoretical results can still be exploited to build high performance artifacts. Also, the ever-ending stimulating relation-

DOI: 10.4018/978-1-61520-703-9.ch001

ship between users, who require better computing services, and providers, who discover new ways to satisfy them, is the motivation to introduce future trends in the domain, which pave the way towards the next generation Cyberinfrastructure. The chapter introduces a comprehensive set of concepts, models, and technologies, which are discussed in details in the next chapters.

BASIC CONCEPTS

There are several definitions of distributed systems. For the purpose of this work, we reproduce two definitions that reflect similar approaches in the study, design, development, implementation, and use of these systems. One definition belongs to Coulouris et al (2001), which state that "We define a distributed system as a collection of autonomous computers linked by a network, with software designed to produce an integrated computing facility." Very common and well known examples are the Internet, the Web, intranets, peer-to-peer systems, mobile and ubiquitous networks, and others. The second definition belongs to Tanenbaum and van

Steen 2007), and describes a distributed system as a "collection of independent computers that appears to its user as a single coherent system." Being independent means that processing units can execute separate programs. On the other hand, they appear as a single system (in other words they present a single system image), which represents an important design goal for the developers of these systems. From the designers' point of view, a distributed system is organized according to a specific paradigm. In distributed file systems, such as the Network File System (NFS), everything is a file. Similarly, distributed systems can be organized as a collection of software objects (like in CORBA, DCOM, etc.), as linked documents (the Web), or as distributed coordination (Jini, for example).

Obviously, a distributed system runs parallel / distributed programs, collectively named concurrent programs. A concurrent program describes a collection of two or more sequential processes that cooperate in performing data transformations. Processes cooperate by communication (sharing some common data) and synchronization (execute actions in a specific order or at specific moments in time). In a parallel program, these processes are executed in parallel on multiple processors. In a distributed program, processes are executed on different computers that communicate through a network. Thus, concurrent programs encompass parallel programs and distributed programs.

Among various distributed system architectures, we can identify two basic models: client-server and peer-to-peer. In client-server systems, there are two kinds of processes that run on different machines. The server process implements and offers a specific service (such as a file service, name service, print service, etc.), while the client process requests a service. The server waits to be invoked by clients. When it receives a request, the server executes the service and sends the result to the requesting client. The client that needs a service makes a request and then waits for the result from the server and uses (consumes) it. A common example of a client-server distributed system is an Intranet with several clients running on different workstations and several specialized servers (print, file, directory, mail, web, etc.) running on more powerful machines.

In peer-to-peer (P2P) distributed systems, processes have equal rights and share resources and services by direct exchanges. In other words, a peer can give some resources (or provide a service) to other peers, and receive other resources (or services) from them. This model is called pure peer-to-peer. Other models exist such as hybrid peer-to-peer, in which there is a special directory server that is used for finding other peers. Once two peers get in contact, they directly exchange resources and services.

Several motivations exist for using distributed systems: reducing the application execution time, increasing systems' reliability, ensure fault tolerance, build functional specialization, and exploit the inherent parallelism of applications. Compute intensive applications can be executed more efficiently if they are divided into several tasks that run in parallel on different computers. Examples of such programs are scientific applications, data mining programs, simulators, etc. Often, applications claim for high reliability (for example an air traffic control system or a nuclear power plant control system) that may be assured through replicating some processes and/or data. If some processors fail, their replicas can replace them. Thus, a failure in one processor does not affect the correct working of the entire system. Applications can be partitioned in several phases with distinct functionalities: computationally intensive, image processing, file processing, print processing, etc. Different parts of the application can be executed on separate specialized hardware, thus increasing the chance to obtain good performance and efficient use of resources. Finally, some applications are inherently parallel. Examples include air traffic control, airline reservation applications that must respond to many concurrent requests and are therefore parallel and often distributed.

There are some other advantages of using distributed systems such as price/performance ratio (it is cheaper to share common resources than buy them for exclusive use), easier user access to remote resources (the network supports the interconnection of users and resources), incremental growth (permits adding to existing infrastructure rather than replacing the existing resources with more powerful ones).

In turn, designers have several goals when building a distributed system. Transparency is equivalent to "appear as a single coherent system". Transparency has several aspects. The most important ones are: the replication (hide that resources are replicated; this means that the result must not be dependent on the particular replica used by a process), concurrency (hide that resources may be shared by several competing users; in other words, the user must not be forced to program specific actions in order to share the same resources with other users), and failure (hide the failure and recovery of resources; in other words, the system must continues to operate in the presence of failures of some components, eventually with degrade of performance; the system re-enters a normal state, without user knowledge, after the failed component has been repaired).

Openness is another important characteristic, which means the system can be extended and re-implemented in different ways. It requires respecting the standards and public interfaces. This permits the interoperation with other components and systems that obey to the same rules, and allows extending the system with new services. Also, applications can move from one system to another without modifications if both systems support the same interface rules (portability).

Scalability is the ability of the system to extend itself without dramatic performance changes. The extension can be in terms of number of users, size of the application, geographic dispersion of users and resources, or number of administrative organizations involved. Solutions are based on asynchronous communication that avoids the long

blockings found in the synchronous communication, on task distribution among different computers, and on components replication. The last solution raises the problem of consistency, which means that different replicas behave similarly.

Security refers to confidentiality (the information can be disclosed only to authorized subjects), integrity (only authorized subjects can change the information), and availability (information can be accessed when needed). The solutions are based on cryptographic algorithms, mechanisms, protocols, and services.

The heart of modern distributed systems is the middleware that brings enhancements to services of network operating systems. The Middleware layer covers the gap between services provided by the platform (Network OS services) and those needed by the Applications. It is essential for supporting the operation of distributed systems, since they must cope with the heterogeneity of components (network protocols, hardware and diverse data representations, operating systems with different solutions for data and resources management, and programming languages that use different representations for characters and data structures).

The middleware is in a continuous evolution. Along with the development of new technologies, new interfaces are added to it. Also, some common and frequently used services evolve from APIs to Operating System components. First generation middleware included network programming services, and primitive services like terminal emulation, file transfer, and e-mail. Next to these, basic client-server services have been developed, like the Remote Procedure Call (RPC), Remote Data Access (RDA), and Message Oriented Middleware (MOM).

In the sequel we provide general descriptions of the most important categories of large scale distributed systems: the Web, Web-based systems, Grids, clouds, and P2P systems. The main criteria used for this categorization is the kind of applications supported. For each category, the characteristics, main applications, specific issues and approaches to solve them are presented. A separate section is devoted to issues that are common to all distributed system categories. These are further discussed in detail in Chapters 3 to 11 of the book. Also, while architectural issues for each distributed system category are approached in the current chapter, the architectural models of large scale distributed systems are the main topic of Chapter 2 of the book.

THE WEB

A very well known, huge distributed system is the Web. It consists of millions of servers distributed worldwide, and millions of clients that access collections of documents from almost any place and any device. The client can be a browser, such as Netscape Navigator or Internet Explorer that makes requests to a Web Server "to retrieve and view documents, to listen to audio streams and view video streams, and to interact with an unlimited set of services." (Tanenbaum & van Steen, 2007) The main issue of the Web system is the time spent for the page download. A low response time can be due to the congestion of the Web server or to the long distance from the Web server to the client. The solutions for accelerating the page download include page caching (in this case the page is obtained from the client cache or from a proxy cache) and server replication (different page requests can be distributed to different servers for load balancing). Another important issue is Web page protection against unauthorized access and attacks to integrity. They can be ensured by the access control to restricted web pages of authenticated clients, and by the use of secure communication between server and clients. In some cases, the servers also authenticate to clients to ensure they are the authorized holder of the Web pages. A third issue is increasing the performance of page search for which high performance search engines are used. Finally, creat-

ing valuable content must be supported by novel efficient methods such as collaborative content creation. Some of the methods that are present in the actual Web system are shortly presented in the sequel.

The Web is mainly based on three open standards: Hypertext Markup Language (HTML) for specifying the contents and layouts of pages, Uniform Resource Locators (URLs) for identifying the documents and other resources, and HyperText Transfer Protocol (HTTP) for communicating between clients and servers. HTTP messages (commands and responses) include headers that permit the control of caching, security, sessions, etc. A server can control the caching of pages in private caches at client, or in shared caches at proxies and servers. Other headers can be used to allow the user to download the most recent version of a document page (cache coherence). The replication can be more complicated like in the Content Delivery Network (CDN) model (Tanenbaum & van Steen, 2007). Here, the pages that are not modified very often are replicated and hosted by special servers, so that the client may access the better (usually the geographically closest) one for downloading. HTTP includes also headers to ensure user authentication and authorization when accessing restricted pages. More than this, when associated with the Transport Layer Security (TLS), HTTP gives raise to Secure HTTP (or HTTPS) that permits mutual authentication of clients and servers, and information exchange over encrypted connections. HTTP is a stateless protocol. Nevertheless, cookies can be used to maintain states in a session. The cookie is a (key, value) pair, which is transmitted by the server and kept by the browser, which includes it in commands that belong to the same session. Two important attributes can be associated with the client and, respectively the server. The plug-in mechanism is used to support the client extensibility, more specific the extension to different document types. The plug-in is a specific piece of software that can be dynamically loaded by the browser to process documents of some MIME type. The plug-in has a standard interface for the browser, which, in turn, has a standard interface for the plug-in. Concerning the server, it can be supported by a cluster, which has a front-end that examines the client requests and distributes them to nodes in the cluster. Cluster nodes can keep different data resources so that the client requests are distributed according to the content requested. Alternatively, the nodes keep similar resources and the front-end distributes the requests so that load balancing is ensured. Different mechanisms are used (such as TCP handoff) to improve the performance of the server. Also, solutions exist to distribute the load of the front-end among several cluster resources (switches, distributors, dispatchers).

The new Web allows the aggregation of information from several sources, new forms of content production and consumption (e.g. social networks), and different types of links over the physical networks (overlays). Other special middleware services refer to groupware (that supports collaborative group applications), mobile computing, distributed multimedia middleware, and others.

Due to Web's large scale and the huge amount of pages available for public access, searching the Web claims for automated tools that help users in retrieving the information they need in their daily activity. This role is fulfilled by search engines like Google, Yahoo!, and many other tools that help the user to locate the pages they are looking for. Search engines (2007) use index databases that keep information about Web pages and allow a fast identification of pages that respond to specific user criteria. The information stored in index databases is accumulated by crawlers that visit Web pages, read the information found there (including meta-data), and return that information back to a repository site where the data is indexed. The crawler uses hyperlinks to visit related pages and perform indexing on all linked sites. Periodically, crawlers re-visit the sites to check for changes in the pages posted there. Indexing can also be done

on information directly submitted by humans. The main problems faced by search engines are related to the high volume of the databases that is collected and searched subsequently, the need to keep the databases up-to-date by frequent re-visits of the Web sites, and the user requirements for high quality responses to their search queries. For the last issue, search engines use different algorithms to find the best pages that match users' queries. Some algorithms count how many times a keyword (or search term) appears on a Web page and in what locations (header or body of the page, first paragraph, etc.). Others consider how pages are linked to one another to determine how important a page is, for a specific subject. Page ranking can be modified by the number of "clickthroughs", which means the number of times the page was selected from the results of search actions.

Web searching in other languages than English is an interesting and actual topic due to the rapid increase of online users in non-English-speaking regions like China, Latin America, and Middle East (Chung, 2008). Several search engines, like Google, AltaVista, Yahoo!, and MSN Search, provide search services to these users. For example, Google can restrict search results to pages in 117 languages, and provides translation between English and 12 other languages. Chung (2008) presents a framework for Web searching in several languages, which includes components for meta-search, language processing, and page treatment (summarization, classification, and visualization) along with domain collections that was used to build three prototype search portals in Chinese, Spanish, and Arabic. The experiments developed on these portals highlighted the usability in supporting multi-lingual Web search, but also the areas for further improvements.

Despite the increased volume of index databases and the higher quality of ranking algorithms, search engines don't provide all the time the results that fit users' expectations. The main reason is that Web pages were designed to be understood and used by people, not to be processed by machines. The

Semantic Web approach tries to make it possible "for the web to understand and satisfy the requests of people, and machines to use the web content" (Berners-Lee et al, 2001). The Semantic Web is based on languages designed for data (Resource Description Framework - RDF, Web Ontology Language - OWL, and Extensible Markup Language - XML) and produce data descriptions that have meaning, can be understood and processed by machines and lead to more meaningful results. RDF together with SPARQL (query language for RDF) and URIs (Universal Resource Identifiers) are used to build data-integration applications (Hendler et al, 2008) by linking data entities and querying databases for retrieving and integrating data from multiple sources. OVL is a language that describes the meaning of the terminology used in Web documents (concepts associated with terms and the relationships between those terms) making possible their correct interpretation and processing by programs.

Another orientation towards increasing the usefulness of search results is seeking information for specific purposes like learning, decision making or other similar complex activities. Information-Seeking Support Systems - ISSS (Marchionini & White, 2009) go beyond the simple search and consider users' prior knowledge and skills, the tasks they must perform, the context they work in (physical, temporal, and social constraints), etc. This extended framework allows the system to provide more targeted information that better serves user goals. At the same time, it asks for more robust models of human-information interaction, new tools and services, and better methods to evaluate information seeking (Marchionini & White, 2009).

Some approaches are used in the emerging Social Web to increase the efficiency of searching documents on the Web. For example, a voting scheme allows users to associate to a page figures that reflect their value or popularity. The system can then calculate average values over a community of users and can be used similar to page ranks. Spar.Tag.us is a social reading and annotation tool that allows tagging and highlighting of web content at paragraph level. It uses a browser extension to extract paragraphs and send them to the SparTags.us server that receives the annotation data added by the user as well. Users who post pages on the Web can add meta-descriptions (for example keywords) that characterize the content of pages and makes them easier to find. The Social Web aims not only to support the search process but also let users socialize on the Web. Users create content and share it with others, like in wikis; also, users collaboratively create content like in Wikipedia. This social nature of the Web, its dynamicity, the unpredictable user behavior, and the large scale claim for an interdisciplinary approach for researching the Web topic, which involve "mathematics, computer science, artificial intelligence, sociology, psychology, biology, and economics." (Hendler et al, 2008)

Apart from the search service, users might want to know when and how Web pages of interest change. Obviously, they might schedule the visits of the pages of interest for finding the last updates. As an alternative, information change monitoring tools can be used to inform the users about fresh changes of Web pages. Several such tools are available that offer different services (some of them advertize when the pages are changed, others also identify the changes) at various performance, quality, and scalability levels. One of the most interesting tool is WebCQ (Liu at al, 2004), which detects changes and promptly notify users about what and how changes have been done.

WEB-BASED SYSTEMS

Web-based client-server applications (or Web Applications) are client-server applications that use the Web browser as client. When the user asks for a service, a standard exchange of messages is started. The browser composes and sends a request message to the Web server. This one analyses the request and directs it to the corresponding application server. This server processes the request and transmits the result back to the Web server, which translates it to a convenient form. Then, the Web server sends the response to the Web client, which displays it to the user. Obviously, the request processing can be very complicated and could involve several application components, such as computational modules, data files, databases, etc. The approach has the advantage of using the ubiquitous standard Web browsers as clients. So, the application can be accessed from many simple or complicated devices. If required by the application, the browser can download and execute more complicated clients. In addition, the pervasive nature of the Internet and the Web stimulated the development of many Web applications, of different categories: commercial (e-business, e-commerce), scientific (e-science), governmental (e-government), educational, organizational, etc.

A common issue of Web application is their easy and rapid development for which several development frameworks have been proposed. Some applications require high client server interactivity. For them, several solutions have been found from which we mention here the rich Internet Applications, RIA. Transparency, flexibility, extensibility, reuse are also important for many applications. Service oriented architecture, SOA is a loosely coupled approach that responds to these requirements and offers platform and location independence, dynamic search and composition of services, adaptation to customer profile, and a low maintenance cost.

Many approaches to Web application development have been proposed. All of them try to make more efficient the development process, by identifying those functional components that are common to all dynamic Web applications. In this category, the following functions are included (Shklar & Rosen, 2003): the interpretation of user requests, authentication and authorization, access to requested data, construction and transmission of the final responses. Also, different approaches

provide solutions for implementing the functionality related to content (produce the data to be transmitted to the client) and presentation (formatting the results). For example, in scripting approaches like CGI (Common Gateway Interface), the code is focused on dynamically producing the content, but is interspersed with output statements that make the page formatting. CGI provides mechanisms for creating and starting the process that gets the request's context information (environment variables) and executes a particular application. Other functions (session management, database access) are supported by specialized packages for languages used in CGI, such as C, Pearl, etc. The same approach is used in the Java servlet API, which makes some improvements over CGI to ensure a more efficient processing of client requests. Completely different is the template approach. SSI (Server-Side Includes) uses directives that allow the inclusion of dynamically created content in HTML pages. Cold Fusion provides tags that allow the inclusion of external resources based on queries that are simple to use and allow data access, iterative result presentation, etc.

Hybrid approaches combine the facilities offered by scripting and template approaches. For example, PHP (PHP Hypertext Processor) makes a clear separation between the blocks that produce dynamic content and those coping with the format. In JSP (Java Server Page), a pre-processor translates the mixed page-like structures into code that is compiled by the server (into Java servlets) and executed.

The separation of content from presentation is realized in the Model-View-Controller - MVC approach. It has the advantage of separating the duties of developers (which are responsible for the business logic and access to content) and page designers (which are responsible for the presentation formatting). These two domains are represented by the Model and View parts of the pattern, while the coordination between the content production and the formatting is made by the Controller (which is also in the charge of developers). The MVC concept leads to a complex design that includes several components and the interactions between them. To easy the design process, Web application development models and guidelines have been proposed, such as JSP Model 2, and application development frameworks have been implemented, such as the Struts framework developed in the Apache Jakarta project (Sklar & Rosen, 2003).

Rich Internet Applications (RIAs) feature a high client – server interactivity and offer, in the form of Web applications, the functionality available on desktops' local software. To achieve the required quality of service, two important mechanisms are used. First, the fat client model is adopted, which implements locally the user interface capabilities. Second, the client interacts asynchronously with the server, which leads to reduced waiting times on both sides (Lawton, 2008). RIA model has several advantages: better distribution of tasks between the client and the server, increased interactivity, reduced latency. Application development is supported by Asynchronous JavaScript and XML (Ajax) platforms, first used by Google (which recently developed the Google Web Toolkit) and afterwards adopted by other vendors that developed their own Ajax based platforms, such as ASP.Net Ajax from Micorsoft. Ajax uses HTTP for asynchronous transfers and partial updates of the page, rather than whole page downloads. Also, it uses JavaScripts that run in the browser and make the applications more responsive to events. Non-Ajax platforms exist as well, such as Flash and Adobe Integrated Runtime (AIR) from Adobe, Silverlight from Microsoft, and Java FX from Sun Microsystems.

Service Oriented Architecture (SOA) received general acceptance in the world of Web applications developers. The service is used as a paradigm for developing a system as a collection of services that coordinate with each other (Papazoglou et al, 2007). A service is offered by a supplier (service provider) and is used by a customer (service consumer). The service is accessed by means of an interface. Usually, providers and consumers don't know each other explicitly so that services need to know what services are available, and how these services can be invoked. The consumer can look for a specific service by sending a request to a discovery service, which will return the identity of a service provider. Than, the consumer interrogates the service provider to find out the service description, builds the service request, transmits it to the provider and gets back the response. Another way to find information about available services is the publish / subscribe service. With this, a description of the service is published when it becomes available, while a potential consumer passes a subscription that describes its needs. The publish / subscribe service sends a notification to the consumer when a service is published that corresponds to its requirements.

SOA is not tied to a specific technology and can be implemented with the Representational State Transfer (REST) architectural style for distributed hypermedia systems, Remote Procedure Call (RPC), Common Object Request Broker Architecture, CORBA (Siegel, 2000), Distributed Component Object Model (DCOM), Web Services, etc. A general view on SOA is included in the SOA Reference Model elaborated by OASIS, which presents an abstract description of model's entities and their relationships, and frames the development of standards for service oriented architectures. W3C elaborated and published several standards related to Web Services. The Web Service Description Language (WSDL) is used to describe Web service's interface, with information about publicly available functions, datatypes for message requests and responses, the transport protocol to be used, and the location of the service (Cerami, 2002). The Universal Description, Discovery, and Integration (UDDI) offers support for publishing and finding Web services. UDDI describes how to build a distributed service directory, how to register services, and how to search existing UDDI data.

The possibility to build Web applications by loosely coupling Web services has significant advantages. Finding and bounding services at runtime allow building very flexible applications that dynamically adapt to user demands by changing the workflow composition of services involved. Also, it is possible to re-use available services for building new applications or easily replace old services with new, higher performance versions. Finally, services can be easily replicated to support fault tolerance, and easily integrated in large systems with complex workflows.

Many large scale client-server applications are offered as services. Good examples include the very popular social network applications Facebook, MySpace and others, which aim at building online communities based on common shared interests, activities, preferences and others. Users are allowed to set up their personal profiles, establish who can have access to them (the "friends"), form groups or join groups of users (personal networks), communicate, collaborate and share content across networks. Other functions refer to receiving recommendations of expert contacts, and awareness of a common context with other peoiple (this contributes to the creation of the trust relationship in a network). Apart from these profile-based services, other types of social network services exist, which are based on content (Flikr is based on photo sharing), mini-communities (PeopleAggregator), virtual representations of the site member (Second Life), mobility (MySpace, Twitter), and others. Social network services can be used by closed groups that belong to an organization or communicate at intranet level. Social network services are growing very fast and attract a very large number of users. Their development and maintenance pose the same problems as other large scale client-server applications. Additional issues are related to specific attributes of collaborative communities and represent challenging research subjects. Examples include the implications of information revelation in social networks on user privacy

(Gross, Acquisti, & Heinz III, 2005), visualization of social network to facilitate the suggestive representation of the community structure and the discovery of people, connections or communities (Herr, & Boyd, 2009), optimization of social network services for mobile use (referinta aici), integration of social networks and web browsing (Golbeck, & Wasser, 2007).

Usually, services are adapted or adaptable to users' profile that includes skills, preferences, space or time contextual information and others. Other services are essentially based on the location information offered by tracking systems like GPS. Spatial alarms fall in this category (Bamba, Liu, Yu, & Iyengar, 2009). They work similar to temporal alarms: the alarm must be set by designating a spatial reference; when a GPS enabled mobile device enters the area the alarm goes off and the user is notified. The alarms can be used in applications like traffic monitoring (traffic information on a specific highway zone), tourist orientation (inform the user about near sightseeing spots), social networking (notify the user if some of its friends are near to his current location), etc. Alarms can be offered as public services. In this case, a server publishes the alarm by topic categories similar to the traffic alarm mentioned above, while the clients may subscribe to public alarms. The alarm service should be scalable and offer a high accuracy (no false or missing notifications). Good results have been obtained by the use of a client-server architecture in which the alarm processing is distributed to the server and the mobile clients (Bamba, Liu, Yu, & Iyengar, 2009).

GRIDS

The original idea of Grid computing, which was borrowed from electrical power grids, was the separation of the production from consumption: users are able to consume electric power without knowing about where the energy was produced. This makes the production more effective by the use of distributed unexploited resources, parallel and aggregate use of resources, load balancing, etc. Also, it makes the consumption more economic (on demand), flexible, and reliable. Grids are used for compute intensive and / or data intensive applications, for remote access to powerful scientific instruments, and in collaborative systems. Grids are used in Virtual Organizations (VOs) that are composed of people from different organizations, working on a common project and sharing resources to fulfill a specific goal (Foster et al, 2001). VOs are dynamic in nature since they exist on the duration of the project, and users can join and leave the VOs at any time. In addition, the resources can change their status, fail, join or leave the Grid. According to this view, the Grid means the "coordinated resource sharing and problem solving in dynamic, multi-institutional virtual organizations"(Foster et al, 2001). Coordinated sharing means that resource owners are able to establish constraints for resource allocation and use, while users can specify the kinds and quantities of resources they need. Coordination is not a trivial problem since users might belong to different control domains (administration units) with different security and payment policies. In addition, the required QoS in terms of response time, throughput, and availability is nontrivial. Similar to other large scale distributed systems, the solutions are based on open standards, which (in this case) are elaborated by the Open Grid Forum (OGF).

In fact, standardization is one of the main issues of Grid infrastructures. Several solutions have been proposed, the most recent being closer to the Web Services standards (OGSA, WSRF). Other important issues relate to security, VO management, data management, task management, resource management for compute-intensive and data-intensive applications. The response consists of many innovations evaluated in experimental platforms and included in Grid middleware. The easy to use gave rise to Grid portals, while the easy to develop led to the de-

velopment of methodologies and support tools for application gridification.

Grid technologies evolved from custom solutions developed at the beginning of '90s, which were built over the Internet protocols, to the actual solutions framed by the Open Grid Service Architecture (OGSA). The evolution was possible due to volunteer work and Grid initiatives such as the Globus Project (which became the Globus Alliance), the Global Grid Forum, and many worldwide Government funded projects. In particular, the open source Globus Toolkit (2009), developed by the Globus Alliance with the participation of other contributors (GT Contributors, 2009), has been used to implement and test different solutions for building Grids. For example, the Globus Toolkit 2.0 was the testbed for a systematic development Grid protocols, APIs, and services, such as Grid Security Infrastructure (GSI), Monitoring and Discovery Service (MDS), Grid Resource Allocation Manager (GRAM), and GridFTP. Globus Toolkit 3.2 experimented essential Grid services included in the Open Grid Service Infrastructure (OGSI) as support of the Open Grid Service Architecture. Also, the proposal of a new concept for Grid services, namely the Web Service Resource Framework (WSRF) was implemented in Globus Toolkit 4.0.

Important projects were dedicated to the development of middleware functions (NSF Middleware Initiative funded by NSF), production of reliable and scalable resources for the European research community (Enabling Grids for E-Science in Europe, EGEE), development of research methods to exploit computational thinking (UK e-Science Programme), etc. Other important projects that contributed to the development of the Grid concept, middleware, frameworks, and solutions are Condor-G (Grid agent for remote access to batch systems), Cactus (Grid portal), UNICORE (general purpose portal infrastructure), Access Grid (group-to-group human interaction through Grid), GridICE, MonALISA, and Ganglia (for grid monitoring), SEE-GRID SCI (providing processing and storage services for eScience research).

Many applications have been built or "gridified" to benefit by the use of large scale and high performance of Grid platforms. Compute intensive applications (in which the processing power is the dominant factor) are mainly simulation studies of very complex systems and phenomena, such as galaxy formation and gravity wave detection. For example, the Grid Physics Network (GriPhyN) and Virtual Data Grid Laboratory (iVDGL) joined to offer computational resources for experiments in physics, astronomy, biology, and engineering. Data intensive applications (in which the bandwidth and latency of accessing data are the dominant factors) include experimental data analysis from physics, astronomy, and other scientific domains. The DataGrid, a project funded by the European Union, had the objective to support intensive computation on large-scale databases (of the order of PetaBytes). Collaborative applications support the shared online use of very expensive apparatus, the co-design of complex engineering artifacts, remote visualization, and others. For example, the Network for Earthquake Engineering Simulation (NEESit, 2009) allows specialists to organize physical and numerical simulations on remotely accessible experimental facilities. Also, Collaborative Advanced Knowledge Technologies on the Grid (CoAKTinG, 2009) supports collaborative mediated spaces for distributed e-Science based on advanced knowledge technologies.

Very often we find hybrid applications in which large amounts of data form the input for very complex transformations. These data-intensive computing applications combine the requirements for manipulating large datasets with those for very complex computation (Gorton et al, 2008). They ask for new scalable algorithms and technologies to search and process large datasets originating from distributed and heterogeneous sources, high-speed memory access to data, new architectures that support large datastreams received from very high speed networks, high performance distributed

file systems, software mobility to support load balancing, and others. Huge amounts of data, with different levels of trust or usefulness and with no standard formats, continue to be produced by different experiments, simulation studies, sensor networks, and social networks users. For example, the experiments with the Large Hadron Collider at the Center for European Nuclear Research will produce 2 Pbytes of raw data per second (Kouzes et al, 2009), which can't be stored by available storage devices. On the other hand, since raw data is not useful to all physicists participating in the experiments, data are filtered, processed in real-time and stored at a rate of 10 Pbytes per year. Other applications, like Internet search, use several data centers distributed over large geographic areas, each one composed of hundreds thousand of nodes. Distributed computing is used to classify, summarize, and annotate the stored data. This helps further search operations for data that fits with some particular interest and satisfy specific criteria such as the provenance of the data, more specific the data originator and the chain of actors (identity and version of the code executed, for example) who processed the retrieved data (Kouzes et al, 2009). To cope with the problem of various formats used for data stored in distributed locations, and for achieving easy access to data and the interoperation of application that process these data, the adoption of standard data representations is highly recommended (Lee & Percivall, 2008). At the data management level, technologies are required to support parallel execution of queries on organized data collections (repositories, relational databases, etc.) that are distributed across multiple sites. Concerning data processing, the scalability of the algorithms used for data analysis is a major concern. Distributed algorithms fit very well the distributed pattern of data. On the other side, they suffer from latency induced by the underlying message passing programming model and the hardware that supports the execution. One solution is the development and use of algorithms that hide the latency by interleaving compute and transfer tasks. Another one is designing new techniques like neural networks and genetic algorithms that help in reducing the complexity. Last but not least, the correct selection of the computational resources to run the applications plays an important role. For example, fine grain parallel applications could be efficiently executed on vector machines rather than on clusters with slow interconnects.

Obviously, systems supporting data-intensive computing must be high performance, offer high security, and provide fault tolerance. Distributed systems have the great advantage that failures can be only partial. This characteristic favored the adoption of specific methods and mechanisms, such as data replication and consistency, fault detection and recovery methods, trust based mechanisms, mutual authentication, etc., to build high-assurance computing platforms. These methods have a counter effect on the performance since they increase the overhead, which becomes more significant with the increase of the systems' scale. Reducing the overhead requires new methods for resource management, load balancing, application scheduling and co-scheduling, advance resource reservation, and others. Since recent large scale applications include modules that can be mixed in flexible combinations to produce meaningful results, workflow creation, management, and monitoring are also important middleware functions that must be exploited (Matsuoka et al, 2008).

Another important issue is the easy to use the Grid facilities. Access tools would let users store and manage large data collections or use high performance applications with minimal training and help. The experience gained with gateways to Grid facilities that are already in place for scientific communities (Wilkins-Diehr et al, 2008) contribute to the improvement of their functionalities and performance.

Concerning the terminology and the former definitions presented in this section, Grid computing is a form of volunteer computing where resource owners allow the use of resources for the benefit of a project. Examples include Rosetta@

home that aims to "predict protein-protein docking and design new proteins with the help of over 84,000 volunteered computers processing over 88 teraFLOPS on average as of April 14, 2009" (Rosetta, 2009), SETI@home used in the Search for Extra-Terrestrial Intelligence (Anderson et al, 2002), and many others. Since Grids offer computing and storage resources like a utility (similar to electrical power, water, gas, etc.), it is also a form of utility computing (Utility, 2009).

CLOUDS

Cloud computing is another computing model under current research and development (Strickland, 2009). The cloud is composed by hardware and software computer resources in data centers, which are accessible remotely through Internet. Interface software to clouds can be as simple as a browser (it can be other software that has networking capabilities) and runs on the user's local computer.

The cloud can include any type of hardware and software resources that might be useful to clients (Hayes, 2008). They are offered according to "on demand" delivery model, which means users have access to resources and use them when needed. Also, the cost is tailored according to resource usage. This is why cloud computing is considered a form of on-demand computing, software as a service, or the internet as platform. Due to the large number of potential (or actual) users, resources to manage the cloud are essential to ensure the promised functionalities and quality of service, such as performance, fault tolerance, security, etc. To satisfy users' requirements, cloud computing applies techniques commonly used in distributed systems like replication, resource management, parallel execution, access control, etc.

Cloud computing model is inspired from the old time sharing systems that provided remote access to large computer systems, through very simple terminals with no local storage capabilities.

Similar to that model, the computation take place in the cloud, while the local client computer can have very limited capabilities for running the cloud interface. In contrast with centralized architecture of time sharing systems, there is a many-to-many relation between clients and cloud's resources: a client may simultaneously access several resources in the cloud, while a resource can serve several clients at a time.

Clouds can offer a large variety of resources. For example, Amazon.com offers (among other things) infrastructure resources (data storage and computing capacity) to be used remotely. The clients can pay for the resources they actually consume (cost per hour) or pay once for a resource reservation and have an important discount for the effective resource usage. This allows great savings contrasted with buying resources that are rarely used, waste physical space for computer installations at client premises, and are hard to maintain. With the cloud approach, users can access very expensive high performance computers they couldn't afford to buy. Also, users have access to several instances representing different storage capacities and processing power. For example, Amazon's Large Instance (Amazon.com, 2009) has 7.5 GB of memory, 4 EC2 Compute Units (2 virtual cores with 2 EC2 Compute Units each), 850 GB of instance storage, on a 64-bit platform. Data storage services can take more elaborated forms. SQL Server Data Service (SSDS, 2009) from Microsoft (Microsoft SQL, 2009) offers on-demand data storage and query processing services based on SQL Server technologies. Customers can use SSDS to store any amount of data in the cloud, query data and modify data as required in different applications. SSDS supports REST and SOAP interfaces. The advantage of using the cloud is the high data availability and reliability.

Clouds can offer operating system facilities inside the browser. For example, the eyeOS (2009) offers file management, system management (packages installer, multiple application instances, etc.), office, network, and desktop facilities in a free software product that is publicly installed on the Company's server or can be installed on another web server controlled by the client. Cloud providers can use a different approach and replace the browser with a more complex interface software that runs on the client machine and directly communicates with the cloud.

Other clouds offer application services. For example, Google offers Google Docs (2009) that includes word processing, spreadsheet, and presentation (similar to Power Point) facilities. Adobe Buzzword is a web-based word processor that allows create and access documents from anywhere. Similar to other cloud applications, it operates in a browser but has the same look and functionality of a desktop word processor. It allows collaborative document editing and has facilities for versioning and tracking changes. Another service offered by Adobe is Photoshop Express (2009), which includes photo storage, sharing and editing facilities. Salesforce.com (2009) offer is focused on business applications offered online, mainly on-demand customer relationship management (CRM) services. The service is easy to use, accessible anywhere, and easily customizable to respond to particular requirements of companies.

Cloud computing has numerous advantages for users and software vendors. Users can reduce the costs of IT hardware and software infrastructure. This is more important for users that need very expensive high performance systems for running rarely used applications. Online services eliminate the efforts for software installation, administration, and maintenance. Software vendors can install their products on machines that correspond to specific requirements, and provide software services to clients that use different technologies. Online services also favor collaborative applications.

Cloud computing comes also with some concerns. One is about security of sensitive assets residing in the cloud and not on the user's local resources, which are more exposed to security attacks. Second, users loose the total control on their data. It is not clear if users moving to another service provider can take the data with them, or if documents that users want to discard aren't preserved by the provider without users' consent. A counterargument is that cloud computing providers want to maintain their reputation on which their business depends. Privacy is another concern. The mechanisms used to preserve it are the authentication, which is usually based on the name-password technique, and authorization. Since hackers can discover names and passwords by using different techniques, such as key logging, the use of these security mechanisms increases the service vulnerability.

Cloud / Utility computing is also a business model for Data Centers that assign parts of their resources to customers, on demand (Lysne, 2008). The customer pays, for a specific period, and only for resources it rented. Users' requirements are diverse in number and types of resources, performance, Quality of Service, security, and others. Usually, the utility computing Data Center sets up virtual hardware and software configurations to run user jobs, such as high performance parallel / distributed applications, or some standard software such as Web servers.

Due to the large variations in user requests, utility computing is confronted with several challenging problems, mainly related to resource management. Resources fall into three categories: compute nodes, storage nodes, and access nodes to external network. They are used according to the following constraints (Lysne, 2008): for each user request, a subset of resources is allocated; for a more effective use of resources, sets of resources allocated to different requests can overlap; applications can be produced by customers, in which case the utility provider has little control on them - consequently, the quality of the software is variable; the presence of several customers sharing common resources should not put on risk the achievement of the required QoS. To answer these challenges, several techniques are used for: finding a flexible resource partitioning that maximizes the resource utilization and reduces the interferences among different jobs; providing additional resources for node replication, in order to support fault tolerance (so that jobs execute to the end even in the case of nodes failures); predict the resources needed by each job for ensuring the response time imposed by customers.

PEER-TO-PEER SYSTEMS

There are many applications that fit well with the peer-to-peer concept (Pourebrahimi et al, 2005). We mention here the compute intensive, collaborative, and content distribution applications. Peer-to-peer is also used to build middleware services such as lookup, monitoring, and routing. Last but not least, peer-to-peer models are at the base of some important characteristics of distributed systems such as fault tolerance, security (in particular, anonymity, intrusion detection, and denial of service), trust (Xiong & Liu, 2002), and reputation.

In distributed computation P2P systems, peers share their available processing power. These systems are based on three important conditions. One refers to the application, which must allow distributing the computation into small, relatively independent tasks that could run simultaneously on small computers and deliver the results to a central coordinator. The second is to convince the owners of those small computers to host the tasks and execute them when their computers have nothing else to do. The third condition is to have a convenient way to implement this approach. SETI@home (Hipschman, R., 2009; SETI@home, 2009) uses P2P to process data in a scientific application, namely the "Search for Extraterrestrial Intelligence" (SETI). The application is executed as a collection of distributed tasks, so that each peer runs a small task that downloads and analyzes radio telescope data. The task is executed as a screen saver program (starts its execution when the processor is idle). It gets a piece of data over the Internet, analyzes the data and returns the result to the coordinator. When the user gets in contact with its computer, the task is suspended and is resumed later when the computer becomes idle again. Similar computation P2P exist, such as genome@home (2009), which is used to design new protein sequences. Other applications include "code breaking, portfolio pricing, risk hedge calculation, market and credit evaluation, and demographic analysis" (Milojicic, 2003).

Collaborative P2P systems provide the infrastructure for real-time collaboration between peers, which may chat, send and receive instant messages, and work in a collaborative workspace. For example, Jabber.org (2009) is an instant messaging service that uses a standard protocol, Extensible Messaging and Presence Protocol (XMPP). In order to start chatting, the user has to create a Jabber account, download a client, and log in. Internet Relay Chat (IRC) was designed for peers to chat with each other (Jolo@EFnet et al, 2005) but has also facilities for sending files (pictures, text files, etc.). Groove Workspace (2009) uses the P2P technology to create a workspace for peers' collaboration. Each workspace can be customized by selecting the appropriate facilities and tools from a large palette that includes file sharing, whiteboard, chat, attendance of meetings and presentations, group calendar, and others.

Content distribution P2P systems support the sharing of digital media and other data files. This basic facility is frequently associated with more complicated ones that allow publishing, updating, indexing, searching, and retrieving data (Androutsellis-Theotokis, 2004). Napster (2009) and Gnutella (2009) allow peers to search for and download files, mainly music files (Milojicic, 2003). Napster used a central server to manage communication between peers (Dufour, 2005). The server had a list of available files (songs) and locations. A user looking for a specific file addressed a query to the server and got a response indicating the location of that file. The file was downloaded directly between peers. Gnutella uses a distributed approach, which is based on an overlay network that interconnects the peers. To find a file, a peer uses query messages that are flooded through the nodes of the overlay network until a proper peer is identified. The transfer is done directly between peers, as before. Gnutella faces the problem of inefficiency since the overlay doesn't map well with the physical network and two neighbors in the overlay could be situated far apart from one another in the physical network. This may lead to long delays for query messages and responses. Improvements in Gnutella are addressed in (Dufour, 2005). Anyway, attempts to make scalable gnutells-like P2P networks exist (Chawathe et al, 2003).

Freenet (Clarke et all, 2001; Clarke et all, 2002) allows the publication, replication, and retrieval of data files. The network is totally decentralized and preserves the anonymity of information publishers and consumers. To this aim, the messages exchanged between peers are encrypted and are routed through several intermediate nodes before delivery. Also, the files are kept in encrypted form in the data store. Another important feature is the policy used in file replication: files are replicated in locations near the peers that are interested in their use, and are deleted from locations where there are no interested users. Peers share bandwidth and a part of their storage space. One particular characteristic is that files are kept in the data storage according to their popularity.

BitTorrent is a P2P system for accessing rich media (large amounts of data) over the Internet. It is based on a protocol that works as follows. When a file provider (called seed) makes a file available to the network, other peers download the file and, at the same time, make the data available to others. A peer that completely downloaded the file might become seed and continue to make data available to others. This replication of the file source contributes to the balancing of the charge and reduces the resource consumption of the original seed. Bit-Torrent software includes a client (the first piece of software developed for the protocol), which has many versions and licenses. The program is "designed to speed up the viewing of streaming video files, downloading software (with or without the BitTorrent protocol) and playing online video games." (BitTorrent, 2009). The new BitTorrent DNA (Delivery Network Accelerator) the client has several advantages: it delivers downloads in parallel from several sources, which decreases the download time; the number of sources increases with the increase in popularity of the streams; it selects from the most proper sources (for example sources that are closer to the destination) to increase the efficiency; the BitTorent protocol itself is efficient since it distributes the download tasks among several peers (a peer downloading a stream will distribute it to other peers; also, it will distribute recently received files).

Voice over IP (VoIP) is a peer-to-peer telefony service that allows making free cals over the Internet. Skype (Skype, 2009) uses a global decentralized user directory, a highly effective routing, and firewall and NAT traversal solutions to offer a scalable telefony service as good as the traditional telefony systems.

PeerCQ (Gedik & Liu, 2003) is a decentralized information monitoring system for heterogeneous peer-to-peer network. Similar to WebCQ, it uses Continual Queries that are executed whenever a trigger condition becomes true and return the part of results that is different from the results of the previous execution. The service is used to track changes in web documents and notify users if the changes satisfy specific conditions. Good performance is obtainen by the use of a totally decentralized architecture and of a service-opartitioning mechanism at the P2P protocol layer. The peer-to-peer model was also used in building middleware (or infrastructure) services that stay at the aim of building distributed applications. Examples include location services, reputation management, anonymity assurance, security, etc. Chord (Stoica et al, 2001) is a scalable peer-to-peer lookup service for Internet peer-to-peer applications. Chord supports one operation, namely "given a key, it maps the key onto a node". This is used to locate the node that stores a particular data item. To do this, a key is associated with each data item, and the (key, data item) pair is stored at the node to which the key maps. Content Addressable Network - CAN (Ratnasamy et al, 2001) proposes a scalable indexing mechanism that allows the mapping of file names to their locations in a large scale distributed system like the Internet. Pastry (Rowstron and Druschel, 2001) is an infrastructure for application level location and routing. In Pastry, each node has a unique nodeId. Given being a message and a key, a Pastry node routes the message to the node which nodeId is numerically closest to the key. Other related works are Tapestry (Zhao et al. 2004) that refers to an infrastructure for fault-tolerant wide-area location and routing, and Kademlia (Mayamounkov and Mazieres, 2002) that describes a scalable peer-to-peer lookup service based on the XOR metric.

Srivatsa and Liu (2005) developed Event-Guard, a framework and defense mechanisms for securing publish-subscribe overlay services. The service model includes publishers, subscribers and routing nodes, each one being a possible threat source. For example, malicious publishers may masquerade as authorized publisher and spam or flood the subscribers with incorrect or duplicate publications; malicious subscribers may try to break the confidentiality (obtain information for which they didn't subscribe); malicious routing nodes may eavesdrop routed messages. EventGuard ensures publishers and subscribers' authentication, confidentiality and integrity of the messages sent by publishers to subscribers, and the availability of the services against DoS attacks. In addition, it introduces a low overhead, has a good scalability, and is easy to use. EventGuard is based on three elements: a set o security guards against possible security threats, a network able to cope with node failures and DoS attacks, and a trusted meta-service to create tokens and keys for controlling the confidentiality.

COMMON ISSUES IN DISTRIBUTED SYSTEMS

At the beginning of this chapter, the main requirements for large scale distributed applications have been presented: achieving high performance, reliability, and fault tolerance; exploiting the functional specialization of system components and the applications' parallelism. To these we added the low development and exploitation cost, easier user access to application components hosted by remote resources, incremental system growth, transparency (of replication, concurrency and failures), openness, scalability, and security. Answering these requirements claims for new approaches, models, technologies, techniques, algorithms, and implementations to exploit communication, storage and processing resources. They are subjects to chapters 3 to 9 of the book. Here we shortly present these important key issues of large scale distributed systems.

Communication plays an important role in distributed systems. No matter if they are client-server or peer to peer systems, components are usually located in different locations and must communicate through the network that connects them. Consequently, communication is essential for the overall performance of distributed applications. Finding new methods for the efficient use of very high performance communication networks for both high volumes of data and high interactive message exchanges is a very important research issue.

Resource management must respond to both the applications' QoS requirements and to constraints stated by resource owners. These make difficult the efficient and balanced resource use which calls for new approaches and methods that often lead to complex multi-criteria optimization problems.

New task scheduling algorithms are also necessary for responding to general requirements like response time reduction. Task scheduling is known to be a NP complete problem even for single-processor systems. For distributed systems, task scheduling must take into consideration not only the estimated task execution times but also the code and data transfer times if tasks are to be run on remote resources, the rapid variation of the resource state and others. New scheduling mechanisms, like resources co-allocation and advance reservation are required to solve complex problems raised by these problems.

Another issue is related to storing large amounts of data and quickly retrieving them when needed. Solutions must be found for distributing data among several repositories, and for fast and reliable data transfer. In addition, storing and retrieving functions are difficult to implement since data are replicated and their consistency must be maintained.

Monitoring means collecting, processing and displaying information about the status and operations of distributed systems. Monitoring can be used in the development phase, for testing, debugging and evaluating components of distributed systems. Also, it is important during the normal operation, for gathering information about the dynamic system behavior. This information can be further used as feedback for resource management and task scheduling or for prediction and learning purposes. The main concerns related to monitoring are data production, collection, and display in the conditions of high accuracy and low overhead induced in the monitored system.

Fault tolerance is another important topic in all distributed system types and it is achieved by replication. So, the same resource type (file, page, processing resource, etc.) or service may be offered by several peers (in a P2P system) or servers (in a client-server system). For statefull resources or services, consistency is one of the most difficult issues. Also difficult is recovery from failures, which is treated according to techniques specific to distributed systems.

Security is another issue common to all distributed system types. The main security attributes (confidentiality, integrity, and availability) are preserved with specific methods that take into account the distribution on large scale of the distributed system components. The most important issues refer to the access control to different system and application components and to secure communication among components.

CONCLUSION

Distributed computing refers to concepts, models, methods, and technologies used in producing integrated computing facilities as collections of autonomous network-interconnected computers. Large scale distributed computing has the additional constraint of scaling, which means that computing facilities' performance doesn't degrade with the increase in the number of computers and users, network size, and volume of datasets they process. Well-known large scale distributed systems are the Internet, the Web, large Enterprise Information Systems, Peer-to-Peer Systems, Grids, Utility and Volunteer Computer Systems, Pervasive Systems, and others.

Large scale distributed computing is used in numerous applications with high QoS requirements in terms of performance, cost, availability, ease of use, reliability and others. Similar new solutions, conceptual approaches, models, architectures, and design methodologies are required by all these application types to cope with common problems such as: the integration of diverse technologies used in different parts of the distributed systems that must inter-operate; tolerance to faults, which have a higher occurrence probability in large systems than in usual, smaller scale computer systems; assurance of confidentiality and protection; efficient use of resources, and scalability. In addition, compute-intensive applications require more processing power, data-intensive applications have specific demands for storing and retrieving data in large repositories, while collaborative applications need the ability to share and co-create knowledge in large organizations and cope with social issues that influence their design and implementation.

Distributed systems can be classified in two broad architectural categories, client-server and peer-to-peer, in which components can play the role of client, server, or both. Both categories share common characteristics: they use centralized, decentralized and distributed solutions; components can be part of the business structure (that perform the tasks specific to the application) or of the management structure (that perform monitoring and control tasks); common approaches (such as service orientation) are used as response to similar demands.

Despite the success registered so far, the large scale distributed computing is a young field of research, with promising results, but very complex at the same time. It is difficult and challenging to predict the impact solutions that we design for, and evaluate in smaller test systems we are familiar with, will have on the large user community of large scale distributed computer systems.

REFERENCES

Amazon.com. (2009). *Amazon Elastic Compute Cloud (Amazon EC2)*. Retrieved April 11, 2009, from http://aws.amazon.com/ec2/

Anderson, D. P., Cobb, J., Korpela, E., Lebofsky, M., & Werthimer, D. (2002). Seti@home: an experiment in public-resource computing. *Communications of the ACM, 45*(11), 56–61. doi:10.1145/581571.581573

Androutsellis-Theotokis, S., & Spinellis, D. (2004). A survey of peer-to-peer content distribution technologies. *ACM Computing Surveys, 36*(4), 335–371. doi:10.1145/1041680.1041681

Bamba, B., Liu, L., Yu, P., & Iyengar, A. (2009). Distributed Processing of Spatial Alarms: A Safe Region-based Approach. In *Proceedings of IEEE Int. Conf. on Distributed Computing (ICDCS 2009)*, June 22-26, Montreal, Quebec, Canada. Retrieved September 2, 2009, from http://www.cc.gatech.edu/~lingliu/papers/2009/Bamba-icdcs09.pdf

Berners-Lee, T., Hendler, J., & Lassila, O. (2001). The Semantic Web. *Scientific American Magazine*, May 17, 2001. Retrieved April 11, 2009, from http://www.sciam.com/article.cfm?id=the-semantic-web&print=true.

BitTorrent. (2009). *BitTorrent*. Retrieved April 11, 2009, from http://www.bittorrent.com/

Cable News Network. (2000). *Open source Napster-like product disappears after release.* Retrieved April 11, 2009, from http://www.cnn.com/2000/TECH/ptech/03/15/gnutella/

Cerami, E. (2002). *Web Services.* New York: O'Reilly.

Chawathe, Y. Ratnasamy, Sylvia, Breslau, L., Lanham, N., & Shenker, S. (2003). Making gnutella-like p2p systems scalable. In *SIGCOMM '03: Proceedings of the 2003 conference on Applications, technologies, architectures, and protocols for computer communications* (pp. 407–418). New York: ACM Press.

Chung, W. (2008). Web searching in a multilingual world. *Communications of the ACM, 51*(5), 32–40. doi:10.1145/1342327.1342335

Clarke, I., Hong, T. W., & Sandberg, O. (2002). Protecting Free Expression Online with Freenet. *Internet Computing, 6*(1), 40–49. doi:10.1109/4236.978368

Clarke, I., Sandberg, O., Wiley, B., & Hong, T. W. (2001). *Freenet: A distributed anonymous information storage and retrieval system.* Retrieved February 12, 2009, from http://www.cs.uiowa.edu/~ghosh/freenet.pdf

CoAKTinG. (2009). *CoAKTinG.* Retrieved April 10, 2009 from http://www.aktors.org/coakting/

Conallen, J. (2000). *Building Web Applications with UML.* Reading, MA: Addison Wesley.

Contributors, G. T. (2009). *GT Contributors.* Retrieved April 10, 2009, from http://www.globus.org/toolkit/contributors.html

Coulouris, G., Dollimore, J., & Kindberg, T. (2001). *Distributed Systems Concepts and Design* (3rd ed.). Reading, MA: Addison-Wesley.

Dufour, A., & Trajkovic, L. (2006). Improving Gnutella Network Performance Using Synthetic Coordinates. In *ACM International Conference Proceeding Series, Vol. 191. Proceedings of the 3rd international conference on Quality of service in heterogeneous wired/wireless networks* (Article 31). New York: ACM. eyeOS. (2009). *Cloud Computing Operating System.* Retrieved April 11, 2009, from http://eyeos.org/

Foster, I., & Kesselman, C. (2001). *The Anatomy of the Grid. Enabling Scalable Virtual Organizations.* Intl J. Supercomputer Applications.

Freenet Project Inc. (2003). *The Free Network Project.* Retrieved February 12, 2009, from http://freenetproject.org/

Gedik, B., & Liu, L. (2003). PeerCQ: A Decentralized and Self-Configuring Peer-to-Peer Information Monitoring System. In *Proceedings of the 23rd International Conference on Distributed Computing Systems* (pp. 490-499). Washington, DC: IEEE. genome@home (2009). *genome@home.* Retrieved April 11, 2009, from http://genomeathome.stanford.edu/

Globus Toolkit. (2009). *Globus Toolkit.* Retrieved April 10, 2009, from http://www.globus.org/toolkit/

Gnutella Developer Forum. (2003). *The Gnutella Developer Forum (GDF).* Retrieved April 10, 2009 from http://groups.yahoo.com/group/the_gdf/

Golbeck, J., & Wasser, M. M. (2007). *Social-Browsing: Integrating Social Networks and Web Browsing.* Retrieved September 11, 2009, from http://trust.mindswap.org/papers/GolbeckWasserWIP.pdf

Google Docs. (2009). *Create and share your work online.* Retrieved April 11, 2009, from http://docs.google.com/

Gorton, I., Greenfield, P., Szalay, A., & Williams, R. (2008). Data-Intensive Computing in the 21st Century. *Computer, 41*(4), 30–32.

Groove. (2009). *Groove Workspace.* Retrieved April 10, 2009 from http://www.groove.net.

Gross, R., Acquisti, A., & Heinz, H. J., III. (2005). Information Revelation and Privacy in Online Social Networks. In *Proceedings of the 2005 ACM workshop on Privacy in the electronic society* (pp. 71-80). New York: ACM.

Hayes, B. (2008). Cloud Computing. *Communications of the ACM, 51*(7), 9–11.

Heer, J., & Boyd, D. (2009). *Vizster: Visualizing Online Social Networks.* Retrieved September 11, 2009, from http://hci.stanford.edu/jheer/files/2005-Vizster-InfoVis.pdf

Hendler, J., Shadbolt, N., Hall, W., Berners-Lee, T., & Weitzner, D. (2008). Web science: an interdisciplinary approach to understanding the web. *Communications of the ACM, 51*(7), 60–69.

Hipschman, R. (2009). *How SETI@home works.* Retrieved April 11, 2009, from http://seticlassic.ssl.berkeley.edu/about_seti/about_seti_at_home_1.html

Jabber. (2009). *Jabber.* Retrieved April 10, 2009, from http://www.jabber.org

Jolo@EFnet, et al. (2005). *IRC File Trading: Geek-centric way to get free stuff?* Retrieved April 11, 2009, from http://www.irchelp.org/irchelp/security/warez.html

Kouzes, R. T., Anderson, G. A., Elbert, S. T., Gorton, I., & Gracio, D. K. (2009). The Changing Paradigm of Data-Intensive Computing. *Computer, 42*(1), 26–34.

Lawton, G. (2008). New Ways to Build Rich Internet Applications. *Computer, 41*(8), 10–12.

Lee, C., & Percivall, G. (2008). Standards-Based Computing Capabilities for Distributed Geospatial Applications. *Computer, 41*(11), 50–57.

Liu, L., Tang, W., Buttler, D., & Pu, C. (2002). Information Monitoring on the Web: A Scalable Solution. *Springer World Wide Web Journal, 5*(4), 263–304.

Lysne, O., Reinemo, S.-A., Skeie, T., Solheim, A. G., Sodring, T., Huse, L. P., & Johnsen, B. D. (2008). Interconnection Networks: Architectural Challenges for Utility Computing Data Centers. *Computer, 41*(9), 62–69.

Marchionini, G., & Ryen, W. (2009). White Information Seeking Support Systems. *Computer, 42*(3), 30–32.

Matsuoka, S., Saga, K., & Aoyagi, M. (2008). Coupled-Simulation e-Science Support in the NAREGI Grid. *Computer, 41*(11), 42–49.

Mayamounkov, P., & Mazieres, D. (2002). Kademlia: A peer-to-peer information system based on the xor metric. In *Proceedings of the 1st International Workshop on Peer-to-Peer Systems* (IPTPS'02), MIT Faculty Club, Cambridge, MA.

Microsoft, S. Q. L. (2009). *SQL Server Data Services FAQ.* Retrieved April 10, 2009, from http://www.microsoft.com/sql/dataservices/faq.mspx

Milojicic, D.S., Kalogeraki, V., Lukose, R., Nagaraja1, K., Pruyne, J., Ichard, B., Rollins, S., & Xu, Z. (2003). *Peer-to-Peer Computing.* HP Laboratories Palo Alto, HPL-2002-57 (R.1).

Napster. (2009). *Napster.* Retrieved April 10, 2009, from http://www.napster.com

NESSit. (2009). *NESS Project.* Retrieved April 10, 2009, from http://it.nees.org/

Papazoglou, M. P., Traverso, P., Dustdar, S., & Leymann, F. (2007). Service-Oriented Computing: State of the Art and Research Challenges. *IEEE Computer, 40*(11), 38–45.

Photoshop Express. (2009). *Photoshop Express.* Retrieved April 11, 2009, from https://www.photoshop.com/express/landing.html

Pourebrahimi, B. Bertels, K.L.M., & Vassiliadis, S. (2005). A Survey of Peer-to-Peer Networks. In *Proceedings of the 16th Annual Workshop on Circuits, Systems and Signal Processing.* ProRisc.

Project jxta (2009). *Project jxta.* Retrieved April 10, 2009, from http://www.jxta.org.

Ratnasamy, S., Francis, P., Handley, M., Karp, R., & Shenker, S. A. (2001). Scalable Content-Addressable Network. In *Proceedings of the 2001 conference on Applications, technologies, architectures, and protocols for computer communications SIGCOMM'01* (pp. 161-172). ACM New York, NY, USA.

Rosetta. (2009). *Rosetta.* Retrieved April 12, 2009, from http://en.wikipedia.org/wiki/Rosetta@home

Rowstron, A., & Druschel, P. (2001). Pastry: Scalable, decentralized object location and routing for large-scale peer-to-peer systems. In *Proc. of the 18th IFIP/ACM International Conference on Distributed Systems Platforms (Middleware 2001),* Heidelberg, Germany, November 2001. Retrieved February 12, 2009, from http://research.microsoft.com/en-us/um/people/antr/pastry/pubs.htm

salesforce.com. (2009). *CRM Solutions & Platform.* Retrieved April 11, 2009, from http://www.salesforce.com/aloha.jsp

Search Engines. (2007). *How Search Engines Work.* Retrieved March 14, 2009, from http://searchenginewatch.com/2168031

SETI@home. (2009). retrieved on February 12, 2009, from http://setiathome.berkeley.edu/sah_about.php

Shklar, L., & Rosen, R. (2003). *Web Application Architecture.* Hoboken, NJ: John Wiley & Sons.

Siegel, J. (Ed.). (2000). *CORBA 3. Fundamentals and Programming.* New York: OMG Press, John Wiley & Sons.

Skype. (2009). *VoIP explained.* Retrieved April 11, 2009, from http://www.skype.com/help/guides/voip/

Srivatsa, M., & Liu, L. (2005). Securing Publish-Subscribe Overlay Services with EventGuard. In *Proceedings of ACM Computer and Communication Security* (pp. 289-298). New York: ACM.

SSDS. (2009). *SQL Server Data Service.* Retrieved April 11, 2009, from http://www.microsoft.com/sql/dataservices/faq.mspx

Stoica, I., Morris, R., Liben-Nowell, D., Karger, D., Kaashoek, M.F., Dabek, F., & Balakrishnan, H. (2001). Chord: A Scalable Peer-to-peer Lookup Service for Internet Applications. *IEEE/ACM Transactions on Networking (TON), 11*(1), 17-32.

Strickland, J. (2008). *How Cloud Computing Works.* Retrieved April 10, 2009, from http://communication.howstuffworks.com/cloud-computing.htm

Strickland, J. (2009). *How Utility Computing Works.* Retrieved April 11, 2009, from http://communication.howstuffworks.com/utility-computing.htm

Tanenbaum, A. S., & van Steen, M. (2007). *Distributed Systems. Principles and paradigms* (2nd ed.). Upper Saddle River, NJ: Prentice Hall.

Utility. (2009). *utility computing* Retrieved April 11, 2009, from http://en.wikipedia.org/wiki/Utility_computing

Wilkins-Diehr, N., Gannon, D., Klimeck, G., Oster, S., & Pamidighantam, S. (2008). TeraGrid Science Gateways and Their Impact on Science. *Computer*, *41*(11), 32–41.

Xiong, L., & Liu, L. (2002). Building Trust in Decentralized Peer-to-Peer Electronic Communities. In Fifth International Conference on Electronic Commerce Research (ICECR-5), Montreal, Canada, October, 2002. Retrieved September 2, 2009, from http://www.cc.gatech.edu/~lingliu/papers/2002/xiong02building.pdf

Zhao, B. Y., Huang, L., Stribling, J., Rhea, S. C., & Joseph, A. D. (2004). Tapestry: A Resilient Global-scale Overlay for Service Deployment. *IEEE Journal on Selected Areas in Communications, 22*(1). Retrieved September 2, 2009, from http://www.cs.berkeley.edu/~adj/publications/paper-files/tapestry_jsac.pdf

Chapter 2
Architectures for Large Scale Distributed Systems

INTRODUCTION

This chapter introduces the macroscopic views on distributed systems' components and their inter-relations. The importance of the architecture for understanding, designing, implementing, and maintaining distributed systems is presented first. Then the currently used architectures and their derivatives are analyzed. The presentation refers to the client-server (with details about Multi-tiered, REST, Remote Evaluation, and Code-on-Demand architectures), hierarchical (with insights in the protocol oriented Grid architecture), service-oriented architectures including OGSA (Open Grid Service Architecture), cloud, cluster, and peer-to-peer (with its versions: hierarchical, decentralized, distributed, and event-based integration architectures). Due to the relation between architecture and application categories supported, the chapter's structure is similar to that of Chapter 1. Nevertheless, the focus is different. In the current chapter, for each architecture the model, advantages, disadvantages and areas of applicability are presented. Also the

DOI: 10.4018/978-1-61520-703-9.ch002

chapter includes concrete cases of use (namely actual distributed systems and platforms), and clarifies the relation between the architecture and the enabling technology used in its instantiation. Finally, Chapter 2 frames the discussion in the other chapters, which refer to specific components and services for large scale distributed systems.

IMPORTANCE OF ARCHITECTURAL MODELS

The essential characteristic of distributed computer systems, which differentiate them from other system types, is the existence of several software components that run simultaneously on different computers and intercommunicate by message exchanges. This characteristic is at the base of several distributed system architectures. Tanenbaum and van Steen (2007) identify two approaches. The first one, related to the logical organization of distributed systems, is the software architecture, which describes "how the various software components are to be organized and how they should interact." For example, the basic client-server model describes the distinct roles of the client and server, and specifies their interaction supported by a request-reply type protocol. The second one is the system architecture, which captures also the physical realization of distributed systems, i.e. the way software components are instantiated and placed on real machines. For example, in a centralized architecture a single machine runs all the server software components that are remotely accessible to clients through communication channels. Software architecture models are useful for the study and design of distributed systems. They are used in early phases of distributed systems' development as a blueprint for the whole software process including concept, design, implementation, testing, and maintenance. The system architectural models are important for distributed system implementation and evaluation. Important characteristics such as performance, efficient use of resources, dependability, fault tolerance, security, and others are strongly determined by the architecture model and the technologies behind it. Anyway, documents that present architectural models often refer to both software architecture (that describes the reference model), and system architecture (that describes implementation issues).

CLIENT-SERVER ARCHITECTURES

The classical client-server model distributes the processing between two processes (it is a two-tiered architecture): the server and the client (see Figure 1). The server implements a specific service, for example retrieving a document from a database. It waits to be invoked by a client. When it receives an invocation, it searches for the specific document requested by the client and offers it as response. The client sends an invocation to the server and waits for the response that includes the requested document. When the client receives the document it can display it for the user. This example corresponds to the thin client model, in which the client implements only the user interface that includes the presentation software. The whole application processing (in general, the application is much more than simply searching for a document) is carried out by the server. Another model is the fat client, in which the client implements a part of the application as well. The model is especially useful for applications that highly interact with the user for which a low response time is required. The disadvantage of the fat client model is that new versions of the application must be installed on each client machine not only on the server, which is not the case for the thin client model.

Very often a server can act also as a client and call another server. This leads to a multi-tiered architecture in which each tier represents an application layer. In a three-tiered architecture we typically find a presentation layer for the interface with the user, a processing layer that contains the application specific functionality, and the data layer that manages the databases containing the application data. There are several advantages of the multi-layered approach: more clear specialization of servers, possibility to distribute the servers to different machines, increase scalability (servers could be added as the demands increase), etc.

The main issues of this architecture are determined by the existence of one server that must respond to many clients' requests. The results

Figure 1. Client-server architecture

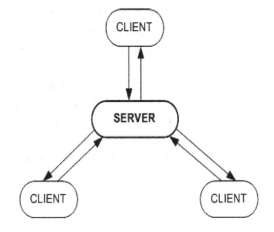

of this centralization are server overloading and network congestion, which cause performance degradation. In addition the centralized server represents a single point of failure, which means lack of robustness. Server replication is used to solve these problems but it needs special mechanisms for keeping replicas' consistency. Anyway, the replication is also a solution to improve the client-server communication since it contributes to congestion avoidance and allows clients to communicate more profitably with those server replicas located in their proximity. Another solution for improving the communication is the use of fat clients that support executing parts of the application at clients sites. Consequently, the load is distributed between servers and clients, which reduces servers' load and improves the performance. Also, the solution favors the client-server communication in highly interactive applications. The bad part is that maintenance becomes more difficult since upgrading the application means also upgrading the many clients that use it. To cope with this problem, in Web based applications, the client is a standard browser which dynamically downloads the application software from the server, when needed. Easy application development and coping with heterogeneity of distributed systems are other issues, which are solved by using specific software development tools and runtime environments. Other problems relate to low cost development, mobile code, and fat clients. Some of them are discussed in the sequel.

The object oriented client/server architecture, which is widely used today, has two forms: distributed classes or distributed objects. If until 1970 only 40% of the budgets of IT departments were spent on software maintenance, in 1990 the percent raised to 90%, mainly because of the orientation to object programming and faster distribution of applications (Schünemann, 2009). Today there is an increasing need for software to access the information stored in various databases or different hardware. The object-oriented client/server architectures came to meet these demands.

In the distributed classes architecture the logical software components are classes implemented on different computers based on their specific behavior. This architecture is based on a peer-to-peer underlying communication layer in order to function. In the distributed objects architecture the logical components of the software application are objects dynamically distributed on various nodes of the underlying network. The fundamental idea is that these distributed objects are not linked to the computers where they were initially created; instead they can migrate wherever they are needed. Such a working environment naturally fits to the peer-to-peer architecture in which the objects can collaborate anywhere in the network. The technology to support this type of architecture is the object request broker, middleware that allows objects to invoke other objects anywhere in the network.

Object-Oriented Client/Server Internet (OCSI) environments combine the object-orientation, client/server model, and Internet concepts to deliver business functionality. In particular, several attempts are underway to combine distributed objects and the Web (the ANSAWEB prototype being developed by the ANSA Consortium or the Microsoft's Active Platform are examples of this).

In the Web-based environment there are various restrictions: the hardware scalability compared to the ever-increasing computation needs of the applications, inclusion of legacy applications, integration of systems based on the supported environments coming from different vendors, supplying security, transactions, and data integrity services. All these constraints pushed the enterprise software on the architectural evolution track that ranges from one-tier to distributed environments based on multiple tiers (or n-tiers) models. For instance, the server side of the three-tier architecture can be divided in two: one layer hosts the Web server delivering services and another for the application server (Schussel, 1995).

The I-net architecture (Kaiser, et al, 1999) is yet another client/server architecture, taken to another level. This architecture represents a new form of data processing in which the client/server system uses the Web browser as client and the Web server as the back-end component. The I-net architecture has several advantages over traditional client/server architectures. A first advantage is the increased efficiency when it comes to costs. The configuration of the system can be done relatively easy, with low cost, because the underlying technologies are based on widely-adopted open-standards. The server application to configure the Web server is available from a wide range of producers. The client machines have Web browsers, which are relatively easy to use, to access the server. The underlying network for I-net use is already deployed in many companies' information systems. A second advantage consists of the hybrid architecture that exploits the performance of both, the client/server and the host models. The I-net architecture is oriented towards ease of use, centralized control of information and simple administration of resources. The possibility of grouping several heterogeneous systems together, in a globally interoperable network, is yet another advantage of the I-net architecture. The I-net architecture was developed from the beginning with the idea of connecting different systems together.

From the software development point of view, the major advantage of I-net is the possibility to create applications for many platforms, without additional costs for creating and distributing several versions of the applications. The updates on the server-side are immediately available for all users. The I-net applications using components on the client-side, for example mini Java-applications or ActiveX controls, can use the automatic download capabilities of the browser to update any component when available. The components working together to ensure the functionality to build I-net applications are: the Web browser, the server components, components adequate to work with distributed systems (middleware components) and server-based components.

The Web browser is currently used as client for obtaining access to the static data hosted on

Web servers, and to interactively modify Web content as well. The Web client/server concept evolved from accessing and displaying static Web page stored on Web servers to interact with real applications that execute the business logic that processes the data stored in databases to dynamically respond to user demands. Today, the data flow came to be bidirectional between the client and the application server.

The Representational State Transfer (REST) architecture is an abstraction of the architectural elements within a distributed hypermedia system (Fielding, 2000). REST ignores the details of component implementation and protocol syntax in order to focus on the roles of components, the constraints upon their interaction with other components, and the interpretation of significant data elements. It encompasses the fundamental constraints upon components, connectors, and data that define the basis of the Web architecture, and thus the essence of its behavior as a network-based application. REST is considered a coordinated set of architectural constraints that attempts to minimize latency and network communication while maximizing the independence and scalability of component implementations. This is achieved by "placing constraints on connector semantics where other styles have focused on component semantics" (Fielding, 2000). REST enables the caching and reuse of interactions, dynamic substitutability of components, and processing of actions by intermediaries, thereby meeting the needs of an Internet-scale distributed hypermedia system.

Several architectural models have been identified for the mobile code. All of them are related to the notion of virtual machine (Tanenbaum, & van Steen, 2007), which is a software implementation of a computer. A piece of code can be migrated from one machine to another if the second machine has the same characteristics as the first one or runs a virtual machine that fulfils this condition. In the Remote Evaluation architectural model (Fuggetta et al, 1998), a client sends a piece of code to a remote server that has the necessary resources to execute it. The results are sent back to the client. Obviously, the execution is constrained by several conditions that refer to the protection of other software running on the server. Anyway, the approach lets clients to run applications for which they don't have enough resources or that might be executed more efficiently on remote servers (for example, the transfer of the code to the remote server is less costly than the transfer of the data to be processed from the server to the local client). In the Code-on-Demand architectural model (Fuggetta et al, 1998), the client downloads a piece of code and executes it locally. This approach dynamically extends the basic functionality of the client and keeps simple its static behavior, while decreasing the load of the server by passing some tasks to the clients. The downloaded code must be executed in a protected environment at the client.

Ryan and Perry (2003) discuss several variations of the client/server architectures for current and Next Generation Internet (NGI) applications, from the perspective of end-users, application developers and service providers. The authors present substantial evidence to show that up until today the move to richer client functionality has been slow for next-generation mobile phones, with tension existing between the needs of various stakeholders such as application users, developers and service providers. This is augmented by the increasing diversity of NGI (Moyer and Umar, 2001), where devices are ever varying along a number of dimensions such as screen size, form factor, processing speed, permanent storage capacity, and power consumption. The authors also present an empirical study, which evaluates the performance of a typical Internet based business scenario, provides evidence to sustain that delegating functionality to clients offers a significant benefit to end users and service providers, thereby potentially justifying additional development effort.

HIERARCHICAL ARCHITECTURES

The idea at the aim of the hierarchical architectures is the realization of the distributed system functionality by composing the functionalities of several layers organized in a stack (Figure 2).

In each layer, the functionality is offered by several components that interact according to a specific protocol, using the services of the layer bellow to offer enriched services to the layer above. The model has the advantage of simplicity since each layer of the hierarchy isolates the lower layers from the upper layers. Consequently, components at one layer can be replaced by new ones (with higher performance) as long as the layer offers unchanged service to the layer above. On the other hand, the performance could be affected by the increased overhead induced by the distribution of the overall functionality into several distinct layers (Cremonesi & Turri, 2006). When combined with the client-server model, the hierarchical architecture is known as multi-tiered architecture.

Although hierarchical architectures are considered separate architecture styles, their use within network-based systems is limited to the combination with the client-server architectures to provide layered-client-server, LCS. Layered-client-server adds proxy and gateway components to the client-server architectures. A proxy acts as a shared server for one or more client components, taking requests and forwarding them, with possible translation, to server components. A gateway component appears to be a normal server to clients or proxies that request its services, but is in fact forwarding those requests, with possible translation, to its "inner-layer" servers. These additional mediator components can be added in multiple layers to add features like load balancing and security checking to the system. Architectures based on layered-client-server are referred to as two-tiered, three-tiered, or multi-tiered architectures (Umar, 1997) and were described in the previous section.

Hierarchical architecture design is focused on protocols that govern the cooperation of compo-

Figure 2. Layers of the hierarchical architecture

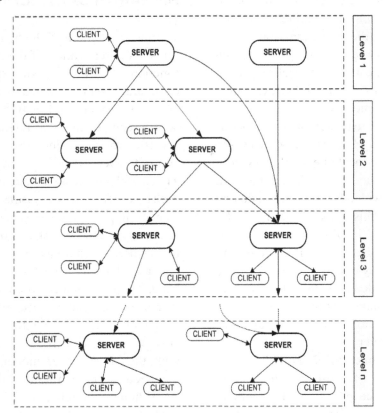

nents in different layers. Hierarchical architectures have several advantages: they simplify the design, based on the well known principle "divide-et-impera"; they support enhancement of components at one layer without need to make changes in other layers of the architecture on condition the cooperation protocols are respected; similarly, different implementations of the same layer can coexist in a distributed system. Hierarchical architectures are difficult to develop and implement. First, not all systems can be organized as layers. Second, even if this is possible, establishing the right layers that satisfy specific high performance requirements or constraints could be difficult and represent an important research issue. One solution could be the self-organizing software architecture (Georgiadis et al, 2002) in which the designer specifies the constraints configurations must obey to and

components self-configure their interactions in accordance with these specifications.

An example of hierarchical architecture is the protocol oriented Grid architecture (Foster, 2001). This is inspired from the ISO OSI and TCP/IP Internet reference models, from which it borrowed the vocabulary (entities, interfaces, protocols, and services), conceptual aspects (the hierarchical organization, the separation of layers, etc.), and the practical approach (Grid APIs & SDKs to facilitate the application writing). In addition, the majority of Grid services and protocols are extensions of the actual network services and protocols, which refer to remote resource access, and communication among Grid entities. New services refer to the issues that Grid computing try to resolve such as the resource brokerage, resource discovery, and allocation.

The model distributes the Grid functionality in five layers (Figure 3). The Fabric layer provides the Grid resources as logical or physical entities. The service primitives available at this layer are used for introspection (discovery of the structure, states, and capabilities of resources), management of the quality of service, and specific operations (for the computational resources these include starting the program execution, its monitoring and control, query service for finding the resource characteristics, load level, etc.)

The Connectivity layer provides the inter-resource communication (data transfer between resources, remote access to a resource, etc.) Also, it includes: user and resource authentication based on the single sign-on paradigm, rights delegation, inter-operation with local security solutions, trust management, and data encryption. The Resource layer is concerned with sharing of a single resource and includes protocols for negotiation, initialization, monitoring, control, log and payment at single resource level. It uses the Fabric services to access and control the local resource, and offers information services (to find out the structure and state of a resource) and management services (for negotiating the access to shared resources, advance reservation, operation control and monitoring, etc.) at the level of an individual resource. The Collective layer offers services and protocols for collections of resources. The services offered at the global level of a VO – Virtual Organization include: directory services (resource discovery), resource co-allocation, scheduling, brokerage, monitoring and diagnosis of the VO resources, data replication. Additional services refer to authorization at VO level, as well as software discovery, payment and accounting. The Application layer includes user applications, SDKs for application development, workflows, and Grid collaborative services.

This architectural model was used for the development of Grid protocols in the Globus Toolkit™ V-2. We mention here the Grid Security Infrastructure (GSI) at the Connectivity level, and several protocols at Resource level: Grid Resource

Figure 3. Grid protocol architecture

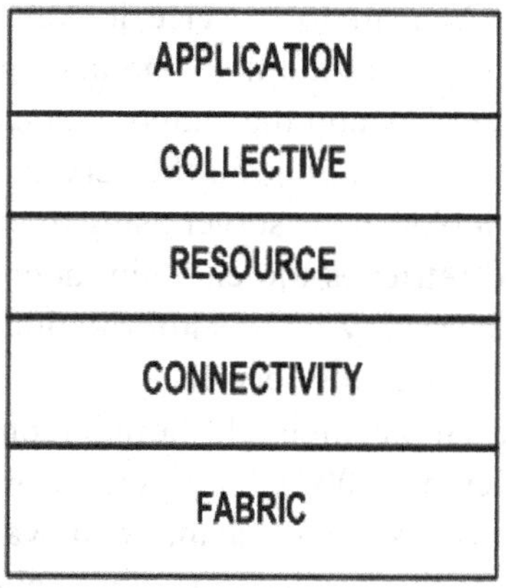

Allocation Management (GRAM), Grid Resource Information Protocol (GRIP), Grid File Transfer Protocol (GridFTP).

SERVICE-ORIENTED ARCHITECTURES

The roots of the Service-Oriented Architecture (SOA) are in the models of Remote Procedure Call (RPC) and Remote Method Invocation (RMI). The first model describes how a program running on one computer can transparently call a procedure located in a different computer, similar to calling a local procedure. The model includes the components and protocol that facilitate the communication between the program (acting as a client) and the procedure (acting as a server) in order to complete the remote call. Also, RPC adopts a language to describe the server interface (XDL - eXternal Data Representation for Sun RPC, IDN - Interface Definition Notation for DCE RPC), the procedures to be followed by the application programmer to develop the server and client code, and the mechanisms used to bind the client to the server at run time. For Sun RPC (Coulouris at al, 2001), the client must know the server machine address. It can use a port mapper program on that machine, and ask for the server's endpoint address to which to connect. In DCE RPC, a very simple mechanism for service lookup is used: the server registers the machine address with a directory service, and the endpoint address with a DCE daemon running on the server machine. The client looks up the server using the directory server, and retrieves the endpoint address from the DCE daemon. With this information in hand, the client invokes the service.

These examples highlight the main components of SOA (Cerami, 2002): the service provider that implements the service and makes it available on the Internet; the service consumer (client) that invoke the available services; the service directory (or registry) that permits the providers to publish services and the clients to find and invoke them; and the transport layer that ensures the exchange of messages between clients and servers. Each service is described by an interface definition, which specifies how the service can be invoked and how the messages exchanged between clients and servers are structured.

Similar mechanisms are used for the Remote Method Invocation. For example, in CORBA (Common Object Request Broker Architecture), which is an OMG (Object Management Group) standard for developing distributed applications, the communication between clients and servers is supported by an Object Request Broker, ORB that uses a specific protocol such as the Internet Inter-Orb Protocol, IIOP (Siegel, 2000). ORB makes transparent to the client several characteristics regarding server objects such as their locations (in the same process as the client, in another process on the same machine, or in a different machine), implementation (what language, operating system, what machine type, what mechanisms for client – server communication were used, etc.) The client executes specific tasks by obtaining a reference of the object and invoking different methods. The server object implements services described by an IDL interface, and is identified by a unique object reference, which is opaque for the client (the client doesn't have direct ac-

cess to the fields of the reference structure). The reference can be obtained at object's creation, by invoking the directory service, by invoking the trading service, or by the notification service to which the client can subscribe. Other services are those for CORBA object Life Cycle, events, time management, security, concurrency control, etc. CORBA introduces the possibility to dynamically build invocations at runtime (not only statically, at compile time), by using a Dynamic Invocation Interface. An Interface Repository (IR) offers to the client information on different existing IDL interfaces, while an Implementation Repository contains information that allows the activation of server objects and processes. The activation and the delivery of invocations to server objects are done by an Object Adapter that fulfils other functions as well. CORBA has been used for the development of many distributed applications. Nevertheless, it is very complex and uses specific protocols for the client-server interaction.

Another approach for the development of distributed systems is the Web service with its related Service Oriented Architecture, SOA. A Web service is specified, as before, by its interface, in a specific language, the Web Service Description Language, WSDL. This describes the Web services in an XML grammar, which makes it possible to be processed by machine. A WSDL specification has two main parts. The first part specifies the service name, the server operations, different type definitions, and message definitions. The second part describes the bindings to specific message formats and communication protocol used, and the address information for locating the service. The first part represents a logical contract offered by the service independently of the location and communication details. This is a very important advantage for developers who need to consider in their application only the logic of the service and not details related to the underlying technology supporting the service implementation.

A typical use of a Web service is presented in Figure 4. Here, a client checks with a Discovery

Figure 4. Typical use of web services

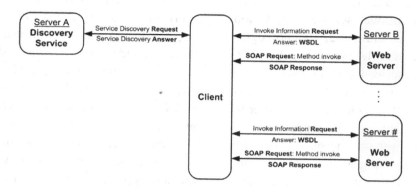

service for the existence of a service that fulfils a specific task. The Discovery service indicates the server that offers the required service. The client contacts the server to obtain a WSDL interface specification. The protocol used in the invocation can be SOAP over HTTP, but other solutions can be used as well.

SOA supports the interoperability of system components, uses standards and common specifications: XML messaging (in particular SOAP), UDDI for service discovery, HTTP and BEEP for message transport. Web services are easy to use, either stand alone or in combination with other Web services. They offer independency from the programming language used for the development. Nevertheless, messaging in XML, which has the advantage of openness, induce a higher overhead than other technologies, such as CORBA, for example. Anyway, many existing CORBA systems can be integrated with the new SOA approaches by using CORBA bindings for WSDL (Vinoski, 2004). This permits the specification of CORBA interfaces in the first part of a WSDL description, and of the communication mechanisms in the WSDL binding definition part.

In addition to functional requirements, the static or dynamic composition of services must often satisfy QoS requirements. This is imperative in mission-critical systems (such as defense, traffic control, healthcare systems, etc) that have high-assurance requirements regarding performance,

reliability, security, dependability and others (Dong et al, 2008). This asks for including the high-assurance requirements representation in the description of service interfaces, and for a method to select those services that together satisfy the global QoS requirements stated by the user. For the first problem, ad hoc, non-standard solutions are used, which makes harder the service discovery. Services composition is a complex problem that claims for exploring different workflows and select the services that satisfies the constraints (Yen et al, 2008). More practical is to make the selection from a small set of possible workflows for which the overall QoS is pre-calculated. Yen et al (2008) propose the use of a decision service that makes the selection. In addition they use reconfigurable services, for which parameters that can be adjusted at runtime are included in the service description.

Actual research in service-oriented computing is conducted along several axis (Papazoglou et al, 2007): service foundations, service composition, service management, and service design and development. For the first axis, the main topics include dynamically creating and configuring optimal service oriented architectures, ensuring end-to-end security, providing uniform access to data, and developing semantically enriched discovery services. Service composition refers to orchestration and choreography. By orchestration, services are connected and coordinated to create higher level business processes. The Business

Process Execution Language for Web Services (BPEL4WS) supports Web service composition (Weerawarana & Curbera, 2002). By choreography externally observable interactions between web services are described. It is supported by the Web Services Choreography Description Language (WS-CDL). Research challenges refer to behavioral and semantic conformance, adaptive processes, QoS awareness, and business-driven compositions. Concerning service management, the challenge is the development of services that are capable of self -configuration, -adaptation, -healing, -optimization, and -protection. Service design and development needs contributions in service-oriented engineering methodologies, development strategies, service versioning, and service governance.

OGSA AND WSRF

The service model has also been used in Grid computing, for building the Open Grid Service Architecture, OGSA. The main purpose was to use the Web service model and standards to specify a set of high level Grid services (for common runtime, monitoring and discovery, execution management, data management, and security) and to integrate them in application development frameworks such as Globus Toolkit 4 (GT4).

This represented the next step in Grid technology, made by OGSA, which was centered on the concept of Grid Services. Grid Services are based on Web Services - technology that has the advantage of standardization, relying on Internet based standards like Simple Object Access Protocol (SOAP) and Web Services Description Language (WSDL). A Grid service is actually a Web service that conforms to a set of conventions and supports standard interfaces (Foster, 2002). The Grid services can maintain an internal state, which distinguishes an instance of the service from others. Most of the Grid software packages adopted the Web Services technology.

The Web services community pointed out some shortcomings of OGSA, and of its implementation support Open Grid Service Infrastructure (OGSI), which are underlined in (Czajkowski, 2004): there are too many functions in a single specification, it does not work well with the existing Web services and XML tools (for example, JAX-RPC), it has too many similarities with the object oriented model (like the existence of instances and of an internal state), and it uses features from WSDL 2.0 which are not supported in WSDL 1.1 (Bokhari, 2008; Berman, 2003).

These issues were addressed with the introduction of the Web Services Resource Framework, WSRF, which defines the notion of WS-resource as an extension of the Web service. Conceptually, a WS-resource is a pair of a Web services and an associated resource (see Figure 5), used to create a stateful web service. While the resource is the entity used to separately keep the service state, a WS-resource invocation identifies both the service and the resource by a WS-addressing endpoint reference (Foster, 2002). This refactoring has been done in three steps (Czajkowski, 2004): the introduction of the WS-Resource concept, a better separation of function and exploitation of other Web services specifications, and a broader view of notification (for the state changes appearing in Web services). OGSA with WSRF aim to exploit the new Web services standards, especially WS-Addressing (standard that describes transport neutral mechanisms to address Web services).

In the WS-Resource Framework, the state is no longer stored within the service, but within the so-called resources. WSRF and Grid services offer equivalent functionality, but WSRF has several advantages, like being easier to implement and exploit with the current Web services tools, and making a clearer separation between the service (which can be a simple message processor, both in WSRF and OGSI) and the resource, which stores the internal state (Bhatti, 2003).

The current state of the art in Grid architecture technologies is represented by the WSRF

Figure 5. Layers of the grid service model

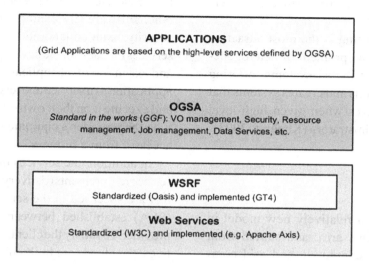

framework, which is being adopted in some of the most important Grid software toolkits and has reached sufficient maturity to be included in enterprise products (e.g., Univa Globus Enterprise) (Alef, 2009). The WSRF could offers a service-oriented based architecture for meta-scheduling in computational Grid (Moltó, 2008) making resource available for users from different VO, using Globus Toolkit 4. Chapter 4 describes the role of WSRF for resource management systems in large scale distributed systems.

Although WSRF and Java-based hosting environment have been successful in dealing with the heterogeneity of resources and the diversity of applications, the current Grid middleware has several limitations to support on-demand resource provisioning effectively (Byun, 2007). For example in DynaGrid project, a new framework for WSRF-compliant applications is adopted (Byun and Kim, 2007). Many new components, such as Service Door, Dynamic Service Launcher (DSL), Client Proxy, and Partition Manager, have been introduced to offer adaptive, scalable, and reliable resource provisioning. The experimental evaluations were performed on a real test bed with practical applications including the Map Reduce application.

Another important aspects added by OGSA are represented by choreography, orchestration and workflow (Peltz, 2002). *Choreography* describes required patterns of interaction among services and templates for sequences (or more structures) of interactions (Zhou, 2009). *Orchestration* describes the ways in which business processes are constructed from Web services and other business processes, and how these processes interact (Turner, 2007).

Workflow is a pattern of business process interaction, not necessarily corresponding to a fixed set of business processes. All such interactions may be between services residing within a single data center or across a range of different platforms and implementations anywhere (Kurdel, 2008). However, a lack of sophisticated coordination mechanisms for specifying workflow deters the widespread adoption of Grid Services. There is a need for a seamless, flexible, demand-based service to enable engineers and scientists to submit jobs to a computational Grid from remote sources in a manner that ensures that jobs are executed in an efficient, controlled method. The solution presented in (Chao, 2006) uses BPEL4WS (Business Process Execution Language for Web Services) as a coordination language to define and manage workflow among Grid Services to meet engineering requirements.

Autonomic computing is the most attractive approach to solving the problem of heterogeneity in large scale distributed systems, offering services-based solutions and creates systems that can manage themselves when given high-level objectives from administrators (Kephart, 2003).

CLOUD

Cloud computing is a relatively new model in the distributed systems area, and started from concepts like utility computing and grid computing. It implies the providing of computing resources (computers, storage and even software) as a service. The aim is to make resources less expensive (the clients are charged only for the amount of resources effectively used, and do not have to deal with their maintenance) and to increase their utilization (resources can be shared by different users and applications). The services are reliable, and are accessible in the Internet on demand, from simple or complex terminals (such as laptops, smart phones, workstations, etc.), from anywhere there is network access. Cloud computing is based on advanced technologies such as virtualization, clustering, distributed and parallel processing and others.

The clouds provide services on various levels that form a multilayered hierarchy. The most important layers are for infrastructure, platform and software services; corresponding with these layers, the concepts promoted by cloud computing are: infrastructure as a service (IaaS), platform as a service (PaaS), and software as a service (SaaS). IaaS delivers virtualized hardware resources such as computers, storage, and bandwidth for Internet access. The user executes specific operating systems and other software on these resources, and pays for their usage rather than purchasing the necessary equipment. PaaS is the delivery of a computing platform that includes not only the infrastructure but also the operating systems and other software (for example a database service, security, team collaboration or other specialized services) needed for the development, deployment, and execution of an application. SaaS licenses an application as a service and lets the users download and execute it on their own computers, or execute it on the provider's equipment (in the cloud) and access it from a browser.

In addition, the services must meet quality of service requirements (delivery time, performance), that are specified in the service level agreement (SLA) established between the client and the provider. To satisfy the clients' performance objectives, the clouds are built on the idea of elasticity – the capability to quickly increase or decrease the number of resources allocated for an application, depending on how the requirements of the application evolve. The cloud platforms usually provide web interfaces that allow the user to configure, control, and scale the capacity of the computing resources and adapt them to variable requirements.

The internal architecture of clouds is inspired from grids and peer-to-peer systems, as the provided functionalities are quite similar. Currently, most of the clouds are composed of a small number of large data centers, placed in different geographic locations. However, there is ongoing research on other architectural alternatives for cloud systems. Grossman et al. (2009) proposed a cloud storage infrastructure, Sector, in which the storage servers are organized in a peer-to-peer overlay that uses the Chord protocol. On top of Sector there is a middleware layer that manages the computing resources, being able to locate data automatically and to distribute the processing operations among the nodes.

Sedayao (2008) introduces a framework for monitoring the performance of a commercial web site, which was built using technologies that are specific to cloud computing and to Service Oriented Architecture. The framework uses web services for tasks like provisioning virtual machines or obtaining geographic information, and was deployed on PlanetLab, a world-wide testbed for distributed systems.

Some of the most important issues concerning cloud computing are resource management, data management, fault tolerance and security. Resource management in clouds is mainly focused on provisioning, not a trivial problem in environments with multiple users that have strict quality-of-service requirements; the resource provisioning solutions often use virtualization as the base technology and take advantage of recent developments that make possible the migration of virtual machines. Cloud computing has brought significant innovations in the data management area, with new database models emerging, that aim to provide better performance than the traditional relational databases (however, at the cost of reduced functionalities); another concern of cloud data management is providing data storage as a service – one of the most popular types of cloud services. Since most of the current cloud applications come from the business area, they have strong fault tolerance requirements; replication is often employed to diminish the effect of failures. Security is a sensitive issue as the users are highly concerned about preserving the privacy of the data that they store in the cloud.

Cloud computing is a new research domain, and many issues need further study. Among the future trends that can be foreseen for cloud systems, we mention the orientation to micro data centers, the emergency of common standards and APIs for accessing cloud resources, the connection of multiple cloud systems into inter-clouds, and the automated resource provisioning. Church et al. (2008) shows that the current large data centers are extremely expensive to maintain; high costs are paid for electricity (especially the cooling systems), for the networking infrastructure, for maintaining the building that hosts the data center etc. The authors bring arguments in favor of geo-diverse, distributed data centers, also known as micro data centers. The micro data centers have a significantly smaller maintenance cost, more fault tolerance and would also bring the benefits of edge processing (allocating resources to process the clients' requests as close as possible from the clients). The interoperability among cloud systems and the possibility to connect them into so-called inter-clouds are issues promoted by several research and industrial groups. In order to achieve these objectives, a first step is establishing a set of common interfaces to access cloud resources; although up to this moment a standard has not

Figure 6. Cloud architecture

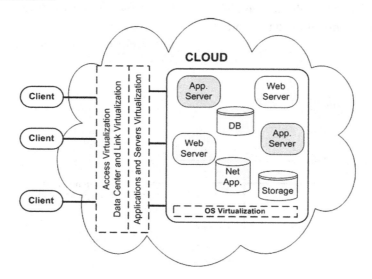

been defined yet, the beginning of standardization work is expected. Another trend for cloud platforms is the automated resource provisioning. While in most of the current cloud platforms the computing resources have to be requested and released manually, the future provisioning systems will be intelligent, having the ability to add and remove resources automatically to an application based on how well it satisfies the Service Level Agreements.

CLUSTERS

A computer cluster is an ensemble of computers (workstations) that are interconnected by a local area network and behave as a single computer system. Clusters were traditionally used for high performance computing (compute clusters), but are now used also for increasing the availability (high availability clusters) or for the load balancing of computer servers (Foster, 2001). High availability clusters have a configuration of a minimum two nodes, which are necessry to provide redundancy and the avoidance of single points of failures. The load balancing and compute clusters include two types of nodes. The master nodes run the file system and the cluster middleware. They fulfill several functions such as load balancing, scheduling, user interface and job queuing. The compute nodes do the application data storage and processing.

According with all this presented aspects, we could design cluster architecture in a modular and open way. In this architecture all components have unique roles and could be organized as a software stack. This stack represents a standard consisting in three tier system architecture (Jaeger-Frank, 2006). This architecture includes back-end compute nodes (computer tier), management nodes (management tier), and front-end access nodes (access tier).

The computer tier consists of many back-end compute nodes, which represents the compute power of the cluster. All tasks are scheduled to run on one or more node in this tier. In this tier, nodes run the daemons associated with message-passing environments and services for system monitoring and automatic control. The tasks are submitted to a node in computing tier using a node from the management tier. After task's execution the computing element reports job completion status and accounting details. Effective scheduling in such cluster architecture can reduce the amount of data transferred across the Grid by dispatching a job to where the needed data are present (Chang, 2007).

The management tier includes a group of servers (one or many) which run the resource management system, hardware diagnosis software, system performance monitor, fault tolerance detector, and system recovery and restore. Other functionalities offer by this tier are: file servers that provide NFS service to other nodes in the cluster, management of operating system

Figure 7. Cluster architecture

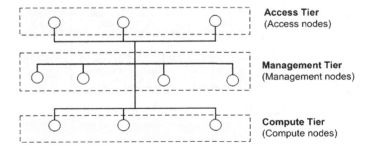

and application software versioning and patch application on other nodes in the cluster, security services. A main strategy for Cluster security could be to adopt both PKI and PMI infrastructures at the grid layer, ensuring that an adequate transfer of authentication and authorization will be made between the Virtual Organization and Resource Provider layers (Laccetti, 2007).

The number of servers in the management tier depends on the type of services to be provided. For example, in small implementation a single node can be chosen to host all management services. This model offers an ease possibility of administration because limited functionality. If the functions and services are provided by multiple servers, the management tier offers a greater scalability and flexibility.

The access tier offers access and authentication services to VOs users. One of the access method is based on telnet, remote login, or ssh. Another access method is based on web services, which permit easy access to the cluster facilities. The external services, like accounting, could be offered at this tier by implementing different type of protocols. The access method should be able to integrate with common authentication schemes such as NIS, LDAP, and Kerberos.

Cluster contains multiple systems implementing various functionalities. Nodes in the access tier are used to submit, control, and monitor jobs; compute tier nodes are used to execute jobs; and management tier nodes run the majority of the software needed to implement the cluster. Table 1 presents the main requirements for each described tier (Jain, 1999).

Cluster computers provide a low-cost alternative to multiprocessor systems for many applications. Building a cluster computer is within the reach of any computer user with solid C programming skills and a knowledge of operating systems, hardware, and networking. On the other hand, Server-Based Computing (Niemi, 2009), replace workstations with thin clients, and offers an effective solution to many IT problems, while free open source software is a cost-efficient alternative to proprietary software.

For complex applications, grid-based On-Line Analytical Processing (OLAP) application, which distributes query computation across an enterprise Grid, represents a viable solution. The idea presented in (Dehne, 2009) follows a two-tiered process for answering queries based on sharing Cached OLAP data between the users at the local grid site and using grid scheduling approaches to

Table 1. Requirements for the nodes in different tiers

Tier	Requirements
Computer	- support a variety of job types - message passing methods - support for distributed memory applications - support for monitoring and nod status - support for job execution status and check-pointing
Management	- dependent on the size of the compute cluster - dependent on the volume of jobs being submitted - support for monitoring - support for different scheduling policies and models - possibilities to be configured to act as compute nodes - dedicated server nodes
Access	- no special configuration - direct access the Cluster Grid - simple operations for introduction or modification of nodes - ease management mechanisms - scalability - reliability

execute the remaining parts of a query amongst a distributed set of OLAP Servers.

For parallel algorithms, a generic framework combining communication models and adaptive approaches to deal with the performance modeling is presented in (Nasri, 2009). The problem associated with the design of efficient parallel algorithms in grid computing environments requires collective communication operations. Experiments performed on a cluster platform prove that the cluster framework provides significant performance, while determining the best combination of model and algorithm depending on the problem and architecture parameters.

Future Clusters solution will allow a VO to take advantage of computational GRIDs without having to develop a custom in-house solution. For example in (Bradley, 2006), GRID Resource Providers are described, which have the role to make resources available on the GRID. It allows companies to make use of a range of resources such as processing power or mass storage. Access to these resources must be controlled, otherwise computational GRIDs will simply evolve to become unable to offer a suitable Quality of Service to any user (Bhatti, 2003).

A new model for resource Cluster organization and management is based on virtualization.

Figure 8. Distributed p2p architecture

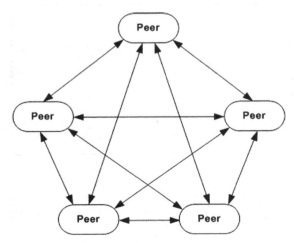

Virtualization can enhance the functionality and ease the management of current and future Cluster Grids by enabling on-demand creation of services and virtual clusters with customized environments, QoS provisioning and policy-based resource allocation. The use of virtual machines is considered in a data-center environment, where a significant portion of resources from a shared pool are dedicated to Grid job processing. The goal of virtualization is to improve efficiency while supporting a variety of different workloads (Cherkasova, 2006).

PEER-TO-PEER ARCHITECTURES

Peer-to-peer architectures are based on components (nodes) that have equivalent application functionalities. In other words, there is no component specialization of the peers, all of them being able to offer and consume (or share), the same kind of resources such as CPU cycles, storage, content, etc. In addition, peers implement special services such as bootstrapping, adding and removing peers, maintaining an index to search for other peers, connecting to and disconnecting from neighbor nodes, encrypting / decrypting the content, and others (Androutsellis-Theotokis & Spinellis, 2004). The absence of a centralized server (Figure 8) makes peer-to-peer architectures more scalable and adaptable to variations in the number of nodes or to network and peer failures (there is no single point of failure). Also distributed are the administration, maintenance and other responsibilities related to systems and their applications. This architecture corresponds to totally de-centralized peer-to-peer systems. To highlight that, in such systems, nodes can equally act as servers and as clients, a peer is also called servent (an abbreviation for server and client). Examples of such systems include Gnutella, Freenet, Chord, and CAN (Pourebrahimi, et al., 2005).

In hybrid peer-to-peer architectures (Figure 9), the nodes are not homogeneous. Maintaining directories with meta-information, used to search for specific content or services, is not done by all nodes. In hybrid centralized architectures, the directory is maintained by a central server. So, a peer must first contact the server to find information about resources shared by active peers, and then interact directly with one of these peers. These architectures suffer from the existence of a single point of failure, a higher vulnerability to security attacks, inefficiency due to the high load of the centralized server, and lack of scalability due to the centralized approach (Pourebrahimi, et al., 2005). On the other hand, the architecture is simple and the discovery service needs a few messages to be exchanged with the centralized server. This architecture is used by Napster (Cable News Network, 2000).

In hybrid peer-to-peer partially centralized architectures, directories are maintained by a group of interconnected supernodes. Each supernode keeps information about the resources shared by local peers connected to it, and acts as a proxy for search requests initiated by these peers and solved by other superpeers. A node must have more bandwidth and processing power than other peers, and a minimum number of clients to become a supernode. Rules can be defined to automatically turn a node into a supernode or back into a regular peer. An example is Kazaa (2009). More recently, Gnutella also adopted the concept of supernode. This architecture avoids the single point of failure (is fault tolerant) and is more scalable since the directory service is distributed among several supernodes.

Many peer-to-peer applications involve searching – locating the peer(s) that store some required data, or that meet some given criteria. The search is usually performed by creating queries that are routed from one peer to another until the suitable one is found.

For example, in Gnutella a search is initiated by a peer that sends queries to the adjacent nodes (nodes to which it is connected directly). Each neighbor node forwards the query to its own neighbors. The process continues until a node that contains the specific file is reached. The query carries different parameters. For example, a Time To Live value indicates how many times a message can be forwarded. Also, a "minimum speed required" parameter can be included in the query, indicating that nodes may respond only if they satisfy this minimum transfer speed for data transfer. The query can include other parameters as well. The node that satisfies the requirements sends an answer in which it includes information about the endpoint connection address at which

Figure 9. Decentralized p2p architecture

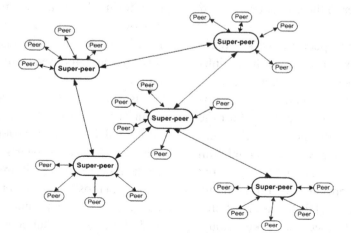

the peer can be contacted. Consequently, a node knows where the content is placed and directly contacts the node for the transfer.

In contrast with this approach, in Freenet (2009) a node that can satisfy a query directly responds with the content. This makes the network less vulnerable since a node has information only about the neighbors and generally does not know where the data is stored in the network. In addition, nodes that forward the content can store this locally and become sources for other queries. If not, nodes can "learn" from past history and direct future queries that ask for the same content on the right path towards the content source.

A key concept in peer-to-peer systems is the topology – the layout of the overlay network that connects the peers. Depending on the degree of determinism in building the overlay, the peer-to-peer systems can be classified as structured or unstructured. In unstructured overlays, there are no rules for establishing links, and a peer that joins the system can connect to any other nodes that are already in the network. Gnutella, discussed above, is an unstructured peer-to-peer system. The disadvantage of such systems is the large overhead associated with query routing, which used to be done by flooding the network. This problem has been overcome by applying better strategies for transmitting the queries, like using parallel random walks through the network or maintaining routing tables that indicate which neighbors are more likely to be closer to the content requested by the query.

In structured peer-to-peer networks, there are specific conventions for establishing links among the nodes, depending on their contents. In this way, the query routing can be done deterministically, and there is an upper bound for the number of hops taken until the desired content is found (usually, it is approximately equal with the logarithm of the network size). The structured peer-to-peer overlays provide the functionality of a distributed hash table (DHT) – a distributed data structure in which the peers store (key, value) pairs and there is an efficient method for retrieving the value associated with a given key. Some well-known structured peer-to-peer systems are Chord, CAN and Tapestry. Some of the more recent research aims to combine the low routing overhead advantage of DHTs with the advantages of using super-peers - better tolerance to churn (nodes that join or leave the system frequently) and handling of nodes heterogeneity. One example is StealthDHT (Brampton et al., 2006), a system in which the super-peers are organized into a DHT and have the function of forwarding messages, while the other nodes only act as clients of the super-peers (not taking part in the DHT).

There are various protocols for communication and membership management in peer-to-peer systems. Since it is impossible for a node to have a global view of the system, the usual approach is that each node maintains knowledge about a small set of other nodes (neighbors) with whom it communicates according to a specific protocol. For example, in Gnutella, a node wishing to join the network must connect to an existing node, by using a protocol that is similar, in many respects, to HTTP. After being admitted in the network, the node can start communicating with other nodes by using the Gnutella protocol, and can accept connections from nodes that wish to join the network.

Among the most important issues in peer-to-peer systems are searching (discussed above), data management, fault tolerance, security and monitoring. In what concerns data management, peer-to-peer systems have been traditionally used for file sharing applications, so there has been a lot of research focused on distributed data storage and retrieval; this has resulted in a large number of distributed hash table types, and also in many solutions for storing data in unstructured or semi-structured peer-to-peer systems. The inherent fault tolerance of peer-to-peer systems has also been extensively studied for its many practical applications, and most of the current overlays are able to deal successfully with churn and even with massive node failures. In what concerns the security, the peer-to-peer systems encounter a broader range of problems than the other types of distributed systems, among which are: malicious nodes that aim to corrupt the overlay, trust issues with the code of the applications and with the shared data, and also the free-riders (users that benefit from a peer-to-peer application without contributing to it). Monitoring has been mostly used so far for detecting and measuring the use of file sharing applications, but another direction is to use the monitoring information for the self-adaptation of the peer-to-peer overlay (to the varying conditions of the network and of other external factors).

Nowadays peer-to-peer systems are often used for disseminating data – for example, media streams or RSS feeds. The most common architecture used in such applications is a multicast tree, and an important problem with this type of overlay is its low resistance to churn. Several improvements have been proposed to increase the tolerance to churn in the tree topologies, one of the most recent ones being presented by Frey & Murphy (2008). They proposed an overlay maintenance protocol in which each node continuously monitors its neighbors, thus being able to detect the failure of its parents in the tree and to actively search for a new parent when this happens.

Freedman et all (2002) present Tarzan, a P2P anonymizing network layer. Tarzan reduces the necessary effort to offer anonymity for existing (peer-to-peer or client-server) Internet applications without modifying them, and with a reasonable overhead. To ensure anonymity, Tarzan uses two main mechanisms: each packet is routed, from source to destination, through a randomly chosen sequence of peers; packets are transmitted in encrypted form, using "mix-style layered encryption", which means that each peer transforms the packet by removing or adding a layer of encryption. Together, these mechanisms create a tunnel for packet transmission. In addition, a Tarzan client must be installed at one end of the tunnel, and a network address translator (which routes the packet to the destination) must be present at the other end.

Trust management in a peer-to-peer community is very important and difficult at the same time. In such communities there is no trusted third party or authority to manage the trust. Consequently, trust management must be based on past experience and information distributed among peers. Xiong and Liu (2002) developed PeerTrust, a P2P system for trust management based on peer reputation. The authors propose a model in which not only the feedback obtained from other peers is used, but also the total number of interactions the feedback is based on (the feedback context), and the level of trust associated with the peer that provides feedback. In a more recent paper, Xiong et al (2007) discuss the problems of feedback scarcity (insufficient feedback) and feedback manipulation by malicious users and provide solutions to improve the trust management process.

Vlachos et al (2004) describe the use of a P2P infrastructure for increasing the resistance of open networks to epidemic type of virus and worm attacks. The solution proposed by the authors is based on a group of specialized peers that detect virus or worm rapid propagation, exchange warning messages describing the attacks identified by the Intrusion Detection System, and adapt the level of security control to the rate of warning messages received.

We are witnessing a trend of broadening the range of peer-to-peer applications, from the traditional file sharing applications to voice over IP, media streaming, distributed web search and many others. This will result in the arising of new research issues and also in increasing the interest for some of the existing ones. For example, two of the research trends are focused on optimizations based on the underlying network topology and on self-organizing peer-to-peer overlays. By designing overlays that are aware of the underlying network topology, the communication performance can be significantly improved and also its cost can be reduced. This approach was taken by Zeinalipour-Yatzi et al. (2007) to construct pFusion, an unstructured overlay which clusters together the nodes that are topologically close to each other. In order to improve the information retrieval, pFusion uses a search mechanism in which the nodes profile the query activity of their neighbors, and use the acquired knowledge when deciding where to forward the queries. Self-organizing peer-to-peer systems represent another trend in the domain, and the objective is the automatic adaptation to various types of changes (in the underlying network infrastructure or performance, in the number and distribution of member nodes, in the users' requests etc.) and to failures. The challenge here is to collect monitoring information that can provide a global view of the system, so that adaptation decisions can be made; the difficulty resides especially in ensuring a reasonably small overhead (in terms of communication and storage) while collecting the data.

CONCLUSION

The macroscopic view of large scale distributed systems is offered by two architectural model types. The software architecture describes the organization and interactions of their software components. It is useful for distributed systems study and design. The system architecture refines the software architecture so that it can be implemented and deployed as computer-based solutions. Two main categories of distributed system architectural models are known, which are based on the client-server and peer-to-peer patterns, respectively. The simplest client-server model distributes the processing between the client and the server. More complex models include several tiers, in which some servers can act also as clients and invoke other services. These models can be implemented based on Object Oriented technologies but other solutions exist as well. Many client-server models are Web-based, in which case the client is implemented in the browser and the application server is added to the Web server. Some models make a more detailed specialization of components, such as the MVC, which distinguishes among the Model, Vie, and Controller components. In the hierarchical models, components can be structured in layers, so that components on one layer can use the services of layers bellow to provide enhanced services to the layers above. A more flexible organization is offered by the SOA, in which the processing is performed by composing self-descriptive services that can be discovered at execution time. This model is being used in numerous Web applications and Grid platforms. A special form of services is offered by Cloud computing, which is based on provisioning computing resources (mainly computers and storage) as services. To support high performance services, clusters can be used, which gather computers (workstations) that are interconnected by a local area network and behave as individual, powerful computer systems. Last but not least, peer-to-peer architectures use components (nodes) that are able to share with other nodes the same kind of resources: CPU cycles, storage, content, etc.

Architectural models are continuously evolving and respond to higher requirements posed by users. In turn, the new architectures stimulate the development of new and more complex applications that offer higher quality services, i.e. services that are closer to users' expectations. Architectural models are at the aim of developing such kind of systems.

REFERENCES

Alef, M., Fieseler, T., Freitag, S., Garcia, A., Grimm, C., & Gürich, W. (2009). Integration of multiple middlewares on a single computing resource. *Future Generation Computer Systems*, *25*(3), 268–274. doi:10.1016/j.future.2008.05.004

Androutsellis-Theotokis, S., & Spinellis, D. (2004). A Survey of Peer-to-Peer Content Distribution Technologies. *ACM Computing Surveys, 36*(4), 335–371. doi:10.1145/1041680.1041681

Berman, F., Fox, G., & Hey, A. J. (2003). *Grid Computing: Making the Global Infrastructure a Reality*. Hoboken, NJ: John Wiley & Sons, Inc.

Bhatti, S. N., Sørensen, S., Clark, P., & Crowcroft, J. (2003). Network QoS for Grid Systems. *International Journal of High Performance Computing Applications, 17*(3), 219–236. doi:10.1177/1094342003173009

Bokhari, S. S., Ferworn, A., & Abhari, A. (2008). Architectural model for grid resources discovery. In H. Rajaei, G.A. Wainer, & M.J. Chinni (Eds.), *Proceedings of the 2008 Spring Simulation Multiconference, Ottawa, Canada* (pp. 1-5). New York: SCS/ACM.

Bradley, A., Curran, K., & Parr, G. (2006). Discovering Resources in Computational GRID Environments. *The Journal of Supercomputing, 35*(1), 27–49. doi:10.1007/s11227-006-0888-0

Brampton, A., MacQuire, A., Rai, I. A., Race, N. J. P., & Mathy, L. (2006). Stealth distributed hash table: a robust and flexible super-peered DHT. In C. Diot, & H. Ammar (Eds.), *Proceedings of the International Conference On Emerging Networking Experiments And Technologies (CoNEXT), Lisboa, Portugal* (pp. 19). New York: Association for Computing Machinery (ACM).

Byun, E., Jang, J., & Kim, J. (2007). Towards adaptive, scalable, and reliable resource provisioning for wsrf-compliant applications. In C. Kesselman, J. Dongarra, & D.W. Walker (Eds.), *Proceedings of the 16th international Symposium on High Performance Distributed Computing (HPDC '07)*, Monterey, California, USA (pp. 217-218). New York: Association for Computing Machinery (ACM).

Byun, E., & Kim, J. (2007). DynaGrid: A dynamic service deployment and resource migration framework for WSRF-compliant applications. *Parallel Computing, 33*(4-5), 328–338. doi:10.1016/j.parco.2007.02.005

Cable News Network. (2000). *Open source Napster-like product disappears after release.* Retrieved April 2, 2009, from http://www.cnn.com/2000/TECH/ptech/03/15/gnutella/

Cerami, E. (2002). *Web Services Essentials*. Sebastopol, CA: O'Reilly.

Chang, R., Chang, J., & Lin, S. (2007). Job scheduling and data replication on data grids. *Future Generation Computer Systems, 23*(7), 846–860. doi:10.1016/j.future.2007.02.008

Chao, K., Younas, M., & Griffiths, N. (2006). BPEL4WS-based coordination of Grid Services in design. *Computers in Industry, 57*(8), 778–786. doi:10.1016/j.compind.2006.04.012

Cherkasova, L., Gupta, D., Ryabinkin, E., Kurakin, R., Dobretsov, V., & Vahdat, A. (2006). Optimizing grid site manager performance with virtual machines. In *Proceedings of the 3rd USENIX Workshop on Real, Large Distributed Systems (WORLDS '06), Seattle, WA, USA* (pp. 5-5). Berkeley: USENIX Association.

Church, K., Greenberg, A., & Hamilton, J. (2008). On Delivering Embarrassingly Distributed Cloud Services. In *Seventh ACM Workshop on Hot Topics in Networks (HotNets-VII)*.

Coulouris, G., Dollimore, J., & Kindberg, T. (2001). *Distributed Systems Concepts and Design* (3rd ed.). Reading, MA: Addison-Wesley.

Cremonesi, P., & Turri, R. (2006). Performance models for hierarchical grid architectures. In *Proceedings of the 7th IEEE/ACM International Conference on Grid Computing, Barcelona, Spain* (pp. 278-285). Washington, DC: IEEE Computer Society.

Czajkowski, K., Ferguson, D., Foster, I., Frey, J., Graham, S., Maguire, T., et al. (2004). *From Open Grid Services Infrastructure to WSResource Framework: Refactoring & Evolution*. Retrieved September 13, 2009, from http://www-106. ibm.com/developerworks/library/ws-resource/ ogsi_to_wsrf_1.0.pdf

Dehne, F., Lawrence, M., & Rau-Chaplin, A. (2009). Cooperative caching for grid-enabled OLAP. *International Journal of Grid and Utility Computing, 1*(2), 169–181. doi:10.1504/ IJGUC.2009.022032

Dong, J., Paul, A., & Zhang, L. J. (2008). High-Assurance Service-Oriented Architectures. *Computer, 41*(8), 27–28. doi:10.1109/MC.2008.298

Erl, T. (2006). *Service Oriented Architecture*. Upper Saddle River, NJ: Prentice Hall.

Fielding, R. (2000). *Architectural styles and the design of network-based software architectures*. Ph.D. thesis, University of California, 2000. Retrieved April 12, 2009, from http://www.ics.uci. edu/~fielding/pubs/dissertation/top.htm

Foster, I., Kesselman, C., Nick, J., & Tuecke, S. (2002). The Physiology of the Grid: An Open Grid Services Architecture for Distributed Systems Integration. *Open Grid Service Infrastructure WG, Global Grid Forum, June 22, 2002*. Retrieved September 13, 2009, from http://www.globus.org/ alliance/publications/papers.php#OGSA

Foster, I., Kesselman, C., & Tuecke, S. (2001). The Anatomy of the Grid: Enabling Scalable Virtual Organizations. *International Journal of High Performance Computing Applications, 15*(3), 200–222. doi:10.1177/109434200101500302

Freedman, M., Sit, E., Cates, J., & Andomorris, R. (2002). Introducing Tarzan, a peer-to-peer anonymizing network layer. In *Lecture Notes in Computer Science, Revised papers from the 1st International Workshop on Peer-to-Peer Systems (IPTPS'02)* (pp. 121-129). London, UK: Springer-Verlag.

Freenet. (2009) *Freenet Project*. Retrieved May 12, 2009, from http://freenetproject.org

Frey, D., & Murphy, A. L. (2008). Failure-Tolerant Overlay Trees for Large-Scale Dynamic Networks. In K. Wehrle, W. Kellerer, S.K. Singhal, & R. Steinmetz (Eds.), *Proceedings of Eighth International Conference on Peer-to-Peer Computing* (P2P'08), Aachen, Germany (pp. 351-361). Washington, DC: IEEE Computer Society.

Fuggetta, A., Picco, G. P., & Vigna, G. (1998). Understanding Code Mobility. *IEEE Transactions on Software Engineering, 24*(5), 342–361. doi:10.1109/32.685258

Georgiadis, I., Magee, J., & Kramer, J. (2002). Self-organising software architectures for distributed systems. In D. Garlan, J. Kramer, & A. Wolf (Eds.), *Proceedings of the first workshop on Self-healing systems,* Charleston, South Carolina (pp. 32 – 38). New York, NY: Association for Computing Machinery (ACM).

Grossman, R. L., Gu, Y., Sabala, M., & Zhang, W. (2009). Compute and storage clouds using wide area high performance networks. *Future Generation Computer Systems, 25*(2), 179–183. doi:10.1016/j.future.2008.07.009

Jaeger-Frank, E., Crosby, C. J., Memon, A., Nandigam, V., Conner, J., & Arrowsmith, J. R. (2006). A three tier architecture applied to LiDAR processing and monitoring. *Science Progress, 14*(3-4), 185–194.

Jain, A. K., Murty, M. N., & Flynn, P. J. (1999). Data clustering: a review. *ACM Computing Surveys, 31*(3), 264–323. doi:10.1145/331499.331504

Jiang, M., & Willey, A. (2005). Service-Oriented Architecture for Deploying and Integrating Enterprise Applications. In *Proceedings of WICSA 2005, 5th Working IEEE/IFIP Conference on Software Architecture, Pittsburgh, Pennsylvania, USA* (pp. 272 – 273). Washington, DC: IEEE Computer Society.

Kaiser, T., Thiesse, F., Sieberath, C., & Vogler, P. (1999). A Reference Model for the Design of I-Net Applications. In De Bra, P., & Leggett, J.J. (Eds.), *Proceedings of the WebNet Conference on the WWW and Internet,* Honolulu, Hawaii, USA (pp. 598-603). Charlottesville, VA: Association for the Advancement of Computing in Eduction (AACE).

Kazaa. (n.d.) *Home page.* Retrieved April 20, 2009, from http://www.kazaa.com/us/index.htm.

Keahey, K., Foster, I., Freeman, T., Zhang, X., & Galron, D. (2005). Virtual Workspaces in the Grid. In J.C. Cunha, & P.D. Medeiros (Eds.), *Proceedings of the 11th International Euro-Par Conference,* Lisbon, Portugal (pp. 421-431). London, UK: Springer.

Kephart, J. O., & Chess, D. M. (2003). The Vision of Autonomic Computing. *IEEE Computer, 36*(1), 41–50.

Kurdel, P., & Sebestyénová, J. (2008). Grid workflows specification and verification. *W. Trans. on Comp., 7*(8), 1199–1208.

Laccetti, G., & Schmid, G. (2007). A framework model for grid security. *Future Generation Computer Systems, 23*(5), 702–713. doi:10.1016/j.future.2007.01.002

Moltó, G., Hernández, V., & Alonso, J. M. (2008). A service-oriented WSRF-based architecture for metascheduling on computational Grids. *Future Generation Computer Systems, 24*(4), 317–328. doi:10.1016/j.future.2007.05.001

Moyer, S., & Umar, A. (2001). The Impact of Network Convergence on Telecommunications Software. *IEEE Communications, 2001*(1), 78-84.

Nasri, W., Steffenel, L. A., & Trystram, D. (2009). Adaptive approaches for efficient parallel algorithms on cluster-based systems. *International Journal of Grid and Utility Computing, 1*(2), 98–108. doi:10.1504/IJGUC.2009.022026

Niemi, T., Tuisku, M., Hameri, A., & Curtin, T. (2009). Server-Based Computing Solution Based on Open Source Software. *Information Systems Management, 26*(1), 77–86. doi:10.1080/10580530802552227

Papazoglou, M. P., Traverso, P., Dustdar, S., & Leymann, F. (2007). Service-Oriented Computing: State of the Art and Research Challenges. *IEEE Computer, 40*(11), 38–45.

Peltz, C. (2003). Web Services Orchestration and Choreography. *IEEE Computer, 36*(10), 46–52.

Pourebrahimi, B., Bertels, K. L. M., & Vassiliadis, S. (2005). A Survey of Peer-to-Peer Networks. In *Proceedings of the 16th Annual Workshop on Circuits, Systems and Signal Processing, ProRisc 2005.*

Ryan, C., & Perry, S. (2003). Client/Server Configuration in a Next Generation Internet Environment: End-User, Developer, and Service Provider Perspectives. In *Proceedings of Australian Telecommunications, Networks and Applications Conference (ATNAC),* Melbourne, Australia.

Schünemann, U. (n.d.). *Comprehensive History of Information and Computing: Electronic Age.* Retrieved May 18, 2009, from http://www.cs.mun.ca/~ulf/csh/commcomp.html

Schussel, G. (1995). *Client/Server Past, Present, and Future.* Retrieved April 5, 2009, from http://news.dci.com/geos/dbsejava.htm

Sedayao, J. (2008). Implementing and operating an internet scale distributed application using service oriented architecture principles and cloud computing infrastructure. In G. Kotsis, D. Taniar, E. Pardede, & I.K. Ibrahim (Eds.), *Proceedings of the Tenth International Conference on Information Integration and Web-based Applications Services (iiWAS'2008),* Linz, Austria (pp. 417-421). New York: Association for Computing Machinery (ACM).

Siegel, J. (Ed.). (2000). *CORBA 3 Fundamentals and Programming*. New York: OMG Press, John Wiley & Sons.

Tanenbaum, A. S., & van Steen, M. (2007). *Distributed Systems. Principles and paradigms* (2nd ed.). Upper Saddle River, NJ: Prentice Hall.

Turner, K. J., & Tan, K. L. (2007). A rigorous approach to orchestrating grid services. *Computer Networks: The International Journal of Computer and Telecommunications Networking*, *51*(15), 4421–4441.

Umar, A. (1997). *Object-Oriented Client/Server Internet Environments*. Upper Saddle River, NJ: Prentice Hall.

Vinoski, S. (2004). *CORBA in a loosely coupled world*. Retrieved September 12, 2009, from http://www.looselycoupled.com/opinion/2004/vinos-corba-infr0908.html

Vlachos, V., Androutsellis-Theotokis, S., & Spinellis, D. (2004). Security applications of peer-to-peer networks. *Computer Networks: The International Journal of Computer and Telecommunications Networking*, *45*(2), 195–205.

Weerawarana, S., & Curbera, F. (2002). *Business Process with BPEL4WS: Understanding BPEL4WS part 1*. Retrieved May 3, 2009, from http://www.ibm.com/developerworks/library/ws-bpelcol1

Xiong, L., & Liu, L. (2004). PeerTrust: Supporting Reputation-Based Trust in Peer-to-Peer Communities. *IEEE Transactions on Knowledge and Data Engineering (TKDE). Special Issue on Peer-to-Peer Based Data Management*, *16*(7), 843–857.

Xiong, L., Liu, L., & Ahamad, M. (2007) Countering Feedback Sparsity and Manipulation in Reputation Systems. In *3rd IEEE Conference on Collaborative Computing: Networking, Applications and Worksharing* (pp. 203-212). Washington, DC: IEEE.

Yen, I.-L., Ma, H., Bastani, F. B., & Mei, H. (2008). QoS-Reconfigurable Web Services and Compositions for High-Assurance Systems. *IEEE Computer*, *41*(8), 48–55.

Zeinalipour-Yatzi, D., Kalogeraki, V., & Gunopulos, D. (2007). pFusion: A P2P Architecture for Internet-Scale Content-Based Search and Retrieval. [IEEE TPDS]. *IEEE Transactions on Parallel and Distributed Systems*, *18*(6), 804–817. doi:10.1109/TPDS.2007.1060

Zhou, J., & Zeng, G. (2009). A mechanism for grid service composition behavior specification and verification. *Future Generation Computer Systems*, *25*(3), 378–383. doi:10.1016/j.future.2008.02.013

Chapter 3
Communication

ABSTRACT

Communication in large scale distributed systems has a major impact on the overall performance and widely acceptance of such systems. In this chapter we analyze existing work in enabling high-performance communications in large scale distributed systems, presenting specific problems and existing solutions, as well as several future trends. Because applications running in Grids, P2Ps and other types of large scale distributed systems have specific communication requirements, we present different the problem of delivering efficient communication in case of P2P and Grid systems. We present existing work in enabling high-speed networks to support research worldwide, together with problems related to traffic engineering, QoS assurance, protocols designed to overcome current limitation with the TCP protocol in the context of high bandwidth traffic. We next analyze several group communication models, based on hybrid multicast delivery frameworks, path diversity, multicast trees, and distributed communication. Finally, we analyze data communication solutions specifically designed for P2P and Grid systems.

INTRODUCTION

Distributed computing offers a natural approach to solving complex data and computation intensive problems. Many approaches to distributed computing have been developed over the past decades. These include *Socket Programming, Remote Procedure Calls (RPC)*, object-oriented technologies such as *DCE, DCOM, CORBA*, Java *RMI*, and *Message-Oriented Middleware (MOM)*. In fact, the trends in the evolution of the large scale distributed systems, such as today's Grids, show that more and more data-intensive applications are migrated towards this environment. The success registered by the large scale distributed computing-intensive applications provided a powerful thrust in this direction. Research communities, such as Biomedical sciences, Earth sciences (like seismol-

DOI: 10.4018/978-1-61520-703-9.ch003

ogy), Astronomy and Astrophysics are today very interested in the subject, due to the massive amount of data they have to deal with. Such communities face challenges such as efficiently streaming data among many participants distributed worldwide or making the backbones of current existing network successfully deal with high amounts of data being transferred in a short amount of time or dealing with the need of the applications to react quickly to errors at the network layer.

In order to face these challenges several developments were made, mostly at the upper layers of the well known ISO/OSI protocols hierarchy: protocols optimized for data transfer over wide area network, data stream distribution through overlay networks for multicast purposes, systems for scheduling the data transfer requests in order to avoid overwhelming the network and storage devices. However, despite the fact that the network bandwidths have grown approximately two orders of magnitude faster than processor speeds over the last two decades, the current distributed systems have treated the network, so far, as a passive and largely featureless substrate for data transport.

HIGH PERFORMANCE NETWORKS AND TECHNOLOGIES

The current Internet architecture was designed as a public **communication environment** for everybody. The Internet by itself is a resource whose fair share is controlled by the used protocols. Because of this, most of the currently available data transfer tools are unaware of the network. They rely on the underlying network protocols to tune their data flow in an acceptable manner for everybody using the network in that moment. Because of this, the Internet architecture is limited in its ability to support, for example, Grid computing applications. Packet switching is a proven efficient technology for transporting burst transmission of short data packets (e.g., for remote login, consumer oriented email and web

applications). Making forwarding decisions every 1500 bytes is sufficient for emails or 10-100 kB web pages. However, this is not an optimal mechanism if we are to cope with data sizes of six to nine orders larger in magnitude. For example, copying with 1.5 Terabytes of data using packet switching requires making the same forwarding decision about 1 billion times, over many routers along the path. Setting circuit or burst switching over optical links is a more effective multiplexing technique.

Over the last few years, optical component technology has rapidly evolved to support multiplexing and amplification of increasing digital modulation rates. Currently, 10 Gigabit Ethernet (GbE) network interfaces are in widespread use, and the costs of these interfaces, as well as 10 GbE ports on switches have dropped. However, because the cost for replacing the current equipment is not justified, given the state of the telecommunications market, for long connections (typically transoceanic connections) SONET optical data transmission technology will remain for several years (SONET, 2006). The cost of the existing 10Gbps network infrastructures has not yet been fully amortized, which makes the Telecom Operators to head towards the so called "next generation SONET/synchronous digital hierarchy (SDH)". This relies on (SONET, 2007):

* GFP – The *Generic Framing Protocol* is designed to transport different packet-switching and TDM technologies over SDH (which is the international standard equivalent of SONET).

* VCAT – The *Virtual Concatenation* creates appropriate sized channels for transporting data over SDH. Only the end nodes of the circuit need to support the protocol. A concatenated payload is created by summing the capacities of the constituting links allowing virtual capacity. As 10 Gbps seems to be the upper limit for transoceanic links, VCAT could be used to transparently

aggregate higher bandwidth links, in order to achieve higher end-to-end transmission rates (for example for transporting data in a very high speed stream between two server-clusters), with a minimal reconstruction effort on the end nodes.

- LCAS – *Link Capacity Adjustment Scheme* combined with VCAT provides "on-the-fly" transport capacity adjustments according to the traffic patterns. With the LCAS, the concept of "Bandwidth on Demand" becomes possible for SDH networks as well.

VCAT is particularly interesting as it is a significant step from the conventional rigid SONET/SDH hierarchy as it provides the capability to deliver fine grained streams of n*51Mbps, whereas conventional SONET/SDH can provide only n*155Mbps streams, with n limited to 1, 4, 16, 32, 64. As a result new products are likely to provide fractional 10GigE services, e.g. 5Gbps, using flow control over the physical 10G interface to regulate the traffic (Cirstoiu, 2008).

Since 2003-2004 a new generation of community-owned or leased wide area optical fiber-based network infrastructures emerged. These are managed by non-profit consortia of universities and regional network providers, to be used on behalf of research and education. Such **network infrastructures** were mainly deployed to cope with the required networking challenges large-scale applications have to meet. The first one consists of providing the networking links capable of sustaining traffic of as much as 100 Gbps, as in the case of the LHC distributed processing (Newman, 2005). The second one consists of developing new tools to move the data through the dedicated links with sufficient efficiency.

This trend, pioneered by C4*net4 in Canada (CANARIE, 2007), has spread to other regions of the world. In U.S. the first network infrastructure of this kind was the "National Lambda Rail" (NLR, 2006), built to accommodate up to 40 10-Gbps

wavelength. In 2005 GEANT 2 was deployed in Europe, connecting 33 European countries (GEANT, 2006). In Japan, 20 Gbps optical backbone came into service in April 2004.

In order to support the large scale distributed infrastructures a number of national or centric based network backbones, as well as continental and intercontinental links and peering points came into existence in the last decade. The U.S.-CERN link ("LHCNet") (Newman, 2005) connecting StarLight (in Chicago) and CERN (in Geneva) is one such initiative, concentrating mostly on supporting the LHC physics experiments in CERN. The Global Ring Network for Advanced Applications Development (GLORIAD) rings the northern hemisphere of the earth in an ambitious effort to link the communities of the three organizing nations – U.S., Russia and China – in close cooperation with core partners in Korea, Netherlands and Canada. StarLight is a research-support facility and a major peering point for US national and international networks. It is based in Chicago, and is designed by researchers for researchers. It anchors a host of regional, national and international wavelength-rich Lambda Grids, with switching and routing at the highest experimental levels. It is also a testbed for conducting research and experimentation with "lambda" signalling, provisioning and management, for developing new data-transfer protocols, and for designing real-time distributed data mining applications (Newman, 2004).

The bandwidth capabilities of the **next-generation networks** have been demonstrated during various challenges. Transfers at 7,2 Gbps have been demonstrated over distances of up to 20,700 km in 2004 (an Internet2 Land Speed Record). During the 2005 SuperComputing Bandwidth Challenge an international team of scientists and engineers led by the California Institute of Technology have achieved a peak throughput of 151 Gbps and an official mark of 131,6 Gbps for several hours at a time. They used 22 optical fiber links and used a FAST TCP protocol (Newman, 2005).

One of the research trends for enabling **high-speed data communications** in support to large scale distributed applications today consists in a forward-looking vision of obtaining much higher capacity networks using many wavelengths. Regarding the actual communication, two terms have appeared to support it: *virtual circuits* when referring to end to end connections which are formed at layer 2 and 3 from the OSI stack, and *lightpaths*, when referring to end to end connections at layer 1.

Another trend in networking is towards *hybrid* networks. Such networks try to combine conventional parts of the network (packet switched) with circuit-oriented segments, where the most demanding applications are matched to dynamically-constructed optical paths to help ensure high end-to-end throughput. Such hybrid networks are supported for example in the context of LHCNet, StarLight or GLORIAD research projects (Newman, 2005).

One other research topic relates to the possibility of enabling a robust and scalable control plane that would establish the path across the optical core of a hybrid network, while automatically configuring the edges to enable the switching onto the Light-Paths. In (Cirstoiu, 2008) the author demonstrates such an approach using a combination of automatic optical-switching control together with a monitoring framework for large scale distributed systems.

Various **communication protocols** for network provisioning are developed today in the context of emerging data-intensive large-scale applications. Such protocols make the switching between routing in layer 3 to direct path selections in the first two layers. Multiprotocol Label Switching (MPLS – RFC 3031) is a connection-oriented, packet-based technology that uses virtual circuits (called LSP – label switched paths). The LSP labels are used by label switch routers (LSR) to switch and forward packets (MPLS, 2007). It can be used to carry IP packets, as well as native ATM, SONET, and Ethernet frames. An important

proposed MPLS capability is the quality of service (QoS) support.

Traffic engineering (Nguyen, 2003) allows a network administrator to make the path deterministic and bypass the normal routed hop-by-hop paths. An administrator may elect to explicitly define the path between stations to ensure QoS or have the traffic follow a specified path to reduce traffic loading across certain hops. In other words, the network administrator can reduce congestion by forcing the frame to travel around the overloaded segments. Traffic engineering, then, enables an administrator to define a policy for forwarding frames rather than depending upon dynamic routing protocols.

One control mechanism to allocate labels to the corresponding traffic flows consists in using the *reservation protocol* (RSVP). Initially defined as a resource reservation setup protocol, RSVP (ReSerVation Protocol) (RFC 2205) was designed to provide diverse levels of Quality of Service (QoS) to traffic flows. This is achieved by making appropriate intra and inter-domain resource reservations. Hence, RSVP facilitates the provisioning of network services for real time and interactive applications such as videoconferencing and IP telephony over the Internet architecture.

Generalized Multi-Protocol Label Switching (GMPLS) (RFC 3945) extends MPLS to provide the control plane (signaling and routing) for devices that switch in any of the packet, time, wavelength, and fiber domains. This common control plane simplifies network operation and management by automating end-to-end provisioning of connections, managing network resources, and providing the level of QoS that is expected in the new, sophisticated applications.

Automatically Switched Optical Networks (ASON) was developed by Study Group 15 of the ITU-T, the ITU's telecoms standardization sector (ASON, 2001). ASON is an architecture that defines the components in an optical control plane and the interactions between those components. It also identifies which of those interactions will occur across a multi-vendor divide, and therefore requires standardized protocols. An Automatically Switched Optical Network is an optical transport network that is capable of dynamically adding and removing connections. This capability is accomplished by using a control plane that performs the call and connection control functions in real time. ASON can be thought of as an improved optical transport network (OTN) that adds sufficient intelligence to the optical nodes to permit dynamic provisioning that can respond to changing traffic patterns. It is an architecture that defines the components of an optical control plane and the interactions between those components. In itself, it does not define any protocols. A key principle of ASON is to explicitly build a framework that supports legacy network equipment.

Based on these **communication protocols**, a number of projects are trying to implement tools for the provision of capacity management (or bandwidth brokerage) services at Layers 1 to 3 of the ISO/OSI network model. Some of the research projects that are currently underway to develop such capabilities are: User Controlled Light Paths (UCLP) in the CANARIE network (UCLP, 2007), Circuitswitched High-speed End-to-End Transport ArcHitecture (CHEETAH) (Zheng, 2005), Automated Bandwidth Allocation across Heterogeneous Networks (AutoBAHN) on GEANT 2 network (GEANT, 2008), Hybrid Optical and Packet Infrastructure (HOPI, 2002), Terapaths (Gibbard, 2006) and LambdaStation (DeMar, 2004).

Dynamic Resource Allocation Controller (DRAC) is a tool developed by Nortel, in collaboration with SURFnet (the Dutch national research and education network) (DRAC, 2004). Their focus is on the flexible provisioning of Layer 1 circuits; although extensions to Layer 2 services are planned to be added to the next versions. The typical service for DRAC is a Level 1 SDH/SONET circuit between two Ethernet ports at the edges of a network. For interconnection to other networks DRAC also supports the concept of ENNI connections to Ethernet, SDH or SONET ports.

The Dynamic Resource Allocation via GMPLS Optical Networks (DRAGON) project is a collaboration among Mid-Atlantic Crossroads (MAX), University of Southern California (USC) Information Sciences Institute (ISI) East and George Mason University (GMU). The goals of the project are to develop infrastructures, technologies, and software to provide dedicated paths across heterogeneous network technologies. The project's target is to accomplish this dynamically in direct response to application requests, on an inter-domain basis with required levels of AAA. The DRAGON project assumes a GMPLS capable optical core network (Lehman, 2006). Optical transport and switching equipment acting as Label Switching Routers (LSRs) provide deterministic network resources at the packet, lambda, and fiber cross connect levels. Current implementations allow to dynamically establishing inter-domain paths across network topologies consisting of Ethernet switches, TDM and optical switches. There are several other areas of work on which are not covered by standards such as domain abstraction for inter-domain advertisements, and Constrained Shortest Path Computation (CSPF) algorithms.

On-demand Secure Circuits and Advance Reservation System (OSCARS) is a project supported by ESnet, whose mission is to provide network services for the Department of Energy, US (Guok, 2006). The project focuses on an automated solution for bandwidth on demand. Initially, this will apply to dynamically setting up MPLS Label Switched Paths (LSPs) to tunnel IP traffic. At a later stage also Layer 2 VPNs will be tackled. For now, OSCARS is a single domain solution, but it is foreseen the support for inter-domain reservations i.e. reservations that span multiple administrative domains.

The OSCARS bandwidth on demand system consists of a front end and a back end. The front end provides the web user interface and the authentication and authorization, which is based on Shibboleth (a standard-based, open source middleware software which provides web single sign-on across or within organizational boundaries). The information entered by the user is stored in a MySQL database to be retrieved later by the back end. The back-end is the portion that actually retrieves and schedules the bandwidth needed. Once the network path is established, and the guarantee for available bandwidth is given, we can make one step further in our attempt to move the data efficiently: choosing which protocols and which tools are available for this purpose.

Currently the most widely used **network protocol** for reliable data transport is Transmission Control Protocol (TCP). It is the most common solution for reliable data transfer over IP networks. Although TCP has proved its remarkable capabilities to adapt to vastly different networks, recent theories (Feng, 2000)(Low, 2003) have shown that TCP becomes inefficient when the bandwidth and the latency increase. TCP's additive increase policy (AIMD: Additive Increase, Multiplicative Decrease) for moderating the window size, based on the often-incorrect presumption that packet losses indicates network congestion, limits the efficient use of the available bandwidth.

To overcome this limitation several new TCP implementations have been proposed: HighSpeedTCP (Floyd, 2003), TCP Westwood+ (Grieco, 2002), H-TCP (Shorten, 2003), FAST TCP (Jin, 2004) or CUBIC (Ha, 2008). Although important progress has been made over the last years, new TCP implementations have to be carefully evaluated before being put into production. Poor implementations or unfair algorithms could cause network collapses.

Another approach to overcome TCP's limitations is to use UDP-based data transport protocols. The best known tool that exploits this idea is UDT (Gu&Grossman, 2008). The advantage of this approach lies in the ease of deployment – since no kernel update is needed. The main disadvantage is the fact that CPU usage is slightly higher in this case, since all the processing requires more

overhead in the user space. On the other hand, TCP stacks are continuously improved within the Linux kernel development, and they will provide the long term solution for this problem.

To support large-scale data driven applications, particularly as the amount of data becomes more prevalent, a large set of subsystems have to be configured and tuned simultaneously. Performing these operations manually, not only demands expensive human expertise, but also limits the maximum practical size of such a system. Also, it becomes difficult to deal with dynamically changing demands and to coordinate the resource requirements of different applications.

It is clear that in order to provide the desired quality of service, the problem of data management has to be tackled at all the layers, in an integrated approach:

- physical layer has to provide the means to move packets in an efficient way, and scalable to the speeds of the next-generation networks;
- hosts have to be properly configured, taking into account the necessities for wide area network transfers (proper network buffer settings and appropriate TCP stacks);
- data movement applications have to know the environment in which they run, and use the proper resources when they are available, in an optimal manner.

Another technique to achieve **high performance data transfer** rate in large scale distributed systems is represented by the adoption of effective **group communication models**. In group communications, multiple peer processes first establish a group and then messages are exchanged among the processes. An efficient and scalable group communication mechanism is essential to the success of large-scale group communication applications. IP Multicast has long been regarded as the right mechanism for this due to its efficiency. In IP Multicast, a packet is sent once by the source, and reaches every destination without unnecessary duplication in the network. However, since its deployment imposes dependency on routers, full deployment has been long in coming. Several alternate approaches to multicast delivery in the network have been proposed in literature.

One deployment practice is to manual configure tunnels to connect several IP multicast enabled "islands" to form what is known as MBone, a static overlay network. However, this approach relies upon coordinated manual configuration of multicast routers on both ends of each tunnel connecting the islands. This makes MBone expensive to set and maintain.

An alternative approach is to let end-host to replicate and forward packets on behalf of the multicast isolated group (Chu, 2002). This solution is expensive because it requires moving the multicast functionality from the network layer to transport or application layer, and it also adds several performance penalties. As end hosts generally do not have the routing information available, solutions implementing this approach must rely on end-to-end measurements to construct the end-host multicast delivery tree. An alternative approach to end host multicast is described in (Banerjee, 2003). The authors present a solution for an application-layer multicast protocol based on probabilistic constructions. The solution, however, focuses mostly on constructing a resilient application-layer multicast protocol that provides fast data recovery when overlay node failures partition the data delivery paths. It does not address the important problem of providing fast communication between the end nodes of the network overlay.

The authors in (Zhang, 2002) proposed a hybrid multicast delivery framework, Host Multicast, to leverage such problems. The solution automates the interconnection of IP-multicast enabled islands, while providing multicast delivery to end hosts where IP multicast is not available. Distributed members self-organize into an efficient, scalable and robust multicast delivery tree. The tree structure is adjusted periodically to accommodate changes in group membership and network topology.

Apostolopoulos (2001) proposed utilizing striped video and multiple descriptions coding (MDC) to exploit path diversity for increased robustness to packet loss. They propose building an overlay composed of relays, and having each stripe delivered to the client using a different source. The work examines the performance of the MDC, but does not describe an infrastructure to actually forward the stripes to the clients. CoopNet (Padmanabhan, 2002) implements such a hybrid system, which utilizes multiple trees and striped video using MDC. When the video server is overloaded, clients are redirected to other clients, thereby creating a distribution tree routed at the server. However, CoopNet uses a centralized algorithm (on the server) to build the multicast trees and does not attempt to manage the bandwidth contribution of individual nodes.

The problem with the tree-based multicast systems such as the ones presented is that they assume that a relatively small numbers of interior nodes carry the load of forwarding multicast messages. This works well when the interior nodes are highly available, dedicated infrastructure routers but it poses a problem for application-level multicast in peer-to-peer systems.

The authors in (Castro, 2003) address this problem by striping the content across a forest of interior-node-disjoint multicast trees that distributes the forwarding load among all participating peers. In their proposed system, named SplitStream, it is possible to construct efficient forests in which each peer contributes only as much forwarding bandwidth as it receives. Furthermore, with appropriate content encodings, SplitStream can be highly robust to failures because a node failure causes the loss of a single stripe on average.

Driven by the success of computing resource sharing as developed in the distributed computing community, in (Sharma, 2005) the authors proposed a new communication paradigm called

distributed communication. Distributed communication enables sharing a set of relatively low-speed WAN channels emanating from communities of multi-homed devices interconnected with a high-speed wireless LAN. The idea is based on the model of task decomposition already adopted in the distributed computing model. Distributed communication is a paradigm that, analogous to distributed computing, considers that (i) communication resources (e.g., channels) are pooled, (ii) networking tasks (e.g., layered video streams) are decomposed into subtasks (e.g., component layers), and (iii) these subtasks are mapped to different channels across multiple hosts with communicated components integrated after delivery. In the case of personal mobile wireless computing devices, multiple wireless communication interfaces have become more prevalent. Often these devices have two distinct types of interfaces: a high-speed LAN interface and a relatively low speed WAN interface. The wireless LAN interface (e.g., IEEE 802.11x) is primarily used to connect to access points that have a wired connection to the Internet. The WAN interface, such as a 2.5G or later generation cellular link, offers near ubiquitous Internet connectivity when a device is out-of-range of an access point. Yet, higher-speed communication can be achieved even when devices are out-of-range of a wireless LAN access point. Ad hoc or mobile collaborative communities can be formed by a group of mobile computing devices in close proximity connected through their compatible high-speed LAN interfaces. By pooling independent communication resources, the community can aggregate the bandwidths of all members' WAN links to achieve higher speed connectivity to all members.

The authors in (Sharma, 2005) also present a prototype bandwidth aggregation system that demonstrates that capturing statistical multiplexing gains is technically feasible. Their design allowed the exploration of link aggregation, highlighting several challenges that should still be addressed. The design of an effective inverse multiplexing system becomes very challenging when the component links are heterogeneous, imperfect, and support time-varying workloads. Links from different service providers may be of dissimilar technologies with different communication characteristics and costs, complicating link selection and task assignment. And even what appear to be similar links offered by the same access provider may introduce thorny problems such as dependent or correlated transmission characteristics or outages.

PEER-TO-PEER COMMUNICATION

By their nature, communication is an inherent aspect of every distributed application. Applications running in Grids, P2Ps and other types of large scale distributed systems have several specific communication requirements. Such requirements include high throughput data transfers, reliable point-to-point messaging and unreliable multicast streaming.

Peer-to-peer (P2P) systems have been widely adopted for communication technologies, distributed system models, applications, platforms, etc (Milojicic, 2002)(Liben-Nowell, 2002). Such systems describe not a particular model, architecture or technology, but rather group a set of concepts and mechanisms for decentralized distributed computing and direct peer-to-peer information and data communication.

The most notable challenge of **peer-to-peer communication** is to deal with the problems associated with the dynamic nature of the peering entities. Within communication itself, as a concept, peer-to-peer technology was used for a long time. Network topologies where the nodes are connected directly (such as meshed topologies and one-to-one connections) have always been part of various communication infrastructures. Flooding or network broadcast are also technologies that support the communication in anonymous peer groups. Network multicast is another peer-to-peer

Figure 1. From physical to logical network topology in the overlay networks.

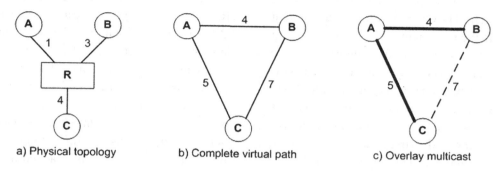

a) Physical topology   b) Complete virtual path   c) Overlay multicast

communication scheme where the user group is known. Group communication and multi-peer communication models apply as well various peer-to-peer principles at the transport layer.

Currently there has been much interest in **P2P network overlays** (distributed systems that are not under any hierarchical organization or centralized control) because they provide (to some extent) a long list of features very attractive to developers of LSDS applications such as: selection of nearby peers, redundant storage, efficient search/location of data items, data permanence or guarantees, hierarchical naming, security. P2P networks can potentially offer an efficient self-organized, massively scalable and robust routing architecture in the context of wide-area networks, combining fault tolerance, load balancing and explicit notion of locality. Currently there is a continuous effort even to include P2P results in defining what is known as mobile peer-to-peer communications – communication services enabled by P2P technologies.

An **overlay network** is a network built on top of another network. The nodes in an overlay network can be thought as being interconnected through a set of logical links. These logical links represent one or more underlying network segments (see Figure 1).

The overlay networks have appeared due to the problems in deploying multicast applications (such as peer-to-peer or video-conferencing applications) over wide area networks. If in intra-domain (within a LAN or a site) multicast

is widely available, the situation is different for inter-domain multicast. Many Internet Service Providers (ISPs) are still reluctant to provide a routing service for this kind of applications due to various technical or marketing reasons. The solution that was widely adopted today to solve the multicast problem was called the tunneling approach. A host having access only to unicast routing contacts a reflector, which is a user-level gateway between the unicast host, a multicast-enabled network or another reflector. The tunnels are established dynamically and they form the overlay network that is used by the application.

All collaborative P2P systems share the problem of locating and addressing peers. In contrast to other types of applications, however, communication here is mostly synchronous amongst an identifiable group (although in some cases systems may provide anonymity to end users). Hence, the addressing problem is related to addressing issues in group and multicast communication. However, in order to provide communication support for modern peer-to-peer application one research issue today is finding good addressing and routing solutions. This should work for highly dynamic group models and also guarantee some degree of anonymity.

According to (Lua, 2005), a generic P2P overlay architecture is generically described as composed of five different layers, each one providing a particular functionality. The network communications layer describes the network characteristics of desktop machines composing the P2P system. The Overlay Nodes Management layer covers the management of peers, including discovery of peers and routing algorithms. The Features Management layer includes security, reliability, fault resiliency and aggregated resource availability aspects of maintaining the robustness of P2P systems. The Services Specific layer provides scheduling of distributed tasks and content and file management. This layer also provides meta-data catalogues, describing the content stored across the P2P peers and also location information. The Application layer is concerned with upper-level tools, applications and services that use the overlay infrastructure.

From the communication perspective, more specifically based on the management of the network topology, **P2P overlay networks** can be either *Structured* or *Unstructured*. A structured P2P overlay network is tightly controlled and the content is placed not at random peers but at specified locations that help in making queries as efficient as possible. Such a system uses a Distributed Hash Table (DHT) as a substrate, in which data location information is placed deterministically. In such systems the data objects are assigned unique identifiers called keys, mapped by the overlay network protocol to a unique peer. Each peer also maintains a small routing table used to forward lookup queries across overlay paths to peers in some progressive manner. DHT-based systems (such as Tapestry, Chord, etc) are an important class of P2P routing infrastructures. They support the rapid development of a wide variety of Internet-scale applications ranging from distributed file and naming systems to application-layer multicast. They also enable scalable, wide-area retrieval of shared information. Although in structured P2P networks the key-based routing facilitates scalability, they incur significantly overheads than unstructured P2P systems for popular content, aspect that makes them in particular unsuitable as protocols for P2P file sharing applications.

The Content Addressable Network (CAN) (Ratnasamy, 2001) is a distributed decentralized P2P infrastructure that provides hash-table functionality on Internet-like scale. CAN is designed to be scalable, fault-tolerant, and self-organizing. The architectural design is a virtual multi-dimensional Cartesian coordinate space on a multi-torus. It routes messages in a d-dimensional space, where each node maintains a routing table with $O(d)$ entries and any node can be reached in $O(dN^{1/d})$ routing hops. Unlike other solutions, the routing table does not grow with the network size, but the number of routing hops increases faster than $logN$. Still, CAN requires an additional maintenance protocol to periodically remap the identifier space onto nodes. CAN has a number of tunable parameters to improve routing performance: Dimensionality of the hypercube; Network-aware routing by choosing the neighbor closest to the destination in CAN space; multiple peers in a zone, allowing CAN to deliver messages to anyone of the peers in the zone in an anycast manner; uniform partitioning allowed by comparing the volume of a region with the volumes of neighboring regions when a peer joins; landmark-based placement causes peers, at join time, to probe a set of well known landmark hosts, estimating each of their network distances. There are open research questions on CAN's resiliency, load balancing, locality, and latency/hopcount costs.

Pastry (Rowstron, 2001) is a scalable, distributed object location and routing scheme based on a self-organizing overlay network of nodes connected to the Internet. Pastry performs application-level routing and object location in a potentially very large overlay network of nodes connected via the Internet. It can support a variety of peer-to-peer applications, including global data storage, data sharing, and group communication and naming. Pastry is completely decentralized, scalable, and self-organizing; it automatically adapts to the arrival, departure and failure of nodes. Experimental results obtained with a prototype implementation on an emulated network of up to 100,000 nodes confirmed Pastry's scalability and efficiency, its ability to self-organize and adapt to node failures, and its good network locality properties. Several application have been built on top of Pastry to date, including a global, persistent storage utility called PAST and a scalable publish/subscribe system called SCRIBE (Rowstron, 2001).

Sharing similar properties as Pastry, Tapestry (Zhao, 2004) employs decentralized randomness to achieve both load distribution and routing locality. The difference between Pastry and Tapestry is the handling of network locality and data object replication. Tapestry's architecture uses a variant of the distributed search technique described in (Plaxton, 1997), with additional mechanisms to provide availability, scalability, and adaptation in the presence of failures and attacks. Plaxton (1997) proposes a distributed data structure, known as the Plaxton mesh, optimized to support a network overlay for locating named data objects which are connected to one root peer. On the other hand, Tapestry uses multiple roots for each data object to avoid single point of failure.

The Chord protocol (Stoica, 2001) uses consistent hashing to assign keys to its peers. Consistent hashing is designed to let peers enter and leave the network with minimal interruption. It is closely related to both Pastry and Tapestry, but instead of routing towards nodes that share successively longer address prefixes with the destination, Chord forwards messages based on numerical difference with the destination address. Although Chord adapts efficiently as nodes join or leave the system, unlike Pastry and Tapestry, it makes no explicit effort to achieve good network locality.

Chord maps keys and peers to an identifier ring and guarantees that queries make a logarithmic number hops and that keys are well balanced. To minimize disruption of keys when peers leave and join the overlay network Chord uses consistent hashing. Also in Chord, the network is maintained appropriately by a background maintenance process, i.e. a periodic stabilization procedure that updates predecessor and successor pointers to cater for newly joined peers. Stoica (2003) demonstrates the advantage of recursive lookups approach considered by Chord over iterative lookups. The authors also propose future work to improve resiliency to network partitions using a small set of known peers, and to reduce the amount of messages in lookups by increasing the size of each step around the ring with a larger fingers in each peer. Alima (2003) proposed a correction-on-use mechanism in their Distributed K-ary Search (DKS), which is similar to Chord, to reduce the communication costs incurred by Chord's stabilization procedure. The mechanism makes correction to the expired routing entries by piggybacking lookups and insertions.

The Kademlia (Maymounkov, 2002) P2P decentralized overlay network assigns each peer a NodeID in the 160-bit key space, and (key,value) pairs are stored on peers with IDs close to the key. A NodeID-based routing algorithm is used to locate peers near a destination key. One of the key architecture of Kademlia is the use of a novel XOR metric for distance between points in the key space. XOR is symmetric and it allows peers to receive lookup queries from precisely the same distribution of peers contained in their routing tables. Kademlia can send a query to any peer within an interval, allowing it to select routes based on latency or send parallel asynchronous queries. It uses a single routing algorithm throughout the process to locate peers near a particular ID.

The Kademlia's XOR topology-based routing resembles very much the first phase in the routing algorithms of Pastry and Tapestry. For these algorithms there is a need for an additional algorithmic structure for discovering the target peer within the peers that share the same prefix but differ in the next b-bit digit. As argued in (Maymounkov, 2002), Pastry and Tapestry algorithms require secondary routing tables of size $O(2^b)$ in addition to the main tables of size $O(2^b log_2^b N)$, which increases the cost of bootstrapping and maintenance. Kademlia resolves this by using the XOR metric.

The Viceroy (Malkhi, 2002) P2P decentralized overlay network is designed to handle the discovery and location of data and resources in a dynamic butterfly fashion. Viceroy employs consistent hashing to distribute data so that it is balanced across the set of servers and resilient to servers joining and leaving the network. It utilizes the DHT to manage the distribution of data among a changing set of servers and allowing peers to contact any server in the network to locate any stored resource by name. Its diameter of the overlay is better than CAN and its degree is better than Chord, Tapestry and Pastry. As demonstrated in (Malkhi, 2002), the routing process in Viceroy requires only $O(logN)$, where N is the number of peers in the network. Peers joining and leaving the system induce $O(logN)$ hops and require only $O(1)$ peers to change their states. Li (2002) describes that limited degree may increase the risk of network partition or limitations in the use of local neighbors. However, its advantage is the constant-degree overlay properties. Kaashoek (2003) highlights about fault-tolerant blind spots of Viceroy and its complexity. Further work were done by Viceroy's authors with proposal of a two-tier, locality-aware DHT (Abraham, 2004) which gives lower degree properties in each lower-tier peer, and the bounded-degree P2P overlay using de Bruijn graph.

Since de Bruijn graphs give very short average routing distances and high resilience to peer failure, they are well suited for structured P2P overlay networks. The P2P overlays previously discussed are 'greedy', and for a given degree, the algorithms are suboptimal because the routing distance is longer. There are increasing P2P overlay proposals based on de Bruijn graphs (Kaashoek, 2003)(Naor, 2003)(Loguinov, 2003)(Fraigniaud, 2004). The de Bruijn graph of degree k (k can be varied) could achieve an asymptotically optimum diameter (maximum hopcounts between any two peers in the graph) of log_kN, where N is the total number of peers in the system. Given $O(logN)$ neighbors in each peer, the de Bruijn graphs' hop count is $O(logN/loglogN)$.

Instead of using DHT as it building block, SkipNet (Harvey, 2003) is an overlay network based on the use of Skip Lists. The skip lists are used to organize peers and data primarily by their sorted string names, rather than by hashes of those names. In this way, Skip Net supports useful locality properties as well as the usual DHT functionality. In addition, (Loo, 2004) proposes the design of a hybrid model by using structured DHT techniques to locate rare object items, and unstructured flooding to locate highly replicated contents.

Andreica (2007) proposed an alternative approach based on lexicographic based routing among peers. The authors proposed a scalable, fault tolerant communication framework oriented towards high volume point-to-point and multicast data delivery. The proposed system uses balanced message flow distribution over multiple paths in order to achieve high throughput and the lexicographic distance between the peer's names in order to guarantee that the message flow converges to destination. The novelty of the communication framework is represented by its focus on high throughput message routing, at the expense of other network metrics. The communication framework distributes the message flow over all these paths in such a way that the total size of the messages forwarded on any path is proportional to the available bandwidth of the path. The system behaves better, in terms of consumed throughput, than other approaches in geographically sparse distributed systems.

Research efforts (Heikkinen, 2008) investigates the possibility of using structured P2P overlay networks in the context of large scale distributed systems integrating even mobile resources. With the emergence of high-end mobile multimedia devices, efficient mobile data transfer technologies, such as 3G HSPA, and alternative network interfaces in mobile devices, such as WLAN, are technical incentives for developing novel mobile services. P2P applications such as Skype already use P2P technologies to facilitate digital communication. This trend is known as mobile P2P communications (or communication services enabled by the P2P technologies). Two promising mobile P2P communication technologies are: mobile P2PSIP and mobile Skype. The former is an open standard proposal currently under development, whereas the latter refers to a group of mobile variants of the proprietary Skype service.

The ongoing P2PSIP standardization effort in the Internet Engineering Task Force (IETF) done by the P2PSIP working group aims to provide a peer-to-peer alternative for the client-server based session initiation protocol (SIP) defined in RFC 3261. According to Bryan (2007), the P2PSIP approach would minimize capital expenses by eliminating SIP servers and reduce operational expenses related to keeping those servers running. P2PSIP would be ideal for adhoc and small-scale systems whereas large deployments would be based on the client-server model due to reasons related to control, charging, legislation and regulation.

Skype is an overlay peer-to-peer network which provides several communications services. Unlike P2PSIP, Skype is a proprietary architecture which is not defined publicly. Baset and Schulz-rinne (2004) analyzed the functionality of Skype by studying the network traffic generated by it. According to them, the Skype network consists of two types of nodes: ordinary hosts and supernodes. Any host may be promoted to supernode status if it has enough resources to contribute to the overlay. Also, centralized nodes called login servers exist in the network. A host joining the network must connect to a supernode and register itself at a login server.

Although mobile P2P communication is a promising technology, its real implications are not yet fully understood (Heikkinen, 2008). The main uncertainties are related to the restrictions posed by both technology and operators. Mobile operators are not willing to let their profits diminish by adopting the bit-pipe business model of

solely acting as a mobile data capacity provider in the near future. Future study could involve formalizing the proposed business implications by using quantitative techno-economic modeling.

P2P network overlays that are based on DHT routing schemes have strong theoretical foundations, guaranteeing that a key can be found if it exists. However, DHT-based systems have a few problems in terms of data object lookup latency (Lua, 2005):

1. For each overlay hop, peers route a message to the next intermediate peer that can be located very far away with regard to physical topology of the underlying IP network. This can result in high network delay and unnecessary long-distance network traffics, from a deterministic short overlay path of $O(logN)$, (where N is the number of peers).

2. DHT-based systems assume that all peers equally participate in hosting published data objects or their location information. This would lead to a bottleneck at low-capacity peers.

P2P DHT-based overlay systems are also highly susceptible to security breach from malicious peers' attacks, such as man-in-the middle and Trojan attacks (Lua, 2005). For additional aspects related to security issues please refer to the security chapter.

The second category of P2P systems, the unstructured ones, was brought into the attention of platform providers and users in 1999, when Napster (Stern, 2000) pioneered the idea of peer-to-peer applications for content and information exchange in the Internet. Napster was the first file sharing system to handle requests for popular content by many peers. Such P2P content-sharing systems are self-scaling in that, as more peers join the system, they add to the aggregate download capability. Thus, unstructured P2P systems are composed of peers joining the network with some loose rules, without any prior knowledge of the underlying topology. In case of unstructured P2P systems the overlay network organize peers in a random graph in flat or hierarchical manners and use flooding or random walks or expanding-ring Time-To-Live (TTL) search on the graph to query content stored by peers. This approach induces problems related to scalability, as the load on each peer grows linearly with the total number of queries and the size of the system (Liven-Nowell, 2002).

Gnutella (Milojicic, 2002) provides a purely distributed file sharing solutions without a central node. In the strict sense Gnutella is not an application but rather a protocol used to search for and share files. To find content and other peers a user has to know the IP address of at least one other Gnutella node. The protocol assumes that a client trying to download a file will initiate a request to the closest node. The request then traverses the entire Gnutella network, effectively flooding the network, which can cause scalability problems.

Chawathe (2003) improves the original Gnutella design using their Gia system, by incorporating adaptation algorithm so that peers are attached to high-degree peers and providing a receiver-based token flow control for sending lookup queries to neighbors. Instead of flooding, they make use of random walk search algorithm and also the system keep pointers to objects in neighboring peers. In addition, the authors proposed that Unstructured P2P overlay like Gnutella can be built on top of Structured P2P overlay to help reduce the lookup queries overhead and overlay maintenance traffic. They used the collapse point lookup query rate (define as the per node query rate at which the successful query rate falls below 90%) and the average hop counts prior to collapse. However, the comparison was done in static network scenario with the older Gnutella and not the enhanced Gnutella version.

FastTrack/KaZaA's peers (Leibowitz, 2003) are differentiated into clients and super-peers. Super-peers are chosen automatically based on their computational power, storage capacity and bandwidth. Clients connect to the closest super-peer, using it for file search and download. As such, peers form a structured overlay of super-peers architecture to make search more efficient. Super-peers are peers with high bandwidth, disk space and processing power, and have volunteered to get elected to facilitate search by caching the meta-data. The ordinary peers transmit the meta-data of the data files they are sharing to the super-peers. All the queries are also forwarded to the super-peer. Then, Gnutella-typed broadcast based search is performed in a highly pruned overlay network of super-peers. The P2P system can exist, without any super-peer but this result in worse query latency. However, this approach still consumes bandwidth so as to maintain the index at the super-peers on behalf of the peers that are connected. The super-peers still use a broadcast protocol for search and the lookup queries is routed to peers and super-peers that have no relevant information to the query.

BitTorrent (Tian, 2006) uses swarming content delivery. All the peers trying to download the same file are part of the same swarm. This file distribution network uses tit-for-tat (peer responds with the same action that its other collaborating peer performed previously) as a method of seeking. In order to download a file, a peer has to contact a central tracker. After that it connects to several randomly chosen peers in the swarm. Files are decomposed into smaller pieces and a client may start sharing the downloaded pieces before downloading the entire file. BitTorrent uses a tit for tat scheme which encourages peers to upload files, not just download them. The protocol is designed to discourage free-riders, by having the peers choose other peers from which the data has been received. BitTorrent is considered one of the first systems from the second generation P2P overlay system, as it achieves higher level of robustness and resource utilization based on its incentives cooperation technique for file distribution.

Overnet/eDonkey (Yang, 2006) is a hybrid two-layer P2P information storage network composed of client and server, which are used to publish and retrieve small pieces of data by creating a file-sharing network. This architecture provides features such as concurrent download of a file from multiple peers, detection of file corruption using hashing, partial sharing of files during downloading and expressive querying methods for file search. To join the network, a peer needs to know the IP address and port of another peer in the network. It then bootstraps from the other peer. The clients connect to a server and register the object files that they are sharing by providing the meta-data describing the object files. After registration, the clients can either search by querying the meta-data or request a particular file through its unique network identifier, thus providing guarantee service to locate popular objects. Servers provide the locations of object files when requested by clients, so that clients can download the files directly from the indicated locations.

(Pouwelse, 2004) presents an insight comparison measurement study of several P2P file-sharing systems, such as BitTorrent, FastTrack/KaZaA, Gnutella, Overner/eDonkey, and DirectConnect, based on five characteristics: popularity, availability, download performance, content lifetime and pollution level. The study showed that availability has a significant influence on popularity of P2P file sharing systems. In systems such as Gnutella and Overnet/eDonkey the responsibility is full or partial distributed among file sharing peers. The availability of content in BitTorrent is unpredictable and vulnerable to potential failures, due to its lack of decentralization. However, BitTorrent is well-suited for download performance due to its advanced download distribution protocol.

One of the most frequent uses of the unstructured P2P systems is the download of files, often very large. More often such files are available at least in part at more than one location on the network. This observation has inspired a number of different algorithms for multi-source file downloading (Byers, 2002). Even if the multi-source download problem looks simple enough, in prac-

tice is complicated by the fact that nodes can join or leave the system, aborting downloads and initiating new requests at any time. Thus, a download algorithm can make very few assumptions about the uptime or bandwidth capacity of participating nodes. An effective multi-source download algorithm should meet two main challenges. First, it should maximize the utility of nodes with partial knowledge of a file to each other. This, in turn, means minimizing the amount of overlapping information nodes are likely to have. This is known as the availability aspect of the algorithm, because it allows nodes with truncated downloads to reconstruct a file even in the event that every source node with the complete file has left the network. The second challenge of a multi-source download algorithm is to make the reconciliation phase as bandwidth-efficient as possible. This phase is an instance of the more general set reconciliation problem (Minsky, 2002). Unfortunately, existing set reconciliation algorithms are not practical for multi-source download algorithms. They are either too computationally costly, suboptimal in terms of message complexity, or simply too complicated to implement.

In (Maymounkov, 2003) the authors proposed an algorithm that combines near-optimal availability with a simple yet practical reconciliation phase not based on the general set reconciliation problem. The approach is made possible by the recent introduction of locally-encodable, linear-time decodable, rateless erasure codes (Luby, 2002). It exploits particular properties of the way file contents tend to disperse over nodes in a peer-to-peer system. The proposed download algorithm shows that rateless codes offer increased file availability and decreased reconciliation costs. Interestingly, the decrease of reconciliation costs is due to the limit on how many streams a cluster of nodes may need. More interestingly, the authors show a solution to avoid difficult information-theoretical problems, like set reconciliation, by making use of a wider range of properties of the underlying peer-to-peer system.

Another research aspect related to unstructured P2P systems is the design of optimum search solutions. According to the study conducted in (Jovanovic, 2001), most of the unstructured P2P networks (such as KaZaA and Gnutella) are not pure power-law networks with Zipf distribution properties. The study revealed that Gnutella networks have topologies that are power-law random graphs. Research on powerlaw networks (Barabasi, 2000) showed that networks as diverse as the Internet tend to organize themselves so that most peers have few links while a small number of peers have a large number of links. Based on this, Adamic (2001) studied random-walk search strategies in power-law networks and discovered that, by changing walkers to seek out high degree peers, the search performance can be greatly optimized. Several search techniques for unstructured P2P networks are discussed in (Yang, 2002): iterative deepening, directed BFS and local indices.

One of the concerns regarding the peer-to-peer systems relates to their capacity to fill the underlying network capacity quicker than content delivery networks or the web traffic. For example, a study conducted in 2002 (Saroiu, 2002a) showed that an average peer of Kazaa peer-to-peer network consumes 90 times more bandwidth than an average web client. Also, the analysis also showed that an organizational peer-to-peer proxy cache has the potential to significantly reduce P2P bandwidth requirements. In another study (Saroiu, 2002b) the authors conducted a measurement study that tried to precisely characterize the population of end-user hosts that participate in these two systems. Their characterization included the bottleneck bandwidths between these hosts and the Internet at large, IP-level latencies to send packets to these hosts, how often hosts connect and disconnect from the system, how many files hosts share and download, the degree of cooperation between the hosts, and several correlations between these characteristics. The measurements showed that there is significant heterogeneity and lack of cooperation across peers participating in these systems. This

implies that any similar peer-to-peer system must be very deliberate and careful about delegating responsibilities across peers. Also, peers tend to deliberately misreport information if there is an incentive to do so. Because effective delegation of responsibility depends on accurate information, this implies that future systems must have built-in incentives for peers to tell the truth, or systems must be able to directly measure or verify reported information.

GRID COMMUNICATION

Unlike P2P overlay networks, Grid systems arise from the collaboration between established and connected groups of systems that include a reliable set of resources to share. In case of high performance computing and parallel processing systems, either Grids, clusters or cloud computing systems, the most common communications approach used in HPC programming is the Message Passing Interface (MPI), which provides a flexible set of node-to-node and collective message passing operations. Except for that, various Grid middlewares, such as Globus, provide various solutions for resource management and discovery, job management, and data transfer and access mechanisms that cross organizational boundaries. Some Globus-related projects also provide communications support for MPI programs running on various Grid nodes. The first implementation, MPICH-G (Foster, 1998), enabled basic MPI functionality and was based on the Nexus communication libraries (Foster, 1997), which supported heterogeneous architectures, multi-threading, and security, but also added overhead. The more recent MPICH-G2 (Karonis, *et al*, 2003) implementation of the MPI standard permits excellent performance on node-to-node and collective MPI operations on machines across the Grid.

Despite the high computing performance orientation of Grid systems, communication delays between Grid computing nodes is a big hurdle due to geographical separation in a realistic Grid computing environments. **Communication schemes** such as broadcasting, multicasting and routing should, therefore, take communication delay into consideration. Such communication schemes in a Grid computing environment pose a great challenge due to the arbitrary nature of its topology. Resource sharing in **Grid computing networks** is not primarily concerned with file exchange but with direct access to computers, software, data and other resources. This sharing is highly controlled, with resource providers and consumers defining clearly and carefully just what is shared, who is allowed to share and the conditions under which sharing occurs. With the traffic increase and the need for its efficient propagation deep into the network, cost effective analytical algorithms are essential for the computation of the performance metrics for Grid computing networks. In (Kouvatsos&Mkwawa, 2003) the authors present such a heuristic algorithm for multicast communication is proposed for Grid computing networks with finite capacity and bursty background traffic. The scheme facilitates inter-node communication for Grid computing networks and it is applicable to a single-port mode of message passing communication. The scheme utilizes a queue-by-queue decomposition algorithm for arbitrary open queuing network models, based on the principle of maximum entropy, in conjunction with an information theoretical decomposition criterion and graph theoretical concepts. Evidence based on empirical studies indicates the suitability of the scheme for achieving an optimal multicast communication cost, subject to system decomposition constraints.

Rapid increases in both the quantity and diversity of data stored on secondary and tertiary storage systems, and in the raw capacity of wide area networks, make it both desirable and feasible, in principle at least, to move large amounts of data across wide area networks. In practice, the orchestration of such transfers is technically challenging. One key issue is the frequent need to exploit parallelism in multiple dimensions, including (depending on context) storage systems, network interfaces, and backbone network trunks. Another is dealing with failures of various sorts. Firewalls, parallel file systems, and other specialized devices can also cause difficulties, as can the need to transform data before and/or after transfer. For these and other reasons, rapid, efficient, and robust wide area end-to-end transport requires the management of complex systems at multiple levels.

Effective end-to-end data transfers thus demand an approach in which file systems, computers, network interfaces, and network protocols are managed in an integrated fashion to meet performance and robustness goals. Furthermore, unless such approaches are encapsulated in software that is both easily usable (by end users and higher-level tools) and portable across different end system and network architectures, they will not be widely used.

The Globus GridFTP framework has a modular structure that allows for the coordination of multiple data streams, the substitution of alternative transport protocols, and other desirable features. These features allow achieving a high fraction of end-to-end bandwidth over both local and wide area networks. The current implementation of GridFTP (Allcock, 2005) provides the first publicly available release of striping. The implementation is based on Globus eXtensible Input/Output (XIO) system (Beck, 2002) and it provides several new clean interfaces for modifying and extending the server. The implementation also provides support for IPv6. The server is faster in both single-process and striped configurations, achieving, for example, speeds of 27.3 Gbit/s memory-to-memory and 17 Gbit/s disk-to-disk over a 60 millisecond round trip time, 30 Gbit/s network.

The Fast Data Transfer (FDT) application is another data transfer server designed to stream data at fast rates in a Grid environment. During the "High Speed Data Gathering, Distribution and Analysis for Physics Discoveries at the Large Hadron Collider" demonstration at SuperComputing 2006 (SC06) Bandwidth Challenge (BWC), an international team of physicists, computer scientists, and network engineers led by the California Institute of Technology joined forces to set new records for sustained data transfer between storage systems. Using FDT for its networking support and LISA as the control plane of the experiment the team achieved a peak throughput of 17.77 Gbps between clusters of servers located at the show floor and at Caltech (Dobre, 2007).

In order to manage a Grid infrastructure, the management of the underlying network that provides the communication support is also a requirement. The **management of the network infrastructure** is important because Grid users access the shared resources through the network and, if the network is congested or unavailable, such access is likely to be compromised. The configuration of the underlying network allows, for example, reservation of network bandwidth and prioritization of critical flows, which is generally proceeded with the use of a QoS provisioning architecture such as DiffServ or IntServ. Currently existing Grid toolkits (such as Globus) do interact with neither the network QoS provisioning architecture nor the network management systems. That leads to a situation where the Grid and network administrators are forced to manually interact with each other in order to proceed with the required configuration of the communication support.

A commonly required network configuration in a Conference Grid, implemented for instance with the AccessGrid toolkit (ACCESS-GRID, 2007), is to reserve network resources for multicast audio and video flows. This configuration must be executed in all administrative domains that are part of the Grid, to guarantee a successful audio and video transmission. The current version of the AccessGrid toolkit considers that all needed configuration and network reservations for the Grid operation were made, which is not always true. A toolkit that explicitly considers an

integrated network infrastructure management is Globus, through its Globus Architecture for Reservation and Allocation (GARA) (Foster, 2004). This architecture provides interfaces for processor and network resources reservations. GARA was implemented in a prototype where configurations are made directly in routers to configure queue priorities of the DiffServ architecture. This implementation considers that the toolkit has permission to directly access and configure the network devices.

Globus, in its management support, also explicitly defines the concept of proxy (an important concept for the Grid policy definitions). A proxy represents a Grid resource that runs determined tasks on behalf of the users and which has the same access rights that are given to the user. Globus implements proxies using credentials digitally signed by users and passed to the remote resources. A possible proxy configuration could be a user accessing a storage server through a process running in a supercomputer. In this case, the supercomputer acts as a user proxy, since it requests actions in name of the user.

Besides the management support provided by the toolkits, policy-based Grid solutions were also proposed by (Sundaram, 2002). Such a policy uses parameters to specify processor execution and memory usage for a user accessing a server during a determined period of time. It is important to note that this approach for Grid policy definition does not allow the specification of network QoS parameters to be applied in the user-server communication and also does not support explicitly the concept of user proxies.

Another proposals using policies for network configuration aiming Grid support are presented in (Yang, 2002) and (Sander, 2001). The solution from (Yang, 2002) specifies an architecture divided in a policy-based management layer (that follows the IETF definitions of PEPs and PDPs), and a layer that uses the concept of programmable networks (active networks represented by a middleware) to automatically configure the network devices. (Sander, 2001) proposes a policy-based architecture to configure the network QoS of different administrative domains members of a Grid using an inter-domain signaling protocol, that sequentially configures an end-to-end communication path (e.g. a user accessing a server). Although both solutions are based on policies, they do not specify how Grid and network policies are defined neither present any facility to allow the integration with the Grid toolkits. Authors in (Neisse, 2004) proposed an architecture that translates Grid policies to network policies through a translation engine based on translation rules. The system interacts with a subset of Grid policies being provided in Globus using web services.

Recent ad hoc implementations of data transferring protocols and implementations for the communication between globally distributed clusters have been developed as well. For example, Harness (Kurzyniec, 2002) allows the use of multiple middleware systems at the same time. The VMI (Pakin&Pant, 2002) middleware communication systems deals with both parallel and distributed paradigms; it is close to VIA, and targets large clusters with SAN rather than WAN. PadicoTM (Denis & Perez, 2004) is also a **Grid communication middleware**. The system combines both parallel and distributed paradigms, by resource abstraction (adaptation), in order to allow the execution of parallel and/or distributed applications without imposing any programming constraints or the use of a particular communication layer. In these systems the middleware systems are decoupled from the actual network so that they can transparently and efficiently utilize any network they are deployed on. Proteus (Chiu, 2002) is a system for integrating multiple message protocols such as SOAP and JMS within one system. It aims at decoupling applications from protocols, which is an approach quite similar to ours, but at a much higher level in the protocol stack.

An ad hoc implementation of data transfers between two clusters has been also proposed in (Klasky, 2003). The system streams gyrokinetic toroidal simulation results from the simulation cluster to a visualization/analysis cluster. To achieve this goal, the authors developed a threaded parallel data approach using Globus and pthreads. However, the approach is tailored to one application, the Gyrokinetic Toroidal Code (GTC). Also the communication framework does not ease the responsibility of the application programmer, as he has to take care of some programming details related with the transfer of the data. The authors in (Fide&Jenks, 2004) further extended the solution, presenting a generic paradigm to support scalable cluster-to-cluster (C2C) communications. The framework handles run-time communications between parallel programs running on distributed clusters, providing easy and efficient programming and achieves cluster-to-cluster communications transparent to the user.

FUTURE TRENDS

The bandwidth capabilities of the next-generation networks have been demonstrated during various challenges. Such networks are mostly based on the use of optical capabilities and multiple wavelengths transport carriers. One of the research trends for enabling high-speed data communications in support to large scale distributed applications today consists in a forward-looking vision of obtaining much higher capacity networks using many wavelengths. Another trend in networking is towards hybrid networks. Such networks try to combine conventional parts of the network (packet switched) with circuit-oriented segments, where the most demanding applications are matched to dynamically-constructed optical paths to help ensure high end-to-end throughput. One other research topic relates to the possibility of enabling a robust and scalable control plane that would establish the path across the optical core of a hybrid network, while automatically configuring the edges to enable the switching onto the Light-Paths.

Another future trend is the research of adequate generic traffic engineering solutions to support the automatic provision of capacity management services. Such systems should consider many parameters, ranging from the state of the physical links and the background traffic to the prioritization of traffic.

The limitations of the TCP protocol when the bandwidth and the latency increase have led to the research of various alternatives. However, in order for them to be widely adopted, they must be thoroughly tested and validated. Each alternative have various problems and, in the future, we expect to see even more alternative proposals, especially since the bandwidth capacity of future networks will grow larger.

In the research community, efforts are being made in improving the lookup properties of Unstructured P2P overlays to include flow control, dynamic geometric topology adaptation, one-hop replication, peer heterogeneity, etc. The research of efficient multicast models for very large distributed systems represents another future trend. Such systems could be based on bandwidth aggregation or various tree schemas.

Future trends in P2P overlay networks consist in the research of adequate algorithms, based on data locality and various other parameters. Future research still needs to be conducted towards finding appropriate solutions of using structured P2P overlay networks in the context of large scale distributed systems integrating even mobile resources. Such resources pose several challenges because of their limited capacities to store data and compute operations. Also, a standardization effort is currently well underway to provide a peer-to-peer alternative for the client-server based session initiation protocol.

In Grid computing environment one of the biggest challenge relates to the large distance between computing nodes. Applications needing to process data must efficiently retrieve the data at fast rates. Currently several bandwidth challenges are being set on an annual-base rate to promote worldwide

the research efforts providing the most notable results in this area. Such efforts are today more critical than ever, not only because of the need to offer efficient data transfers to the end-users before the widely-adoption of Grid computing, but also because of the social impacts of the Internet and the increase in network traffic that impose challenges to service providers.

CONCLUSION

In this chapter we analyzed current existing work in enabling high-performance communications in large scale distributed systems, presenting specific problems and existing solutions, as well as future trends. By their nature, communication is an inherent aspect of every distributed application. Applications running in Grids, P2Ps and other types of large scale distributed systems have several specific communication requirements. For this reason we presented different the problem of delivering efficient communication in the case of P2P and Grid systems.

As more and more data-intensive application are migrated towards large scale distributed systems, scientists face challenges such as efficiently streaming data among many participants distributed worldwide or making the backbones of current existing network successfully deal with high amounts of data being transferred in a short amount of time or dealing with the need of the applications to react quickly to errors at the network layer. Such challenges are dealt using protocols optimized for data transfer over wide area network, data stream distribution through overlay networks for multicast purposes, systems for scheduling the data transfer requests in order to avoid overwhelming the network and storage devices. However, despite the fact that the network bandwidths have grown approximately two orders of magnitude faster than processor speeds over the last two decades, the current distributed systems have treated the network, so far, as a passive and largely featureless substrate for data transport.

As applications running in large scale distributed systems are deployed at a larger rate, needing the transfer of data from possible distant nodes at a high rate, various high performance networks and technologies appeared in the last years. Over the last few years, optical component technology has rapidly evolved to support multiplexing and amplification of increasing digital modulation rates. Currently, 10 Gigabit Ethernet (GbE) network interfaces are in widespread use, and the cost of these interfaces, as well as 10 GbE ports on switches has dropped. One of the research trends for enabling high-speed data communications in support to large scale distributed applications today consists in a forward-looking vision of obtaining much higher capacity networks using many wavelengths. Such solutions are based on forward-looking vision of obtaining much higher capacity networks using many wavelengths or on the use of hybrid networks. Such solutions are completed by the adoption of a robust and scalable control plane that would establish the path across the optical core of a hybrid network, while automatically configuring the edges to enable the switching onto the Light-Paths.

Traffic engineering allows a network administrator to make the path deterministic and bypass the normal routed hop-by-hop paths. An administrator may elect to explicitly define the path between stations to ensure QoS or have the traffic follow a specified path to reduce traffic loading across certain hops. Several state-of-the-art protocols were developed in the last years to support this: RSVP, GMPLS or ASON. Based on these protocols, we analyzed a number of projects that are trying to implement tools for the provision of capacity management (or bandwidth brokerage) services at Layers 1 to 3 of the ISO/OSI network model. We also presented several protocols designed to overcome the current limitation of the TCP protocol in the context of high bandwidth traffic.

We next analyzed several group communication models. One deployment practice is to manual configure tunnels to connect several IP multicast enabled "islands" to form what is known as MBone, a static overlay network. However, this approach relies upon coordinated manual configuration of multicast routers on both ends of each tunnel connecting the islands. This makes MBone expensive to set and maintain. We analyzed alternative approaches, based on hybrid multicast delivery frameworks, path diversity, multicast trees, distributed communication.

The most notable challenge of peer-to-peer communication is to deal with the problems associated with the dynamic nature of the peering entities. Within communication itself, as a concept, peer-to-peer technology was used for a long time. Network topologies where the nodes are connected directly have always been part of various communication infrastructures. Flooding or network broadcast are also technologies that support the communication in anonymous peer groups. Network multicast is another peer-to-peer communication scheme where the user group is known. Group communication and multi-peer communication models apply as well various peer-to-peer principles at the transport layer. P2P networks can potentially offer an efficient self-organized, massively scalable and robust routing architecture in the context of wide-area networks, combining fault tolerance, load balancing and explicit notion of locality. Currently there is a continuous effort even to include P2P results in defining what is known as mobile peer-to-peer communications. We analyzed several of the proposed solutions in this area, highlighting their pros and cons.

Unlike P2P overlay networks, Grid systems arise from the collaboration between established and connected groups of systems that include a reliable set of resources to share. In case of large scale distributed systems the most common communications approach used in HPC programming is the Message Passing Interface (MPI). Various Grid middlewares, such as Globus, provide various solutions for resource management and discovery, job management, and data transfer and access mechanisms that cross organizational boundaries. Some Globus-related projects also provide communications support for MPI programs running on various Grid nodes. Despite the high computing performance orientation of Grid systems, communication delays between Grid computing nodes is a big hurdle due to geographical separation in a realistic Grid computing environment. Communication schemes such as broadcasting, multicasting and routing should, therefore, take communication delay into consideration. Such communication schemes in a Grid computing environment pose a great challenge due to the arbitrary nature of its topology. We analyzed various data communication solutions specifically designed for Grid systems.

We believe communication to be an important and active research domain in today's large scale distributed systems being deployed all around the world. The solutions being analyzed are in their vast majority theoretical and work still needs to be done in deploying the proposed solutions into real world scenarios. We believe this to be happening, as large scale distributed systems gain more and more attention from user communities that pose requirements such as efficient communication.

REFERENCES

Abraham, I., Malkhi, D., & Dubzinski, O. (2004). Land: Stretch (1+epsilon) locality aware networks for dhts. In J. I. Munro (Ed.), *Proceedings of the Fifteenth Annual ACM-SIAM Symposium on Discrete Algorithms, SODA 2004* (pp. 550 - 559). New Orleans, LA: ACM Press.

ACCESS-GRID. (2007). *The access grid user documentation*. Retrieved February 12, 2009, from http://www.accessgrid.org/docs/documentation-index.html

Adamic, L., Lukose, R., Puniyani, A., & Huberman, B. (2001). Search in power-law networks. *Physical review. E, Statistical, nonlinear, and soft matter physics, 64*(4/2), 046135.

Alima, L., El-Ansary, S., Brand, P., & Haridi, S. (2003). Dks(n,k,f): a family of low communication, scalable and fault-tolerant infrastructures for p2p applications. In *Proc. of the 3rd IEEE/ACM International Symposium on Cluster Computing and the Grid, CCGrid 2003* (pp. 344–350). Monterey, CA: IEEE Computer Society.

Allcock, W., Bresnahan, J., Kettimuthu, R., Link, M., Dumitrescu, C., Raicu, I., & Foster, I. (2005). The Globus Striped GridFTP Framework and Server. In *Proc. of the 2005 ACM/IEEE conference on Supercomputing* (pp. 54). Washington, DC: IEEE Computer Society.

Andreica, M. I., Legrand, I. C., & Tapus, N. (2007). Towards a Communication Framework based on Balanced Message Flow Distribution. In *Proc. of The International Conference on "Computer as a Tool", EUROCON 2007* (pp. 495-500). Warsaw, Poland: IEEE Computer Society.

Apostolopoulos, J. G. (2001). Reliable video communication over lossy packet networks using multiple state encoding and path diversity. In *Proc. Of Visual Communication and Image Processing* (pp. 392–409). San Francisco: ACM Press.

ASON. (2001). *Rec. G.8080/Y.1304 Standard Specification, Architecture for the Automatically Switched Optical Network, ITU-T*. Retrieved March 21, 2009, from http://www.itu.int/news-archive/press_releases/2001/29.html

Banerjee, S., Lee, S., Bhattacharjee, B., & Srinivasan, A. (2003). Resilient Multicast using Overlays. *ACM SIGMETRICS Performance Evaluation Review archive, 31*(1), 102 – 113.

Barabasi, A., Albert, R., Jeong, H., & Bianconi, G. (2000). Power-law distribution of the world wide web. *Science, 287*(1), 2115a. doi:10.1126/science.287.5461.2115a

Baset, S. A., & Schulzrinne, H. (2004). *An analysis of the Skype peer-to-peer Internet telephony protocol.* Technical Report CUCS-039-04, Columbia University, New York, NY.

Beck, M., Moore, T., & Plank, J. (2002). An End-to-End Approach to Globally Scalable Network Storage. *ACM SIGCOMM Computer Communication Review, 32*(4), 339–346. doi:10.1145/964725.633058

Bryan, D. A. (2007). P2PSIP: on the road to a world without servers. *Business Communications Review, 37*(3), 40–44.

Byers, J., Considine, J., Mitzenmacher, M., & Rost, S. (2002). Informed Content Delivery Across Adaptive Overlay Networks. *IEEE/ACM Transactions on Networking (TON), 12*(5), 767 – 780.

CANARIE. (2007). *CANARIE deployed CAnet 4.* Retrieved February 21, 2009, from http://www.canarie.ca/canet4/index.html

Castro, M., Druschel, P., Kermarrec, A.-M., Nandi, A., Rowstron, A., & Singh, A. (2003). *SplitStream: High-bandwidth multicast in a cooperative environment. Proc. of the nineteenth ACM symposium on Operating systems principles, SOSP '03 (pp. 298 – 313).* Lake Bolton, NY: ACM Press.

Chawathe, Y., Ratnasamy, S., Breslau, L., Lanham, N., & Shenker, S. (2003). Making gnutella-like p2p systems scalable. *Proc. of the 2003 conference on Applications, technologies, architectures, and protocols for computer communications* (pp. 407-418). Karlsruhe, Germany: ACM Press.

Chiu, K., Govindaraju, M., & Gannon, D. (2002). The proteus multiprotocol library. In *Proceedings of the 2002 Conference on Supercomputing (SC '02).* Baltimore, MD: ACM Press.

Chu, Y.-H., Rao, S. G., & Zhang, H. (2002). A Case for End System Multicast. *IEEE Journal on Selected Areas in Communications, 20*(8), 1456–1471. doi:10.1109/JSAC.2002.803066

Cirstoiu, C. (2008). *Optimizations in Distributed Systems. Optimization Framework for Data Intensive Applications in Large Scale Distributed Systems.* Doctoral Thesis, University Politehnica of Bucharest, Romania.

DeMar, P., & Petravick, D. (2004). LambdaStation: A forwarding and admission control service to interface production network facilities with advanced research network paths. In Aimar, A., Harvey, J., & Knoors, N. (Eds.), *Computing in High Energy and Nuclear Physics, CHEP 2004* (p. 1300). Interlaken, Switzerland: CERN Publishing.

Denis, A., & Pérez, C. (2004). Network Communications in Grid Computing: At a Crossroads Between Parallel and Distributed Worlds. In *Proc. of the 18th International Parallel and Distributed Processing Symposium, IPDPS '04* (pp. 95). Santa Fe, New Mexico: IEEE Computer Society.

Dobre, C., Voicu, R., Muraru, A., & Legrand, I. C. (2007). A distributed agent based system to control and coordinate large scale data transfers. In *Proc. of the 16th International Conference on Control Systems and Computer Science, CSCS17 (pp.* 415-419). Bucharest, Romania: IEEE Computer Society.

DRAC. (2004). *Dynamic Resource Allocation Controller (DRAC).* Retrieved February 12, 2009, from http://www.nortel.com/drac

Feng, W., & Tinnakornsrisuphap, P. (2000). The Failure of TCP in High-Performance Computational Grids. *Proceedings of the 2000 ACM/IEEE conference on Supercomputing* (pp. 37). Dallas, TX: IEEE Computer Society.

Floyd, S. (2003). *HighSpeed TCP for Large Congestion Windows, RFC 3649.* Retrieved March 14, 2009, from http://www.ietf.org/rfc/rfc3649.txt

Foster, I., Fidler, M., Roy, A., Sander, V., & Winkler, L. (2004). End-to-end quality of service for high-end applications. *IEEE Computer Communications. Special Issue on Network Support for Grid Computing, 24*(1), 1375–1388.

Foster, I., Geisler, J., Gropp, W., Karonis, N., Lusk, E., Thiruvathukal, G., & Tuecke, S. (1998). Wide-area implementation of the message passing interface. *Parallel Computing, 24*(12), 1735–1749. doi:10.1016/S0167-8191(98)00075-1

Foster, I., Geisler, J., Kesselman, C., & Tuecke, S. (1997). Managing multiple communication methods in high-performance networked computing systems. *Journal of Parallel and Distributed Computing, 40*(1), 35–48. doi:10.1006/jpdc.1996.1266

Fraigniaud, P., & Gauron, P. (2003). *The content-addressable networks d2b*. Technical Report 1349, Laboratoire de Recherche en Informatique, Universite de Paris Sud, France.

GEANT. (2006). *The GEANT2 network description*. Retrieved February 12, 2009, from http://www.geant2.net

GEANT. (2008). *Automated Bandwidth Allocation across Heterogeneous Networks on Geant2 network*. Retrieved March 12, 2009, from http://www.geant2.net/

Gibbard, B., Katramatos, D., Yu, D., & McKee, S. (2006). TeraPaths: End/to-End Network Path QoS Configuration Using Cross-Domain Reservation Negotiation. In 3rd Intl. Conf. on Broadband Communications, Networks and System, BROADNETS 2006 (pp. 1-9). San Jose, CA: IEEE Computer Society.

Grieco, L. A., Mascolo, S., & Di Sciascio, E. (2002). A mathematical model for the steady state throughput of the Westwood TCP congestion control algorithm. In *Proceedings of the 24th International Conference on Information Technology Interfaces, ITI 2002* (pp. 487- 492). Cavtat, Croatia: IEEE Computer Society.

Gu, Y., & Grossman, R. (2008). *Using UDP for Reliable Data Transfer over High Bandwidth-Delay Product Networks*. Unpublished manuscript submitted to Computer Communication Review.

Ha, S., Rhee, I., & Xu, L. (2008). CUBIC: A new TCP-Friendly high-speed TCP variant. *ACM SIGOPS Operating Systems Review, 42*(5), 64–74. doi:10.1145/1400097.1400105

Harvey, N. J. A., Jones, M. B., Theimer, M., Saroiu, S., & Wolman, A. (2003). Skipnet: A scalable overlay network with practical locality properties. In *Proc. of the 4th USENIX Symposium on Internet Technologies and Systems (USITS)* (pp. 9). Seattle, WA: ACM Press.

Heikkinen, M. (2008). *Mobile Peer-to-Peer Communications: an overview*. Finland: Research Seminar on Telecommunications Business, Telecommunications Software and Multimedia Laboratory, Helsinki University of Technology.

HOPI. (2002). *Hybrid Optical and Packet Infrastructure Standard Specification*. Retrieved February 08, 2009, from http://networks.internet2.edu/hopi

Jin, C., Wei, D.X., & Low, S.H. (2006). FAST TCP: motivation, architecture, algorithms, performance. *IEEE/ACM Transactions on Networking (TON), 14*(6), 1246 – 1259.

Jovanovic, M. A., Annexstein, F., & Berman, K. (2001). *Scalability issues in large peer-to-peer networks - a case study of gnutella*. Technical Report from University of Cincinnati.

Kaashoek, F., & Karger, D. (2003). Koorde: A simple degree-optimal hash table. In *Proceedings of the 2nd International Workshop on Peer-to-Peer Systems, IPTPS 03* (pp. 313-324). Berkeley, CA: ACM Press.

Karonis, N., Toonen, B., & Foster, I. (2003). MPICH-G2: A Grid-Enabled Implementation of the Message Passing Interface. *Journal of Parallel and Distributed Computing, 63*(5), 551–563. doi:10.1016/S0743-7315(03)00002-9

Klasky, S., Ethier, S., Lin, Z., Martins, K., McCune, D., & Samtaney, R. (2003). Grid-Based Parallel Data Streaming Implemented for the Gyrokinetic Toroidal Code. In *Proc. of the SuperComputing Conference, SC2003: High Performance Networking and Computing* (pp. 24). Washington, DC: IEEE Computer Society.

Kouvatsos, D. D., & Mkwawa, I. M. (2003). Multicast communication in grid computing networks with background traffic. *IEEE Software, 150*(4), 257–264. doi:10.1049/ip-sen:20030810

Kurzyniec, D., Sunderam, V., & Migliardi, M. (2002). On the viability of component frameworks for high performance distributed computing: A case study. *IEEE International Symposium on High Performance Distributed Computing, HPDC-11* (pp. 275 – 283). Edimburg, Scotland: IEEE Computer Society.

Lehman, T., Sobieski & J., Jabbari, B. (2006). DRAGON: a framework for service provisioning in heterogeneous grid networks. *IEEE Communications Magazine, 44*(3), 84–90. doi:10.1109/MCOM.2006.1607870

Leibowitz, N., Ripeanu, M., & Wierzbicki, A. (2003). Deconstructing the Kazza network. In Proc. *of the third IEEE Workshop on Internet Applications* (pp. 112-120). San Jose, CA: IEEE Computer Society.

Li, X., & Plaxton, C. (2002). On name resolution in peer to peer networks. In *Proc. of the 2nd ACM International workshop on principles of mobile computing* (pp. 82–89). Monterey, CA: ACM Press.

Liben-Nowell, D., & Balakrishnan, H. (2002). Observations on the dynamic Evolution of Peer-to-Peer Networks. *Lecture Notes in Computer Science, 2429*(1), 22–33. doi:10.1007/3-540-45748-8_2

Loguinov, D., Kumar, A., & Ganesh, S. (2003). Graph-theoretic analysis of structured peer-to-peer systems: routing distances and fault resilience. *Proc. of the ACM SIGCOMM* (pp. 395–406). Karlsruhe, Germany: ACM Press.

Loo, B. T., Huebsch, R., Stoica, I., & Hellerstein, J. M. (2004). The case for a hybrid p2p search infrastructure. In *Proc. of the 3rd International Workshop on Peer-to-Peer Systems, IPTPS* (pp. 23-30). San Diego, CA: IEEE Computer Society.

Low, S. H., Paganini, F., Wang, J., & Doyle, J. C. (2003). Linear Stability of TCP/RED and a Scalable Control. *Computer Networks Journal, 43*(5), 633–647. doi:10.1016/S1389-1286(03)00304-9

Lua, E. K., Crowcroft, J., Pias, M., Sharma, R., & Lim, S. (2005). A survey and comparison of peer-to-peer overlay network schemes. *IEEE Communications Surveys and Tutorials, 7*(2), 72–93. doi:10.1109/COMST.2005.1610546

Luby, M. (2002). LT Codes. In *The 43rd Annual IEEE Symposium on Foundations of Computer Science, FOCS'02* (pp. 271). Vancouver, Canada: IEEE Computer Society.

Malkhi, D., Naor, M., & Ratajczak, D. (2002). Viceroy: a scalable and dynamic emulation of the butterfly. In *Proc. of the ACM Symposium on Principles of Distributed Computing, PODC'02* (pp. 183–192). Monterey, CA: ACM press.

Maymounkov, P., & Mazieres, D. (2002). Kademlia: A peer-to-peer information system based on the xor metric. In Proc. of the International workshop on Peer-to-Peer Systems, IPTPS (pp. 53-65). Cambridge, MA: IEEE Computer Society.

Maymounkov, P., & Mazieres, D. (2003). Rateless Codes and Big Downloads. In *Proc. of the 1st international MobiSys workshop on Mobile opportunistic networking* (pp. 91-98). San Juan, Puerto Rico: IEEE Computer Society.

Milojicic, D., Kalogeraki, V., Lukose, R., Nagaraja, K., Pruyne, J., Richard, B., Rollins, S., & Xu, Z. (2002). *Peer-to-Peer Computing.* HP Technical Report.

Minsky, Y., & Trachtenberg, A. (2002). *Practical Set Reconciliation.* Tech. Rep. BU-ECE-2002-01, Dept. Elec. Comput. Eng. Boston, MA: Boston University.

MPLS. (2007). How MPLS Works. *MPLS Experts.* Retrieved February 07, 2009, from http://www.mpls-experts.com

Naor, M., & Wieder, U. (2003). A simple fault tolerant distributed hash table. In *Proc. of the 2nd International Workshop on Peer-to-Peer Systems, IPTPS 03 (*pp. 88–97). Berkeley, CA: IEEE Computer Society.

Neisse, R., Granville, L. Z., Janilce, M., Almeida, B., & Tarouco, L. M. R. (2004). Managing Grids Communication Infrastructure through Policy Translations. In *Proc. of IEEE Workshop on IP Operations and Management* (pp. 278- 282). Beijing, China: IEEE Computer Society.

Newman, H. B. (2005). *Networking for High Energy and Nuclear Physics.* USA: ICFA SCIC Report, California Institute of Technology.

NLR. (2006). *Official web site of National Lambda Rail, NLR.* Retrieved February 20, 2009, from http://www.nlr.net

Padmanabhan, V., Wang, H., Chou, P., & Sripanidkulchai, K. (2002). Distributing streaming media content using cooperative networking. In *Proc. of the 12th International Workshop on Network and Operating Systems Support for Digital Audio and Video, NOSSDAV '02* (pp. 177 – 186). Miami Beach, FL: ACM Press.

Pakin, S., & Pant, A. (2002). VMI 2.0: A dynamically reconfigurable messaging layer for availability, usability, and management. In *Workshop on Novel Uses of System Area Networks, SAN-1* (pp. 12-19). Cambridge, MA: IEEE Computer Society.

Plaxton, C., Rajaraman, R., & Richa, A. (1997). Accessing nearby copies of replicated objects in a distributed environment. In *Proc. of the 9th Annual ACM Symposium on Parallel Algorithms and Architectures* (pp. 311 – 320). Newport, RI: ACM Press.

Pouwelse, J. A., Garbacki, P., Epema, D., & Sips, H. (2004). *A measurement study of the bittorrent peer-to-peer file sharing system.* Technical Report PDS-2004-007, Delft University of Technology Parallel and Distributed Systems Report Series, Holland.

Ratnasamy, S., Francis, P., Handley, M., Karp, R., & Shenker, S. (2001). A scalable content-addressable network. *Proc. of the 2001 conference on Applications, technologies, architectures, and protocols for computer communications* (pp. 161 – 172). San Diego, CA: ACM Press.

Rowstron, A., & Druschel, P. (2001). Pastry: Scalable, distributed object location and routing for large-scale peer-to-peer systems. In *Proc. of IFIP/ACM International Conference on Distributed Systems Platforms (Middleware)* (pp. 329 – 350). Heidelberg, Germany: ACM Press.

Rowstron, A., Kermarrec, A.-M., Druschel, P., & Castro, M. (2001). Scribe: The design of a large-scale event notification infrastructure. *Lecture Notes in Computer Science, 2233*(1), 30–43. doi:10.1007/3-540-45546-9_3

Sander, V., Adamson, W., Foster, I., & Alain, R. (2001). End-to-end Provision of Policy Information for Network QoS. In *Proc. of 10th IEEE International Symposium on High Performance Distributed Computing* (pp. 115). San Francisco: IEEE Computer Society.

Saroiu, S., Gummadi, K. P., Dunn, R. J., Gribble, S. D., & Levy, H. M. (2002a). An Analysis of Internet Content Delivery Systems. In *Proc. of the 5th symposium on Operating systems design and implementation* (pp. 315 – 327). New York: ACM Press.

Saroiu, S., Gummadi, P. K., & Gribble, S. D. (2002b). *A Measurement Study of Peer-to-Peer File Sharing Systems. Technical Report #UW-CSE-01-06-02, Department of Computer Science & Engineering.* Seattle, WA: University of Washington.

Sharma, P., Lee, S.-J., Brassil, J., & Shin, K. G. (2005). Distributed Communication Paradigm for Wireless Community Networks. *2005 IEEE International Conference on Communications, ICC 2005, 3*(1), 1549 – 1555.

Shorten, R. N., Leith, D. J., Foy, J., & Kilduff, R. (2003). Analysis and design of congestion control in synchronised communication networks. *Proc. of the 12th Yale Workshop on Adaptive and Learning Systems, 17*(1), 1-14.

SONET. (2006). *Synchronous Optical Network (SONET) standard description.* Retrieved February 12, 2009, from http://www.iec.org/online/tutorials/sonet/topic01.html

SONET. (2007). *Making SONET Ethernet-Friendly, GFP, VCAT, LCAS.* Retrieved March 20, 2009, from http://www.lightreading.com/document.asp?doc_id=30194&print=true

Stern, R. (2000). Napster: a walking copyright infringement? *IEEE Micro, 20*(6), 4–5. doi:10.1109/40.888696

Stoica, I., Morris, R., Karger, D., Kaashoek, M. F., & Balakrishnan, H. (2001). Chord: A scalable peer-to-peer lookup service for Internet applications. In *Proc. of the 2001 conference on Applications, technologies, architectures, and protocols for computer communications* (pp. 149-160). San Diego, CA: ACM Press.

Stoica, I., Morris, R., Karger, D., Kaashoek, M. F., & Balakrishnan, H. (2003). Chord: A scalable peer-to-peer lookup protocol for internet applications. IEEE/ACM Transactions on Networking, 17 – 32.

Sundaram, B., & Chapman, B. M. (2002). Xml-based policy framework for usage policy management in grids. In *Proc. of the 3rd International Workshop on Grid Computing (Grid'02)* (pp. 194-198). Berlin: Springer Verlag.

Tian, Y., Wu, D., & Ng, K.-W. (2006). Analyzing Multiple File Downloading in BitTorrent. In *International Conference on Parallel Processing, ICCP 2006* (pp. 297-306). Columbus, OH: IEEE Computer Society.

UCLP. (2007). *User Controlled LightPath Provisioning Standard Specification.* Retrieved February 15, 2009, from http://www.canarie.ca/canet4/uclp/

Yang, B., & Garcia-Molina, H. (2002). Improving Search in Peer-to-Peer Networks. *Proc. of the 22nd IEEE International Conference on Distributed Computing Systems, ICDCS'02* (pp. 5). Vienna, Austria: IEEE Computer Society.

Yang, J., Ma, H., Song, W., Cui, J., & Zhou, C. (2006). Crawling the eDonkey Network. In *Fifth International Conference on Grid and Cooperative Computing Workshops, GCCW'06* (pp. 133-136). Hunan, China: IEEE Computer Society.

Yang, K., Galis, A., & Todd, C. (2002). Policy-based active grid management architecture. In *10th IEEE International Conference on Networks* (pp. 134-145). Singapore: IEEE Computer Society.

Zhang, B., Jamin, S., & Zhang, L. (2002). Host Multicast: A Framework for Delivering Multicast to End Users. In *Proc. of the Twenty-First Annual Joint Conference of the IEEE Computer and Communications Societies, INFOCOM 2002* (pp. 1366- 1375). New York: IEEE Computer Society.

Zhao, B. Y., Huang, L., Stribling, J., Rhea, S. C., Joseph, A. D., & Kubiatowicz, J. D. (2004). Tapestry: A resilient global-scale overlay for service deployment. *IEEE Journal on Selected Areas in Communications, 22*(1), 41–53. doi:10.1109/JSAC.2003.818784

Zheng, X., Veeraraghavan, M., Rao, N. S. V., Wu, Q., & Zhu, M. (2005). CHEETAH: Circuitswitched high-speed end-to-end transport architecture testbed. *IEEE Communications Magazine, 43*(8), s11–s17. doi:10.1109/MCOM.2005.1497551

Chapter 4
Resource Management

INTRODUCTION

The resource management is an important component in LSDS implemented for a variety of architectures and services. This chapter considers the management of distributed resources, virtual resources and provides the requirements for resource management in large scale distributed system. A resource management system is defined as a service that is provided by a distributed network component system that manages a pool of named resources that is available such that a system-centric or job-centric performance metric is optimized. Due to issues such as extensibility, adaptability, site autonomy, QoS, and co-allocation, resource management systems is more challenging in large scale distributed computing environments. The taxonomy of resource management systems (RMS) for very large-scale network computing systems presents the variety of requirements for this tool. The taxonomy could be used to identify architectural approaches and issues that have not been fully explored in the research.

DOI: 10.4018/978-1-61520-703-9.ch004

The resource management system could support different users constrains, so the multiple policies is provided. In general, requiring the RMS to support multiple policies can compel the scheduling mechanisms to solve a multi-criteria optimization problem. An important subject presented in this chapter is Agents Frameworks for resource management that offer a mechanism for distributes resources management. The chapter ends with presentation of WSRF (Web Services Resource Framework) that is the new solution for resources management based on SOA (**OGSA** – Open Grid Service Architecture). Resource management in Grid implies a quite large number of functionalities, from resource discovery to scheduling, execution management, status monitoring and accounting. In this section, we shall focus on scheduling systems, and we shall present the monitoring functionalities and the Grid information systems in a further section. We shall introduce here some general issues, and then we shall present taxonomy of the scheduling systems and some details regarding the scheduling mechanisms used in the most important current Grid projects.

Wieder et al. (2006) distinguishes between two cases of Grid systems with respect to their requirements on resource management capabilities.

Case 1 is Specialized Grids for dedicated purposes, which are centered on a single or limited application domain and require high efficiency in execution. The Resource Management System (RMS) is adapted to the special application, its workflow and the available resource. Thus, the interfaces to the resources and the middleware are built according to the given requirements caused by the application scenario. While the Grid RMS is highly specialized, the handling for the user is often easier as the know-how of the application domain has been built into the system.

Case 2 is a Generic Grid Middleware, which has to cope with the complete set of the requirements to support applicability. The Grid RMS is open for many different application scenarios. In comparison to the specialized Grids, generic interfaces are required that can be adapted to many front- and backend. However, the generic nature of this approach comes at the price of additionally overhead for providing information about the application. For instance, more information about a particular job has to be provided to the middleware, such as a workflow description, scheduling objectives, policies and constraints.

The application-specific knowledge cannot be built into the middleware, and therefore must be provided at the frontend level. In this case, the consideration of security requirements is an integral aspect, which is more difficult to solve. It is possible to hide the additional RMS complexity of generic Grid infrastructures from the users or their applications by specialized components, which might be built on top of a generic middleware. Nevertheless, it can be concluded that in general a generic Grid middleware will carry additional overhead with less efficiency at the expense of broader applicability.

REQUIREMENTS FOR RESOURCE MANAGEMENT IN LSDS

Current research is mostly focusing on presented Case 1 in which solutions are built for a dedicated Grid scenario in mind. As mentioned before, these systems are usually more efficient and will therefore remain the favorite solution for many application domains. That is, Case 1 will not become obsolete if corresponding requirements and conditions exist. However, for creating future generation Grids suitable solutions are required for Case 2.

One of the most important components of a RMS is the scheduler, which distributes the applications on the Grid resources and usually also handles the execution management. We shall present as follows a brief taxonomy for scheduling systems.

A criterion by which we can classify the **scheduler**s is their organization. We can distinguish three categories of schedulers: centralized, hierarchical and decentralized. Most of the scheduling systems developed so far follow the centralized approach, in which the decisions about the place where a job should be executed are taken by a single entity. The decentralized model usually involves a multi-agent system, in which both the resources and the users are represented by agents, which negotiate the conditions of jobs' execution.

Another criterion used to classify the schedulers is the way they perform the state estimation of the system. The state estimation could be done in predictive way (estimation based on heuristics, price model or/and machine learning) or in non-predictive way (considering heuristics or/and probability distribution). Some of the schedulers attempt to predict the load on the resources in the future or the execution time of the jobs, others take into account only the present information. However, the available information is always partial or stale, due to the propagation delay in large distributed systems (Darbha & Agrawal, 1998).

Some of the schedulers provide a **rescheduling** mechanism, which determines when the current schedule is re-examined and the job executions reordered. The rescheduling taxonomy divides this mechanism in two conceptual mechanisms: periodic/batch and event-driven online. Periodic or batch mechanism approaches group resource request and system events which are then processed at intervals that may me periodic triggered by certain system events. The other mechanism performs the rescheduling as soon the system receives the resource request.

The **scheduling policy** can be fixed or extensible. The fixed policies are system oriented or application oriented. The extensible policies are ad-hoc or structured. In a fixed approach, the policy implemented by the resource manager is predetermined. Extensible scheduling policy schemes allow external entities the ability to change the scheduling policy.

The main requirements for a Resource Management Systems, according with Krauter (2002) refer to:

- *Adaptability* considers different type of systems like Grids, P2P systems, web-based systems.
- *Scalability* offers solutions for resource management in the context of dynamic environment.
- *Interoperability* among systems with different administrative policies (while preserving autonomy) represents the support for decentralization.
- *Economy of Computation* defines a pricing model for resource utilization of users from different VO.
- *Fault Tolerance* provides methods that ensure continued systems operation in the event of individual failures by providing redundant system elements.
- *High Level language support* offers a variety of application development possibility for different types of users. This could be considered a top services offered by a resource management system.
- *Extensible with other tools*
- *Security* is the support for protecting users' information and systems' information and data from unauthorized access.
- *Co-Scheduling* is a key concept to allocate distributed resources based on scheduling in computer multitasking and multiprocessing operating system design, and in real-time operating system design. It refers to the way processes are assigned priorities in a priority queue.
- *Support for QoS* represents the concept of applying and ensuring specific, quantifiable performance levels on a distributed system.
- *Reservation guarantee*
- *Stability*
- *Monitoring and storing of dynamic information*
- *Reliability* ensures properties with respect to the delivery of data to the intended recipient(s), as opposed to an unreliable protocol, which does not guarantee that data will be delivered intact, or that it will be delivered at all.

Resource management in a peer-to-peer system is based on a network management model in which each node is considered having equivalent capabilities and responsibilities. P2P architecture classification is based on the network and application (Qadri et al., 2008).

An example of a pure P2P file sharing network was the original design of Gnutella (released March 2000) in which the search function and content storage were totally decentralized, meaning that each function was conducted at the individual peer level (Stutzbach & Rejaie, 2005). This design suffered from several technical weaknesses that have diminished its role as a competitive distribution platform (see Figure 1).

One of the important aspects in P2P architecture is Collaborative Distributed Computing.

Figure 1. Pure peer network (early Gnutella)

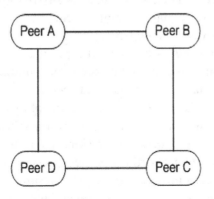

Figure 2. Centrally coordinated peer network (Napster)

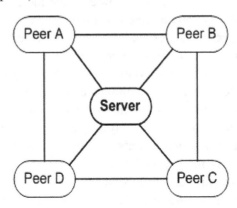

It combines the idle or unused CPU processing power and/or free disk space of many computers in the network. Collaborative computing is most popular with science and biotech organizations where intense computer processing is required. The Instant Messaging allows users to send different types of messages in real-time. The Affinity Communities is the group of P2P networks that is based around file-sharing and became widely known and talked about due to the public legal issues surrounding the direct file sharing group, Napster (see Figure 2). Affinity Communities are based on users collaborating and searching other user's computers for information and files (Gummadi et al., 2002).

The fault tolerant architecture for P2P systems is presented in Figure 3. The Hierarchical Peer Network considers different super-nodes which represents the communication point with clients.

P2P and Grid architectures differ from Web-based systems' architecture where some computers are dedicated to serving the others. In the modern approach, the web applications are based on services. An overview over standards-based web services shows that they differ in technology and in the applicability area. The success of the web services technology is conditioned by the existence of general open standards, available to any developer or user. The development of web services and application must satisfy certain requirements: a web service must be able to answer

to any client, regardless of the platform on which it is developed. A client must be able to retrieve the servers that can respond to its request through a web service (Kolici et al., 2008).

The web service standards were defined to improve the interoperability and availability for users from different domains. Serving as a base for the development of Grid systems and applications, the Internet offers the support for the web services functionality. The diagram below, reproduced from (Tanenbaum, 2002), describes the client-server model which is the base for web services design.

The communication between the service providers and the client's needs a common terminology; so that the exchanged information is understood by both of the parties in an effective manner (the XML standard offers the solution for this problem). Simple Object Access Protocol (SOAP) is a common protocol for representing the messages exchanged by web services (SOAP, 2009). The language which describes web services is Web Services Description Language (WSDL, 2009). Universal Description, Discovery and Integration (UDDI) define the way in which the providers publish details about the services and the clients obtain the published information (UDDI, 2009).

The current requirements in developing Grid application impose the compliance with the stan-

Figure 3. Hierarchical peer network (Kazaa, Grokster)

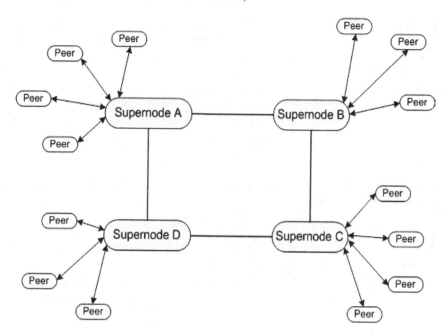

dards described above. The applications that are currently designed for an architecture that includes support for web services are from various domains like economy (Buyya, 2002), industry and science (for example, simulations and data processing in nuclear physics and complex systems physics).

Table 1 presents some characteristics for different type of LSDS middleware for Cluster, Grids, Web-based systems, Cloud Computing, P2P. The characteristics are presented from the applications side and include scope of the system, architecture, development models and technologies, supported platform.

VIRTUAL RESOURCES

Virtualization denotes the ability of resources to support multiplexing and polymorphism (i.e. to simultaneously appear as multiple resources with possibly different functionalities). Virtualization technologies are available or emerging for all the resources needed to construct virtual grids which

would ideally inherit the above mentioned properties. In particular, these technologies enable the creation of dynamic pools of virtual resources that can be aggregated on-demand for application-specific user-specific grid-computing. This change in paradigm from building grids out of physical resources to constructing virtual grids has many advantages but also requires new thinking on how to architect, manage and optimize the necessary middleware (Adabala et al., 2005).

The properties of virtual resources in distributed environments are:

- *Excellent isolation*, enhanced security, audit forensics
- *Fine-grain enforcement potential*
- *Customizable software configuration*: library signature, OS, maybe even 64/32-bit architectures
- *Serialization property*: for example, VM images (include RAM), can be copied.
- *The ability to pause and resume computations* is support for migration.

Table 1.

	Cluster	Grid	Web-based system	Cloud Computing	P2P
Scope	High Performance Computing	Workflow execution	Client-Server Application	SOA Applications	File sharing Applications
Architecture	Centralized	Decentralized	Hierarchical	Hierarchical, Decentralized	Centralized, Hierarchical, Decentralized
Development model	Execution Job Object	Abstract Job Object	RPC based Object (RMI, Corba)	Web Services Object	Component Object
Development technology	Java, C/C++, Perl, Python	Java, C/C++, Perl, Python	Java, C/C++, C#	J2EE,.NET, WebSpere, Azure	Java, C++, C#
Supported platform	Unix, MacOS	Unix, MacOS	Unix, Windows, MacOS	Platform independent	Platform independent
Users and applications	SEE-GRID, EuroGrid, Grid Interoperability Project (GRIP)	EGEE, AppLeS, Ninf, Nimrod-G, NASA IPG, Gridbus Broker, eScience (UK), EU Data Grid.	Web 2.0 & 3.0 Applications (CSS, DHTML, JSP, Servlets, EJB, SaaS)	Identity (OAuth, OpenID), Integration (Amazon Simple Queue Service), Payments (Amazon Flexible Payments, Google Checkout, PayPal), Mapping (Google Maps, Yahoo! Maps), Search (Google Custom Search, Yahoo! BOSS), Others (Amazon Mechanical Turk)	Kazza, Napster, Gnutela

A *virtual workspace* is an abstraction of an execution environment that can be made dynamically available to authorized clients by using well-defined protocols. There are two dimensions considered in virtual workspaces: software configuration and resource quota (CPU, memory, etc.). Some examples of workspaces are: a physical machine configured to meet TeraGrid requirements, a cluster of virtual machines configured to meet OSG requirements, a cluster of physical machines running a hypervisor.

Virtual Cluster is an abstraction of virtual workspace by deploying a cluster with scheduling (PBS/Torque) implementations, configuring networking and shared storage, offering image propagation with main deployment cost. Figure 4 describes the interaction between physical resourced, virtual resources and applications.

Xen is the powerful open source industry standards for virtualization, offers a powerful, efficient, and secure feature set for virtualization

of x86, x86_64, IA64, PowerPC, and other CPU architectures. It supports a wide range of guest operating systems including Windows, Linux, Solaris, and various versions of the BSD operating systems (Barham et al., 2003).

Adabala (2005) describes the distributed architecture of the *In-VIGO* (In Virtual Information Grid Organizations) grid-computing system. The novelty of In-VIGO architecture is the extensive use of virtualization technology, emerging standards for grid-computing and other Internet middleware.

The *Virtuoso* project explores two different perspectives: resource capability by developing mechanisms that will make it easy for resource owners to carefully control when and how the resources are used by virtual machines and application necessity by considering measurement and prediction of static and dynamic resource availability to include virtual machines (Shoykhet et al., 2004).

Figure 4. Resource virtualization

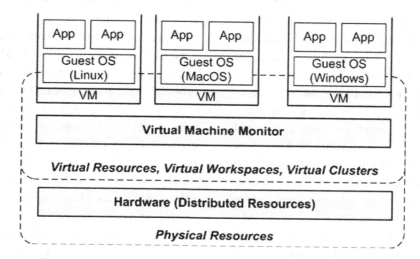

DISTRIBUTED RESOURCES AND EXISTING RMS TOOLS

A model for resource organization in LSDS is based on *tiers*. The functionality of each tier in the architecture is based on individual hardware and software components that can be combined to create a complete Cluster Grid solution. Hardware requirements, networking options, software integration, resiliency, and interoperability are discussed to provide readers a sound basis for the design and implementation of their own Cluster Grid solution. The tier architecture includes front-end access nodes, middle-tier management nodes, and back-end compute nodes (Figure 5).

The *access* tier provides access and authentication services to the Cluster Grid users. Conventional access methods, such as telnet, rlogin, or SSH, can be used to grant access. Alternatively, Web-based services can be provided to permit easy or tightly-controlled access to the facility.

Protocols can also be implemented to allow external services like accounting or analysis programs. Any access method should, of course, be able to integrate with common authentication schemes such as NIS, LDAP, and Kerberos. Furthermore, facilities for mapping external user

Figure 5. Distributed resource layers and tier layers

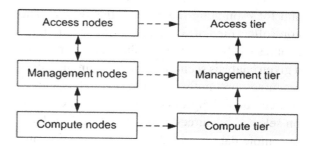

identities to a local identity can be considered. This middle tier includes one or more servers which run the server elements of client-server software such as Distributed Resource Management (DRM), hardware diagnosis software, and system performance monitors.

At the management layer, one of the most popular resource management systems is **Condor**. The software of a Condor pool is divided into two parts. The first part does job management, keeping track of a user's jobs. The other part of the Condor software does resource management, keeping track of which machines are available to run jobs, how the available machines should be utilized given all the users who want to run jobs on them, and when a machine is no longer available (Frey et al., 2006). Condor works with grid resources, allowing users to effectively submit jobs, manage jobs, and have jobs executed on widely distributed machines, all this being based on estimate the system state.

Another resource management project is **TORQUE**, which is available as open source and provides control over batch jobs and distributed compute nodes. It is a community effort based on the original PBS project and, with more than 1,200 patches, has incorporated significant advances in the areas of scalability, fault tolerance, and feature extensions contributed by NCSA, OSC, USC, the U.S. Dept of Energy, Sandia, PNNL, U of Buffalo, TeraGrid, and many other leading edge HPC organizations (TORQUE, 2009). TORQUE is a centralized system, in which a controller is responsible for the system-wide decision-making and for estimating the state of the system. The controller mediates access to distributed resources by discovering suitable data sources for a given analysis scenario, suitable computational resources, optimally mapping analysis jobs to resources, deploying and monitoring job execution on selected resources, accessing data from local or remote data source during job execution and collating and presenting results.

In **MOAB**, a cluster management solution that integrates scheduling, managing, monitoring and reporting of cluster workloads, we find a simplified and unified management across one or multiple hardware, operating system, storage, network, license and resource manager environments. "*Its task-oriented graphical management and flexible policy capabilities provide an intelligent management layer that guarantees service levels, speeds job processing and easily accommodates additional resources*" (MOAB, 2009). The precursor to MOAB is **MAUI**, "*an optimized, configurable tool capable of supporting an array of scheduling policies, dynamic priorities, extensive reservations, and fairshare capabilities*" (MAUI, 2009). Features like virtual private clusters, basic trigger support, graphical administration tools,

and a Web-based user portal are present both in Moab and Maui.

A project based on the meta-scheduling concept is **GridWay**. Built on top of **Globus** services, it performs job execution management and resource brokering, allowing unattended, reliable, and efficient execution of jobs, array jobs, or complex jobs on heterogeneous, dynamic and loosely coupled Grids (Badia et al., 2008). "*GridWay performs all the job scheduling and submission steps transparently to the end user and adapts job execution to changing Grid conditions by providing fault recovery mechanisms, dynamic scheduling, migration on-request and opportunistic migration*" (GridWay, 2009). The model of this scheduler is based on a flexible mechanism and allows different scheduling policies, which can determine the relative ordering of requests and jobs when rescheduling.

RESOURCE MANAGEMENT POLICIES

For a general purpose a resource management approach should make some assumptions about and have few restrictions to the types of applications that can be executed. These assumptions represent the based for defining *policies*. Interactive tasks, distributed and parallel applications, as well as non-interactive batch tasks, should all be supported with good performance. This property is a straightforward one, but to some extent difficult to achieve. Because different kinds of tasks have different attributes, their requirements to the scheduler may contradict. For example, a real-time task, requiring short-time response, prefers space-sharing scheduling; a non-interactive batch task, requiring high-throughput, may prefer time-sharing scheduling. To achieve the general purpose, a tradeoff may have to be made. The scheduling method focused on parallel tasks, while providing an acceptable performance to other kinds of tasks.

Efficiency of resource management system has two meanings: one is that it should improve the performance of scheduled tasks as much as possible; the other is that the scheduling should incur reasonably low overhead so that it won't counterattack the benefits.

The *fairness* refers to sharing resources among users' raises new challenges in guaranteeing that each user obtains her fair share when demand is heavy. In a distributed system, this problem could be exacerbated such that one user consumes the entire system. There are many mature strategies to achieve fairness on a single node.

The *dynamics* of the resource management systems and scheduling models means that the allocation algorithms employed to decide where to process a task should respond to load changes, and exploit the full extent of the resources available.

For the *transparency* of resource allocation process the behavior and result of a tasks execution should not be affected by the host(s) on which it executes. In particular, there should be no difference between local and remote execution. No user effort should be required in deciding where to execute a task or in initiating remote execution; a user should not even be aware of remote processing, except maybe better performance. Further, the applications should not be changed greatly. It is undesirable to have to modify the application programs in order to execute them in the system.

AGENT BASED PLATFORM FOR RESOURCE MANAGEMENT

In order to use the shared resources provided in a distributed environment and to enable high-performance computing, the monitoring service plays an essential role in a scheduling system.

The Grid Monitoring Service has the specific purpose to collect information regarding the status of the Grid global system and obtain real-time information about the various site facilities, networks, and about state of the current activities performed in the system. The monitoring information gathered is used by our method with the purpose to develop, based on the genetic algorithm, automated decisions that maintain and optimize the assignation of tasks on the resources of the computational Grid. The motivation for using monitoring in scheduling system can be summarize as follows:

- *Performance Tuning*. The meta-scheduling environment changes dynamically due to the variable load on the system and the network. The monitoring system could be an effective means for performance tuning and application steering.
- *Performance Evaluation*. The monitoring information can also be used to evaluate the scheduling performance in real-time mode.
- *Fault Recovery*. A monitoring system can be used effectively to classify and report all failures during the application scheduling and execution, so recovery procedure can be manually or automated initiated.
- *Correctness Checking*. A monitoring system can be used as a verification technique to ensure the consistency with a formal specification, for example enabling interaction with various scientific workflow specification languages.
- *Resource Utilization - Accounting*. The monitoring information is essential for recording resource (hardware, software, network etc.) usage at all levels.
- *Debugging and Testing*. A monitoring system could offers information about a centralized **scheduler** or isolated system.

For dynamic and decentralized **agent**-based resource allocation, a monitoring system must meet some important requirements:

- *Scalability*. The monitoring system should scale with the number of nodes in the system and with number of scheduling agents.

- *Extensibility*. The monitoring system should be extensible in the types of parameters that are monitored and the parameters collecting process. The monitoring system should consider different type of requests from scheduling agents.
- *Portability*. The monitoring system should be portable to a variety of clusters architectures.
- *Overhead*. The system should guarantee a low per-node overhead in monitoring system.
- *Robustness*. The monitoring system should recover from node and network failures of various types: network errors, timing errors, response errors, byzantine errors, physical errors, life cycle errors, interaction errors.
- *Accuracy*. The monitoring system must provide real-time and history, correct information, up to date offering global views of how large systems perform.

The techniques for collecting and publishing monitoring information consider the data collection engines (Hawkeye, PBS, **Condor**, SNMP), the data handling (filters, database push / pull mechanism), and registration and discovery monitoring services, which must consider replication of registration and discovery services and policies.

For monitoring, the agent architecture could use **MonALISA** (Newman et al., 2003) distributed service system, which provides reliable real-time information, such as systems information for computer nodes and clusters, network information (traffic, connectivity, topology, etc.) for WAN and LAN, monitoring information about the performance of applications, jobs or services. MonALISA has been used in several large scale distributed systems in which it proved its reliability and scalability.

The *resource allocation process* could be described as follows. Users submit Scheduling requests. A near-optimal schedule is computed by the **scheduler** based on the scheduling requests and the Monitoring data provided by the Grid Monitoring Service (MonALISA). The schedule is then sent as a Request for task execution to the Execution Service. The user receives feedback related to the solution determined by the scheduler, as well as to the status of the executed jobs in the form of the Schedule and task information. Furthermore, the system can integrate new hosts in the scheduling process, or overcome failure situations by means of the Discovery Service. The Scheduling request contains a description (in XML) of the tasks to be scheduled. This way, a user may ask for the scheduling of more than one task at a time. Various parameters have been taken into account for task description: resource requirements (CPU Power, Free Memory, and Free Swap), restrictions (deadlines) and priorities. The assignment of a task on a given computing node must be conditioned by meeting the resource requirements.

The Grid Monitoring Service has the specific purpose to obtain real-time information in a heterogeneous and dynamic environment such as a Grid. It uses the MonALISA distributed service system in conjunction with ApMON (Legrand, 2005), which is a library that can be used to send any status information in the form of UDP datagrams to MonALISA services. MonALISA provides system information for computer nodes and clusters, network information for WAN and LAN, monitoring information about the performance of applications, jobs or services. It proved its reliability and scalability in several large scale distributed systems. We have deployed the existing implementation of the MonALISA Web Service Client to connect to the monitoring service via proxy servers and obtain data for the genetic algorithm. Task monitoring is achieved by means of a daemon application based on ApMON. This daemon provides information regarding task status parameters on each node (amount of memory, disk and CPU time used by the tasks).

The up-to-date information offered by the Grid Monitoring Service leads to realistic execution times for assigned tasks.

The monitoring information about computers in the cluster is used for fitness computation in the genetic algorithm. We have enriched the existing implementation of the MonALISA Web Service Client to connect to the monitoring service via proxy servers and obtain data for the genetic algorithm. The up-to-date information leads to realistic computed execution times for assigned schedules, as proved by the experimental results.

The existing Web Service, "MLWebService", is integrated with the MonALISA service, as well as with the MonALISA Repository. The existing implementation was adapted to meet the necessities of the genetic algorithm. Each of the nodes executing the Genetic Algorithm runs a client application requesting and receiving the parameters needed in order to monitor data. Gathering monitoring data from the MonALISA service can be possible using a feature based on the WSDL/ SOAP technology of the Web Service.

Given its capability to dynamically load modules that interface existing job monitoring with batch queuing applications and tools (e.g. **Condor**, PBS, SGE, LSF), the Execution Service can send execution requests to an already installed batch queuing system on the computing node to which a particular group of tasks was assigned. Sets of tasks are dynamically sent on computing nodes in the form of a specific command. The time ordering policy established in the genetic algorithm for tasks assigned on the same processor is preserved at execution time.

Lookup processes are triggered by the Discovery Service and determine the possibility of achieving a decentralized schedule by increasing the number of hosts involved in the genetic scheduling. The apparition or dysfunction of agents in the system can easily be intercepted, resulting in a scalable and highly reliable optimization tool. If one agent ceases to function, the system as a whole is not prejudiced, but the probability of reaching a less optimal solution for the same number of generations increases.

The functionality of the **scheduler** relies on a communication model in which two different entities are involved: Brokers and Agents. The Brokers collect user requests for task allocations (Task Description Files), parse them and create an object, batch of tasks, which contains the tasks to be scheduled. Then the Brokers forward the requests to Agents. Each Agent executes the scheduling algorithm.

The Broker develops communication in two directions: with the user on one side and with the Agents on the other side. The Broker has a listener to the input, which receives the requests from users. These requests are XML files that contain description of the tasks to be scheduled. This offers the possibility to request the scheduling of a batch of tasks. The Broker creates objects that represent the tasks requirements that are going to be sent to the Agents in the negotiation phase. The Broker is responsible for the selection of the best resources. The Broker could have the following main components: user interface, broker module, scheduling module, negotiation module and rating module. The Agent could have the following module: agent service module, evaluation module, cluster status module, agent scheduler and rating module.

The description of a scheduling request specifies the tasks' requirements together with other information of interest such as the task ID, path to the executable, the arguments, the input data file, the output and error files, and the arriving time. The task description adopted in the system is presented below.

The requirements specified for each task include:

- resource requirements (CPU Power, Free Memory, Free Swap);
- restrictions (deadlines);
- priorities.

Some functional and descriptive information about the task are indicated in the XML description, such as:

- the *path* to the executable;
- the *arguments* received by the executable, in case they are needed;
- the *input* file received by the program;
- files for redirection of: *output*, and *error;*
- arriving date (*arrivingDate*) and time (*arrivingTime*) of the task, for a possible insertion in the task queue ordered by arriving time.

Requirements are specified for each task, as follows:

- *memory*, disk space (*swapSpace*) and CPU power (*cpuPower*) requirements;
- processing time (*processingTime*), which is an initial value of the time necessary for the task to be processed in the conditions specified by the memory and CPU power requirements;
- deadline restrictions (*deadlineTime*), representing the date and time by which the task must finish execution;
- schedule priority (*schedulePriority*), representing a priority associated with the task, and denoting its precedence over other tasks considered for allocation, which have a smaller priority.

Moreover, the task description specifies the number of executions of the specific task that may occur. A user may ask for the scheduling of more than one task at a time. The assignment of a task to a given computing node is conditioned by meeting the resource requirements. The study is focused on classes of independent tasks, as described in (Maheswaran et al., 1999), which avoids communication costs due to dependencies. It is considered a model based on a real scenario in which groups of tasks are submitted by independent users, to be executed on a group of nodes.

WEB SERVICES RESOURCE FRAMEWORKS

Resource management could be done using new technique based on Web Services. For Grid systems, **Globus** offer a novel solution for resource specification.

The Globus Toolkit includes software services and libraries for distributed security, resource management, monitoring and discovery, and data management. Its latest version, GT4, includes components for building systems that follow the Open Grid Services Architecture (**OGSA**) framework defined by the Global Grid Forum (GGF), of which the Globus Alliance is a leading member. The toolkit includes software for security, information infrastructure, resource management, data management, communication, fault detection, and portability. It is packaged as a set of components that can be used either independently or together to develop applications. Every organization has unique modes of operation, and collaboration between multiple organizations is hindered by incompatibility of resources such as data archives, computers, and networks. The Globus Toolkit was conceived to remove obstacles that prevent seamless collaboration. Its core services, interfaces and protocols allow users to access remote resources as if they were located within their own machine room while simultaneously preserving local control over who can use resources and when.

GT4's components and software development tools also comply with the Web Services Resource Framework (WSRF), a set of standards in development in OASIS (Foster, 2005). WSRF provides the stateful services that **OGSA** needs. In Figure 6: WSRF specifies stateful services (as opposed to those services simply 'being required' by OGSA). Another way of expressing this relation is that,

Figure 6. Relationship between OGSA, GT4, WSRF, and Web Services

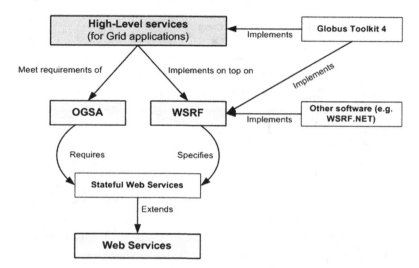

while OGSA is the architecture, WSRF is the infrastructure on which that architecture is built on.

Most of **Globus** services are implemented on top of WSRF (the toolkit also includes some services that are not implemented on top of WSRF and are called the non-WS components). The Globus Toolkit 4, in fact, includes a complete implementation of the WSRF specification. This part of the toolkit (the WSRF implementation) is a very important part of the toolkit since nearly everything else is built on top of it. However, it's worth noting that it's also a very small part of the toolkit (Boverhof, 2005).

Foster (2005) consider that "*Monitoring and discovery are two vital functions in a distributed system, particularly when that system spans multiple locations, as in that context no one person is likely to have detailed knowledge of all components. Monitoring allows us to detect and diagnose the many problems that can arise in such contexts, while discovery allows us to identify resources or services with desired properties*" (see Figure 7). The LSDS monitoring has the specific purpose to collect information regarding the status of the Grid global system and obtain real-time information about the various site facilities, networks, and about state of the current activities performed in the system. The monitoring information gathered is used by our method with the purpose to develop, based on the genetic algorithm, automated decisions that maintain and optimize the assignation of tasks on the resources of the computational resources. The monitoring information is used by WSRF component to specify the status of resources.

CONCLUSION

The evolution of distributed systems and specific technologies imposes new scheduling methods, adapted to the user requirements and resource constraints. The optimization of decentralized scheduling in LDSD environments considers multi-criteria constraints for objective function in scheduling algorithm. The decentralized strategies place the scheduling component on the top of LSDS architecture in the global Grid.

The analysis of algorithms for independent and dependent task scheduling offers a selection base of the "best" algorithm. A comparative evaluation was performed for different scheduling strategies, using a series of performance metrics and a simulation tool.

Figure 7. GT4 monitoring and discovery infrastructure

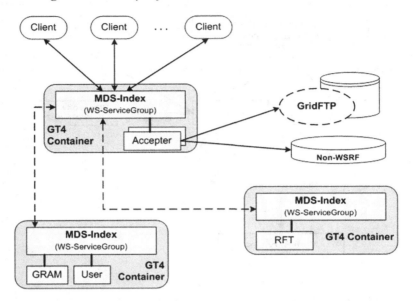

In LSDS environments, various real applications require dynamic scheduling for the optimized assignment of tasks. Monitoring information could be used for scheduling, and offers a solution for decentralized resources allocation strategies. The use of the MonALISA monitoring system facilitates rapid integration of sites that appear dynamically during the execution of applications. The validation of decentralized scheduling model in real environments was made using monitoring information.

The resource allocation algorithms are difficult to implement because the resources are owned by different organizations that have their own policies and charging mechanisms. The complexity of the applications increases when the users specify constraints like deadlines and time limitations. An agent platform designed for the scheduling process offers a reliable and fault tolerant communication system for task scheduling according to the users' requirements and resources' constraints. This decentralized scheduler adapts to the changes in the system, such as load and resource availability changes, using monitoring information. Also, it ensures the quality of offered services. The communication model based on negotiation offers the possibility to minimize the costs associated to task execution and maximize the provider profits.

REFERENCES

Adabala, S., Chadha, V., Chawla, P., Figueiredo, R., Fortes, J., & Krsul, I. (2005). From virtualized resources to virtual computing grids: the In-VIGO system. *Future Generation Computer Systems*, *21*(6), 896–909. doi:10.1016/j.future.2003.12.021

Badia, R. M., Du, D., Huedo, E., Kokossis, A., Llorente, I. M., Montero, R. S., et al. (2008). Integration of GRID Superscalar and GridWay Metascheduler with the DRMAA OGF Standard. In E. Luque, T. Margalef, & D. Benítez (Eds.), *Proceedings of the 14th international Euro-Par Conference on Parallel Processing* (LNCS 5168, pp. 445-455). Berlin: Springer-Verlag.

Barham, P., Dragovic, B., Fraser, K., Hand, S., Harris, T., Ho, A., et al. (2003). Xen and the art of virtualization. In *Proceedings of the Nineteenth ACM Symposium on Operating Systems Principles* (pp. 164-177). New York: ACM.

Boverhof, J. (2005). *Python WSRF Programmers' Tutorial (Tech. Rep.)*. Lawrence Berkeley National Lab, Computational Research Department.

Darbha, S., & Agrawal, D. P. (1998). Optimal Scheduling Algorithm for Distributed Memory Machines. *IEEE Transactions on Parallel and Distributed Systems*, 9(1), 87–95. doi:10.1109/71.655248

Foster, I. (2005). Globus toolkit version 4: Software for service-oriented systems. In *IFIP International Conference on Network and Parallel Computing* (LNCS 3779, pp. 2-13). Berlin: Springer-Verlag.

Frey, J., Tannenbaum, T., Foster, I., Livny, M., & Tuecke, S. (2006). Condor-G: A computation management agent for multi-institutional grids. *Cluster Computing. Springer Netherlands*, 5(3), 235–247.

GridWay. (2009). *Metascheduling Technologies for the Grid*. Retrieved September 13, 2009, from http://www.gridway.org

Gummadi, P. K., Saroiu, S., & Gribble, S. D. (2002). A measurement study of Napster and Gnutella as examples of peer-to-peer file sharing systems. *SIGCOMM Comput. Commun. Rev*, 32(1), 82–82. doi:10.1145/510726.510756

Kolici, V., Xhafa, F., Matsuo, K., Durresi, A., Barolli, L., & Miho, R. (2008). A P2P system based on JXTA-overlay and its application for end-device control. In *Proceedings of the 6th international Conference on Advances in Mobile Computing and Multimedia* (pp. 364-369). New York: ACM.

Krauter, K., Buyya, R., & Maheswaran, M. (2002). A taxonomy and survey of grid resource management systems for distributed computing. *Software, Practice & Experience*, 32(2), 135–164. doi:10.1002/spe.432

Legrand, I. (2005, September). *End user agents: extending the intelligence to the edge in distributed service systems*. Paper presented at the Fall 2005 Internet2 Member Meeting, Philadelphia.

Maheswaran, M., Ali, S., Siegel, H. J., Hensgen, D., & Freud, R. F. (1999). Dynamic mapping of a class of independent tasks onto heterogeneous computing systems. *Journal of Parallel and Distributed Computing*, 59(2), 107–131. doi:10.1006/jpdc.1999.1581

Maui Cluster Scheduler. (2009). *Center for HPC Cluster Resource Management, Scheduling, and Grid Scheduling Research and Development*. Retrieved September 13, 2009, from http://www.clusterresources.com/products/maui

MOAB Cluster Suite (2009). *Center for HPC Cluster Resource Management, Scheduling, and Grid Scheduling Research and Development*. Retrieved September 13, 2009, from http://www.clusterresources.com/products/moab-cluster-suite.php

Newman, H., Legrand, I., Galvez, P., Voicu, R., & Cirstoiu, C. (2003, March). *Monalisa: A distributed monitoring service*. Paper presented at CHEP conference, La Jolla, California.

Qadri, N. N., Alhaisoni, M., & Liotta, A. (2008). Mesh based P2P streaming over MANETs. In *Proceedings of the 6th international Conference on Advances in Mobile Computing and Multimedia* (pp. 29-34). New York: ACM.

Shoykhet, A., Lange, J., & Dinda, P. (2004). *Virtuoso: A System for Virtual Machine Marketplaces* (Technical Report NWU-CS-04-39). Evanston, IL: Northwestern University.

Stutzbach, D., & Rejaie, R. (2005). Characterizing the two-tier gnutella topology. *SIGMETRICS Perform. Eval. Rev*, 33(1), 402–403. doi:10.1145/1071690.1064275

Tanenbaum, A. S., & van Steen, M. (2002). *Distributed Systems. Principles and paradigms*. Upper Saddle River, NJ: Prentice Hall.

TORQUE resource manager. (2009). *Center for HPC Cluster Resource Management, Scheduling, and Grid Scheduling Research and Development*. Retrieved September 13, 2009, from http://www.clusterresources.com/pages/products/torque-resource-manager.php

Vaughan-Nichols, S. J. (2006). New Approach to Virtualization Is a Lightweight. *Computer, 39*(11), 12–14. doi:10.1109/MC.2006.393

Wieder, P., Waldrich, O., & Ziegler, W. (2006). Advanced Techniques for Scheduling, Reservation, and Access Management for Remote Laboratories. In *Proceedings of the Second IEEE international Conference on E-Science and Grid Computing* (December 04 - 06, 2006). Washington, DC: IEEE Computer Society.

Chapter 5
Scheduling

INTRODUCTION

This chapter presents the scheduling problem in large scale distributed systems. Most parts of the chapter are devoted to discussion of scheduling algorithms and models. The main challenges of scheduling problem are approached here. The implementation issues are also covered.

The chapter has three parts. The first part covers basics like scheduling models, scheduling algorithms for independent tasks and DAG scheduling Algorithms for tasks with dependencies. The first part of the chapter presents a classification of scheduling problems, methods that are relevant for the solution procedures, and computational complexity. The scheduling models are presented based on systems architecture described in Resource Management chapter. This firs part also provides a critical analysis of most important algorithms from different points of view, such as static versus dynamic policies, objective functions, applications models, adaptation, QoS constraints and strategies dealing with dynamic behavior of resources.

DOI: 10.4018/978-1-61520-703-9.ch005

The second part covers new scheduling mechanism like resources co-allocation and advance reservation. Multi-criteria optimization mechanisms for users and systems constrain (e.g. load-balancing, minimization of execution time) are described and analyzed in this chapter. This part uses algorithm and methods to highlight the importance of these topics. The dynamic scheduling is also the subject of this part. It is also presented the implementation issues for scheduler tools. Since it is not possible to cover the whole area of scheduling in one chapter, some restrictions are imposed. Firstly, the chapter presents only Scheduling for Large Scale Distributed Systems (LSDS), without single system scheduling. Secondly, some interesting topics of fault tolerance (re-scheduling) are not analyzed in this chapter.

The scheduling is presented using a higher level abstraction for the distributed systems by ignoring infrastructure components such as authentication, authorization, and access control. A very good definition for the distributed system that can be used in this chapter for understanding scheduling problem keys is given in (Baker et al., 2002): "*A type of parallel and distributed system that enables the sharing, selection, and aggregation of geographi-*

cally distributed autonomous and heterogeneous resources dynamically at runtime depending on their availability, capability, performance, cost, and users' quality-of-service requirements".

More applications are turning to LSDS computing to meet their computational and data storage needs. Single sites are simply no longer efficient for meeting the resource needs of high-end applications, and using distributed resources can give the application many benefits. Effective LSDS computing is possible, however, only if the resources are scheduled well.

In scheduling context *a task* could to be defined, for an user, as anything that needs a resource, from a bandwidth request, to an application, to a set of applications (for example, a parameter sweep). In the same context, *a resource* could be anything that can be scheduled: a machine, processors, disk space and memory, a QoS network.

Scheduling is a key concept for multitasking and multiprocessing design in large scale distributed systems and a most important aspect in real-time system design. *Scheduling* is the process of assigning tasks on compute resources according with a task policy and ordering communication between tasks. This assignment is carried out by software known as a *scheduler*. The scheduling process is also known as the allocation process of computation and communication in time. (Ramin & Wieder, 2005).

In manufacturing, the scope of scheduling is to minimize the production time and costs (in many case the cost is represented by money), by offering a production facility what to make, when, with which staff, and on which resources (Blazewicz et al., 2001). Production scheduling aims to maximize the efficiency of the operation and reduce costs.

The scheduling process is described by a *scheduling algorithm*, which is a procedure used by a scheduler to determine when a task can run (Roehrig & Zeigler, 2002). There exist different algorithms for independent tasks and dependent tasks. All scheduling algorithms use in tasks as-

signment different policies. A *scheduling policy* is a set of rule defined by users or imposed by recourses administrators. In most cases, the scheduler uses an internal queue for tasks management. A *scheduling queue* is a collection of tasks within the (batch) queuing system. Roehrig et al. explain that each queue has a set of associated attributes that determine which actions are to be performed upon each task within the queue. Typical attributes include queue name, queue priority, resource limits, destination(s), and task count limits. Selection and scheduling of tasks is implementation-defined.

The background for scheduling problems is described by resources environment, **task** characteristics and assignment policies. The Table 1 presents in the first part a description the resources environment. It states a general commitment about the resources (represented by processors) and their relation to the tasks: whether there are one or more processors, whether they have identical or uniform speed on not, whether the environment is a certain shop system and what network topology the processors are connected by. The second one specifies the characteristic of tasks. It is mainly concerned with the admissibility of preemptions, precedence constrains, release times, bounded processing time and deadlines (Berman, 1998).

According with these aspects about environment and tasks the optimality criteria could be described. These criteria represent the main focus of scheduling policies. First the policies for task processing consider the following aspects: tasks can be processed on any single processor, tasks require fixed numbers of processors, linear speedup, processing times are in the inverse ratio to number of assigned processors, processing times are an arbitrary function of the number of assigned processors, tasks require sub-hypercube of a hypercube network, tasks require sub-meshes of a mesh (array), there is exactly one fixed sub-graph specified for each task, or there are sets of possible sub-graphs specified for each task. In the case of communication tasks, the delays are also important. The scheduling policies can consider no

Table 1. Background of scheduling in LSDS

Resources environment	Parallel processors	Single processor
		Identical processors
		Uniform processors
		Unrelated processors
	Multipurpose machines	Multipurpose machines with identical speeds
		Multipurpose machines with uniform speeds
	Dedicated processors	General shop system
		Job shop system
		Flow shop system
		Open shop system
		Mixed shop system
	Communication network topology	Negligible communication delays
		Arbitrary communication links
		Line (one-dimensional mesh)
		Closed line topology
		Multi-dimensional mesh
		Multi-dimensional hypercube
		Tree-structured network
	Simultaneousness of processing and communication	Parallel processing and communication possible
		No overlapping of processing and communication
Task characteristics	Preemption	No preemption allowed
		Preemptions are allowed
		Divisible tasks (preemptions are allowed)
	Additional resources	No additional resources
		Specified resource constrains
	Precedence constrains	Independent tasks
		Arbitrary precedence constrains (DAG) Unconnected activity networks
		Precedence constrains forming an in/out tree
		Precedence constrains forming either an in-tree or out-tree
		Tree or out tree
		Set of chains
		Series-parallel graph
	Release times	All tasks are released at time t = 0.
		Release time may be specified for each task
	Processing times	Task heaving arbitrary processing times
		Constant processing time
		Bounded processing time
	Deadlines	No deadlines (although due dates may still be specified)
		Deadlines may be specified
	No-wait property on dedicated processors	Assuming buffers or unlimited capacity
		No buffering, tasks must immediately proceed
		Processing on consecutive processors

Figure 1. Scheduling model properties

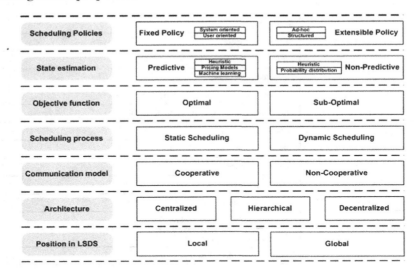

communication delays, equals delay or different delays. Another important policy refers to fault tolerance. It considers task duplication that could be allowed or not (Streit, 2002).

In LSDS scheduling process involves three main phases described in (Schopf, 2004): first, **resource** discovery, which generates a list of potential resources; second, information gathering about those resources and selection of a best set of resources according with users requirements; third, task execution (system preparation and submission), phase which includes task staging and system cleanup. Because each of the main phases includes some steps, it produces many levels and it's difficult to implement all steps in a real environment.

The next section presents the possibility to be considered in a design process for a scheduler according with a global view of for distributed systems. Using it, it is possible to choose for different properties and models.

SCHEDULING MODELS

A *scheduling model* consists of **scheduling policy**, a program model, a performance model, and a performance measure method. A scheduling model specify the position of scheduler in LSDS, the scheduler architecture, the communication model between entities involved in scheduling, the process type: static or dynamic, the objective function, the state estimation, and the scheduling policies (see Figure 1).

First, a scheduler in LSDS could work local or global. This is the position of schedulers in LSDS. The *local scheduler* uses a single CPU (a single machine) and determines how the tasks are allocated in time and executed on it. It is represented by scheduler from system operating kernel. The *global scheduler* uses information about system and its components to allocate tasks to multiple resources and try to optimize this process according with specified performance objectives. It is represented by Grid scheduler.

Next, the scheduler architecture is very important because it split the schedulers in tree classes: centralized, hierarchical and decentralized (Hamscher et al., 2000).

In the *centralized* scheduler all tasks are sent to the one entity in the system. This entity is called central server or master or coordination. There is a queue in on this entity for holding all the pending tasks. When a **task** is submitted to the scheduler, it may not be scheduled at once; it will be put in the queue and waiting for scheduling and resource allocation. The main problem with centralized scheme is that is not very scalable with increasing number of resources. For example, if a network failure appears and the master is not accessible or responds very slow, the system availability and performance will be affected. As an advantage, the scheduler is able to produce very efficient schedules at local level, because the master has an overview on the available resources and on pending applications (Czajkowski et al., 1998). This type of scheduler is recommended for homogenous systems like massive multiprocessors machine or clusters.

The hierarchical scheduler is organized on different levels having a tree structure (Wedde et al., 2004): the higher-level components manage direct larger sets of resources and indirect a smaller set of resources using lower-level components. The lower-level components could be local schedulers in clusters that provide to the higher-level components the possibility to schedule a set of task on the managed resources. **Hierarchical scheduling**, in comparison with the centralized scheduling, addresses the scalability and the problem of single-point-of-failure. Hierarchical scheduling uses some of the advantages of the centralized scheme: higher-level components have a local scheduler and some resources (preferred to be homogenous) managed in a centralized way. One of the issues with the hierarchical scheme is that it does not provide site autonomy yet.

The *decentralized scheduler* has multiple components (site) that work independent and collaborate for obtaining the schedule (Arora et al., 2002). Each site in the LSDS could be a local scheduler and a computational resource in the same time. The schedule requests could be processed by local scheduler or transferred to other local scheduler where different scheduling policies are possible. In this way, the decentralized scheduler delivers better fault-tolerance and reliability than the centralized scheme, but the lack of a global

scheduler, which knows the information of all applications and resources, usually results in low efficiency.

The next attribute for scheduling process is the collaboration mode between involved entities. If a **distributed scheduling** architecture adopted, the next issue that should be establishes is the working way: cooperatively or independently (non-cooperatively). In the non-cooperative case, individual entities work as autonomous entities and obtain their optimum objects independent of the decision on the rest of system. This model is very good for application-level schedulers in LSDS which are coupled with an application and optimize their private individual objectives. In the cooperative case, each entity works to a common system-wide goal. The cooperative model requires a communication protocol. An example of **cooperative scheduling** is presented in (Shan, 2004), where is presented a distributed Grid scheduler based on client-server model. The obtained results are compared with centralized scheduling and local scheduling and prove that decentralized cooperative model are more efficient that centralize or non-cooperative scheduler.

Static or dynamic scheduling is used for efficient planning in distributed systems. In the case of *static scheduling*, information regarding all resources in the LSDS as well as all the tasks in an application is assumed to be available by the time the application is scheduled. In the static model, every task comprising the task is assigned only once to a resource. For this reason, the assignment of an application to corresponding resources is said to be static. Accordingly, a realistic prediction of the cost of the computation can be made in advance of the actual execution.

By contrast, when talking about *dynamic scheduling*, the basic idea is to perform task allocation *on the fly* while other applications are in execution. This is useful in the case where tasks arrive in a real-time mode. Dynamic scheduling is usually applied when it is difficult to estimate the cost of applications, or jobs are coming online dynamically (in this case, it is also called online scheduling). A good example of these scenarios is the job queue management in some meta-computing systems like Condor and Legion. Dynamic task scheduling has two major components (Rotithor, 1994): system state estimation (other than cost estimation in static scheduling) and, decision making.

System state estimation involves collecting state information throughout the LSDS and constructing an estimate. On the basis of the estimate, decisions are made to assign a task to a selected resource. Since the cost for an assignment is not available, a natural way to keep the whole system healthy is by balancing the loads of all resources. The advantage of dynamic load balancing over static scheduling is that the system need not be aware of the run-time behavior of the application before execution. It is particularly useful in a system where the primary performance goal is maximizing resource utilization, rather than minimizing runtime for individual tasks. If a resource is assigned too many tasks, it may invoke a balancing policy to decide whether to transfer some tasks to other resources, and which tasks to transfer. According to who will initiate the balancing process, there are two different approaches: sender-initiated where a node that receives a new task but doesn't want to run the task initiates the task transfer, and receiver-initiated where a node that is willing to receive a new task initiates the process.

In the case that all information regarding the state of resources and the tasks is known, an optimal assignment could be made based on some criterion function, such as minimum make-span and maximum resource utilization. But due to the NP-Complete nature of scheduling algorithms and the difficulty in Grid scenarios to make reasonable assumptions which are usually required to prove the optimality of an algorithm, current research tries to find suboptimal solutions, which can be further divided into the following two general categories: *approximate* and *heuristic* algorithms.

The *approximate* algorithms use formal computational models, but instead of searching the entire solution space for an optimal solution, they are satisfied when a solution that is sufficiently "good" is found. In the case where a metric is available for evaluating a solution, this technique can be used to decrease the time taken to find an acceptable schedule. The factors which determine whether this approach is worthy of pursuit include (Chen & Maheswaran, 2002): availability of a function to evaluate a solution, the time required to evaluate a solution, the ability to judge the value of an optimal solution according to some metric, availability of a mechanism for intelligently pruning the solution space.

The other branch in the suboptimal category is called heuristic. This branch represents the class of algorithms which make the most realistic assumptions about a priori knowledge concerning process and system loading characteristics. It also represents the solutions to the scheduling problem which cannot give optimal answers but only require the most reasonable amount of cost and other system resources to perform their function. The evaluation of this kind of solution is usually based on experiments in the real world or on simulation. Not restricted by formal assumptions, heuristic algorithms are more adaptive to the Grid scenarios where both resources and applications are highly diverse and dynamic, so most of the algorithms to be further discussed are heuristics.

Some of the schedulers provide a rescheduling mechanism, which determines when the current schedule is re-examined and the task executions reordered. The rescheduling taxonomy divides this mechanism in two conceptual mechanisms: periodic/batch and event-driven on line. Periodic or batch mechanism approaches group resource request and system events which are then processed at intervals that may me periodic triggered by certain system events. The other mechanism performs the rescheduling as soon the system receives the resource request.

The **scheduling policy** can be fixed or extensible. The fixed policies are system oriented or application oriented. The extensible policies are ad-hoc or structured. In a fixed approach, the policy implemented by the resource manager is predetermined. Extensible scheduling policy schemes allow external entities the ability to change the scheduling policy.

Inspired for the real live, there are a few economic models that can be applied in Grid systems. The main characters in those models are the producers (resource owners) and the consumers (resource users). The main models are: commodity market (flat or supply-and-demand driven pricing) model, posted price model, bargaining model, tender/contract-net model, auction model, bid-based proportional resource sharing model (Buyya et al., 2002).

SCHEDULING ALGORITHMS FOR INDEPENDENT TASKS

Scheduling algorithm could be view, according with used objective function, form tow perspective: systems and applications.

From the systems point view, when as a set of independent tasks arrives a common strategy is to assign them according to the load of resources in order to achieve high system throughput.

From the point of view of applications, some static heuristic algorithms based on execution cost estimate can be applied (Braun et al., 2001).

One of the scheduling algorithms for independent tasks is Minimum Execution Time (MET). This algorithm assigns each task to the resource with the best expected execution time, no matter whether this resource is available or not at the present time. The objective function for MET is to give each task its best machine. This can cause a severe load imbalance among machines. Even worse, this heuristic is not applicable to heterogeneous computing environments where resources and tasks are characterized as consistent, which

means a machine that can run a task faster will run all the other tasks faster (Zhan et al., 2007).

Another important algorithm is Minimum Completion Time (MCT) that is also presented by Zhan et al. (2007). This algorithm assigns each task, in an arbitrary order, to the resource with the minimum expected completion time for that task. It is possible that some tasks to be assigned to machines that do not have the minimum execution time for them. The objective function for MCT is to combine the benefits of opportunistic load balancing (OLB) and MET, while avoiding the circumstances in which OLB and MET perform poorly (Hak & Jin, 2004).

Scheduling algorithms for independent task use heuristics for objecting function. The important used heuristics are Min-min, Max-Min, XSuffrage, and Duplex. Another important strategies for independent tasks are genetic algorithms, simulated annealing, A*.

Min-min finds the minimum completion time for each task. The task with the overall minimum completion time is selected and assigned to the corresponding resources. Last, the newly mapped task is removed, and the process repeats until all tasks are scheduled. Min-min heuristic is based on the minimum completion time (MCT). Min-min schedules the tasks in the order that changes the machine availability status by the least amount that any assignment could.

Max-min finds the set of minimum completion time. The task with the overall maximum is selected and assigned to the corresponding resources. Last, the newly mapped task is removed, and the process repeats until all tasks are scheduled. Max-min heuristic attempts to minimize the penalties incurred from performing tasks with longer execution times.

XSuffrage is described by Maheswaran et al. (1999). A task is assigned to a certain host and if it does not go to that host, it will suffer the most. For each task, its suffrage value is defined as the difference between its best MCT and its second-best MCT. Tasks with high suffrage value take precedence. But when there is input and output data for the tasks and resources are clustered, conventional suffrage algorithms may have problems. If the resources are clustered, and nodes in the same cluster are with near identical performance, then the best and second best MCTs are also nearly identical which makes the suffrage close to zero and gives the tasks low priority.

The *Duplex* heuristic is a combination of the Min-min and Max-min heuristics. The Duplex heuristic performs both of the Min-min and Max-min heuristics and then uses the better solution. Duplex exploits the conditions in which either Min-min or Max-min performs better.

Genetic Algorithms (GA) are a technique used for searching large solution spaces (Zomaya & Hwei, 2001). Multiple possible mappings of the meta-task are computed, which are considered chromosomes in the population. Each chromosome has a fitness value, which is the result of an objective function designed in accordance with the performance criteria of the problem (for example max-span). At each iteration, all of the chromosomes in the population are evaluated based on their fitness value, and only the best of them survive in the next population, where new allocations are generated based on crossover and mutation operators. The algorithm usually stops when a predefined number of steps are performed, or all chromosomes converge to the same mapping.

Simulated Annealing (SA) is an iterative technique that considers only one possible solution (mapping) for each meta-task at a time. This solution uses the same representation as the chromosome for the GA. SA uses a procedure that probabilistically allows poorer solutions to be accepted to attempt to obtain a better search of the solution space (Cooper et al., 2004). This probability is based on a system temperature that decreases for each iteration. As the system temperature decreases, poorer solutions are less likely to be accepted. The initial temperature of the system is the max-span of the initial mapping, which is randomly determined. At each iteration,

the mapping is transformed in the same manner as the GA, and the new max-span is evaluated. If the new max-span is better (lower), the new mapping replaces the old one. If the new max-span is larger, a uniform random number in the [0, 1) interval is generated.

A* heuristic is a search technique based on a tree, which has been applied in various task allocation problems (Michalewicz & Fogel, 2000). The A* heuristic begins at a root node that is a null solution. As the tree grows, nodes represent partial mappings (a subset of tasks is assigned to machines). With each child added, a new task is mapped. Each parent node generates μ children, where μ is the number of possible mappings for a task. After a parent node has done this, the parent node becomes inactive. A pruning process is performed to limit the maximum number of active nodes in the tree at any one time. Moreover, each node, n, has a cost function.

The mapping heuristics described are not exhaustive, which means they do not cover all the search space. The methods presented are a representative set of several different approaches, including greedy (A*), and biologically-inspired techniques (genetic algorithms, simulated annealing). The A* heuristic is equivalent to an exhaustive search if the tree is not pruned, but the time taken by the algorithm would be too large.

GA usually finds the best mappings compared to the heuristics described (Zomaya, 2001). The main difference from Simulated Annealing is that SA allows poorer solutions to be accepted at intermediate stages, and as a result it allows some very poor solutions in the initial stages, from which it can never recover.

Min-min and Max-min provide good results in some cases, and have the advantage of a shorter execution time, comparative to the other techniques described. The advantage of Max-min over Min-min is that it attempts to minimize the penalties due to performing tasks with longer execution times first. In the case of a meta-task with many tasks with very short execution times and one task with a very long execution time, it would be better to map the task with the longer execution task first. In this way, the small tasks may run concurrently with the larger one, while with Min-min, the small tasks are executed first and then some of the processors would be idle while the large task is executed. In such situations, the Max-min heuristic may give a mapping with a more balanced load across machines and a better max-span.

The next section presents the solution for scheduling problem in the case of dependencies between tasks. Some algorithms are mentioned and the properties of this class of algorithms are discussed.

DAG SCHEDULING ALGORITHMS

Any parallel application can be modeled by a **DAG** (Directed Acyclic Graph). Although application loops cannot be explicitly represented by the DAG model, the parallelism in data-flow computations in loops can be exploited to subdivide the loops into a number of tasks by the loop-unraveling technique. The idea is that all iterations of the loop are started or fired together, and operations in various iterations can execute when their input data are ready for access. In addition, for a large class of data-flow computation problems and many numerical algorithms (such as matrix multiplication), there are very few, if any, conditional branches or indeterminism in the program. Thus, the DAG model can be used to accurately represent these applications so that the scheduling techniques can be applied. Furthermore, in many numerical applications, such as Gaussian elimination or fast Fourier transform (FFT), the loop bounds are known during compile time. As such, one or more iterations of a loop can be deterministically encapsulated in a task and, consequently, be represented by a node in a DAG. The node and edge weights are usually obtained by estimation using profiling information of operations such as numerical operations, memory access operations, and message-passing primitives.

In a general representation, jobs are split into sub-jobs which are split into tasks, the atomic unit of an application. Tasks forming a job contain dependencies if a precedence relation can be established among them. The model applied in this case is a **DAG** where a node represents a task and a directed arc represents the order of precedence between the nodes it connects.

We must follow the steps of analyzing the workflow of the application, planning the tasks accordingly, as well as allocating the resources so that the structure of the workflow is respected. An important issue is obtaining the maximum parallelism possible therefore there must be a trade-off between the computational cost and the communication cost.

The **DAG scheduling** problem is a NP-complete problem. A solution for this problem is a series of heuristics, where tasks are assigned priorities and places in a list ordered by priority. The method through which the tasks are selected to be planned at each step takes into consideration this criterion, thus the task with higher priority receives access to resources before those with a lower priority. The heuristics used vary according to job requirements, structure and complexity of the **DAG** (Simion et al., 2007).

Once the priority mechanism is established, we must take into consideration those tasks that have all dependencies solved (the tasks they depend on have been executed), and minimize the time associated to the critical path. For example, HEFT (Heterogeneous Earliest Finish Time) selects at each step the task with the highest "upward rank" (the maximum distance from the current node to the finish node given by the computational and communication cost).

Based on these algorithms, the goal is to analyze the performance of the planning criteria and if possible, optimize the task scheduling by combining the best characteristics of a set of algorithms to obtain a hybrid algorithm with better overall results.

The Figure 2 presents the DAG Scheduling properties. We have multiple criteria for algorithm selection. Fist we must choose between centralized or decentralized architecture. In the case of dependability we could approach an arbitrary graph structure or a restricted graph. Arbitrary approach is more general. At this level we must describe the communication model and costs. It is possible to consider resources with communication and without communication. The cost, in the case of communication, could be uniform or arbitrary. A fault tolerance is considers, so it is possible to choose for tasks duplication. Then we could have a limited number of resources or a restriction for resources. The last case is a challenge to develop a good scheduling algorithm.

MULTI-CRITERIA OPTIMIZATION FOR SCHEDULING

Optimization criteria represent the basic aspects which can be taken into consideration when designing Grid scheduling algorithms: minimization of the maximum lateness, minimization of the cost, maximization of the profit, maximization of personal or general utility, maximization of resource utilization, fairness, maximization of robustness and predictability.

In general we are looking for a feasible solution to scheduling problem. This is a schedule which meets all the requirements and constrains posed by the problem definition. In addition we may define an objective function that has to be optimized.

There are bottleneck objectives (for instance the max-span and the maximum lateness) and sum objectives (the sum of completion times or the number of tardy tasks). The letter ones may also appear in:

- Maximum completion time (max-span).
- Mean / sum of completion time.
- Mean / sum of weighted completion time.
- Mean / sum of flow time.
- Mean / sum of weighted flow time.
- Maximum lateness.
- Mean / sum of tardiness.
- Number of late tasks.
- Total weight of late tasks.

Optimizing a certain sum objective is equivalent to solving the corresponding mean (average) objective since they differ only in a constant factor.

Figure 2. DAG scheduling properties

GRID Communication	Node arbitrary conected	Node fully conected
GRID Resources	Limited number of processors	Unlimited number of processors
Fault tolerance strategy	With duplication	Without duplication
Communication costs	Uniform communication costs	Arbitrary communication costs
Communication model	With communication	Without communication
Graph stucture	Arbitrary graph structure	Restricted graph structure
Tasks dependencies	Depended tasks	Independent tasks
Scheduling model	Centralized Scheduling	Decentralized Scheduling

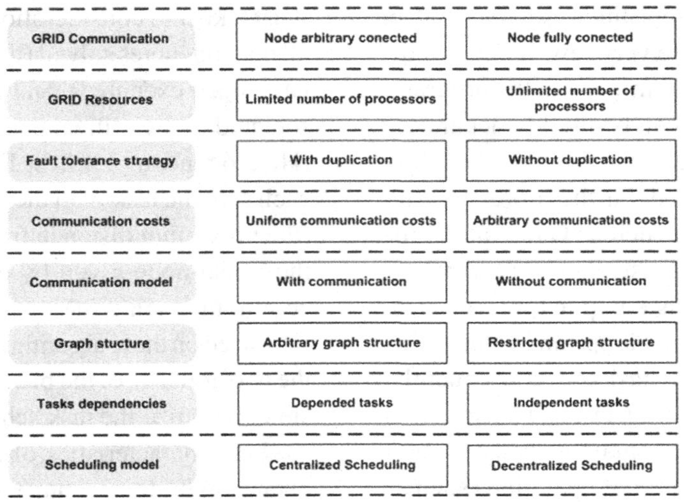

LOAD BALANCING

Just like the case of traditional distributed systems, **load balancing** becomes an important aspect in scheduling in LSDS. Solution based on multi-agent computing on a cluster of workstations is widely envisioned to be a powerful paradigm for building useful distributed applications. With different characteristics between ordinary processes and agents, it is both interesting and useful to investigate whether conventional load-balancing strategies are also applicable and sufficient to cope with the newly emerging needs, such as coping with temporally continuous agents, devising a performance metric for multi-agent systems, and taking into account the vast amount of communication and interaction among agent (see Figure 3).

The communication protocol that ensures load-balancing is a two-phase protocol (see Figure 3): connection establishment and negotiation phase. In the first phase the Broker sends multiple (n) requests to Agents. The Broker will receive response only from m Agents (the number of responses, m is less or equal to n). The last step in this phase is to select the best first x o offers that are with at most w% worse than the best offer. The number of selected offers after first phase will be established by the users at runtime. The second phase, as mentioned, is the negotiation phase. In this phase the Broker begins the negotiation with the best first x offers. It will receive y new o offers from the Agents (y is less or equal to x). After the Broker decides what offer to select, it sends to the Agents a message to inform if their offer was selected or not for the renegotiation step. If the Broker wants to announce the Agent that was chosen for the renegotiation step will send an object representing the offers evaluation made by it; if the Broker wants to announce the Agent that it had not been selected for the next phase it will send a NACK message. The winner Agent selected from the list of o offers after renegotiation phase will send back to the Broker am confirmation message. If the Agent can't execute the task, the Broker will choose the next best offer. Then, the Broker will submit the job to the Agent. A close TCP connection packet could be sent by the Agent to the Broker after it receives the job. After TCP connection is closed by the Agent, the Broker will receive notifications about the state of the executing job using UDP messages (Pop, 2008).

According to how the dynamic load balancing is achieved, there are four basic approaches:

Figure 3. Agent framework: General architecture and communication model

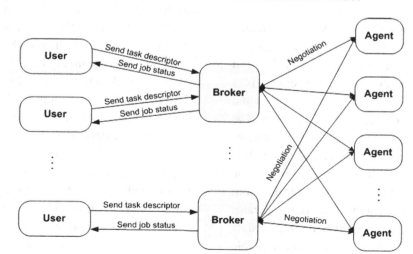

- Unconstrained First-In-First-Out (FIFO, also known as First-Come-First- Served) (Maheswaran et al., 1999)
- Balance-constrained techniques (Chen & Maheswaran, 2002)
- Cost-constrained techniques (Kurowski et al., 2004)
- Hybrids of static and dynamic techniques (Spring & Wolski, 1999).

CO-ALLOCATION

Co-allocation is a scheduling method which ensures that a given set of resources is available for use simultaneously. Co-allocation has a strategy which schedules tasks with dependencies, with main purpose the efficiency of the schedule, in terms of load balancing and minimum time execution of tasks. In this case, load balancing refers to a balanced assignment of depended tasks to resources, without overloading a resource or overusing it, in comparison to the others.

Co-allocation receives as input a set of tasks with dependencies and provides as output a schedule which maps tasks to resources, a resource being mapped to several tasks. A condition the schedule must fulfill is that all the tasks must finish their execution before a deadline; the schedule must be an efficient one, in terms of execution time of the tasks (Bucur & Epema, 2007).

Co-allocation, designed as a dynamic scheduling method, is based on agent system (see Figure 5.3) with a structure composed by a broker and an agent (Driss et al., 2005). The broker provides the interface with the user. Its role within the algorithm is different from that of an agent. *The broker* receives a set of tasks with dependences from the user and provides, in the end, a schedule of the given set on the available resources. The broker doesn't maintain state information about the resources of the system, but communicates with the agents to find it. *The agent* maintains state information about the resources it is responsible

for. A resource consists in one or more CPU's. Co-allocation is a decentralized method, which means that every agent keeps information about the local resources it manages and it's responsible for them (as opposed to a centralized strategy which requires the presence of an entity which manages all the resources of the system). Another important function of an agent is to communicate with the broker. Due to the decentralized strategy that Co-allocation uses, the method is more reliable than a centralized one, being less subject to single point faults.

Co-allocation uses an algorithm that consists in three phases. First phase is represented by task clustering, the second by dynamic scheduling inside the cluster and the third by dynamic scheduling between clusters (Neeraj et al., 2007).

Task clustering is the first phase of the co-allocation algorithm. The broker receives as input a set of dependable tasks described in JSDL format (Anjomshoaa et al., 2005) and provides as output a set of clusters. The broker builds the set of tasks and then initiates the clustering algorithm. A cluster is a set of tasks, representing a part of the initial DAG. The clustering algorithm works in this way: initially, each node is a cluster and every step combines the clusters from the precedent step, based on the dependencies between the combined clusters; a condition every step must check and accomplish is that the graph formed by the clusters doesn't have any cycles; if that happens, the cluster which leads to a cycle, isn't combined with another cluster. In order to obtain a schedule with the property of load balancing, the clusters should contain almost the same number of tasks. The broker tries to build each cluster based on task dependencies, so that it contains the maximum number of tasks. The equivalent graph, which has clusters as nodes, has edges which connect the clusters, corresponding to the initial DAG. In order to keep the DAG concept, an edge in the DAG of clusters, has as maximum value for its cost, the sum of the costs of all the edges from the initial DAG which connect the nodes from the two clusters.

Dynamic Scheduling inside a cluster is the second phase. It begins with the distribution of each cluster to a corresponding agent. The broker sends each cluster to an agent that must schedule the cluster's tasks on its local resources. While distributing the clusters, the broker computes the number of tasks sent to each agent and always sends the current cluster to the agent that received the minimum number of tasks. Therefore, the initial set of tasks is evenly distributed between the agents. All the agents work simultaneously, scheduling the tasks based on the dependencies between them and ignoring the dependencies between clusters. Therefore, each agent will begin the scheduling phase starting with time 0. The dynamic scheduling inside a cluster uses a version of the hybrid remapper algorithm. The algorithm has a dynamic nature because the tasks cannot be scheduled prior to the algorithm; the resources change in time, a task scheduled at each step depends on the tasks scheduled at the precedent steps.

Dynamic Scheduling of the clusters is the last phase of the algorithm. It schedules the graph of clusters, based on the dependencies between the clusters. The broker decomposes the cluster DAG into levels; then, it receives replies from the agents that scheduled the clusters of the first level and builds the final schedule, maintaining for each task the node it was scheduled on, start time and end time; for the next levels, the broker sends to the agent that scheduled the cluster, the (end time + communication time) for each task the tasks of the cluster depend on; the agent delays the start time of each scheduled task according to the information received from the broker, sending a reply with the scheduling it has made.

ADVANCE RESERVATION

Advance Reservation refers to the process of requesting various resources in LSDS for use in the future. This method allows resources to be reserved in advance for a designated set of tasks. It uses a decentralized algorithm in which every resource in the environment maintains its state information locally. As opposed to a centralized strategy, which involves the presence of a single centralized entity which holds information about the state of all resources, the decentralized strategy is less subject to a single point of failure, because the responsibility is distributed evenly between the resources (Foster et al., 2000).

The main purpose of **Advance Reservation** is to obtain an efficient schedule, in terms of resource load and balancing: the optimal schedule would consist in a balanced assignment of tasks to resources, without overloading a resource or overusing it, in comparison to the others (Naiksatam et al., 2005). The optimality criterion by which a schedule in evaluated is the property of load balancing of resources. This criterion was chosen because a balanced workload across the LSDS has a very important influence on the efficiency of a scheduling algorithm. The load balancing of resources ensures that the resources are used in an efficient way, by exploiting at the maximum all the available resources. Secondly, by using all the available resources, the completion time of the tasks that need to be scheduled reduces considerably.

Some other dynamic online scheduling algorithms, such as those in (Aggarwal et al., 2003) and (Mateescu, 2003), consider the case of resource reservation which is popular in Grid computing as a way to get a degree of certainty in resource performance. Algorithms in these two examples aim to minimize the make-span of incoming jobs which consist of a set of tasks. Mateescu (2003) uses a resource selector to find a co-reservation for jobs requiring multiple resources. The job queue is managed in a FIFO fashion with dynamic priority correction. If co-reservation fails for a job in a scheduling cycle, the job's priority will be promoted in the queue for the next scheduling round. The resource selector ranks candidate resources by their number of processors and memory size.

Advance reservation receives as input, a set of tasks and provides as output a schedule, which consists in mappings of each task on the suitable resource of the Grid, the mappings are called reservations.

The dynamic table represents a structure which maintains state information about every resource of the system. State information refers to the usage of each resource: for each resource, the dynamic table contains an entry, which monitors the evolution in time of the resource; this monitoring refers to what tasks are scheduled on a specific resource; the interval of time each task requires in order to be executed; for each interval, the degree of usage of that resource, in other words the load of the resource, on that interval. An interval is described by its inferior limit – start time, its superior limit – end time and a vector of tasks which are scheduled to be run during that interval, in other words, all the reservations made on that interval, on that resource. If more than one task has the same execution interval, they can be scheduled on the same processing resource, as long as the following two conditions are accomplished: the number of tasks on that interval isn't greater than MAX_TASKS; the load of the resource on that interval, increased by the tasks scheduled on it, isn't greater than MAX_LOAD; the usage of the processing resource during this interval.

Each resource has associated a vector of intervals, which are kept in increasing order, after start time. The increasing order is useful in the process of making reservations, when an agents needs to build the specific interval/intervals for a given task. Therefore, the dynamic table is a mapping between each local resource and a vector of intervals. It contains all the reservations the agents make on the system's resources.

The dynamic table represents a dynamic structure because it undergoes changes, in time. Its content modifies every time an agent makes a reservation. Initially, the dynamic table contains, for each local resource, the interval [0, INFINITE], where INFINITE represents a constant which defines the maximum superior limit for an interval. Every time an agent makes a reservation, the dynamic table changes, because a new interval must be added to the vector of intervals of a resource or the old intervals must be changed (the limits, the vector of tasks and the usage must be modified).

The dynamic table is kept distributed among all the agents of the system. Each agent maintains the part of the dynamic table which corresponds to its local resources. The table isn't managed by the broker because the broker can belong to a different VO than the rest of the agents, as well as the agents can belong to different VOs. An agent isn't aware of other resources, it can monitor only the local resources it was designated to manage. On the other hand, Advance Reservation is a decentralized strategy, which means there isn't any entity (agent or broker) which maintains information about all the resources of the system.

The strategy is based on the use of the following entities (see Figure 3):

- *Broker*: It represents an entity designated to provide the interface with the user. A broker also communicates with both the other entities in the system, called the agents. It receives a set of tasks from the user, sends it to every agent, waits for replies from all agents, decides the final schedule and provides a reply to the user. A broker has an important role in the scheduling algorithm, but doesn't actually run it, as it doesn't maintain state information about any resource.

- *Agent*: an agent maintains state information about the nodes it is designated to handle. It monitors its local resources and makes reservations on them. A reservation consists in a mapping of a task on a resource. An agent also communicates with the broker, receiving tasks and sending replies.

The system the strategy runs on is built as follows:

- The elementary entity of the system is the node. A node consists in one or more central processing units (CPU's). A node is also called a resource.
- A set of nodes forms a cluster.
- A set of clusters forms a farm.

IMPLEMENTED SCHEDULER

This section describes a major project for scheduling in Grid systems: Condor. Condor is a centralized scheduler that provides a job queuing mechanism, scheduling policy, priority scheme, resource monitoring, and resource management. Users submit their serial or parallel jobs to Condor, Condor places them into a queue, chooses when and where to run the jobs based upon a policy, carefully monitors their progress, and ultimately informs the user upon completion (Thain et al., 2003).

Condor has the capability to detect that a machine running a Condor job is no longer available (perhaps because the owner of the machine came back from lunch and started typing on the keyboard). It can checkpoint the job and move the jobs to a different machine which would otherwise be idle. Condor continues job on the new machine from precisely where it left off.

In those cases where Condor can checkpoint and migrate a job, Condor makes it easy to maximize the number of machines which can run a job. In this case, there is no requirement for machines to share file systems (for example, with NFS or AFS), so that machines across an entire enterprise can run a job, including machines in different administrative domains.

Condor can be a real time saver when a job must be run many (hundreds of) different times, perhaps with hundreds of different data sets. With one command, all of the hundreds of jobs are submitted to Condor. Depending upon the number of machines in the Condor pool, dozens or even hundreds of otherwise idle machines can be running the job at any given moment.

Condor does not require an account (login) on machines where it runs a job. Condor can do this because of its remote system call technology, which traps library calls for such operations as reading or writing from disk files. The calls are transmitted over the network to be performed on the machine where the job was submitted.

It provides powerful resource management by match-making resource owners with resource consumers. This is the cornerstone of a successful HTC (High-Throughput Computing) environment. Other compute cluster resource management systems attach properties to the job queues themselves, resulting in user confusion over which queue to use as well as administrative hassle in constantly adding and editing queue properties to satisfy user demands. Condor implements ClassAds, a clean design that simplifies the user's submission of jobs.

ClassAds work in a fashion similar to the newspaper classified advertising want-ads. All machines in the Condor pool advertise their resource properties, both static and dynamic, such as available RAM memory, CPU type, CPU speed, virtual memory size, physical location, and current load average, in a resource offer. A user specifies a resource request ad when submitting a job. The request defines both the required and a desired set of properties of the resource to run the job. Condor acts as a broker by matching and ranking resource offer ads with resource request ads, making certain that all requirements in both ads are satisfied. During this match-making process, Condor also considers several layers of priority values: the priority the user assigned to the resource request ad, the priority of the user which submitted the ad, and desire of machines in the pool to accept certain types of ads over others.

Condor includes "DAGMan" which provides a mechanism to describe job dependencies, and the ability to use Condor as the front-end to submit jobs to other distributed computing systems (such as Globus).

Condor-G is a version of Condor based on Globus. Condor-G works with grid resources, allowing users to effectively submit jobs, manage jobs, and have jobs execute on widely distributed machines. Condor-G lets you submit jobs into a queue, have a log detailing the life cycle of your jobs, manage your input and output files, along with everything else you expect from a job queuing system.

Condor uses the Globus toolkit to provide underlying software needed to utilize grid resources, such as authentication, remote program execution and data transfer. Condor's capabilities when executing jobs on Globus resources have significantly increased. The same Condor tools that access local resources are now able to use the Globus protocols to access resources at multiple sites.

Condor-G is a program that manages both a queue of jobs and the resources from one or more sites where those jobs can execute. It communicates with these resources and transfers files to and from these resources using Globus mechanisms. (In particular, Condor-G uses the GRAM protocol for job submission, and it runs a local GASS server for file transfers).

Condor-G allows the user to treat the Grid as a local resource, and the same command-line tools perform basic job management such as: submit a job, indicating an executable, input and output files, and arguments; query a job's status; cancel a job; be informed when events happen, such as normal job termination or errors; obtain access to detailed logs that provide a complete history of a job.

FUTURE TRENDS

Many models and algorithms for LSDS scheduling are developed using classic algorithms for traditional systems. Three heuristics are used for scheduling of tasks with precedence orders in heterogeneous parallel and distributed systems: list heuristics, duplicated heuristics and clustering heuristics. Almost all algorithms in the current literature refer to list algorithms. The ideas behind the latter two categories have many advantages in the LSDS scenario. Since all of these heuristics consider complex application models, where tasks can be fine granular and with data and control dependency, there is great potential for using these heuristics in LSDS computing.

The dynamism in the LSDS requires the assumptions approximation algorithms optimizing. To deal with performance variation, resource information and prediction are recently used. As the techniques in this field develop, better performance knowledge prior to the task scheduling stage can be expected. Current scheduling algorithms consider a snapshot value of the prediction when they make the estimate, and assume that value is static during the job execution period. This might be a waste of the prediction efforts which can actually provide continuous variation information about the system. So, heuristics that can exploit multiple stage prediction information should be designed.

Another issue is to reestablish approximating for make-span optimization based on performance predictions. For example, if we know the range of performance fluctuation is bounded, we can find a bound for the ratio of real make-span to optimal finish time accordingly.

The problem with current rescheduling algorithms is high cost and lack of consideration of dependent tasks. For jobs whose make-spans are large, rescheduling for the original static decisions can improve the performance dramatically. However, rescheduling is usually costly, especially in DAGs where there are extra data dependencies among tasks compared to independent applications.

In addition, many other problems also exist, for example when the rescheduling mechanisms should be invoked, what measurable parameters should decide whether a rescheduling is profitable, and where tasks should be migrated. Current research on DAG rescheduling leaves a wide open field for future work.

QoS is the concern of many Grid applications. Most current research concentrates on how to guarantee the QoS requirements of the applications like (Huedo et al., 2004), but few of them study how the QoS requirements affect the resources assignment and then the performance of the other parts of the applications.

Scheduling algorithms in traditional computing paradigms barely consider the data transfer problem during mapping computational tasks, and this neglect will be costly in the Grid scenario. Only a handful of current research efforts consider the simultaneous optimization of computation and data transfer scheduling, which brings opportunities for future studies.

Although the LSDS have the characteristics of heterogeneity and dynamicity, these features are not flatly distributed in resources, but are rather distributed hierarchically and locally in many cases, due to the composition of the resources. Current resources are usually distributed in a clustered fashion. Resources in the same cluster usually belong to the same organization and are relatively more homogeneous and less dynamic in a given period.

Inside a cluster, communication cost is usually low and the number of applications running at the same time is usually small. These distribution properties might bring another possibility for new algorithms to deal with the challenges. For example, by taking multiphase or multilevel strategies, a scheduler can first find a coarse scheduling in the global and then a fine schedule in a local cluster.

This type of strategy has the following advantages: At the higher level, where fine resource information is harder to obtain, the global scheduling can use coarse information (such as load balancing, communication delay of WAN links) to provide decentralized load balancing

mechanisms. At the lower level, it is easy for local scheduling to utilize more specific information (such as information from a local forecaster) to make adaptive decisions.

CONCLUSION

In Large Scale Distributed Systems, various applications, most of them being real-time applications, require dynamic scheduling for optimized assignment of consisting tasks. A number of different scheduling model and algorithms was presented here. The performance metrics can be taken into account in order to design a feasible scheduling algorithm. Those performance metrics can also represent optimization criteria and are based on various constraints such as deadline restrictions, guaranteed completion time, average service time, start and end time, etc. Some of the metrics that can be used to measure the performances of a Grid scheduling algorithm are: the global job success rate (percentage of co-allocated jobs that were started successfully before their deadline), the local job kill rate (the percentage of local jobs that have been killed), the total load (the average percentage of busy processors over the entire system), the global load (the percentage of the total computing power that is used for computing the global jobs), the processor wasted time (the percentage of the total computing power that is wasted because of claiming processors before the actual deadlines of jobs), max-span (the total execution time of tasks in the system, and is practically equal to the largest processing time over all processors), average processor utilization (a measure of the average times of utilization of processors, relative to the maximum execution time) and load-balancing (measure of the uniformity of the tasks disposal on the processors, with the purpose to obtain similar execution times on processors, and reduce idle times and overloading).

All this criteria and metrics represent the measure effective computing power that the scheduler has been able to get from the distributed system and managed for tasks execution.

In distributed system middleware a large number of tools are available for scheduling. For cluster scheduling we have PBS, Condor, Sun Grid Engine, and LSF. These tools are included in the centralized scheduling class. Inter-cluster scheduling, known as meta-scheduling are studied, so a number of meta-scheduling research projects are under development, like GridWay (that is an incubator project in Globus), Globus CSF. Still there is no meta-scheduler used on a large scale. A problem that must to be solved for this type of scheduling is scalability. It is an aspect more important in the context of heterogeneous systems (that require a simultaneous management of multiple clusters) and middleware tools.

REFERENCES

Aggarwal, A. K., & Kent, R. D. (2005). An Adaptive Generalized Scheduler for Grid Applications. In *Proc. of the 19th Annual International Symposium on High Performance Computing Systems and Applications* (pp.15-18), Guelph, Ontario Canada.

Anjomshoaa, A. Brisard, F., Drescher, M., Fellows, D., Ly, A., McGough, S., Pulsipher, D., & Savva, A. (2005). *Job Submission Description Language (JSDL) Specification, Version 1.0* (GFD-R.056), Global Grid Forum.

Arora, M., Das, S. K., & Biswas, R. (2002). A Decentralized Scheduling and Load Balancing Algorithm for Heterogeneous Grid Environments. In *Proceedings of International Conference on Parallel Processing Workshops* (pp. 499-505), Vancouver, British Columbia Canada.

Baker, M., Buyya, R., & Laforenza, D. (2002). Grids and Grid Technologies for Wide-area Distributed Computing. *Journal of Software-Practice & Experience*, *32*(15), 1437–1466. doi:10.1002/spe.488

Berman, F. (1998). High-Performance Schedulers. In Foster, I., & Kesselman, C. (Eds.), *The Grid: Blueprint for a Future Computing Infrastructure* (pp. 279–309). San Francisco: Morgan Kaufmann Publishers.

Blazewicz, J., Ecker, K. H., Pesch, E., Schmidt, G., & Weglarz, J. (2001). *Scheduling Computer and Manufacturing Processes*. Berlin: Springer.

Braun, R., Siegel, H., Beck, N., Boloni, L., Maheswaran, M., & Reuther, A. (2001). A Comparison of Eleven Static Heuristics for Mapping a Class of Independent Tasks onto Heterogeneous Distributed Computing Systems. *Journal of Parallel and Distributed Computing*, *61*(6), 810–837. doi:10.1006/jpdc.2000.1714

Bucur, A., & Epema, D. (2007). Scheduling Policies for Processor Co-allocation in Multi-cluster Systems. *IEEE Transactions on Parallel and Distributed Systems*, *18*(7), 1045–1065. doi:10.1109/TPDS.2007.1036

Buyya, R., Abramson, D., Giddy, J., & Stockinger, H. (2002). Economic Models for Resource Management and Scheduling in Grid Computing. [CCPE]. *The Journal of Concurrency and Computation: Practice and Experience*, *14*(13-15), 1507–1542. doi:10.1002/cpe.690

Chen, H., & Maheswaran, M. (2002). Distributed Dynamic Scheduling of Composite Tasks on Grid Computing Systems. In *Proc. of the 16th International Parallel and Distributed Processing Symposium* (pp. 88-97), Fort Lauderdale, Florida USA.

Cooper, K., Dasgupta, A., Kennedy, K., Koelbel, C., Mandal, A., Marin, G., et al. YarKhan, A., & Dongarra, J. (2004). New Grid Scheduling and Rescheduling Methods in the GrADS Project. In *Proc. of the 18th International Parallel and Distributed Processing Symposium* (pp.199-206), Santa Fe, New Mexico USA.

Czajkowski, K., Foster, I., Karonis, N., Kesselman, C., Martin, S., Smith, W., & Tuecke, S. (1998). *Resource Management Architecture for Meta-computing Systems* (LNCS 1459). Berlin: Springer.

Driss, A., Jung-Lok, Y., Jin-Soo, K., & Maeng, R. S. (2005). Resource Co-Allocation: A Complementary Technique that Enhances Performance in Grid Computing Environment. In *Proceedings of the 2005 11th International Conference on Parallel and Distributed Systems* (pp. 36-42). Washington, DC: IEEE Computer Society.

Foster, I., Roy, A., & Sander, V. (2000). A Quality of Service Architecture That Combines Resource Reservation and Application Adaptation. In *Proc. 8th Int. Workshop on Quality of Service* (pp. 181-188), Pittsburgh, PA, USA.

Hak, D. K., & Jin, S. K. (2004). An Online Scheduling Algorithm for Grid Computing Systems. In *Grid and Cooperative Computing* (*Vol. 3033*, pp. 34–39). Berlin, Heidelberg: Springer.

Hamscher, V., Schwiegelshohn, U., Streit, A., & Yahyapour, R. (2000). Evaluation of Job-Scheduling Strategies for Grid Computing. In *Proceedings of GRID 2000, First IEEE/ACM International Workshop* (pp. 191-202), Bangalore, India.

Huedo, E., Montero, R. S., & Llorente, I. M. (2004). Experiences on Adaptive Grid Scheduling of Parameter Sweep Applications. In *Proc. of the 12th Euromicro Conference on Parallel, Distributed and Network-Based Processing* (pp. 28-33), A Coruna, Spain.

Kurowski, K., Ludwiczak, B., Nabrzyski, J., Oleksiak, A., & Pukacki, J. (2004). Improving Grid Level Throughput Using Job Migration and Rescheduling. *Science Progress*, *12*(4), 263–273.

Maheswaran, M., Ali, S., Siegel, H. J., Hensgen, D., & Freund, R. F. (1999). Dynamic Matching and Scheduling of a Class of Independent Tasks onto Heterogeneous Computing Systems. *Journal of Parallel and Distributed Computing*, *59*(2), 107–131. doi:10.1006/jpdc.1999.1581

Mateescu, G. (2003). Quality of Service on the Grid via Meta-scheduling with Resource Co-Scheduling and Co-Reservation. *International Journal of High Performance Computing Applications*, *17*(3), 209–218. doi:10.1177/1094342003173006

Michalewicz, Z., & Fogel, D. B. (2000). *How to Solve It: Modern Heuristics*. New York: Springer-Verlag.

Naiksatam, S., Figueira, S., Chiappari, S. A., & Bhatnagar, N. (2005). Analyzing the advance reservation of light paths in lambda-grids, Cluster Computing and the Grid. *CCGrid IEEE International Symposium* (Vol. 2, pp. 985-992). Washington, DC: IEEE Computer Society.

Neeraj, N., Patel, R. B., & Bhat, V. K. (2007). Distributed Parallel Resource Co-Allocation with Load Balancing in Grid Computing. *IJCSNS International Journal of Computer Science and Network Security*, *7*(1), 695–703.

Pop, F. (2008). Communication model for decentralized meta-scheduling in Grid Environments. In *Proceedings of The Second International Conference on Complex, Intelligent and Software Intensive System, Second International Workshop on P2P, Parallel, Grid and Internet computing* (pp. 315-320). Washington, DC: IEEE Computer Society.

Ramin, Y., & Wieder, P. (2005). *Grid Scheduling Use Cases, Open Grid Forum Document (Tech. Rep.). Grid Scheduling Architecture Research Group*. GSA-RG.

Roehrig, M., & Ziegler, W. (2002). *Grid Scheduling Dictionary of Terms and Keywords (Tech. Rep.)*. Open Grid Forum Document, Grid Scheduling Dictionary Working Group.

Rotithor, H. G. (1994). Taxonomy of Dynamic Task Scheduling Schemes in Distributed Computing Systems. *IEEE Proc. on Computer and Digital Techniques, 141*(1), 1–10. doi:10.1049/ip-cdt:19949630

Schopf, J. M. (2004). Ten actions when Grid scheduling: the user as a Grid scheduler. In Nabrzyski, J., Schopf, J. M., & Weglarz, J. (Eds.), *Grid Resource Management: State of the Art and Future Trends* (pp. 15–13). Norwell, MA: Kluwer Academic Publishers.

Simion, B., Leordeanu, C., Pop, F., & Cristea, V. (2007). A Hybrid Algorithm for Scheduling Workflow Applications in Grid Environments (ICPDP). In *Proceedings of On the Move to Meaningful Internet Systems 2007: CoopIS, DOA, GADA, and ODBASE and IS* (*Vol. 4804*, pp. 1331–1348). Berlin: Springer Verlag. doi:10.1007/978-3-540-76843-2_15

Spring, N., & Wolski, R. (1998). Application Level Scheduling of Gene Sequence Comparison on Metacomputers. In *the Proc. of 1998 International Conference on Supercomputing* (pp. 141-148). Association for Computing Machinery.

Streit, A. (2002). A Self-Tuning Job Scheduler Family with Dynamic Policy Switching. In *Proc. of the 8th International Workshop on Job Scheduling Strategies for Parallel Processing* (LNCS 2537, pp. 1-23). New York: Springer.

Thain, D., Tannenbaum, T., & Livny, M. (2003). Condor and the Grid. In Berman, F., Hey, A. J. G., & Fox, G. (Eds.), *Grid Computing: Making the Global Infrastructure a Reality* (pp. 299–336). Hoboken, NJ: John Wiley.

Wedde, H., Farooq, M., & Lischka, M. (2004). An Evolutionary Meta Hierarchical Scheduler for the Linux Operating System. In Goldberg, D. (Ed.), *Genetic and Evolutionary Computation – GECCO 2004* (pp. 1334–1335). New York: Springer.

Zhan, G., Siwei, L., & Ding, D. (2007). A Scheduling Mechanism Considering Simultaneous Running of Grid Tasks and Local Tasks in the Computational Grid. In *International Conference on Multimedia and Ubiquitous Engineering* (pp. 1100-1105). Washington, DC: IEEE Computer Society.

Zomaya, A. Y., & Hwei, Y. (2001). The Observations on Using Genetic Algorithms for Dynamic Load-Balancing. *IEEE Transactions on Parallel and Distributed Systems, 12*(9), 899–911. doi:10.1109/71.954620

Chapter 6
Data Storage, Retrieval and Management

INTRODUCTION

The latest advances in network and distributed-system technologies now allow integration of a vast variety of services with almost unlimited processing power, using large amounts of data. Sharing of resources is often viewed as the key goal for distributed systems, and in this context the sharing of stored data appears as the most important aspect of distributed resource sharing. Scientific applications are the first to take advantage of such environments as the requirements of current and future high performance computing experiments are pressing, in terms of even higher volumes of issued data to be stored and managed. While these new environments reveal huge opportunities for large-scale distributed data storage and management, they also raise important technical challenges, which need to be addressed. The ability to support persistent storage of data on behalf of users, the consistent distribution of up-to-date data, the reliable replication of fast changing datasets or the efficient management of large data transfers are just some of these new challenges.

In this chapter we discuss how the existing distributed computing infrastructure is adequate for supporting the required data storage and management functionalities. We highlight the issues raised from storing data over large distributed environments and discuss the recent research efforts dealing with challenges of data retrieval, replication and fast data transfers. Interaction of data management with other data sensitive, emerging technologies as the workflow management is also addressed.

DATA STORAGE

Many approaches to build highly available and incrementally extendable distributed data storage systems have been proposed. Solutions span from distributed storage repositories to massively parallel and high performance storage systems. A large majority of these aim at a virtualization of the data space allowing users to access data on multiple storage systems, eventually geographically dispersed.

DOI: 10.4018/978-1-61520-703-9.ch006

Independent of the technical solutions adopted, the common objective is to build the storage infrastructure able to support intensive computation on large datasets, of peta-byte order, across widely distributed organizations.

Current storage facilities are developed to address scientific communities' rapidly advancing needs, while taking advantage of the equally rapid evolution of network technologies in order to provide the most effective solutions with adequate up-to-date performance. As these systems are architected and operated to guarantee full performance to support both large-scale data management and real-time traffic, one of the main concerns are the high demanding requirements expected to be dealt with. We outline in the following the main challenges addressed by distributed storage systems.

Providing *high availability* proves to be the main issue in such environments: the storage should remain available, in a transparent fashion to the users, whenever any single or multiple storage units (disks, servers, tapes, etc.) fail. This translates into *high resilience* levels expected from the storage infrastructure, i.e. the fail of a large number of storage units is tolerated without affecting the overall system's availability and *consistency*. The resilience level is closely coupled to the manner in which the distributed storage system handles *corruption* of the storage units or even users: this can take various forms ranging from hardware faults, software bugs to malicious intrusions or behavior. The term used in literature for these issues is *arbitrary* (or byzantine) *faults* and if not treated accordingly, affected systems can deviate from their implemented behavior. Approaches include the use of fault thresholds for long-term storage with service splitting (Chun et al., 2009) and also algorithms that combine strong consistency and liveness guarantees with space-efficiency (Dobre et al., 2008).

However, unless we are dealing with an ideal model, faults cannot be ignored so a reliable system should implement support for *fault tolerance*. To

deal with these problems, data should be stored using some redundant techniques, so that any information from a faulty element can be recovered. Fault tolerance is generally addressed in I/O systems using replication or RAID (Redundant Array of Inexpensive Disks) based approaches. The latter ones are suitable for storage systems based on commodity disks with higher capacity but lower reliability, leading to more frequent rebuilds and to a higher risk of unrecoverable media errors. Current solutions include additional levels of redundancy inside the disk through intradisk redundancy schemes, on top of the RAID redundancy across multiple disks for increased reliability (Dholakia et al., 2008). RAID systems are generally used for their increased performance due to striping and for the redundancy achieved through mirroring or erasure codes. Still, residing at a single physical location makes them vulnerable in the presence of single points of failures: the disk controller, the network interface, etc. In contrast, high performance storage systems use *replication* as a reliable fault tolerance technique: copies of the stored data are kept in several places, called replicas, along with some directory information about data – location mappings, called replica catalogs. Replication will be further discussed in Section 4 of this Chapter.

Another issue which needs to be addressed by a reliable distributed storage system is *asynchrony*. As users interface with the storage through heterogeneous networks, access delays are likely to incur and difficult to predict. These delays are further increased by storage latency. One approach is to access data in the file system cache or high-speed storage first, and consequently the total I/O workloads can be reduced and performance improved. To achieve these, one needs latency data estimations, which allow users and applications to make better data access decisions based on those retrieval time estimates. Such approaches doubled by efficient concurrency control (Ermolinksiy et al., 2009) improve the overall application performance with more predictable behavior in the presence of asynchrony and even failures.

Fairness is also desirable in such environments, allowing many users to access a storage system in a distributed fashion while conserving efficiency. Solutions make use of local latency estimates at hosts to detect overload or try to limit the host issue queue lengths to provide fairness across hosts (Gulati et al., 2008). *Access control* should further be supported and also mapped to the traditional storage model: with many readers and eventually fewer writers. Moreover, the system has to take into account the inherent *intermittence* of the communication and the *transient* nature of the clients.

As the storage systems are deployed in *heterogeneous* environments, they deal with managing their distributed resources using *meta-data* and providing means to manipulate it. Meta-data contains information about accessing and managing the data stored in the storage systems. (Chervenak et al., 2001) makes an important distinction between storage and metadata. While in some cases (i.e. the storage into databases) the combination of metadata and storage into the same abstraction has some advantages, separation of these concepts at the architectural level is however better suited in distributed environments. The authors highlight that this clear separation increases flexibility of the system's implementation while alleviating the impact on others implementations that combine metadata access with storage access.

Enhancing storage systems with meta-data capabilities aims at addressing another requirement imposed by the distributed nature of the large scale environments: *transparency*. Indeed, users should not be aware of the different locations or the specific devices used to store data and should rather be presented a uniform view of data, complemented with *uniform mechanisms* for retrieval. This translates into *neutrality* requirements imposed on mechanisms and policies: it enables their implementation through interfaces that capture and hide the specificities of low-level

components and also via high-level procedures. Hence, application specific behaviors are only supported of the higher architectural levels. Such approaches stimulate a wide adoption with the reuse of low-level components, without compromising from the range size of supported applications.

Clearly, compliance with all the above requirements is hard to achieve. There are many tradeoffs: for instance, providing stronger consistency or additional resilience impacts complexity. However, these principles should drive the design of any reliable storage system in order to meet the complex and stringent performance demands of now-days applications.

Storage Systems

Storage systems are responsible with accessing for read/write purposes, creating, deleting, initiating third-party transfers and handling data, which can reside in conventional or high performance parallel file systems, distributed databases or other storage systems. In fact, this approach allows us to broader the common definition of the storage systems, and to further consider the systems implemented by any storage technology, which support the functionalities previously mentioned. Therefore, we are not aiming at direct mapping between storage systems and some low-level storage devices, but rather consider all the technologies able to meet the performance requirements. We detail in the following some of the most important solutions available for large scale distributed environments.

The High Performance Storage System (HPSS 7.1, 2009) is a hierarchical storage system, which manages data over its life cycle; it basically aggregates the capacity and performance of various storage devices into a single virtual file system. The used model keeps active data on highest performing media and inactive data on less effective devices such as tape or low cost, high capacity disks. This model translates into a layered architecture with the local files system on top of the hierarchy, the high speed shared disks and the high capacity shared disks on the intermediate layers and the primary and remote tape libraries on the bottom layer. Transport of data through these layers is automatic and transparent to the client, in such way that the asynchronous migrate and purge allows lower levels to be used as backup for the higher levels. This hierarchical storage model trades low latencies over high capacities as it puts on top levels the high speed medias. Such systems are then well suited and widely adopted in high performance computing environments and are relatively uncommon in business application where simpler backup and restore strategies are sufficient. HPSS provides long term retention and rapid staging in conjunction with a metadata architecture suitable for medium and coarse-grain file access.

The HPSS components (HPSS Core Server, Metadata DB2 server, HPSS Mover Cluster, Data Disks and Tapes) are connected over a Storage Area Network (Oguchi, 2009). A typical HPSS working scenario involves the following steps: a client issues an access request (read/write) to the Core Server; the Core Server then accesses the metadata information on disk to find location information about the required data and consequently commands Mover to stage file from tape to disk; the Mover stages the file, next the Core Server sends back to the client the lock and the ticket. Now either the client accesses the data directly from the shared disk over the Storage Area Network, or the Mover accesses instead and send the information to the client over his Local Area Network.

The storage system is further enhanced with a large set of user and file system interfaces ranging from simple ftp, samba or nfs to higher performance Grid FTP, parallel ftp, client API, local file movers and third party SAN. The Parallel FTP interface uses similar ftp semantics to support parallel files, servers, clients and WAN transfers at high data rates. The Client API consists of a superset of POSIX read/write interface allowing parallelism. In addition to the original Mover-based disk sharing presented in the previ-

ous working scenario, disks may also be accessed directly over a SAN or LAN. While the LAN access support large number of clients and uses commodity TCP/IP infrastructure, the SAN access is usually limited to a hundred clients and uses more expensive fibre channel switches. However, LAN access to data is recommended for large High Performance Computing clusters.

HPSS addresses the high availability requirements providing hardware redundancy for the core servers and investing the data movers with the ability to configure redundancy mechanisms. Arguably, the authors consider HPSS as the most scalable disk-and-tape system anywhere. Indeed, its cluster and metadata architecture support horizontal scaling to tens of petabytes and hundreds of millions of files benefiting from gigabytes per second data rates. Extension is achieved easily by adding new heterogeneous components. HPSS is now deployed on several large sites: 3.9 PB of data stored in over 66 million files at National Energy Research Scientific Computing Center (as of January 2009), 11+ PB of data stored at Los Alamos National Laboratory (LANL), 7+ PB of data at Lawrence Livermore Lantional Lab (LNL), 3.6 PB at Stanford Linear Accelerator Center (SLAC), 3 PB at CEA Computer Center in France, etc. (all as of 2007).

Castor - CERN Advanced STORage manager (Ponce et al., 2009) is another hierarchical storage management system developed at CERN to address the increased needs of High Energy Physics community for resources able to deal with the data intensive experiments. The system provides a managed storage service for all physics data at CERN, using transparent tape media management, automated disk cache management and a unique global namespace. The goal is to fulfill the Tier-0 and Tier-1 storage requirements for LHC experiments at CERN: this involves support for a Central Data Recording (CDR), data reconstruction and data export to Tier-1 centers.

The Castor (now at version 2) architecture is based on 5 components disposed on three layers: on top of the hierarchy is the Client API, the interface of the storage systems with the users; the intermediate layer consists of the Stager logic and the Central services (e.g. NameServer); the base layer holds the Tape archive subsystem and the Disk cache subsystem. State and handling information are stored in a Relational Database Management System, namely status information about running processes that have stateless components. The Client allows basic interaction with the server in order to get the system's functionalities. To this end, one can either use the command line interfaces for users (supporting stager and RFIO commands) or the Client API written in C to communicate with other third-party applications. The Client interface handles status checks, updates and file retrieval from the tape or disk servers using Rfio, Root, Xrootd and GridFTP.

The Central Services include the DriveQueueManager, a daemon for tape queue management, the VolumeManager, an archive of all tapes available in the libraries, the Castor User Privileges, an authorization daemon providing rights to users and administrators for tape related operations, and the NameServer. The latter is a database implementing a hierarchical view of the name space. It further stores the file location on tertiary storage if the file has been migrated from the disk pool in order to make space for more current files. Files may be segmented or be made up of more than one contiguous chunk of tape media. This allows the use of the full capacity of tape volumes and permits file sizes to be bigger than the physical limit of a single tape volume. Additionally, it provides the ability to create directories and files, change ownership, and stores tape-related information as well.

The Stager acts as a disk pool (a collection of file systems) manager whose functions are to allocate space on disk, to store files, to maintain a catalogue of all the files in its disk pools and to clear out old or least recently used files in these pools when more free space is required. The decisions are taken at the database level (using stored procedures) or by external plugins (schedulers, expert systems); typical decisions include: preparation of migration or recall streams, weighting of file systems used for migration/recall and garbage collection decisions. All these actions are performed by dedicated stateless daemons. These stateless components ensure easy restart and parallelization in the absence of a single point of failure. Moreover, the Stager being split in many independent services makes it fully scalable and able to distinguish between queries, user requests and administrator requests – thus allowing transparent access control, as we required at the beginning of this Chapter. Optimization is achieved by means of minimal footprint of inactive requests: these are not instantiated in terms of processes until they run, but are rather stored in the database and scheduled while waiting for resources.

The disk access uses scheduling for all user requests while the tape archive allows dynamic migration or recall streams to or from it and is able to deal with multiple concurrent requests for the same volume. The disk and tape layer provide support for volatile storage (with garbage collection and without migration), durable storage (without garbage collection and without migration) and permanent storage (with garbage collection and migration). Resiliency against hardware failures is addressed by the database and the replication of all daemon; the database is further regularly backed-up.

Current Castor development (Duellmann, 2008) aims at enabling tape aggregation, redundancy and clustering based on name location. The authors also evaluate larger DataBase cluser per VOs and work on increased consistency using the DataBase constraints. The CASTOR storage system is now used by all LHC experiments at CERN: LHCb, ATLAS, CMS, ALICE and also by a Tier 1 Centre – CNAF; it currently stores more than 17PB of data in 119 million files, as of April 2009 (CASTOR Website, 2009). However, compared to HPSS, the system offers fewer interfaces, as the CASTOR name space can be viewed and manipulated only through CASTOR client commands and library calls. This approach prevented a wider adoption from the scientific communities.

Enstore (Bakken et al., 2008) is the Fermilab Mass Storage System providing distributed access and management of data stored on tape. Also a hierarchical storage manager, the system supports random access of files, but also streaming, the sequential access of successive files on tape. Its main software components are the pnfs namespace – a virtual file system package maintaining file grouping and structure information via a set of tags, the encp – a program for copying files to and from media libraries, the servers (cofiguration, library managers, movers, logging, accounting, etc.) and the administrations tools. Pnfs provides a hierarchical namespace for Enstore users and also manages the file metadata. Encp is the system's user interface and is similar to standard UNIX 'cp' command. Scalability and availability are achieved by spreading the server processes across multiple nodes.

Access to Enstore is typically granted via dCache caching system using its supported protocols: kerberizedftp, dcap – a native dCache protocol, gridftp, weakftp, http etc. dCache stores users' files on RAID disks pending transfer to Enstore, while files already written to storage media that get downloaded to the dCache from Enstore are stored on ordinary disks. Hence, performance is improved for highly active files by avoiding the need of reading from tape every time a file is needed. The caching system easily scales as nodes are added. dCache can work on top of Enstore or as a standalone configuration which will be further discussed in the 'Data Retrieval' section of this Chapter.

The infrastructure composed by Enstore and dCache provides a data throughput sufficient for transferring data from experiments' data acquisition systems. The system is currently used for local HEP experiments (CDF, D0, minos, mini-boone) generating more than 1 PB data / year and 25 TB/ day peak transfers, also by remote HEP experi-

ments: Tier 1 for CMS generating more than 3.5 PB / year (Oleynik, 2005). Fermilab mass storage system currently stores 17 PB of user data on tape, as of April 2009 (Enstore Website, 2009).

OppStore. The traditional distributed data storage model, as presented in the above examples, basically uses high-performance dedicated servers with secondary and tertiary disk or tape storage, data replication and meta-data catalogues. These systems target high-performance computing platforms, with applications that require very large amounts (terabytes or petabytes) of data and run on supercomputers connected by specialized high-speed networks. However this infrastructure proves very expensive both in deployment and production (e.g. high maintenance costs, energy consumes etc.) and is therefore only available in some supercomputing centers. As opposed to this model, comes a different, more exotic approach to dealing with large amounts of data: the opportunistic Grids (Goldchleger et al., 2004), a class of computational grids, which focus on the usage of idle resources from shared machines. These machines normally have large quantities of unused storage space that could be used when the machines are idle, allowing opportunistic grids to share not only computational cycles, but also storage space. OppStore (De Camargo et al., 2007) is a middleware that provides reliable storage using the free storage space from shared grid machines. The storage is thus transparently accessed from any grid machine, allowing easy data sharing among grid users and applications. The system uses a two-level peer-to-peer organization to connect grid machines in a scalable and fault-tolerant way. The systems uses the concept of virtual ids to deal with resource heterogeneity, allowing the creation of virtual spaces located on top of the peer-to-peer routing substrate. These virtual spaces enable the middleware to perform heterogeneity-aware, load-balancing selection of storage sites using multiple simultaneous metrics.

OppStore implements two types of storage: ephemeral and perennial. The first mode stores two replicas of the file on machines from the same cluster where the storage request was issued. This approach suites data this is likely to be used in the same cluster and within a short period (e.g. storage of application checkpoints). The latter mode aims at data storage for longer periods; files are thus encoded into redundant fragments, using an optimized version of information dispersal algorithms.

However, this type of approach raises particular challenges as the shared machines often fail and frequently change their state from idle to occupied, compromising their execution of applications. Unlike dedicated resources, whose mean time between failures are typically very high, non-dedicated resources can become unavailable with a high frequency rate, some machines being even unavailable more than they are available. Fault tolerance mechanisms, such as checkpoint-based rollback recovery, can help guarantee that applications execute properly amid frequent failures. In this scenario, the fault tolerance mechanism must save generated checkpoints on a stable storage medium. But a dedicated checkpoint server can easily become a bottleneck as grid size increases. Moreover, when using an opportunistic computing environment, relying on such dedicated systems increases hardware costs and contradicts the objective of such a system, which is to use the idle time of shared machines. Hence the authors suggest using the grid's shared nodes as the storage medium for checkpoints, thus storing and retrieving data in the nodes' shared disk space: store multiple replicas of checkpoint data, so recovery of the stored data is possible even when part of the data repositories are unavailable. Another approach is to break data into several fragments, adding some redundancy, to enable data recovery from a subset of the fragments and consequently reconstruct the fragments that were stored on machines departed from the grid.

The authors propose such a fragment recovery mechanism in order to achieve redundancy (De Camargo et al., 2009). The system uses heartbeats as a way to monitor node departures and, consequently, false departure detections can happen in the case of transient network failures. To minimize the impact of transient departures and false node departure detection, the beginning of the reconstruction algorithm is delayed until a significant number of fragments are lost, in the hopes that some of the nodes have left the grid only temporarily or that the departure was a false detection: the reconstruction threshold is the minimum number of fragments that need to be available. However this approach significantly affects the overall efficiency of the redundancy mechanism. Moreover, the fragment reconstruction operation itself is expensive, since it is necessary to reconstruct the original file for every lost fragment. Therefore, depending on the amount of stored data and the rate of machine departures, the generated traffic may make the distributed storage of data infeasible. The strategy proposed by the authors is to keep an extra copy of each stored fragment in another machine from the same cluster where it is stored. Thus the fragments lost due to machine departures are reconstructed from the other "close" copy of the fragment. Still, this strategy is based on the assumption that free disk storage space and intra-cluster network bandwidth are less scarce than the inter-cluster network bandwidth.

As a conclusion, we observe that there are various solutions to implement reliable distributed storage systems for high performance computing applications, ranging from high performance servers to commodity solutions harnessing available resources. The choice depends on the requirements and the environment of the targeted applications. Lightweight simple solutions often work the best, especially in the case of smaller of highly distributed sites. WAN-aware architectures should also be considered, as they are best suited for scaling to high performance computing data production requirements.

Storage Resource Management

As seen from the previous section, large data stores use heterogeneous main storage devices along with secondary and possibly tertiary media, as disk or tape systems. All these devices need to be managed and to efficiently interact with the other services (replica management, directory services, scheduling etc.). Hence the manifest need for resource management or brokering. Hence, Storage Resource Management's (SRM) role is to provide a global view of the storage infrastructure, to monitor the status of all resources, to ensure availability, to implement some level of active management based on the collected information and to optimize the efficiency and speed with which the available storage space is utilized in a storage area network (SAN). In SANs, storage is seen as a server independent logically managed component, rather than an individual entity attached to a server as in the traditional approach; hence, the management of distinct functionality services across IP networks is simplified. Functions of an SRM program include data storage, data collection, data backup, data recovery, SAN performance analysis, storage virtualization, storage provisioning, forecasting of future needs, maintenance of activity logs, user authentication, protection from unauthorized intrusions and management of network expansion.

In recent years, the SRM evolved from simple storage monitoring and reporting tools to advanced frameworks allowing management of the system, the fabric, the application and the storage devices, alerting, trend analysis, reports, backup and recovery of data and even event prediction. This constant evolution was recognized and supported by the Open Grid Forum through creation of a specific working group - the OGF Grid Storage Management Working Group (OGF SRM WG Website, 2009). A complete specification and implementation (Badino et al. 2008) was further developed for the DataGrid. The goal is to implement the required functionality and standardize the interface of SRMs as Grid middleware components.

Observing that the concept of a storage resource is flexible, the authors identify several types of SRM (Shoshani et al., 2002), according to their targeted media: SRM managing disk caches (reffered to as Disk Resource Manager - DRM), SRM managing a tape archiving system (reffered to as Tape Resource Manager - TRM) or a combination of both (reffered to as a Hierarchical Resource Manager). Moreover, an SRM at a certain site should be able to manage multiple storage resources and handle access and replication across these several storage systems. SRMs should also provide a uniform interface that abstract from current or future hardware configurations. It is worth mentioning that SRMs do not perform file transfers but rather invoke specific middleware components (sych as GridFTP) to perform file transfer, and in general they interact with the mass storage system to perform file archiving and file staging. We detail in the following the main functionalities of the indicated SRM types:

- **DRM** – manages dynamically a single shared disk cache, which can be a single disk, a collection of disks, or a RAID system. Its role is to manage the disk cache based on some client resource management policies set by administrators. It supports cache management policies to minimize repeated file transfers to the disk cache from remote grid sites; these policies are based either on history traces or anticipated requests.

- **TRM** – acts as a middleware interface to systems that manage robotic tapes. Its role is to accept requests for file transfers from clients, queue such requests in case the Mass Storage System (MSS), as HPSS described in the previous sections, is busy or temporarily down, and apply a policy on the use of the MSS resources. As in the case of a DRM, the policy may restrict the number of simultaneous transfer requests by each client, or may give preferential access to clients based on their assigned priority.

- **HRM** – is a TRM that has a staging disk cache for its use, therefore is often viewed as a combination of DRM and TRM. Its role is to use the disk cache for pre-staging files for clients and for sharing files between clients. This functionality proves rather useful taking into account that robotic tape systems are mechanical in nature and they have latency of mounting a tape and seeking the location of a file. Pre-staging masks this latency.

SRM interfaces were developed for all major storage systems (HPSS, CASTOR, Enstore, etc.). Moreover, proprietary SRM solutions exist as stand-alone products, or as part of an integrated program suite. Solutions vary in the offered components, but most provide a framework for automating the analysis of storage, access, capacity, utilization and availability statistics. HP's SRM solution is Storage Essentials (HP, 2008) which provides storage management for heterogeneous environments (direct attached storage, storage area network, network attached storage), provisioning, metering, reports, business application, backup monitoring and end-to-end performance management. IBM also provides a Storage Manager in its Tivoli software suite (IBM, 2009). The system provides policy-managed backup, archive, space-management, topology mapping, monitoring, reporting and configuration management.

Comparing the available SRMs implementations we observe how diverse storage systems can be integrated under uniform metadata and policy driven access mechanisms. Their main advantages include: the streaming model offered to clients - that is, their ability to provide a stream of files to client programs, rather than all the files at once; they also deal transparently with network and storage devices failures. However, best performance is achieved when SRMs are shared by communities of users that are likely to access the same files (as in HPC experiments).

Distributed File Systems

Distributed file systems support the sharing of information in the form of file instances, as basic data units, throughout distributed environments. In an ideal case, the file service would provide transparent access to files stored at remote servers with performance and reliability similar to files stored on local disk. As this is hard to achieve in the context of large scale distributed systems, we review some key requirements needed to be addressed by a well-designed file system able to deal with such challenges. (Coulouris et al., 2005) presented a first set of such requirements. However, these are quite general and usually available for any distributed service. In fact, many of the requirements and issues of the design of distributed services were first observed in the early development of distributed file systems.

Access transparency is a major challenge and clients should be unaware of the distribution of files; they should instead use a single set of operations for data access. Considering that the file service is usually one of the most heavily loaded service in the distributed environment, access should be complemented with *performance and scalability transparency*: client programs should continue to perform at required parameters while the load on the service varies or the service is expanded by incremental growth. *Concurrency* control is another issue, not trivial to deal with, in a system which supports frequent concurrent file updates. *File replication* has several benefits: on one hand it enables multiple servers to share the load generated by clients accessing the same set of file, and on the other, it enhance the overall scalability and *fault tolerance* by allowing clients to use other servers that hold copies of the targeted file when one has failed. Other aspects that need consideration are: *consistency* (in issues related to delays in propagation of modifications), *security* (using authenticated access control) and *efficiency* (in the context of the diversity of client's goals and behaviors).

We extend these requirements with new ones, extracted from observing the recent storage infrastructure deployments and their specific application use-case scenarios (large datasets, Virtual Organizations, mass storage systems etc.):

- **Location Transparency** – access to files should be granted independent of the client's location. Data location transparency should be further supported through the use of data set names rather than file names or URLs.
- **Resource and Access Functions Transparency** – they are achieved using high level I/O optimizations like collective I/O and data sieving.
- **Single Logical Namespace** – the use of logical namespaces provides a logical view of the files independent of their stored location in the distributed environment. The single view also removes the ambiguity of the location of files and makes it easy for applications to retrieve the files from any computational machine as they all share the same view of the location
- **Manageability** – the system should handle different types of users, privileges, access rights, jobs and usage scenarios. Also, it should allow easy integration with different Virtual Organizations.
- **Interoperability with Grid Applications** – needed by file services which are deployed over grid middleware and needing interfaces with grid services (e.g. Grid Security Infrastructure, Replica Catalogs, etc.)

Recent design advances in distributed file systems considered these requirements and have exploited the increasing capacities of storage systems, higher bandwidth connectivity and new techniques of data organization on disks and tapes to achieve high performance, fault tolerance and scalability. We examine some of these current solutions.

NFS v4.1 - The Network File System version 4.1 (Shepler et al., 2008) is considered one of the most important technological update and the first performance improvement to NFS in the last years. The IETF working group developing NFS had as goal to exploit the results emerged from file server design over the past decade, such as the use of callbacks and or lease to maintain consistency. The new NFS version keeps all the previous features: simplified error recovery, independence of transport protocols and operating systems for file access, clear design. Unlike earlier versions, however, it now supports recovery from server faults by allowing file systems to be moved to new servers transparently, integrates file locking, has stronger security, enhances scalability by using proxy servers and includes delegation capabilities to enhance client performance for data sharing applications on high-bandwidth networks. Moreover, NFS 4.1 is aware of distributed data using faster and optimized compound RPC calls, discovers the inactive clients through client to server pings, and enforces security with GSS authentication, built in mandatory security on file system level and support for ACLs, thus making it ideal for Grid and highly distributed systems.

However, the key component of NFS 4.1 is parallel NFS – pNFS (Pariseau, 2008), which provides parallel I/O to file systems accessible over NFS. Parallel NFS provides a specification for placing a metadata server outside the data path of servers attached to a multi node storage system. In this manner, storage nodes can be held together with another clustered file system, while pNFS exposes the block mapping of files and objects to the client. The client then receives those blocks through multiple parallel network channels and reassembles them for presentation to the user. This allows striping single files across multiple NFS servers. Such approach is very similar to RAID

0, presented in the first section of this Chapter, which dramatically increases performance by allowing multiple disk drives to serve up data in parallel. pNFS extends the solution to multiple storage devices connected to an NFS client over a network. It also addresses on of the key requirements mentioned above through standardization of parallel I/O and by supporting client access to storage devices directly and in parallel. This eliminates the scalability and performance issues associated with NFS servers deployed.

Aggregation and location transparency are smoothly addressed: the unified namespace used by NFS 4.1 enables the aggregation of large numbers of heterogeneous NFS servers under a single namespace. While NFSv3 servers' access control was limited to groups and users, the newest version includes access control of individual files or applications; file and directory delegations allow greater number of NFS clients to access a single NFS share. As the protocol is able to handle large files and many concurrent users, concerns are raised on the connectivity side, namely if pNFS is can pick up the advantages of high speed networks. To this end (Chai et al., 2007) proved that pNFS handles very well high speed networks such as InfiniBand, and achieves up to 5 times higher throughput compared with using GigE as the transport. Encouraged by the little overhead added by the pNFS, the authors indicate it as a parallel solution for cluster.

However, a potential drawback could be pNFS requiring users to deal with multiple NFS servers. Depending on how well the NFS vendor integrates these servers, the management overhead may scale with the number of storage devices that are configured for parallel access. It is therefore advised to use tightly integrated servers that provide a true single system image as opposed to a cluster of servers that are merely duct-taped together. Hence pNFS is not yet suited for environments where improved performance for large, sequential files with parallel access is needed. Moreover, since it's a new technology, although the pNFS extension

has the support of NAS hardware vendors, it's not yet clear how soon application and operating system vendors will support pNFS.

The IBM General Parallel File System – GPFS (Fadden, 2008) is a file management infrastructure, providing concurrent high-speed file access to applications executing on multiple nodes of clusters. Besides file storage capabilities, GPFS provides storage management, information life cycle management tools, centralized administration and allows for shared access to file systems from remote GPFS clusters.

According to high performance file systems' requirements, GPFS handles metadata information in a scalable fashion, by allowing all nodes of the cluster accessing the file system to perform file metadata operations. This approach is different from the cluster file systems' implementations, which typically use a centralized metadata server handling fixed regions of the file namespace. A centralized metadata server can often become a performance bottleneck for metadata intensive operations and can represent a single point of failure. GPFS solves this problem by managing metadata at the node which is using the file or in the case of parallel access to the file, at a dynamically selected node which is using the file.

The system also implements Information Lifecycle Management (ILM) through policy-driven automation and tiered storage management. It actively uses storage pools which allow creation of groups of disks within the file system. This is an important feature in the context of High Energy Physics experiments as it allows modeling the tiers of storage and administrative regions inside a Virtual Organization by grouping disks based on performance, locality, targeted applications or reliability characteristics. Hence, the use of storage pools, filesets and user-defined policies provides the ability to better match applications specific requirements. To support the storage capabilities the system matches equal performance from I/O by: striping data across multiple disks attached to multiple nodes; high performance metadata (inode) scans; supporting a large block size, configurable by the administrator, to fit I/O requirements; utilizing advanced algorithms that improve read-ahead and write-behind file functions and using block level locking based on a very sophisticated scalable token management system to provide data consistency while allowing multiple application nodes concurrent access to the files. Coherency and consistency are maintained using sophisticated byte level locking, token management and logging (Schmuck et al. 2002).

One can easily observe that GPFS is better suited for parallel applications that need concurrently read or update a common file from multiple nodes in the cluster. In fact it is wider deployed than other existing file systems: interfaces for HPSS are developed to achieve synergy between the file system and the mass storage. Goals include extending GPFS pool concept to tape and other long term storage, the use of the rule-based ILM to centralize ILM administration, providing backup for GPFS that makes effective use of ongoing file migration to tape under ILM control, and most of all, aiming at unprecedented scalability.

Hadoop Distributed System. In contrast with the previous examples, we present the Hadoop Distributed File System – HDFS (Wheeler, 2008), an open source file system designed to run on inexpensive commodity hardware. The system organizes file in a hierarchical namespace for storage and retrieval and provides high throughput access to application data. HDFS supports hardware transparency as it runs in user space, as contrasted to the other filesystems which are inextricably linked to their operating systems' kernel; therefore HDFS can run on any operating system supported by Java. HDFS implements replication mechanisms for data across multiple machines in a cluster. This scheme provides not only fault tolerance, but also the potential for extremely high capacity storage given that the overall capacity will be based on all usable space of all disks across all machines. HDFS also assumes that the data will be written only once and is able to gain extra performance by optimizing for subsequent reads while disallowing subsequent writes.

Hadoop's file system architecture is built around a master / slave model with a single NameNode (plus a seconday NameNode for checkpointing), as a master server that manages the file system namespace and regulates access to files by clients, and a number of DataNodes, usually one per node in the cluster, which manage storage attached to the nodes that they run on. DataNode are thus responsible for low-level operations including block creation, deletion, reads and writes. A NameNode keeps track of which DataNodes have which blocks of data and uses this information to manage the hierarchy of the overall file system. Being open source, HDFS is widely adopted and due to the use of commodity components is actively developed in business environments also. Yahoo! is the greatest contributor and the largest user (4000 nodes and 16 PB of raw disk capacity) but is also deployed at Google, Facebook, ImageShack, Last.fm.

We conclude this section observing that file systems and their mass storage systems integration are still under continuous efforts of research and development. Solutions exist and range from high performance proprietary file systems to low-cost hardware based, open source projects. In order to achieve better integration however, there is a constant need for joint work between storage software providers.

Peer-to-Peer Storage

Peer-to-Peer (P2P) systems need a separate discussion as they have particular architectures that influence their exposed properties in the storage context. They benefit from harnessing unsued storage and network resources from clients that voluntarily join the system, self-configuration and automatic load balancing, robustness due to self-organization after failures, and good scalability by using of symmetric algorithms. However they expose major disadvantages, which make difficult the design of a reliable P2P storage system: clients are highly transient, storage is inherently unreliable and the lookup algorithms have long latencies. We distinguish between two models of P2P storage: data publishing and storage sharing, each imposing different requirements on the underlying P2P infrastructure. While file publishing needs equality search and keyword search capabilities, and less sophisticated fault-tolerance mechanisms, storage sharing requires complex fault tolerance support and simple queries.

Concerning the data availability in P2P storage systems (Xin et al. 2004) makes another important distinction between: data reliability (the probability that data is not irretrievably lost) and data availability (the probability that data is not accessible). Data reliability depends on the long-term behavior of a node, whereas data availability is mostly determined by the current behavior of a node. A node that is up for small periods of time contributes much to data reliability but little to data availability. Because of the cyclic behavior of peers in a global P2P system, a node that is up at one time might be down at other time; thus, data availability depends on the status of the nodes on which data is stored. Data is viewed as nomad, and redundancy is necessary to provide fault tolerance and highly availability of data access. Different redundancy scheme exist, ranging from simple replication to fragmentation and erasure codes. Designing P2P storage systems that can implement all the properties previously described is exceedingly difficult. A number of efforts have been made to achieve most of the goals. However, most of these systems utilize specific properties or mechanisms and specialize in particular fields. We examine some of these systems in the following subsections.

PAST (Druschel et al., 2001) is a large scale P2P persistent storage management system. It organizes all machines at a single level and stores data directly in the machines that perform message routing. Consequently, each node arrival and departure requires that large amounts of data are transferred to compensate for changes in machine organization, suffering from the problems described by (Blake et al. 2003). The system relies on Pastry (Rowstron et al., 2001) for resource location and underlying connections. Pastry is a P2P routing substrate that implements a distributed hash table used to routing files to storage. Indeed, several copies of data are disseminated on different nodes. However, there is little support for load distribution, only for storage request forwarding being implemented. For instance, PAST stores a single large file without breaking it into smaller chunks, which raises important efficiency and fault tolerance problems. Also, the system does not consider machine heterogeneity.

OceanStore (Rhea et al., 2003) creates a global-scale persistent storage for nomadic data by distributing data on server peers. It uses Plaxton trees and Bloom filters to perform data locations. Any computer can ad hoc join the infrastructure. In exchange for economic compensation, participants in OceanStore contribute remote storage or provide local user access. By supporting nomadic data, this system provides highly available storage utility, especially for ubiquitous computing. Moreover, OceanStore uses an Introspection mechanism which is a learning process making the system able to take smart decisions based on access patterns. Since nodes cannot be individually trusted, several redundancy techniques are implemented: replication or erasure coding. The first approach needs some consideration: to allow data updates in the presence of file replicas, Byzantine agreements protocols are used. Finally, the introspection mechanisms are employed to cluster related files and for replica management. In the latter approach (erasure coding), each data object is broken into n fragments by using an erasure coding scheme so that m out of n fragments suffice to reconstruct the object. Each data object thus is versioned and spread over hundreds or thousands of servers randomly in read-only form. However keeping track of the sites where each object lives causes much system overhead. Also, the system does not consider node heterogeneity and does not employ load-balancing algorithms when selecting data storage sites.

Ubiquitous Storage - Us (Soyez et al., 2007) aims is data durability. Unlike OceanStore, where data is distributed on server peers, data is distributed on end user peers: each Us peer is both storage space consumer and storage space provider. The main goal of Us is to provide a virtual storage device to each user which insures data durability. Us shares common features with OceanStore as the data dissemination and data redundancy that enhance scalability. The drawback however is that Us faces a higher failure rate of peer because the number of peers is a several order of magnitude greater than the number of peers in OceanStore. Moreover, peers are less robust than OceanStore servers. To tackle these problems, redundancy is implemented using optimized erasure codes. When a peer fails, a reconstruction process rebuilds lost data with help from others peers, but using this technique, systems have to handle a continuous large number of reconstructions to insure data durability. To minimize end user traffic due to the reconstruction process, distribution strategies take into account new measures like the maximum disturbance cost of a peer during the reconstruction process. The disturbance cost is indicated by the number of data communication requests, which are issued from a single peer for rebuilding lost data. Hence these optimizations of the redundancy mechanisms make Us more reliable than OceanStore.

PeerStore (Landers et al., 2004) is another a P2P distributed storage system. It decouples fragment location from its identifier, storing the file index and fragments separately. This eliminates the maintenance due to data misplacement caused by node joins and departures and also make Peer-Store suitable for ubiquitous systems. However, it recovers lost fragments caused by departures in a lazy way, compromising the immediate recovery of stored files. This characteristic makes it less suitable for very dynamic environments, such as opportunistic grids.

Although this last association (between P2P and Grid systems) may sound surprising for these two seemingly different paradigms, we find enough arguments for their convergence in the storage context: they both may use inexpensive commodity hardware and both deal with efficient handling of heterogeneous storage resources. (Foster et al. 2003) even foresees a smooth convergence of the communities, each gradually adopting the advantages of the other one.

DATA RETRIEVAL

Reliable retrieval of data is a cornerstone of distributed systems. Experience with data grids and intensive data applications showed that reliability goals are difficult to achieve. Many problems were encountered with data retrieval – particularly that driven by grid jobs themselves (Stewart et al., 2007): when jobs triggered a data transfer from a remote site they would be unaware if the file requested was already in transit, usually requested by another job; file transfers were triggered without any controls on resources at the source and destination, often leading to overloading of storage elements at sites and consequent failures. Besides these issues, the ever faster processing speeds have imposed the need for faster I/O for retrieval of huge datasets. Data-intensive applications require large amounts of data on a timely basis for appropriate functioning without delays due to data unavailability.

Applications and distributed mass storage systems applied several techniques for maximizing the retrieval data rate achieved across WANs, SANs and LANs. Both hardware and software optimization mechanisms were exploited for this purpose. We showed in the previous section that multithreaded parallel streaming has also been proven as a good and inexpensive way for aggregating I/O. Other enhancement techniques such as buffering, prefetching, and proper cache replacement policies are considered very supportive in improving applications' performance. However, prefetching and cache management are considered to be application- dependant features (Malluhi et al., 2002), therefore an optimal prefetching algorithm for one application may be the worst for another one with different data type and/or access patterns.

Another observation that may be speculated is that in high performance computing environments applications usually require access to only subsets of the distributed datasets since handling the whole dataset at once, if possible, considerably degrades the performance of the client machines. One aiming at designing a reliable retrieval system should then consider that users needn't spend long time waiting for retrieving the whole dataset, if only partial data is needed at any time. Therefore, mass storage system should provide clients with data retrieval APIs that allow partial data transfers. Some storage systems have provided low-level block accesses, which resulted in reducing the startup time required by the applications. Other systems just stripe the dataset into several blocks that are equal to the number of data nodes used in distributing the data object (Chen et al. 2002, Ye et al. 2006). This restriction limits the use of the storage system to file transfer since handling large data chunks may not be useful. It may also result in long network latencies and degrades the positive threads overlapping.

Xrootd (Yang et al., 2008) is a file retrieval server initially developed for the Root analysis framework to ostensibly serve root files. However, the server is agnostic as to file types and provides byte level access to any type of file. The xrootd server is designed to provide POSIX-like for retrieving files and access their enclosing directory namespace. The architecture is extensible, relying on a run-time plug-in mechanism so that new features can be added with a minimum of disruption. The architecture abstracts physical and logical file systems through appropriate plug-ins, and implements the retrieval functionality using a Protocol plug-in. The xrootd protocol is

optimized for lowest possible latency for network data access and allows request multiplexing on a single connection. In asynchronous request mode, multiple requests may be issued concurrently. This allows for parallel as well as pipelined data access to one or more files. Latency is further decreased due to the use of an optimistic run-to-completion transaction model in which, as long as the client issues requests within a reasonable time window, a thread is dedicated to the client; hence no overhead from OS thread switching and network polling.

Xrootd is widely adopted in mass storage devices and is currently deployed in production at CERN, with Castor. Within the ALICE experiment, the xrootd server proved robust, efficient and scalable while the xrootd protocol was well integrated with experiment applications and showed good performance in streamed and random access modes (Duellmann, 2008). Extensions deployed for the ALICE experiment include plug-ins for user authentication (Kerberos, GSI), low latency files access through reads bypass of LSF I/O scheduling latencies and support for multiple pools and services classes from one xrootd setup. The aimed goals of this deployment are to implement full disk management and directly provide online name space (consistent with tape) as xrootd extensions; also to refocus Castor stager on tape-to-disk transfers. Current research involves new plug-ins for I/O scheduling and disk-to-disk copies inside Xrootd, bandwidth reservation needed for tape transfers and Tier0 transfers, and coexistence of Xrootd managed pools with LSF scheduled pools.

dCache (dCache Website, 2009) is a storage software providing mechanisms for storing and retrieving large amounts of data distributed over a large number of heterogeneous server nodes (the only requirement being Java). It provides a single rooted namespace view of all of the files that it manages, completely decoupled from storage and allows access to these files using a variety of a protocols, including SRM. dCache is architected around a set of domains with specific roles such as dealing with file retrieval requests from clients, updating the filesystem namespace or facilitating communication between domains. The disk storage is partitioned into a set of disk pools, each of which can be assigned properties for file control based on specific client policies. Data retrieval is achieved in LANs through dCache access protocol or xroot and in WANs through a proprietary implementation of GridFTP or SRM. Recent research permitted the possibility to configure multiple I/O queues. Such a system allows for WAN and LAN file access to be separated, preventing the (slower) WAN I/O from blocking (fast) user access to files across the LAN.

dCache has been deployed in production at more than 40 sites. They range from small single machine installations that are present at some Tier-2 sites, all the way up to large LHC experiment specific centers such as that at Fermilab. This diversity in composition of these sites gives us a good indication on system's capabilities. Indeed, this dCache installation at Fermilab is composed of more than 690 pools, with 4.8 PB of disk storage and 17 PB of data stored on tape, as of April 2009 (Millar, 2009; Enstore Website, 2009).

In P2P environments, data retrieval is one of the most important issues. As resources are distributed in diverse peers, an efficient mechanism for object location becomes the deciding factor in the performance of such data retrieval systems. Solution should be capable of retrieving any given data item in a large P2P system in a scalable fashion, without any centralized server and adapting to a changing network topology. Most of the existing algorithms for the lookup problem rely on a simple and general interface, a distributed hash table (DHT). Data items are inserted in a DHT and found by specifying a unique key for that data. To implement a DHT, the underlying algorithm must be able to determine which node is responsible for storing the data associated with any given key. To solve this problem, each node maintains information (e.g., the IP address) of a small number of other nodes ("neighbors") in the

system, forming an overlay network and routing messages in the overlay to store and retrieve keys (Balakrishnan et al., 2003).

DATA TRANSFER

Much of data storage and retrieval systems' performance is in conjunction with their data movement capabilities. The tiered data distribution model of today's intensive computing applications involves dissemination of data from the production sites to the storage and processing sites across a highly geographical distributed hierarchy of tiers. In order to harness all the advantages of the always rapid advancing network technologies (among the latest we note GigaByte, InfiniBand and optical networks), applications must rely on robust and efficient data transfer protocols. As we will see in this section, this proves to be a non trivial task.

Indeed, recent experiences with Grids and High Energy Physics experiments at CERN revealed numerous issues related to data transport across widely heterogeneous networks. For instance, much effort is spent on bulk transfers (Paisley et al., 2006), which originated from a historical view of the WAN and can affect the QoS delivered to other users of the network. Solutions to this problem vary from identifying the applications that produce the bulk traffic (usually at bounded set: SRMs, GridFTP) using detection methods based on application signatures (which proves however difficult to achieve in real-time) to using large relatively cheap network capacities for bulk transfers. Other issues comes from the observation that although some file systems (as Hadoop) rely on the paradigm that "moving computation is cheaper than moving data", that is not generally true in supercomputing applications. Hence a manifest need for significant storage resources near the computing elements. Moreover, data transport in these environments cannot capitalize on opportunistic resources and movement of data can result in large wasted network bandwidth unless much of the data is reused. Missing files problems require significant bookkeeping efforts; large jobs startups delays are frequent until all of the required data arrives; the transport proves sometimes unstable, with high latencies and unpredictable for real-time access.

To address these challenges, recent research efforts are underway. We divide the proposed solutions into two categories:

- **Low-level** – dealing with performance issues such as delay, loss, switching / routing, TCP, FastTCP and UDP dynamics, system and network tuning.
- **High-level** – addressing problems by improved protocols, parallel transfers, P2P, grid techniques, abstract storage services.

In this section we concentrate on the latter category, and discuss several protocols, p2p and grid solutions, examining how they cope with the above challenges and studying their compliance with the distributed systems' general requirements.

The Grid File Transfer Protocol – GridFTP (Allcock et al., 2003) is a set of extensions to the FTP that define a general-purpose mechanism for secure, reliable, high-performance data transfer. The protocol is part of the Globus Toolkit 4 (Foster, 2005) and enables efficient data transfer between end-systems by employing techniques like multiple TCP streams per transfer, striped transfers from a set of hosts to another set of hosts, and partial file transfers. GridFTP is based on TCP but it further allows multiple TCP streams creation between the source and the destination in order to offset the network congestion and improve throughput. The use of multiple streams in parallel, however, does not affect the routing or take into account network parallelism.

GridFTP was early adopted by large communities and deployed with much enthusiasm as it is basically the first transfer protocol to address the specific HPC needs. The protocol is thus continuously updated, many interfaces with

storage and retrieval systems are developed, and various extensions are built to address specific applications. An example is the Globos Striped GridFTP framework (Allcock et al., 2005), a set of client and server libraries designed to support the construction of data-intensive tools and applications. The GridFTP server proved faster than other FTP servers in both single-process and striped configurations, achieving high speeds both in memory-to-memory and disk-to-disk transfers. Moreover the server can easily scale and supports thousands concurrent clients without excessive load. The authors argue that this combination of performance and modular structure make the Globus GridFTP framework both a foundation on which to build tools and applications, and a testbed for the study of innovative data management techniques and network protocols.

Recent developments (Bresnahan et al., 2007) in the GridFTP framework take advantage of the latest developments in networking infrastructure and transport protocols to better serve scientific communities. Some of these new features are: GridFTP Pipelining, which improves the performance many small files transfers; GridFTP over UDT, which can provide significantly higher end-to-end performance than GridFTP over TCP, particularly on wide area networks; split DSI for GridFTP, which can help overcome some of the TCP limitations and can also help to avoid some bottleneck links; network provisioning, which allows for binding of GridFTP transfers to optical paths; GridFTP over Infiniband, which enables GridFTP to take advantage of the recent developments in Infiniband over SONET to achieve high performance on wide area networks; new functionalities that allow clients to use any FTP client to invoke data transfers with the previously described GridFTP server.

However, GridFTP currently does not incorporate optimizations which affect network routing or take into account any network parallelism. Hence, there is still place for improvement. (Khanna et al., 2008a) explored the use of two key optimizations, namely, multi-hop path splitting and multi-pathing and proposed optimization algorithms which can exploit these optimizations to maximize file transfer throughput. These optimizations were implemented using GridFTP as the underlying protocol and the authors observed that the proposed solutions yield significant performance improvements for communication patterns like 1-to-all broadcast, all-to-1 gather, data redistribution. In contrast, for scenarios involving data replication, no significant improvement was observed.

Another concern in GridFTP is the heterogeneous nature of the environment and dynamic availability of shared resources, which need to be considered at the time of the data transfers. (Khanna et al., 2008b) proposes a solution that takes into account the dynamically changing network bandwidth. To this end the authors develop an algorithm that dynamically schedules a batch of data transfer requests with the goal of minimizing the overall transfer time. The proposed algorithm performs simultaneous transfer of chunks of files from multiple file replicas, if the replicas exist; the dynamicity of the bandwidth is considered when adaptively selecting replicas to transfer different chunks of the same file by taking. GridFTP is the underlying mechanism for data transfers and the history traces from previous GridFTP transfers are sued to make new estimations on network bandwidth and resource availability.

(Kourtellis et al., 2008) makes a detailed workload analysis of the performance and reliability of the GridFTP, based on traces of reported data from different distributed installed components. The authors focus on three aspects: quantification of the volume of data transferred during the monitored interval (1.5 years) and characterization of user behavior; understanding of how tuning capabilities are used; finally, the quantification of the user base as recorded in the database and the prediction of usage trends. The analysis revealed a small use of the tuning parameters (i.e. users tend not to set the buffer size explicitly leaving it to the OS) and also confirmed the large adoption of

GridFTP both in terms of IPs (users) / domains (Virtual Organizations) and volume transferred.

The Reliable File Transfer Service – RFT (Madduri, 2006) is a file transfer service component of the Globus Toolkit 4. It was developed to address some of the GridFTP drawbacks: no support for web services, the need for clients to maintain open socket connections to the server throughout the transfer, which proves inconvenient for long transfers. To solve these issues, RFT build a service interface based on web services protocols that persists the transfer state in reliable storage. It uses standard SOAP messages over HTTP to submit and manage a set of 3rd party GridFTP transfers, providing also an interface to control various transfer parameters of the GridFTP control channel like TCP buffer size, parallel streams, etc. From this point of view, RFT is a Web Services Resource Framework (WSRF) compliant web service that providing scheduling functionalities for data management.

Fast Data Transfer (FDT Website, 2009) is a new application for efficient data transfers, capable of reading and writing at disk speed over Wide Area Networks (WAN), with standard TCP. FDT is developed within the MonALISA monitoring framework (presented in the next Chapter) to support efficient large scale data transfers and also to help in the active monitoring of the available bandwidth between sites. FDT can be used as an independent application but it can also be controlled and managed by the MonALISA system to provide effective data transfer services. The application is based on an asynchronous, flexible multithreaded system and is using the capabilities of the Java NIO libraries. Its main features include: streaming datasets (lists of files) continuously, using a managed pool of buffers through one or more TCP sockets, the use of independent threads to read and write on each physical device, data transfers in parallel on multiple TCP streams, when necessary, the use of appropriate-sized buffers for disk I/O and for the network, restoring the files from buffers asynchronously and resuming file transfer sessions without loss, when needed.

FDT can be used to stream a large set of files across the network, so that a large dataset composed of thousands of files can be sent or received at full speed, without the network transfer restarting between files. The FDT architecture allows to plug-in external security APIs and to use them for client authentication and authorization. Currently FDT supports several security schemes like IP filtering, SSH, GSI-SSH, Globus-GSI, and SSL. The application enjoys a wide adoption as it very easy to use and portable, being written in Java. Performance evaluation showed very good results both in memory-to-memory tests (achieving 9.4 Gb/s throughput over 10 Gb links) and in disk-to-disk tests conducted over the USLHCNet network. In the last scenario, FDT proved capable to transfer data over WAN at the limit of the disks IO rate showing rates decreasing in time as the write speed on normal disks decreased (as the disks were filled).

BitTorrent (Cohen, 2003) is an incentive P2P file sharing and transfer system. In this highly adopted approach, files are split up into fixed-size chunks (on the order of a thousand per file), and the downloaders of a file barter for chunks of it by uploading and downloading them in a tit-for-tat-like manner to prevent parasitic behavior. Each peer is responsible for maximizing its own download rate by contacting suitable peers, and peers with high upload rates will with high probability also be able to download with high speeds. When a peer has finished downloading a file, it may become a seed by staying online for a while and sharing the file for free, i.e., without bartering.

In contrast to previous examples, BitTorrent is not aimed at improving the performance of single file transfers, but rather targeted at swarm optimization, namely, many users requesting the same files. In addition, BitTorrent does not perform any explicit multi-swarm optimization. This approach radically differs from the grid perspective in which the goal is to perform makespan optimization where the global objective of minimizing the time

is more important than each site's local benefits. Parallelism is also supported by BitTorrent as a source peer can upload data to other peers simultaneously, the chosen peers being the ones which provide the highest upload rates to the source peer. In addition, it also incorporates the concept of optimistic unchoking where in periodically, a source peer chooses a randomly selected peer from the set of requesting ones and starts uploading to it. This allows a site to discover peers that possess the data of interest and that may be able to upload to it at higher rates regardless of the site's upload rate. Recent BitTorrent development addressed issues like multiple trackers per torrent, tracker-less torrents using a DHTs, peer exchange, data encryption and web seeding.

REPLICATION

Replication is a key to providing enhanced performance, high availability and fault tolerance in distributed storage systems. It typically means the maintenance of several copies of data across multiple systems. By means of *performance* enhancement, replication is used for storing data that is likely to be reused and avoid latencies of fetching it form the originating resources or for workload sharing between servers in the same cluster (domain). However, there are limits to the effectiveness of replication as a performance-enhancement technique, especially in environments with frequent updates of data, where overhead is incurred from protocols designed to ensure that clients receive up to date data. Data replication also enables increased *availability* when used at a number of failure-independent servers. Still, highly available data does not necessarily mean strictly correct data. *Correctness* concerns the freshness of the data supplied to users and the effects of users' operations on data. Other common requirements imposed to data replication are *consistency*, that is the compliance between (possibly conflicting) operations upon a set of replicated data and its correctness specifications, and also *transparency*, namely, clients should not be aware of the existence of several copies of data.

Since replication implies that identical data copies exist, replicas need to be uniquely identified through logical and physical filenames. Moreover, there is a manifest need for a service responsible with naming and locating replicas. (Allcock et al., 2002) identified the major components of a high performance data replication system and their basic functionalities:

- **Replica Management** – the service should create new copies of a complete or partial collection of files, register the copies with a naming and location directory service, allow users and application to query the directory to find all the existing copies of a particular file or collection of files;

- **Replica Catalog** – stores naming and location information about the registered data; provide mappings between logical names for files or collections and one or more copies of those objects on physical storage systems; the authors proposed a set of three types of entries for data registration within the catalog: logical collections (user defined group of files, suitable for handling large amounts of data and having the advantage of reducing both catalog entries and the number of catalog manipulation operations), locations (mappings between logical collections and their particular physical instances), and logical files (optional entry suitable for individual files).

The presented prototypes were implemented within the Globus Toolkit (GT) and continuously evolved along with GT new releases. In the current GT version 4.2, the replica management service is implemented by the Data Replication Service – DRS (Chervenak et al., 2008). DRS allows user to identify files, replicate and transfer them and across the network and to register them into the Replica Location Service. Throughout the replication operations, the service maintains state about each file, including which operations on the file have succeeded or failed. The DRS is implemented as a Web Service and it thus exposes the previous functionality through a WS-Resource ("Replicator"), which represents the current state of the requested replication activity. This allows users to query or subscribe to various Resource Properties in order to monitor the state of the resource and control the replication request's behavior.

The Replica Catalog was initially implemented as a simple, centralized service based on LDAP technology. This approach however revealed some serious limitations when deployed in production (Stockinger et al., 2003): performance quickly deteriorates with number of entries, due to the chosen LDAP schema and it translates into low response times; the centralized, not-scalable LDAP architecture is a single point of failure; although there exist some few command lines tools for catalog query, there is no support for high level tools for catalog browsing; the fixed LDAP based schema organized in collections, locations and logical files is note extendible. Therefore, to address these issues, since GT3 the Replication Catalog was updated to the Replication Location Service – RLS (Chervenak et al., 2004). RLS provides a mechanism for registering the existence of replicas and discovering them. It consists of two types of services, a catalog service and an index service. The Local Replica Catalog (LRC) maintains a catalog of replica information in the form of mappings from logical names for data items to target names. These target names may represent physical locations of data items, or an entry in the RLS may map to another level of logical naming for the data item. The other component, the Replica Location Index (RLI) aggregates and answers queries about mappings held in one or more LRCs. An RLI server contains a set of mappings from logical names to LRCs.. In a typical use case scenario the LRC sends an index of its contents to its associated RLI service as well as multiple remote RLI services at collaborating sites. Clients interested in a particular logical name will first query a RLI service to find the LRC services, then they will query one or more LRC services to find the target names (which may correspond to storage location URLs).

The RLI distributed state is maintained using a soft state update mechanism. An advantage of using soft state update protocols resides in relaxing the persistence requirements on RLI state: if an RLI fails and later resumes operation, its state can be reconstructed using soft state updates. Soft state updates may optionally be compressed to reduce the amount of data sent from LRCs to RLIs and reduce storage and I/O requirements on RLIs. To this end, several algorithms were used, including compression based on logical collections and the use of Bloom Filter compression, in which bit maps are constructed by applying a series of hash functions to logical names. Compared to the old Replica Catalog, experimental results showed that RLS' performance scales well for individual servers with millions of entries and up to 100 requesting threads; moreover the distributed RLS index scales well when using Bloom filter compression for wide area updates.

Along with Globus solutions, there is a continuous research effort in enhancing replication mechanism with features compliant with the requirements indicated at the begining of this section. One concern is related to the selection of the best candidate site where replicas should be placed. (Rahman et al. 2007) uses a multi-objective model to tackle this problem. The multi-objective model considers the objectives of p-median and p-center models simultaneously to select the candidate sites that will host replicas. The objective of the p-median model is to find the locations of p possible candidate replication sites by optimizing total (or average) response time; where the p-center model finds p candidate sites by optimizing maximum response time. In addition, observing that candidate sites currently holding replicas may not be the best sites to fetch

replica on subsequent requests due to dynamic latencies, the authors propose a dynamic replica maintenance algorithm that re-allocates to new candidate sites if a performance metric degrades significantly over last K time periods. These models were further validated with different performance metrics, e.g. total file transfer time, the number of local and remote file access, with accuracy (Rahman et al., 2009).

(Ramabhadran et al., 2008) studies the problem of guaranteeing data durability (Chun et al., 2006) in distributed storage systems based on replication. This proves to be difficult because the data lifetimes may be several orders of magnitude larger than the lifetimes of individual storage units, and the system may have little or no control over the participation of these storage units in the system. The authors use a model-based approach to develop engineering principles for designing automated replication and repair mechanisms to implement durability in such systems. In (Duminuco et al., 2007) it is discussed the moment when data should be replicated. Since node failures can be either transient or permanent, deciding when to generate the replicas is not trivial. In addition, failure behavior in terms of the rate of permanent and transient failures may vary over time. The authors propose a new technique to deal with these issues, combining advantages from both reactive approaches (in which new redundant fragments are created as soon as failure is detected) and proactive approaches (which create new fragments at a fixed rate depending on the knowledge of failure behavior). The proposed solution is based on an ongoing estimation of the failure behavior that is obtained using a model that consists of a network of queues; hence the solution combines adaptiveness of reactive systems with smooth bandwidth usage of proactive systems.

The specific problems of replication in P2P environments are addressed in (Brinkmann et al., 2008). Starting from the observation that in small or mid-sized environments with heterogeneous peers, the Consistent Hashing used by many P2P systems as underlying DHT does not use efficiently the available storage, the authors propose a peer-replication strategy, which is able to ensure an optimal capacity efficiency, even in case of data replication. The strategy can retrieve all copies inside the view of a client by introducing a small number of additional communication rounds. The trade-off between the proposed strategy and Consistent Hashing is the number of required communication rounds vs. the quality of the data distribution. The authors show that a very small number of additional communication rounds enables us a significant increase of the capacity efficiency.

DATA MANAGEMENT

With the increasing number of resource intensive experiments accessing or computing on vast amounts of data, the effective data management problem is becoming increasingly important. Although this problem has been addressed in the existing literature at different levels, there is still little consensus over how to balance the ease-of-use and efficiency. Recent advances in the high performance parallel file systems have been presented in the first section of this chapter. As denoted by (Choudhary et al., 1999) however, there still exist important obstacles to preventing the file systems from becoming a real solution to the high-level data management problem in large scale distributed environments. Considering the huge volumes of data that are handled, data management must offer a high degree of control, to ensure that data is placed correctly for processing and safe keeping; but also offer a view at a sufficiently high level to ensure that data placement can be managed efficaciously.

We presented in the previous sections how data storage, retrieval and replication are handled in large distributed environments, focusing on grids and other computing and data intensive environments. We examine in more detail in this section data management in P2P environments and present the latest advances in workflow data management, a topic of increasing interest in recent years.

P2P Data Management

Continuous research is underway to meet the challenges imposed by P2P systems concerning high level data sharing services, efficiency and security. (Daswani et al., 2003) summarized the main requirements as follows:

- **Autonomy** – is an inherent P2P requirement which translates in the data management context in the possibility of peers to control the data they store and which other peers can store its data, e.g. some other trusted peers.
- **Query expressiveness** - the query language should allow the user to describe the desired data at the appropriate level of detail; examples of simple queries are the key look-ups.
- **Efficiency** – the management system should make the efficient use of the P2P system resources (bandwidth, computing power, storage) as they are usually limited; this translates in lower cost and higher throughput of queries
- **Quality of service** - refers to the user-perceived efficiency of the system, e.g. completeness of query results, data consistency, data availability, query responses time, etc.
- **Fault-tolerance** - efficiency and quality of services should be provided despite the transient nature of peers and their dynamic nature; solution is to rely on data replication.
- **Security** – already hard to achieve in P2P systems due to the lack trusted servers, in data management it also concerns access control, e.g. enforcing intellectual property rights on data contents.

(Valduriez et al., 2003) studied how the above requirements can be achieved depending on the different P2P architectures. To this end, the authors identified three main architectural categories within they conducted their study. In *unstructured systems* each peer can directly communicate with its neighbors. This approach means high autonomy, as each peer only needs to know its neighbors, and simple data search, by flooding the network with queries, each peer processing and redirecting the incoming queries to its neighbors. However, the incompleteness of the results can be high since some peers containing relevant data or their neighbors may not be reached because they are either off-line. Still, since all peers are equal and able to replicate data, fault-tolerance is very high.

Structured systems are based on distributed hash tables (DHT) which provide a hash table interface with put(key, value) and get(key) primitives, where key is typically a file name and each peer is responsible for storing the values (file contents) corresponding to a certain range of keys. There is an additional overlay routing scheme that delivers requests for a given key to the peer responsible for that key, and which causes inherent overhead. Clearly, autonomy is lower that in structured cases since peers are responsible for storing the values corresponding to their range of keys.

Super-peer systems are hybrids between previous categories and client-server systems. While in previous systems all peers are equal, in this case, some peers, the super-peers, act as dedicated servers for some other peers and can perform complex functions such as indexing, query processing, access control, monitoring and metadata management. Obviously, in order to eliminate the single points of failures super-peers should be replicated or organized in a P2P fashion and communicate with one another in sophisticated ways. Thus, global information is always partitioned or replicated across all super-peers. The main advantage of super-peer is efficiency and quality of service. A requesting peer simply sends the request, which can be expressed in a high-level language, to its responsible super-peer(s) which can then find the relevant peers either directly through its index or indirectly using its neighboring super-peers. Access control can also be better enforced since directory and security information can be maintained at the super-peers. However, autonomy is restricted since peers cannot log in freely to any super-peer.

A popular example of such super-peer system is Tribler (Pouwelse et al., 2007), a social-based P2P file-sharing system implemented as a set of extensions to BitTorrent. The authors carried out some performance tests, which showed that the super-peer system enables fast data discovery at a low additional overhead brought by the Tribler protocol on top of BitTorrent, and significant improvement in data transfers (downloads).

Workflow Data Management

Scientific applications benefit from the new emerging workflow technologies to achieve their performance requirements. Nevertheless, many challenges remain in the area of workflow data management. (Deelman et al., 2008) makes a complex analysis of these issues focusing on the specific data related problems in each phase of the workflow lifecycle: the workflow generation phase where the analysis is defined, the workflow planning phase where resources needed for execution are selected, the workflow execution part, where the actual computations take place, and the result, metadata, and provenance storing phase.

During workflow creation, the input data and workflow components need to be discovered. Solutions to this challenge rely on maintaining metadata catalogs to store attributes that describe the contents of data sets and provenance catalogs store information about computations and workflows. The workflow engines query these catalogs in order to resolve the appropriate mappings or to optimize service binding decisions. Metadata catalogs are usually deployed by the application communities to store information with a specific semantic relevant to the targeted application.

During workflow mapping and execution, data need to be staged-in and staged-out of the computational resources. At this stage, specific workflow characteristics of data access need to be taken into account by the data placement service. Serious efforts are underway to optimize workflow engine behavior. (Chervenak et al., 2007) observes that data items are usually accessed in related collections rather than individually, hence it makes sense for the placement service to place them together in a collection on a storage system to enhance workflow execution. In addition, another important consideration for the workflow engine is the frequency pattern of the data access: data is usually accessed in bursts, with many data placement operations taking place during the stage in (or stage out) phase of execution. (Singh et al., 2007) examines the issue of minimizing the amount of storage space that a workflow requires for execution, also called the workflow data footprint, To do this, the authors add a cleanup job for a data file when that file is no longer required by other tasks in the workflow or when it has already been transferred to permanent storage. The purpose of the cleanup job is to delete the data file from a specified computational resource to make room for the subsequent computations. Since a data file can be potentially replicated on multiple resources (in case the compute tasks are mapped to multiple resources) the decisions to add cleanup jobs are made on a per resource basis and take into account dependencies. The algorithm is applied after the executable workflow has been created but before the workflow is executed.

Finally, as data are produced, they need to be archived with enough metadata and provenance information so that they can be interpreted, eventually reused and shared among collaborators. We examine in the following the data management capabilities of some important workflow engines.

Pegasus (Deelman et al., 2005) is a scientific workflow system for end-to-end execution of application workflows, which uses abstract to concrete mapping of workflows expressed in Virtual Data Specification - VDS (Zhao et al., 2006). The main purpose of this specification is to enable discovery and sharing of datasets among users. As a part of the mapping, Pegasus automatically manages data generated during workflow execution by staging them out to user-specified locations, by registering them in data registries, and by capturing their provenance information. Moreover, (Chervenak et al., 2007) combined the functionality of the Data Replication Service (DRS) for data placement with that of the Pegasus system for workflow management. The goal was to demonstrate that data-intensive workflows may execute faster with such asynchronous data placement than with on-demand staging of data by the workflow management system. In this scenario, the data placement is based on a priori knowledge of the files to be used during workflow execution. Consequently, requests are sent to DRS to move these files to a storage system associated with the cluster where workflow execution will take place. This data movement takes place asynchronously with respect to the execution of the workflow. Datasets found at the launch of the Pegasus using queries to replica catalogs. If the data items are available on the storage system associated with the computational cluster where the workflow will run, then Pegasus accesses the data sets via symbolic links to that storage system. Thus, Pegasus avoids explicitly staging the data onto computational resources at run time. However, a drawback is that the workflow engine is centralized and hence does not scale.

Stork (Kosar et al., 2004) introduces a specialized scheduler for data placement activities. The authors consider that data placement jobs should be treated differently from computational jobs, since they may have different semantics and different characteristics. Starting from this consideration, Stork has optimized support for data management and access. Thus, it can control the number of concurrent requests coming to any storage system it has access to, and makes sure that neither that storage system nor the network link to that storage system get overloaded. It can also perform space allocation and de-allocations to make sure that the required storage space is available on the corresponding storage system.

Inform (Dasgupta et al., 2007) aims at developing new capabilities for co-ordinated co-scheduling of job executions and data movement. The solution is based on the DECO algorithm (Agarwal et al., 2006), which provides a holistic approach for addressing the problem of optimal co-scheduling job executions and data transfers in grids. The authors enhance this algorithm with support for inter-job dependencies.

In summary, we observe that most scientific workflow engines lack specific support for data handling or provide basic functionalities not always adapted to the high performance computing applications' requirements. Each of these projects addresses many interesting aspects of grid workflow systems. However, because of their inherent non-standardized methodologies, collaboration for leveraging their respective data management strengths or for alleviating problems becomes very difficult.

CONCLUSION

In this chapter we presented the particular challenges of data handling in large scale distributed environments. We discussed solutions for storage, management, retrieval, transfer and replication in various distributed systems ranging from expensive high performance super storage to commodity hardware. We analyzed their most recent or representative implementations. We were further interested by the specific mappings between requirements and solutions in different environments like Grids, P2P systems or workflows.

We argue that new storage architectures and data management solutions will accelerate progress on petascale data intensive computing

by enabling the integration of currently disjoint approaches, encouraging standardization and also revealing technology gaps that require further research and development.

REFERENCES

Agarwal, V., Dasgupta, G., Dasgupta, K., Purohit, A., & Viswanathan, B. (2006). Deco: Data replication and execution co-scheduling for utility grids. *Proceedings of ICSOC*.

Allcock, B., Bester, J., Bresnahan, J., Chervenak, A. L., Foster, I., & Kesselman, C. (2002). Data management and transfer in high-performance computational grid environments. *Parallel Computing, 28*(5), 749–771. doi:10.1016/S0167-8191(02)00094-7

Allcock, W. (2003 April). *GridFTP: Protocol Extensions to FTP for the Grid*. Argonne National Laboratory.

Allcock, W., Bresnahan, J., Kettimuthu, R., & Link, M. (2005). The Globus Striped GridFTP Framework and Server. In *Proceedings of the 2005 ACM/IEEE Conference on Supercomputing (November 12 - 18, 2005). Conference on High Performance Networking and Computing*. Washington, DC: IEEE Computer Society.

Badino, P., Barring, O., Baud, J.-P., Donno, F., Perelmutov, T., Petravick, D., et al. (2008 May). *The Storage Resource Manager Interface Specification Version 2.2*. Retrieved April 14, 2009, from http://sdm.lbl.gov/srm-wg/doc/SRM.v2.2.html

Bakken J., Berman, E., Huang, C.H., Moibenko, A., Petravick, D., Rechenmacher, R., & Ruthmansdorfer, K. (2008 March). *Enstore Technical Design Document, Joint Projects Document JP0026*.

Balakrishnan, H., Kaashoek, M. F., Karger, D., Morris, R., & Stoica, I. (2003). Looking up data in P2P systems. *Communications of the ACM, 46*(2), 43–48. doi:10.1145/606272.606299

Blake, C., & Rodrigues, R. (2003). High availability, scalable storage, dynamic peer networks: pick two. In *HotOS'03: Proc. of the 9th Workshop on Hot Topics in Operating Systems*.

Bresnahan, J., Link, M., Khanna, G., Imani, Z., Kettimuthu, R., & Foster, I. (2007). Globus GridFTP:what's new in 2007. In *Proceedings of the First international Conference on Networks For Grid Applications (Lyon, France, October 17 - 19, 2007)*. Brussels, Belgium: ICST (Institute for Computer Sciences Social-Informatics and Telecommunications Engineering).

Brinkmann, A., & Effert, S. (2008). Data replication in p2p environments. In *Proceedings of the Twentieth Annual Symposium on Parallelism in Algorithms and Architectures* (Munich, Germany, June 14 - 16, 2008). New York: ACM.

Castor Website. (n.d.). Retrieved April 14, 2009 from http://castor.web.cern.ch/castor/

Chai, L., Ouyang, X., Noronha, R., & Panda, D. K. (2007). pNFS/PVFS2 over InfiniBand: early experiences. In *Proceedings of the 2nd international Workshop on Petascale Data Storage: Held in Conjunction with Supercomputing '07* (Reno, Nevada, November 11 - 11, 2007). New York: ACM.

Chen, J., Akers, W., Chen, Y., & Watson, W., III. (2002). Java Parallel Secure Stream for Grid Computing. In *Proceedings of the 6th Joint Conference on Information Sciences*.

Chervenak, A., Deelman, E., Livny, M., Su, M., Schuler, R., Bharathi, S., et al. (2007). Data placement for scientific applications in distributed environments. In *Proceedings of the 8th IEEE/ACM international Conference on Grid Computing (September 19 - 21, 2007)*. Washington, DC: IEEE Computer Society.

Chervenak, A., Foster, I., Kesselman, C., Salisbury, C., & Tuecke, S. (2001). The Data Grid: Towards an Architecture for the Distributed Management and Analysis of Large Scientific Datasets. *Journal of Network and Computer Applications*, *23*, 187–200. doi:10.1006/jnca.2000.0110

Chervenak, A., Schuler, R., Kesselman, C., Koranda, S., & Moe, B. (2008). Wide area data replication for scientific collaborations. *Int. J. High Perform. Comput. Netw.*, *5*(3), 124–134. doi:10.1504/IJHPCN.2008.020857

Chervenak, A. L., Palavalli, N., Bharathi, S., Kesselman, C., & Schwartzkopf, R. (2004). Performance and Scalability of a Replica Location Service. In *Proceedings of the 13th IEEE international Symposium on High Performance Distributed Computing* (June 04 - 06, 2004). Washington, DC: IEEE Computer Society.

Choudhary, A., Kandemir, M., Nagesh, H., No, J., Shen, X., Taylor, V., et al. (1999). Data Management for Large-Scale Scientific Computations in High Performance Distributed Systems. In *Proceedings of the 8th IEEE international Symposium on High Performance Distributed Computing* (August 03 - 06, 1999). Washington, DC: IEEE Computer Society.

Chun, B., Dabek, F., Haeberlen, A., Sit, E., Weatherspoon, H., Kaashoek, M. F., et al. (2006). Efficient replica maintenance for distributed storage systems. In *Proceedings of the 3rd Conference on Networked Systems Design & Implementation - Volume 3* (San Jose, CA, May 08 - 10, 2006). Berkeley, CA: USENIX Association.

Chun, B., Maniatis, P., Shenker, S., & Kubiatowicz, J. 2009. Tiered fault tolerance for long-term integrity. In M. Seltzer & R. Wheeler, (Eds.), *Proceedings of the 7th Conference on File and Storage Technologies* (San Francisco, California, February 24 - 27, 2009) (pp. 267-282). Berkeley, CA: USENIX Association.

Cohen, B. (2003 May). Incentives Build Robustness in BitTorrent. *Workshop on Economics of Peer-to-Peer Systems*, Berkeley, CA, USA.

Coulouris, G., Dollimore, J., & Kindberg, T. (2005). *Distributed Systems: Concept and Design* (4th ed.). Reading, MA: Addison Wesley.

Dasgupta, G. B., & Viswanathan, B. (2007). INFORM: integrated flow orchestration and meta-scheduling for managed grid systems. In *Proceedings of the 2007 ACM/IFIP/USENIX international Conference on Middleware Companion* (Newport Beach, California, November 26 - 30, 2007). New York: ACM.

Daswani, N., Garcia-Molina, H., & Yang, B. (2003). Open problems in data-sharing peer-to-peer systems. *Int. Conf. on Database Theory. dCache Website.* (2009). Retrieved April 14, 2009 from http://www.dcache.org

De Camargo, R. Y., Filho, F. C., & Kon, F. (2009). Efficient maintenance of distributed data in highly dynamic opportunistic grids. In *Proceedings of the 2009 ACM Symposium on Applied Computing* (Honolulu, Hawaii) (pp. 1067-1071). New York: ACM.

De Camargo, R. Y., & Kon, F. (2007). Design and Implementation of a Middleware for Data Storage in Opportunistic Grids. In *Proceedings of the Seventh IEEE international Symposium on Cluster Computing and the Grid* (May 14 - 17, 2007) (pp. 23-30). Washington, DC: IEEE Computer Society.

Deelman, E., & Chervenak, A. 2008. Data Management Challenges of Data-Intensive Scientific Workflows. In *Proceedings of the 2008 Eighth IEEE international Symposium on Cluster Computing and the Grid* (May 19 - 22, 2008) (pp. 687-692). Washington, DC: IEEE Computer Society.

Deelman E., Singh, G., Su, M., Blythe, J., Gil, Y., Kesselman, C., Mehta, G., Vahi, K., Berriman, G.B., & Good, J. (2005). A framework for mapping complex scientific workflows onto distributed systems. *Scientific Programming, 13*.

Dholakia, A., Eleftheriou, E., Hu, X., Iliadis, I., Menon, J., & Rao, K. (2008). A new intra-disk redundancy scheme for high-reliability RAID storage systems in the presence of unrecoverable errors. *Trans. Storage, 4*(1), 1–42. doi:10.1145/1353452.1353453

Druschel, P., & Rowstron, A. (2001). *PAST: A large-scale, persistent peer-to-peer storage utility*. HotOS VIII.

Duellmann, D., CERN Storage Update, *HEPiX Fall2008*, Academia Sinica, Taipei, Taiwan

Duminuco, A., Biersack, E., & En-Najjary, T. (2007). Proactive replication in distributed storage systems using machine availability estimation. In *Proceedings of the 2007 ACM CoNEXT Conference* (New York, New York, December 10 - 13, 2007). New York: ACM.

Enstore Website. (n.d.). Retrieved April 14, 2009, from http://www-isd.fnal.gov/enstore/

Ermolinskiy, A., Moon, D., Chun, B., & Shenker, S. (2009). Minuet: rethinking concurrency control in storage area networks. In M. Seltzer & R. Wheeler (Eds.), *Proceedings of the 7th Conference on File and Stroage Technologies* (San Francisco, California, February 24 - 27, 2009) (pp. 311-324). Berkeley, CA: USENIX Association.

Fadden, S. (2008 November). *An Introduction to GPFS Version 3.2.1* [White Paper].

Foster, I. (2005). Globus toolkit version 4: Software for service-oriented systems. In Jin, H., Reed, D. A., & Jiang, W. (Eds.), *NPC, ser. Lecture Notes in Computer Science* (*Vol. 3779*, pp. 2–13). Berlin: Springer.

Foster, I., & Iamnitchi, A. (2003). On Death, Taxes and the Convergence of Peer-to-Peer and Grid Computing. *IPTPS 2003.*

Goldchleger, A., Kon, F., Goldman, A., Finger, M., & Bezerra, G. C. (2004, March). InteGrade: Object-oriented grid middleware leveraging idle computing power of desktop machines. *Concurrency and Computation, 16,* 449–459. doi:10.1002/cpe.824

Gulati, A., & Ahmad, I. (2008). Towards distributed storage resource management using flow control. *SIGOPS Oper. Syst. Rev., 42*(6), 10–16. doi:10.1145/1453775.1453779

HP. (2008 June). *Storage Essentials – Delivering on the promise of Storage Automation.* Retrieved April 14, 2009, from http://www.hp.com/go/storageessentials

HPSS 7.1 High Performance Storage System User Guide, Release 7.1. (2009 February). Retrieved April 14, 2009, from http://www.hpss-collaboration.org/hpss/users/docs/AdobePDF/7.1/users_guide.pdf

IBM. (2009). *Release notes - Tivoli Storage Manager Server Version 6.1.* Retrieved April 14, 2009, from http://publib.boulder.ibm.com/infocenter/tsminfo/v6/

Khanna, G., Catalyurek, U., Kurc, T., Kettimuthu, R., Sadayappan, P., Foster, I., & Saltz, J. (2008). Using overlays for efficient data transfer over shared wide-area networks. In *Proceedings of the 2008 ACM/IEEE Conference on Supercomputing* (Austin, Texas, November 15 - 21, 2008) (pp. 1-12). Piscataway, NJ: IEEE Press.

Khanna, G., Catalyurek, U., Kurc, T., Kettimuthu, R., Sadayappan, P., & Saltz, J. (2008 April). A Dynamic Scheduling Approach for Coordinated Wide-Area Data Transfers using GridFTP. In *Proceedings of the 22nd IEEE International Parallel and Distributed Processing Symposium* (IPDPS 2008).

Kosar, T., & Livny, M. (2004). Stork: Making data placement a first class citizen in the grid. *Proc. of the 24th ICDCS.*

Kourtellis, N., Prieto, L., Iamnitchi, A., Zarrate, G., & Fraser, D. (2008). Data transfers in the grid: workload analysis of globus GridFTP. In *Proceedings of the 2008 international Workshop on Data-Aware Distributed Computing* (Boston, MA, USA, June 24 - 24, 2008) (pp. 29-38). New York: ACM.

Landers, M., Zhang, H., & Tan, K.-L. (2004). Peerstore: Better performance by relaxing in peer-to-peer backup. In *P2P '04: Proc. of the 4th Int. Conf. on Peer-to-Peer Computing* (pp. 72–79). Washington, DC: IEEE Computer Society.

Madduri, R. (2006). *Reliable File Transfer Service (RFT). GlobusWorld, 2006.* Argonne National Laboratory, University of Chicago.

Malluhi, Q., & Zeyad, A. (2002). DTViewer: A High Performance Distributed Terrain Image Viewer with Reliable Data Delivery. In *Proceedings of the 2nd International Workshop on Intelligent Multimedia Computing and Networking (IMMCN 2002).*

Millar, P. (2009 February). dCache. In *3rd Terena TF – Storage Meeting,* Dublin.

OGF SRM WG. (n.d.). Retrieved April 14, 2009, from http://sdm.lbl.gov/srm-wg/

Oguchi, M. (2009). Research works on cluster computing and storage area network. In *Proceedings of the 3rd international Conference on Ubiquitous information Management and Communication* (Suwon, Korea, January 15 - 16, 2009) (pp. 366-375). New York: ACM.

Oleynik, G. (2005). *Fermilab Mass Storage System.* Retrieved April 14, 2009, from http://storage-conference.org/2005/presentations/oleynik.ppt

Paisley, J., & Sventek, J. (2006). Real-time detection of grid bulk transfer traffic. In *The Tenth IEEE/IFIP Network Operations and Management Symposium 2006* (NOMS 2006), April 2006, Vancouver, British Columbia, Canada.

Pariseau, B. (2008 August). *What is Parallel NFS and will it assist storage virtualisation?* Retrieved April 14, 2009, from http://searchstorage.techtarget.com.au/articles/26445-What-is-Parallel-NFS-and-will-it-assist-storage-virtualisation-Ponce, S. (2009). CASTOR developments: status and plans. *Castor External Operation Meeting* (February 18-19, 2009).

Pouwelse, J., Garbacki, P., Wang, J., Bakker, A., Yang, J., & Iosup, A. (2007). Tribler: A social-based peer-to-peer system. *Concurrency and Computation, 19*, 1–11.

Rahman, R. M., Barker, K., & Alhajj, R. (2007). Study of Different Replica Placement and Maintenance Strategies in Data Grid. In *Proceedings of the Seventh IEEE international Symposium on Cluster Computing and the Grid* (May 14 - 17, 2007) (pp. 171-178). Washington, DC: IEEE Computer Society.

Rahman, R. M., Barker, K., & Alhajj, R. (2009). Performance evaluation of different replica placement algorithms. *Int. J. Grid Util. Comput., 1*(2), 121–133. doi:10.1504/IJGUC.2009.022028

Ramabhadran, S., & Pasquale, J. (2008). Durability of replicated distributed storage systems. In *Proceedings of the 2008 ACM SIGMETRICS international Conference on Measurement and Modeling of Computer Systems* (Annapolis, MD, USA, June 02 - 06, 2008) (pp. 447-448). New York: ACM.

Rhea, S., Eaton, P., Geels, D., Weatherspoon, H., Zhao, B., & Kubiatowicz, J. (2003, March). Pond: the OceanStore Prototype. In *Proceedings of the 2nd USENIX Conference on File and Storage Technologies* (FAST '03).

Rowstron, A., & Druschel, P. (2001). *Pastry: Scalable, Distributed Object Location And Routing For Large-Scale Peer-To-Peer Systems*. IFIP/ACM Middleware.

Schmuck, F., & Haskin, R. (2002). GPFS: A Shared-Disk File System for Large Computing Clusters. In *Proceedings of the Conference on File and Storage Technologies (FAST'02)*, 28–30 January 2002, Monterey, CA (pp. 231–244).

Shepler, S., Eisler, M., & Noveck, D. (2008 December). *NFS Version 4 Minor Version 1*. Retrieved April 14, 2009, from http://www.ietf.org/internet-drafts/draft-ietf-nfsv4-minorversion1-29.txt

Shoshani A., Sim, A., & Gu, J. (2002). Storage resource managers: Middleware components for grid storage. *MSS 2002*.

Singh, G., Vahi, K., Ramakrishnan, A., Mehta, G., Deelman, E., & Zhao, H. (2007). Optimizing workflow data footprint. *Sci. Program., 15*(4), 249–268.

Soyez, O., Randriamaro, C., Utard, G., & Wlazinski, F. (2007). Dynamic Distribution for Data Storage in a P2P Network. *GPC, 2007*, 555–566.

Stewart, G. A., Cameron, D., Cowan, G. A., & McCance, G. (2007). Storage and data management in EGEE. In L. Brankovic, P. Coddington, J. F. Roddick, C. Steketee, J. R. Warren, & A. Wendelborn (Eds.), *Proceedings of the Fifth Australasian Symposium on ACSW Frontiers - Volume 68* (Ballarat, Australia, January 30 - February 02, 2007). Darlinghurst, Australia: Australian Computer Society.

Stockinger, H. (2003). Grid data management in action: experience in running and supporting data management services in the EU DataGrid Project. In *Computing in High Energy Physics* (CHEP 2003), La Jolla, California, March 24-28, 2003.

Valduriez, P., & Pacitti, E. (2005). Data Management in Large-scale P2P Systems. In *High Performance Computing for Computational Science* (LNCS 3402). Berlin/ Heidelberg: Springer.

Website, F. D. T. (n.d.). Retrieved April 14, 2009, from http://monalisa.cern.ch/FDT/

Wheeler, T. (2008 November). *Exploring Scalable Data Processing with Apache Hadoop*. Retrieved April 14, 2009, from http://jnb.ociweb.com/jnb/jnbNov2008.html

Xin, Q., Schwarz, T. J. E., & Mille, E. L. (2004). Availability in Global Peer-To-Peer Storage. In *Proc. WDAS 2004*.

Yang, W. (2008 November). Introduction to the XrootdFS. *OSG Site Administrator's Workshop*.

Ye, W., & Gu, N. (2006). An Approach for Robust Distributed Data Retrieval in Data Intensive Grid Environments. In *1st International Symposium on Pervasive Computing and Applications*, 3-5 Aug. 2006, Urumqi (pp. 194-199).

Zhao, Y., Wilde, M., Foster, I., Voeckler, J., Dobson, J., Gilbert, E., Jordan, T., & Quigg, E. (2006). Virtual data grid middleware services for data-intensive science: Research articles. *Concurr. Comput.: Pract. Exper., 18*.

Chapter 7
Monitoring and Controlling Large Scale Systems

INTRODUCTION

The architectural shift presented in the previous chapters towards high performance computers assembled from large numbers of commodity resources raises numerous design issues and assumptions pertaining to traceability, fault tolerance and scalability. Hence, one of the key challenges faced by high performance distributed systems is scalable monitoring of system state. The aim of this chapter is to realize a survey study of existing work and trends in distributed systems monitoring by introducing the involved concepts and requirements, techniques, models and related standardization activities.

Monitoring can be defined as the process of dynamic collection, interpretation and presentation of information concerning the characteristics and status of resources of interest. It is needed for various purposes such as debugging, testing, program visualization and animation. It may also be used for general management activities, which have a more permanent and continuous nature (performance management, configuration management, fault man-

agement, security management, etc.). In this case the behavior of the system is observed and monitoring information is gathered. This information is used to make management decisions and perform the appropriate control actions on the system. Unlike monitoring which is generally a passive process, control actively changes the behavior of the managed system and it has to be considered and modeled separately. Monitoring proves to be an essential process to observe and improve the reliability and the performance of large-scale distributed systems.

There are a number of fundamental issues related to monitoring of distributed systems. In a distributed environment a large number of events are generated by the system components during its execution or interaction with external objects (e.g. users or processes). Monitoring such events is necessary for observing the run-time behavior of large scale distributed systems and providing status information required for debugging, tuning and managing such applications (Al-Shaer et al., 1997). However, error/failure events (due to software bugs or improper implementation) or events that convey the application status are more likely to appear and can be dispersed over many different

DOI: 10.4018/978-1-61520-703-9.ch007

locations and application entities. This makes the tasks of testing, debugging, monitoring and the management decisions process (e.g. fault recovery or performance tuning procedures) much harder to achieve in distributed environments. Furthermore, the correlated monitored events, either simple (local) or complex (global) events, are generated concurrently and could be distributed in various locations in the applications environment, which complicates the management decisions process and thereby makes monitoring systems an intricate task. For example, application errors related to the communication operations obviously involve observing the sender(s) and the receivers(s). Similarly, the knowledge of application performance is also distributed in the application environment. For instance, calculating the average load of the system must involve all participant machines. As monitoring data may encounter network latency, delays in transferring it from the place of production to the place of storage are inherent which means it could be out of date. Hence, it proves difficult to obtain a global, consistent view of a distributed system. Clock skewing problems and variable delays in reporting events may result in recording events in the incorrect order. Another problem is that the large volume of event traffic which flows in the system may swamp the monitoring process, therefore the monitoring systems should scale gracefully with the number of nodes of the distributed system. Moreover, as the monitoring system shares the resources with the observed system, intrusiveness becomes a key issue which may alter the accuracy of the monitoring process.

In order to overcome these problems, one should design a monitoring system with respect to a set of requirements which we detail in the next section. We further discuss in this chapter the existing architectural models and the implemented solutions.

MONITORING REQUIREMENTS

Due to the distributed nature and the large number of participants or application entities, reliability and performance of specific applications become critical issues. The wide geographical distribution and large interaction of such applications may sometimes increase the possibility of failures/ errors or performance bottlenecks. Unlike centralized or isolated applications, large scale systems are likely to deal with different environments that may be dynamically changing. For these reasons, observing the run-time behavior is essential to discover reliability and performance problems and initiate the proper reactions to alleviate these problems. These actions are performed either at run-time such as fault recovery and applications steering or at development-time such as fixing bugs and design enhancements. The system developers or managers (could be human or software components) require feedback information on the system behavior for testing and debugging purposes or for fault recovery and performance tuning procedures. Monitoring distributed systems is an effective means to observe applications at run-time and provide this feedback information to the system developers and system managers in order to improve reliability, robustness and performance of large scale systems.

In general, monitoring is essential to improve the quality of any process (e.g. management process and production control process). Similarly, in software systems, the process of developing, maintaining and operating distributed applications can be complex. An efficient monitoring of these applications is an essential mechanism to produce good quality applications (e.g. reliable, robust, secure, high-performance). The necessity of monitoring significantly increases when using large-scale distributed systems since they are more susceptible to many issues such as reliability and performance and also more difficult to debug and steer. We can summarize the motivation for monitoring complex systems as follows.

Debugging and Testing. Unlike centralized or isolated systems, bugs or incorrect behavior in LSD systems may be related to multiple components distributed across the application environment. In addition, related events are generated simultaneously. In this environment, it would be difficult or may be infeasible for the system developers to track the state of the system and collect information on the runt-time functional behavior of the system for debugging and testing purposes.

Performance Tuning. The environment of distributed systems (i.e. local/wide area networks or Internet) changes dynamically due to the variable load on the system and the network. For example, a congested link at this moment may not be congested after sometime. Systems need to adapt to the changes in the network or system status in order to maintain a good performance during its execution. This may support improving or maintaining the quality of the services (e.g. fast response) provided by distributed applications and thereby meet the users/customers satisfaction. The monitoring system is an effective means for performance tuning and application steering. The management decisions of the monitoring applications (e.g. tuning) may be based on set of correlated events which are concurrent and distributed in the environment. Therefore, the reactive control monitoring application of the system should be able to request the monitoring of specific local or global events that could effect the performance of the application and adjust the application control parameters to adapt to the new conditions. For example, it may be desirable to dynamically adjust the sending rate in multicast group to the average of the receiver rates (instead of going with the slowest receiver as most reliable multicast protocol do). The reactive control module may get a continues feedback on this global event or it may get informed only when the average of the receivers rate goes beyond a threshold values. In either case, the monitoring system is essential for providing such information at run-time, which can be used (by reactive control components, for example) subsequently for control decisions.

Fault Recovery. Faults occur during the execution of large scale systems because of problems in the environment (e.g. wrong system or network configuration), software bugs or improper user operations (Kandaswamy et al., 2008). It is important for the application developers and the system managers to know the source of any failure in order to improve the robustness and the reliability of the application. The proposed monitoring architecture can be used effectively to classify and report all failures during the application execution so recovery procedure can be manually initiated. Furthermore, the proposed monitoring architecture supports an automatic fault recovery service where corresponding recovery procedures are initiated automatically if a failure detected. Therefore, the monitoring architecture provides a centralized control of application failures that are distributed in the environment.

Security. The monitoring system can be used to detect and report security violation events such as repeated illegal login or attempt to unauthorized file access. The monitoring mechanisms identify these events based on specific pattern or set of values revealed by the application itself.

Correctness Checking. The monitoring architecture can be used as a verification technique to ensure the consistency with a formal specification – enabling interaction with various scientific workflow specification languages (Zhou et al., 2007). The feedback information on the run-time behavior supplied by the monitoring is analyzed by software verification tools to discover any inconsistency.

Performance Evaluation. The monitoring technique can also be used to evaluate the applications performance at run-time. The monitoring mechanism is used to extract data from the application during its execution which is later analyzed to assess system performance (Hui, 2007). Usually, such monitoring techniques require some hardware support to assure accuracy and efficiency. For portability and flexibility purposes, our proposed architecture does not use any special hardware for event detection or filtering techniques. However, if this is desired, the monitoring architecture can be easily extended to support this applications.

Resource Utilization – Accounting. Essential for recording resource (hardware, software, network etc.) usage at all levels. In a Grid environment, the role of a usage accounting system is to collect information regarding the amounts of resources consumed by the users, which represent virtual organizations. Besides providing statistical information, an accounting system can also be the base for managing Grid resources upon an economic model (Ainsworth, 2005).

When building distributed systems it is often observed unexpectedly low performance, the reasons for which are usually not obvious. The bottlenecks can be in any of the following components: the applications, the operating systems, the disks or network adapters, the network switches and routers, etc. The solution should be highly instrumented monitoring systems with precision timing information and analysis tools.

Traditionally, high performance computing has focused on scalability as the primary design challenge. The architectural shift towards increasingly distributed and loosely coupled systems, however, has raised an additional set of challenges. These new challenges arise as a result of several factors: increased physical distribution, long running distributed services, and scaling and evolution of systems over time. Increased physical distribution implies multiple, independently failing and unreliable components. This, in turn, requires designing applications whose management overheads scale slowly with the number of nodes. Long running distributed services imply the need to be highly available to clients of the service. This, in turn requires applications to be robust to a variety of different types of failures. Finally, the scaling and evolution of systems over time implies that hardware and software will change. This, in turn, requires addressing issues

of extensibility and portability. Hence, there are a number of fundamental challenges associated with monitoring of distributed systems, which we review in brief:

- No single point of observation as well as the need for no single point of failure
- Diversity of hardware and software systems, different policies and decision making mechanisms as a distributed monitoring infrastructure can be extended outside the border of a single organization and span multiple administrative domains across the Internet, as it is often the case of large scale collaborations
- Scalability - large number of event producers and consumers which need to be handled: the high volume of events which is generated continuously in real-time may easily swamp the monitoring system.
- Correlated events may be concurrent and distributed
- Delays in transferring information from the place it is generated to the place it is used means that it may be out of date. This means it is very difficult to obtain a global, consistent view of all components in a distributed system. Variable delays in reporting events may result in recording events as having occurred in the incorrect order and so some form of clock synchronization is necessary to provide a means of determining causal ordering. However, this is not considered a major issue in some monitoring applications such as debugging and and performance tuning because they are not time-sensitive application such as performance evaluation or instantaneous reactive control mechanism which require monitoring interaction in order of ms (milliseconds).
- Updates are frequent. Unlike the more static forms of "metadata," dynamic performance information is typically updated

144

more frequently than it is read. Since most existent information-base technologies are optimized for query and not for update, they are potentially unsuitable for dynamic information storage.

- Performance information is often stochastic. It is frequently impossible to characterize the performance of a resource or an application component by using a single value. Therefore, dynamic performance information may carry quality-of-information metrics quantifying its accuracy, distribution, lifetime, and so forth, which may need to be calculated from the raw data.
- Monitoring Intrusiveness. The monitoring system may itself compete for system resources (i.e. computation or network resources) with the monitored objects.

In order to overcome these high challenges a distributed controlling and monitoring system must meet some important requirements:

- **Scalability**. The system should be able to analyze and process vast amounts of data. It should scale gracefully with the number of nodes in the system. Clusters today, for example, commonly consist of hundreds or even thousands of nodes. Grid computing efforts will eventually push these numbers out even further. This implies that a high-performance filtering mechanisms is required to reduce the event traffic and distributing the monitoring operations.
- **Accuracy**. The system should provide real-time and history, correct information, up to date offering global views of how large systems perform.
- **Integration**. It should facilitate interaction with other grid technologies and middleware (security infrastructure, resource brokers, schedulers, etc.)
- **Robustness**. The system should be robust to node and network failures of various

types. As systems scale in the number of nodes, failures become both inevitable and commonplace. The system should localize such failures so that the system continues to operate and delivers useful service in the presence of failures.

- **Extensibility**. The system should be extensible in the types of data that are monitored and the nature in which such data is collected. It is impossible to know a priori everything that ever might want to be monitored. The system should allow new data to be collected and monitored in a convenient fashion.
- **Manageability**. The system should incur management overheads that scale slowly with the number of nodes. For example, managing the system should not require a linear increase in system administrator time as the number of nodes in the system increases. Manual configuration should also be avoided as much as possible.
- **Standardization**. Data used by the system should employ standard representations.
- **Portability**. The system should be portable to a variety of operating systems and CPU architectures.
- **Overhead.** The system should incur low per-node overheads for all scarce computational resources including CPU, memory, I/O, and network bandwidth. For high performance systems, this is particularly important since applications often have enormous resource demands. The monitoring system should be highly re-configurable to handle dynamic consumer requests (runtime add, delete and modify) with minimal performance overhead.

There are currently several classes of distributed systems and levels where monitoring systems are being used: Clusters – with specific approach of local administrators, and Grids – with a specific Virtual Organization monitoring approach.

Each class of systems presents a different set of constraints and requires making different design decisions and trade-offs in addressing the key design challenges. The constraints revolve primarily around how these systems are physically organized and distributed and what types of resources are scarce and/or expensive to use.

- **Clusters**: Clusters are characterized by a set of nodes that communicate over a high bandwidth, low latency interconnect such as Gigabit Ethernet. In these systems, nodes are frequently homogeneous in both hardware and operating system, the network rarely partitions, and, almost universally, the system is managed by a single administrative entity.
- **Grids**: Grids can be characterized as a set of heterogeneous systems federated over a wide-area network. In contrast to the general Internet, such systems are usually interconnected using special high speed, wide-area networks (e.g. Abilene, Gloriad, USLHCNet networks) in order to get the bandwidth required for their applications. These systems also frequently involve distributed management by multiple administrative entities, such as Virtual Organizations. The monitoring needs are sensitively different, with an accent on accounting resources, global usage statistics, security issues and economic sustainability.

ARCHITECTURAL MODELS FOR MONITORING SYSTEMS

Before we describe the architectural models in terms of their functions and implementations, we shall introduce some important distinctions between different types of monitoring in order to understand how they map to these models. A first approach is the status monitoring which examines the behaviour of the targeted system in terms of its status and a set of events – status changes. Depending on the observed objects we distinguish *system state* and *application state monitoring*: while the first is interested in parameters which usually define the machine behavior (ex: load, storage, memory), the latter examines parameters related to the running applications (ex: running status, errors, consumed resources). (Mansouri, et al. 1993) further identifies other types of monitoring: *time-driven monitoring* is based on acquiring periodic status information providing instantaneous views of how the targeted systems perform. *Event-driven monitoring* provides a dynamic view of system activity as only information about the changes in the system are collected (events of interest). We continue by examining the architectural models which suit these approaches and meet the requirements and constraints presented in the previous section.

Monitoring large scale distributed systems typically includes four stages (Mansouri, et al. 1993): (i) generation of events, that is, sensors enquiring entities and encoding the measurements according to a given schema; (ii) processing of generated events is application-specific and may take place during any stage of the monitoring process, typical examples include filtering according to some predefined criteria, or summarizing a group of events (i.e., computing the average); (iii) distribution refers to the transmission of the events from the source to any interested parties; (iv) finally, presentation typically involves some further processing so that the overwhelming number of received events will be provided in a series of abstractions in order to enable an end-user to draw conclusions about the operation of the monitored system. A presentation, typically provided by a GUI application making use of visualization techniques, may either use a real-time stream of events or a recorded trace usually retrieved from an archive. However, in the context of grids, we generalize the last stage as consumption since the users of the monitoring information are not necessarily humans and therefore visualization may not be involved.

Several architectural models for monitoring systems were developed over the last years, ranging from centralized client-server solutions to decentralized client-server or fully decentralized solutions. Centralization in this context reffers to the entities fulfilling the stages previosuly described which may or may not be centralized. While most architectural models use several data producers, some have only one data collector / presenter and hence a centralized component based on the client-server paradigm (ex: Hawkeye, presented in this Chapter). However, in globally distributed environments where system and network failures are the rule rather than the exception, centralized control of information proves to be a weakness. The monitoring system should exhibit its minimalist behavior for a maximum possible subset of the targeted entities even in the precense of the failures of certain information access points. Hence the dependability of the monitoring system can only be achieved if the data providers and controllers are themselves distributed, and geographically reside as close to the observed systems as possible. Moreover, the monitoring should be performed in as decentralized fashion as possible under the constraints of the underlying resources' architecture. We present three architectural models used by current monitoring systems supporting both centralized and decentralized implementations: the de facto standard as proposed by the Open Grid Forum; the relational model further developed starting from this standard; the functional model which is widely used.

GGF Grid Monitoring Architecture

In this section, we provide a brief overview of the Grid Monitoring Architecture (GMA) (Aydt et al., 2001) put together by the Global Grid Forum to encourage implementations (i.e., it is not a

standard) and further applications use. The main components of GMA are as follows:

- A producer is a process implementing at least one producer Application Programming Interface (API) for providing events.
- A consumer is any process that receives events by using an implementation of at least one consumer API.
- A registry is a lookup service that allows producers to publish the event types they generate, and consumers to find out the events they are interested in. Additionally, a registry holds the details required for establishing communication with registered parties (e.g., address, supported protocol bindings, security requirements). Even for systems with no notion of events, registries can be useful for producers and consumers discovering each other.

After discovering each other through the registry, producers and consumers communicate directly (i.e., not through the registry). GMA defines three types of interactions between producers and consumers. Publish/subscribe refers to a three-phase interaction consisting of a subscription for a specific event type, a stream of events from a producer to a consumer, and a termination of the subscription. Both the establishment and the termination of a subscription can be initiated by any of the two parties. A query/response is an one-off interaction initiated by a consumer and followed by a single producer response containing one or more events. Finally, a notification can be sent by a producer to a consumer without any further interactions.

In addition to the three core components, the GMA defines a republisher (referred as compound component or intermediary) and a schema repository:

- A republisher is any single component implementing both producer and consumer interfaces for reasons such as filtering, aggregating, summarizing, broadcasting, and caching.

- A schema repository holds the event schema, that is, the collection of defined event types. If a system is to support an extensible event schema, such a repository must have an interface for dynamic and controlled addition, modification and removal of any custom event types.

Republishers and the schema repository are considered as optional components, though one can easily see that they are essential parts of any sophisticated monitoring framework. The schema repository may be part of the registry, but in any case these two components must be replicated and distributed to allow for distribution of load and robustness.

The GMA, being an architecture, does not define implementation details such as employed data model, event schema, protocol bindings, registry engine and so on. Probably the most important feature of the GMA is the separation of the discovery and retrieval operations (i.e., discover from the registry and retrieve from producers or republishers). Because GMA's components are fairly general, we correlate its main components to the phases of the monitoring process. A sensor must generate events (i.e., the first phase of monitoring), may process them and may make them available to local consumers only (e.g., through a local file); a producer may implement its own sensors, may process events (generated by built-in or external sensors) and must support their distribution to remote consumers, hence the producer interface; a republisher must apply some type of processing to collected events and make them available to other consumers; a hierarchy of republishers consists of one or more republishers; finally, a consumer may apply some processing before presenting the results to the end-user or application.

GMA was rather defined to provide a minimal specification than a standard. Hence, there is a natural concern for implementation issues related to this specification that are critical for proper functioning of a performance monitoring system developed based on this architecture. Some important characteristics that need to be followed and which relate GMA to the requirements presented in the previous section are discussed in (Tierney, 2002). We observe several strategies that are recommended, all focused on fault tolerance, scalability and security. In case of monitoring servers failure, they should be able to automatically restart from check-pointed internal data, directory service failures can be avoided through replication, network failures through reconnection and synchronization. To asses dynamic performance fluctuations, the data management system must control its own execution and resources. To facilitate scaling, an important consideration is hierarchical control mechanisms for coordinating the resource load generated by the producers.

Relational Architecture

A relational implementation of GMA components and their interfaces is R-GMA (Relational Grid Monitoring Architecture). The information and monitoring system appears like one large relational database which can be queried as such. Hence, anyone supplying or obtaining information from R-GMA does not need to know about the Registry, the Consumers and the Producers and the way they are managed behind the scenes. This approach allows both static and dynamic data handling as Producers have two important views: database producers for static data stored on disk in relational databases and stream producers for dynamic data stored in memory buffers.

Using this model, producers use SQL statements to announce their data availability ("create tables") and publish monitoring data ("insert into") while consumers collect the data using queries ("select"). In order for a component to act as either a consumer or a producer, it has to instantiate a remote object (agent) and invoke methods from the appropriate (consumer or producer) API. This schema allows for dynamic creation and dropping of new relations in addition to the core set. The relations and views are further stored by the registry which also holds the global schema. The registry is centralized although efforts for a distributed implementation are under way. A mediator uses the information available in the registry and cooperates with consumers to dynamically construct query plans for queries that cannot be satisfied by a single relation (i.e., involving "joins" from several producers).

(Zhang et al., 2003) proved the stability of RGMA implementation but, on the other hand, stressed its performance problems. RGMA can be used as a standalone grid information service assuming information providers and consumers use the RGMA APIs. Conceptually, RGMA provides access to the information of a Virtual Organization's resources creating the impression of having one RDBMS per VO; there are plans for extending this concept across VOs. Overall, the system has a potential for good scalability given the (under development) replication of the global schema and the registry, and the combination of data sources into a hierarchy of republishers. However, this is not a general distributed RDBMS system, but a way to use the relational model in a distributed environment where global consistency is not important.

Hierarchical Architecture

Besides the layered architecture models, a new model converges from recent research, centering on a hierarchy of components and services. This hierarchical approach is best suited for efficient data collection, federation and aggregation. The model is based on creating a tree of monitoring connections while keeping the monitored system's load at a minimum and transmitting changes in monitoring levels to the local monitors. The hierarchical connection structure allows for efficient data aggregation, aiming to reduce the load of the monitoring system.

Ganglia (Massie et. al., 2004) implements this hierarchical architecture targeting at federation of clusters and using a tree of point-to-point connections. Each leaf represents a node in a specific cluster being federated, with nodes higher up in the tree specifying aggregation points and logically representing sets of clusters. Multiple cluster nodes are specified for each leaf to ensure reliability. Aggregation at each point in the tree is done by polling child nodes at periodic intervals. Monitoring data from both leaf nodes and aggregation points is then exported using the same mechanism, namely a TCP connection to the node being polled followed by a read of all its monitoring data.

The Globus Toolkit's Monitoring and Discovery System MDS (Czajkowski et. al., 2007) also forms a hierarchical structure and uses a pull model for data propagation. Since Globus MDS-4 subscription is also supported. MDS2 has a hierarchical structure that consists of three main components. A Grid Index Information Service (GIIS) provides an aggregate directory of lower-level data. A Grid Resource Information Service (GRIS) runs on a resource and acts as a modular content gateway for a resource. Information providers (IPs) interface from any data collection service and then talk to a GRIS. Each service registers with higher- level services using a soft-state protocol that allows dynamic cleaning of dead resources. MDS4 implements a standard Web services interface to different local monitoring tools and various information providers. Besides the implemented query / subscription / notification protocols and interfaces defined by the WS Resource Framework (WSRF), MDS4 also provides higher level services: an Index service, which collects and publishes aggregated information about information sources, and a Trigger service, which collects resource information and performs actions when certain conditions are triggered. These services are built on a common Aggregation Framework infrastructure that provides common interfaces and mechanisms for working with data sources, following the hierarchical model.

Functional Components

Abstracting from the models presented above, one can easily determine the basic components of any (generic) monitoring system for large scale distributed systems. These components are derived from the four activities usually involved by a distributed monitoring process: Production - monitoring information is generated and collected by clients or by intermediate systems; Processing - the report information on the system activities are processed to produce the required monitoring format. This may include merging of traces, validation, database updating, combination, correlation and filtering of the reported monitoring information; Dissemination - monitoring reports are disseminated to the appropriate users, managers or processing agents; Presentation - the gathered and processed information is displayed to the user in the proper format.

The activities described above may at first appear to be a layered model with production as the lowest layer and presentation using the services of the lower layers. However, a generalized monitoring system may need to perform these activities in various places and in different orders to meet the requirements mentioned at the beginning of this section. For instance, processing and dissemination may be omitted and information displayed directly. Therefore a more convenient technique for modeling the architecture of a general monitoring system is to abstract from these activities the functional components: Sensors, Collecting / Publication Interfaces, Discovery, Storage, Analysis / Processing of data, Visualization. These components support various implementations and may be omitted according to different specifica-

tions. Their functions are a core set of reference models used by any generic monitoring system.

TECHNIQUES FOR COLLECTING AND PUBLISHING DATA

Independent of the architectural model used, the main process of a distributed monitoring system is the task of retrieving, organizing, and providing monitoring information. There is a continuous research effort to optimize this stage and methodologies exist that act as viable approaches (strictly) depending on the requirements of a particular system. In the following, we distinguish between three important steps related to monitoring data retrieving which we discuss in detail: collection, handling and discovery.

Data Collection

At this level, a specific component gathers data obtained either directly or by a monitoring tool. Usually direct retrieving of monitoring data involves parsing applications' and services' log files, inspecting system files or pushing results from external applications, e.g. MonALISA (MonALISA Website, 2009), or protocols (ex: SNMP for network links, routers and switches monitoring) in order to acquire the interesting parameters to be published. The preferred solution to implement this is to develop monitoring modules for specific needs, easy to integrate into the existing monitoring framework. A monitoring module is a dynamic loadable unit which executes a procedure (or runs a script / program, performs a request) to collect a set of parameters (monitored values) by properly parsing the output of the procedure. In general a monitoring module is a simple application, which is using a certain procedure to obtain a set of parameters and report them in a simple, standard format. Monitoring modules can be used for pulling data and in this case it is necessary to execute them with a predefined frequency (i.e. a pull module which queries an webservice) or to "install" (has to run only once) pushing scripts (programs) which are sending the monitoring results (via UDP or TCP/IP) periodically back to the main monitoring service (the collection engine). Allowing to dynamically load these modules from a (few) centralized sites when they are needed makes much easier to keep large monitoring systems updated and to provide new functionalities dynamically. Users can also implement easily any new dedicated modules and use them to adapt the framework. This approach is successfully used by the MonALISA monitoring system and therefore the number of tracked parameters has continuously evolved. Moreover, the types of monitored parameters are quite diverse, closely related to the fields where the systems is used: system parameters, network, jobs, user accounting, VO accounting, P2P key parameters, physical sensors, etc.

The second approach is to use the information provided by an existing monitoring tool and push its results back into the monitoring framework. The core of such an implementation consists of a module capable of interfacing monitoring applications and tools. We review some of the most frequently used tools and batching systems providing monitoring information, stressing their capabilities and performance.

Condor (Condor Website, 2009) is a workload management system specialized for compute intensive jobs, and one of the advantages it has over other batch queuing systems is the ability to perform opportunistic computing (harnessing CPU power from idle desktop workstations). Another strengths of Condor are: ClassAds - the flexible mechanism for matching resource requests with resource offers, the dynamic checkpointing and migration, the mechanism for Globus interface, its coherence with gLite MD. However, Condor is not optimal to parallel appplications, checkpointing only works for batch jobs while it needs complex configuration. (Reilly et al., 2009) explored whether the information provided by Condor could

be used for provenance and further developed a system that transparently gathers provenance while jobs run in Condor. Transparent provenance gathering requires that the application not to be altered in order to run in the provenance system.

Hawkeye (Hawkeye Website, 2009) is a tool designed for grid and distributed applications, not only being flexible and easy to deploy but also providing automated detection and timely alerts of problems. Hawkeye is based on Condor technology and uses ClassAds and match-making mechanisms for collecting, storing, and using information about computers and further management of systems. The system monitors various attributes of a collection of systems: system load, I/O, usage, watching run-away processes, monitoring the health of the job pool, the status of the grid sites, the grid modules check on jobs etc. In short, Hawkeye is essentially a Condor that has been modified to achieve monitoring and publish information in ClassAds. Indeed, the system works by configuring Condor such that it periodically executes specified program(s). These programs are typically scripts which produce output in the form of ClassAd attribute/value pairs. These pairs are then added (using defined naming conventions) to the machine ClassAd. The machine ClassAd then contains attributes which may be used in expressions (such as START and SUSPEND, as well as the submit description file REQUIREMENTS expression). However, (Zhang et al. 2007) observed the Hawkeye Manager performs poorly in the response transmission and connection phases, but has the best performance when searching for ClassAds in the processing phase. Hawkeye is currently being used to monitor systems on the US/CMS test bed but is also integrated in other monitoring tools (ex: MonALISA uses special Hawkeye modules to collect information). However, there hasn't more development on the project since 2006 while the modules date back from 2004.

Portable Batch System – PBS (Feng et al., 2007) is based on the client-server model, with a client making job execution requests to a batch server and the server handling the execution of the jobs in a cluster by placing them in queues. Among the features that PBS provides are the possibility to set priorities for jobs and to specify interdependencies between them, automatic file staging and multiple scheduling algorithms. The system has the advantage of being configurable over a wide range of high power computer architectures, from heterogeneous clusters of loosely coupled workstations, to massively parallel supercomputers. It supports both interactive and batch mode, and has a user friendly graphical user interface. Recently the focus of development has shifted to clusters and basic parallel support has been added. In addition, the Maui scheduler has been ported to act as a plugin scheduler to the PBS system. This combination is proving successful at scheduling jobs on parallel systems. Indeed, (Stefano et al., 2008) proposes a model of advanced reservations, based on monitoring information obtained from PBS. However, since PBS was not designed for a cluster-like computer, it lacks many important features. For instance, while the resource manager and scheduler are able to reserve multiple processors for a parallel job, the job startup, including the administrative scripts, is performed entirely on one node.

Sun Grid Engine – SGE (SGE Website, 2009) is an open source resource management system able to schedule the allocation of various distributed resources, like processors, memory, disk space, and software licenses. Its features include resource reservation, job checkpointing, the implementation of the DRMAA job API and multiple scheduling algorithms, flexible scheduling policies. It allows monitoring and controlling of jobs and queues and also provides accounting information through special plug-ins (ex: APEL, producing CPU job accounting records). (Stosser et al., 2008) uses this information to build discriminatory pay-as-bid market mechanism for scheduling that outperforms traditional approaches like market-based proportional. SGE is currently used in the EGEE grid, however its SGE Information Provider needs to improve its flexibility and take into account overlapping queues / virtual queues definitions.

Load Sharing Facility – LSF (Lumb et al., 2004), a commercial resource management system, has as its core the Platform Enterprise Grid Orchestrator (EGO), which by virtualization and automation provides a way to orchestrate all the enterprise applications into a single cohesive system. The main advantages of using LSF are: its flexible job scheduling policies, the advanced resource management (using checkpointing and job migration, load balancing), the good graphical interfaces to monitor cluster functionalities and also its easy integration with Grid. However, it is an expensive commercial product and also not suitable for small computing clusters.

Ganglia is a scalable distributed monitoring system for high-performance computing systems such as clusters and grids. It is based on a hierarchical design targeted at federations of clusters which was detailed in the previous section. The system relies on a multicast-based listen/announce protocol to monitor state within clusters and uses a tree of point-to-point connections amongst representative cluster nodes to federate clusters and aggregate their state. Ganglia provides more than 34 metrics on all platforms and also additional platform dependent metrics are available. Moreover new metrics can be defined with gmetric extension program. Its main advantages are: availability on many platforms, wide use with many users and setups, global and local views available, highly customizable via modules, fine granular statistics, monitored data stored in Round Robin Databases, easily extendible, adding new data types is trivial. However, there is no official support available, its focus is mainly on monitoring and less on accounting, no automatization supported while some setups require extensive work and the monitoring daemon (gmond) being basically a distributed redundant database, which can imply more overhead than necessary.

Table 1. Resource Managers and the metrics they provide.

Job Manager	CPU Time	Run Time	Job Size	Disk Space
Condor	Yes	Yes	Yes	Yes
PBS	Yes	Yes	No	No
SGE	Yes	No	Yes	No
LSF	Yes	Yes	Yes	No

Some issues highlighted within Ganglia's current architecture have proven to be important milestones for all major monitoring systems: limitation on metrics having to fit within a single IP datagram, the lack of a hierarchical namespace, lack of timeouts on monitoring data, large I/O overheads incurred by the use of RRDtool, and lack of access control mechanisms on the monitoring namespace. Some of these issues (e.g. lack of timeouts) have since been addressed. Still, some unsolved issues likely require more fundamental changes to Ganglia's architecture. In the context of deploying Ganglia to Internet level scalability comes as the main obstacle: both for monitoring within a single cluster and for federating multiple clusters over the wide-area. The authors admit that within a single cluster the quadratic message incurred by a multicast-based listen/announce protocol will not scale properly to thousands of nodes. Consequently, some amount of symmetry at the lowest level is likely to be lost to support emerging clusters of the envisioned scale. For federation of multiple clusters, monitoring through straightforward aggregation of data also presents scaling problems, the authors observe. Scalable monitoring across thousands of clusters in the wide-area will likely require use of some techniques, as proven by Ganglia's deployment on PlantetLab: combination of summarization, locally scoped queries, and distributed query processing (Harren et al. 2002, Renesse et al. 2003). Self-configuration while federating at this scale will also require substantial changes to the original

Ganglia architecture since manual specification of the federation graph will not scale.

We summarized in Table 1 the metrics we can obtain from various resource managers:

In P2P environments, collecting and publishing monitoring information proves to be a non trivial task due to the particular nature of these systems: huge number of nodes, low reliability, variable quality of service and high mobility of nodes. Several efforts have been undertaken to monitor P2P systems ranging from measuring churn-related user behavior (e.g., distribution of lifetime, inter-arrival delays, and availability) (Chu et al. 2002, Dunn et al. 2005, Saroiu et al. 2005, Stutzbach et al. 2006), to topology observation (e.g., degree distribution and clustering coefficients) (Liang et al. 2006, Stutzbach et al. 2005) and traffic flow rate inspection (Sen et al. 2004). Of particular interest, considering the nodes' high volatility, is the monitoring of lifetimes in P2P networks. Recent work of (Wang et al. 2009) show that the traditional method relying on the create-based sampling exhibits an inherent tradeoff between overhead and accuracy which limits its improvement. Instead they propose a robust and bandwidth-efficient sampling mechanism for estimating peer and link lifetime distributions in unstructured P2P networks. This approach keeps track of only residual lifetimes of peers and uses a simple renewal-process model to recover the actual lifetimes from the observed residuals. The authors show that for reasonably large systems, the proposed method can reduce bandwidth consumption by several orders of magnitude compared to prior approaches while simultaneously achieving higher accuracy. However, although experiments run over Gnutella network proved that the probability for the network to disconnect at the super-peer level is below 10^{-64} leaves may be isolated with a non-negligible probability, having only one or two attachment points.

Collection of frequent monitoring updates from a large number of P2P nodes may also be affected by scalabillity issues. (Ratnasamy et al.

2001) proposes a solution which may be adopted in large scale P2P monitoring environments. Observing that flooding the network with monitoring updates is clearly not scalable, the authors propose a scalable indexing mechanism: Content Adressable Network which basically describes a distributed hash table. Their work addresses the key problems in the design of P2P monitoring systems: scalable routing of messages and indexing. Simulation results validate the scalability of the system: for a CAN with over 260,000 nodes, the latency of the routing was less than twice the IP path latency. However the systems still supports improvement regarding security in the presence of malicious nodes.

Handling Monitoring Data

The transmission of monitoring data events from the source to any interested parties is generally granted using several basic models: push/pull mechanisms, data filters, periodic/aperiodic, unicast/one-to-many.

Push/Pull Models. While being the most common mechanisms used by a broad variety of monitoring systems, they become a de-facto standard for monitoring data access. With the "pull" approach, the final data consumer has an active role interacting with the interested data, and is responsible for pulling it (from a browser or an application). The "push" mechanism usually relies on a publish / subscribe notification service. In these approaches, the client applications connect directly with each data producer they are interested in for receiving monitoring information. The clients can further get real-time of historical data using a matching scheme for requesting or subscribing to selected measured values. The matching scheme depends on the data representation models, which will be discussed in the next section. However, in most monitoring systems and independent of the representation model, the matching with the attribute description of the measured values the client is interested in further imposes additional conditions and constraints for selecting the desired values. The subscription requests should create dedicated threads to serve each client performing the matching test for all the queries submitted by clients with the measured values in the data flow. The system is then responsible to send the selected results back to the client using various transmission mechanisms (usually compressed serialized objects). Having independent threads per client allows sending the information they need, fast, in a reliable way and not affected by communication errors which may occur with other clients. In case of communication problems these threads will try to reestablish the connection or to clean-up the subscriptions for a client or a service which is not anymore active.

Monitoring data requests with the push/pull matching mechanism makes also possible the using of the WSDL/SOAP binding from clients or services written in other languages. The attributes of the interested monitoring values are described in WSDL and any client can create dynamically and instantiate the objects it needs for communication. However, currently the Web Services technology does not provide the functionality to register as a listener and to receive the future measurements a client may want to receive. This motivates the approach of periodic vs. aperiodic monitoring data requests. These models are intensively used by monitoring engines like GridIce (Aiftimei et al., 2007) or MonALISA as the main solution for data distribution. Although the matching of the queries is implemented differently (GridIce uses GLUE schema for data representation while MonALISA a proprietary regular expression predicate) the core of the dissemination engine rests the same at a high architectural level.

Data Filters. They are an alternative to the traditional push/pull model which collects large amounts of monitoring information. Filters insert a selection mechanism into the monitoring service, collecting only the relevant information for consumers. In order to decrease the transmission of unneeded monitoring data, these models usually include a subscription mechanism. This allows clients to select the collectors from which they are interested in receiving data instead of receiving it from every collector in the system. The consumers express their monitoring demands through a filter program which contains information about their monitoring requests. This is similar to a subscription process aiming at an event-driven model. The monitoring services receive the monitoring demands and configure their components accordingly. This has the advantage of relieving the consumers from receiving and processing a large volume of monitoring data as it is the case in push/pull approach which may overwhelm the consumers as well as the network links. Compared to the previous model, filters introduce a higher control on the granularity of the monitoring process by limiting the monitoring operations on observing specific system components or events. They also enhance applications' performance and reliability providing faster responses since the reaction can be instant. However, the preferred solution used by current monitoring systems is composing the push/pull approach for data collection with data filtering. Indeed, in RGMA users can easily model their requests with custom 'select' queries: in order to act as a data consumer they instantiate a remote object (agent) and invoke methods from the appropriate consumer API. The global

schema includes a core set of these relations, while new relations with filtering arguments can be dynamically created and dropped by consumer and producers. Republishers can further be defined as one or more SQL queries that provide a relational view on data received by producers or other republishers.

In MonALISA clients can send several types of requests to the services: history requests, served from the service local database and subscription for new data events. Filtering is expressed with a set of predicates written using regular expressions with a simple syntax. The general filtering and data collection model used by the vast majority of monitoring systems (MonALISA included) is presented in Figure 1.

New custom filters can be implemented and deployed dynamically, producing derived values that can be stored along or instead of the original values. Hence the custom filters can be implemented to intercept received data (or particular cuts in it) and act on the values. For instance, when monitoring the ALICE experiment (ALICE Website, 2009) special filters were developed to store all the names of raw data files produced by the experiment in separate database tables, while the size and count values go to the default storage structures and the standard views are used to display them.

Figure 1. Monitoring data handling at collection site

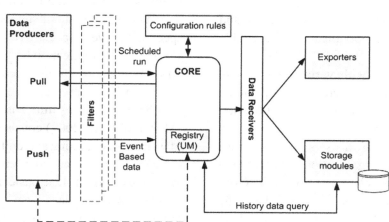

In Ganglia, the mechanisms used for data handling highlighted new issues when deployed on wide area networks: in these scenarios the assumption that wide-area bandwidth is cheap when aggregating data does not hold. New efforts are underway to make more judicious use of network bandwidth, for instance the use of zlib compression has demonstrated reductions in bandwidth by approximately an order of magnitude.

Registration and Discovery Services

Once the important monitored events are detected and the status reports are generated, in order to achieve dissemination to the appropriate users or processing agents one must rely on a discovery service. Its role is to discover the monitoring services and to consequently mediate the interaction between data consumers and data producers: while the first use the service to find the appropriate monitoring information sources the latter registers with the data they are able to provide. This proves not to be a trivial task in a distributed environment where nodes and sites change quickly their statuses and thereby an automated resource and service discovery process must be performed and launched at a frequency compatible with the dynamic of the distributed system's elements. We can easily observe the issues to which a reliable registration and discovery service should cope in such an environment:

- The distributed nature of the users and resources often doubled by unreliable network;
- Many resources with variable status: the resources to be discovered come up and go down without any centralized notification or co-ordination;
- Variable grouping of users and resources: many Virtual Organizations involve and sometimes an unclear partition of the Grid;
- Heterogeneous security approaches: the numerous production sites involved in

a grid have their own security policies and system administration principles and procedures, which can eventually be out-sourced; a global discovery system must be efficient and not intrusive with respect to security policies and should not interfere with site local rules like logging and auditing.

One of the key concepts the R&D Service relates to is the Virtual Organization. The service should work well in environments spanning various VOs, which group together resources and users in related communities. As VOs enable sharing of resources and stress the non-locality of participants, they have an inherent dynamic nature which has to be handled by the R&D system: VOs come and go, resources can join and leave VOs, resources can change status and fail, they have community-wide goals and must not interfere with each other. Scalability in this context implies not only large numbers of users and independent resources but also service dependability, ensuring as much function possible, a "graceful degradation of service" (Clifford, 2004), tolerating partitions and pruning failures. Although resources have discovery information (published by themselves – e.g. WSRF based services – or collected by a separate probe – e.g. GridFTP) there is a need for a separate service to collect and publish this information in order not to increase the local load. Hence some additional requirements needed by a reliable R&D system: support for community specific discovery, specialized views and policies, scalability and replication for fault tolerance purposes. We explore how these requirements are met by some of the most common used R&D services.

The Monitoring and Discovery System 4 (MDS4 Website, 2009) consists of a framework of web services aiming at monitoring and discovering services and resources on Grids. Integrated in Globus Toolkit 4, it basically implements a standard Web Services based interface to local monitoring tools and various information sources.

MDS services provide query and subscription interfaces to highly heterogeneous resources data and a trigger interface configurable to take action when specific conditions are satisfied. The services included in the WS MDS implementation acquire their information through this extensible interface which can be used to: query WSRF services for resource property information, execute a program to acquire data, or interface with third-party monitoring systems. As mentioned in the previous paragraph, distributed computing resources have the ability to publish discovery and monitoring data. MDS4 addresses these particular systems, publishing data available to multiple users at multiple sites. As such, as the authors observe, it is not an event handling system, like NetLogger, or a cluster monitor on its own, but can interface to more detailed monitoring systems and archives, and can publish summary data using standard interfaces.

MDS4 is built around a layered architecture also denoted in the Globus literature as a "protocol hourglass", using standard schemas (e.g. GLUE, presented in the next section) and WS standard interfaces for subscription, registration and notification. At the higher level reside the applications that use the information from the sources the MDS4 interacts with: schedulers, portals, warning systems, etc. At the lower level, MDS4 interfaces with various information providers using a uniform interface which translates diverse schemas into standard (whenever possible) XML schemas. Currently these information providers can be cluster monitors (Ganglia, Hawkeye, Clumon and Nagios), services (GRAM, RFT, RLS) or queuing systems (PBS, LSF, Torque). The Hawkeye Information Provider gathers data about Condor pool resources using the XML mapping of the GLUE schema and reports it to a WS GRAM service, which publishes it as resource properties. The Ganglia information providers do the same for cluster data from resources running Ganglia. The WS GRAM is the job submission service component of GT4; its WSRF service publishes

information about the local scheduler. WSRF is also used fir publishing by the RFT – Reliable File Transfer service component of the GT4 and CAS – Community Authorization Services with information identifying the VO that is serves.

Based on these low-level components MDS4 also provides two higher level WSRF services: an Index Service, collecting and publishing aggregated data from the various sources and providing the query/ subscription interface to the data, and a Trigger Service, performing pre-configured actions when certain coditions are met. The Index Service is a registry similar to UDDI, but much more flexible. Indexes collect information and publish that information as resource properties. Clients use the standard WSRF resource property query and subscription/notification interfaces to retrieve information from an Index. Indexes can register to each other in a hierarchical fashion in order to aggregate data at several levels. Indexes are "self-cleaning"; each Index entry has a lifetime and will be removed from the Index if it is not refreshed before it expires. The Trigger Service collects information and compares that data against a set of conditions defined in a configuration file. When a condition is met, or triggered, an action takes place, such as emailing a system administrator when the disk space on a server reaches a threshold. All these services are built on the Aggregator Framework, a software infrastructure used to build services and collect data. To this end, the Index and Trigger services act as aggregator services which have several components in common: Aggregator Sources – the interface to collect XML data, the configuration mechanism for the Aggregator Sources, limited lifetime for registrations. Deployment on TeraGrid and Earth Science Grid proved a high degree of stability and scalability for the Index service with respect to the number of concurrent queries and number of client, with no noticeable performance or usability degradation (Schopf et al., 2004).

JINI technology (JINI Website, 2009) comes as a natural choice for use in discovery services in large scale distributed environments. It enables service bases architectures, provides spontaneous networking (assembled into working group of objects - Federations), abstracts the distinction between hardware and software (through objects), and also provides a distributed computing infrastructure to make writing distributed programs easier. Moreover, JINI offers a Lookup Service for service finding and resolution, which makes it suitable for monitoring services registration and discovery purposes. The lookup service in JINI acts as a repository of available services which maps interfaces indicating the functionality provided by a service to sets of objects that implement the service. In addition, descriptive entries associated with a monitoring service allow more fine-grained selection of data producer services based on some user defined properties. The lookup service is built around a hierarchical model, as objects in a lookup service may be federated with other lookup services. The basic lookup service interface provides registration, access, update, search and removal. The JINI discovery protocols are used to find and join group of services, which advertise their capabilities. It is based on UDP multicast and establishes a reference with lookup services; this multicast mechanism allows Jini clients and services on relatively close (related to multicast TTL limits on the network) network segments to find each other without prior knowledge. The unicast discovery is also supported and the locator mechanism allows prior knowledge to be used to directly access a Jini lookup service which can be used to find services of interests. Hence to find a service, a JINI client locates it by querying a LookUp service by type, then the code moves from service to client via LookUp service and finally the code needed to use the service is dynamically loaded on demand.

The main design issue of JINI in this context remains, as in MDS case, scalability: JINI was initially designed to be used in LAN settings, dependant on multicast. The infrastructure for supporting JINI communities distributed over wide

are networks is poor and this comes as a critical research topic for the widespread take up of JINI in distributed environments. Solutions used in this case include overlapping LookUp services, P2P technology with JXTA technology, JINI gateways or designing new protcolos (Baker et al., 2009). For instance, MonALISA adopted JINI for a fully distributed and replicated implementation of the LookUp services used by the monitor clients and sensors.

In MonALISA services are able to discover each other in the distributed environment and to be discovered by the interested clients. Each MonALISA service registers itself with a set of Lookup Services as part of one or more groups and it publishes some attributes that describe itself. Consequently any interested application can request MonALISA services based on a set of matching attributes. The registration uses a lease mechanism provided by JINI. If a service fails to renew its lease, it is removed from the LUSs and a notification is sent to all the services or other application that subscribed for such events. Remote event notification is used in this way to get a real overview of this dynamic system. Lookup services maintain replicated information so a monitoring service has to be registered in two or more distributed lookup services, because if one fails responding, interested clients can find the services registered in the other online lookup services. Thus, the single point of failure problem can be avoided and a more reliable network for registration of services can be achieved in the distributed environment. The JINI technology used allows dynamically adding and removing Lookup Services from the system. Security is addressed by restricting services' registration based on authorized X.509 certificates.

In RGMA, the Registry was responsible for data registering and discovery. As in MonALISA, users don't interact directly with it, instead their agents do it on their behalf. RGMA registry abstract differently interaction with consumer agents depending on the type of their query: continuous or one-time. While for one-time queries the agent should consult the registry each time the query is run, in continuous scenarios the query is registered by the agent. Then the registry ensures that throughout the lifetime of the consumer, it can receive all of the data the query asks for: the consumer is notified as new relevant publishers are registered or dropped.

STANDARDS AND SOLUTIONS FOR REPRESENTING THE MONITORING INFORMATION

Each information source publishes its monitoring information using a specific format according to some schema. Due to diversity of data producers and grid resources which may define different schemas, important collaborative efforts are underway to define common schemas (e.g. GLUE, CIM) and abstract modeling for distributed resources. Such a schema should meet some key-requirements (Burke et al., 2008): adequate size – in order to capture all the relevant information but abstracting from all unnecessary details; flexibility – to be able to represent the heterogeneous software and resources in use; precision – as the semantics should be clearly defined; simplicity – the attributes are to be easy to understand and use; calculability - the attributes must be capable of being calculated in real systems in a relatively short time; extensibility – to allow evolution over time with as little overhead as possible. As the authors denote, these properties are to some extent in tension with each other so it will generally be necessary to find a reasonable compromise, as in the schemas presented in the following.

The GLUE Schema (Glue Schema Website, 2009) is an abstract modeling for Grid resources and mapping to concrete schemas that can be used in Grid Information Services; it creates a standardization framework for publication of information about Grid sites. The schema is defined using a subset of UML, in terms of objects with attributes and relations to other objects. Although there are several mappings into LDAP, relational (R-GMA), XML and Condor ClassAds, these intended implementations are significantly different and impose constraints on the possible structure of the schema. The schema specification presents a description of core Grid resources at the conceptual level by defining an information model, that is an abstraction of the real world into constructs that can be represented in computer systems (e.g., objects, properties, behavior, and relationships). Thus the proposed information model is not tied to any particular implementation and can be profitably used to exchange information among different knowledge domains. From a high level we distinguish four categories of the schema, in which parameteres are grouped. The GlueSite is an administrative concept used to aggregate a set of services and resources usually installed and managed by the same set of administrators. The GlueSite can further aggregate GlueServices (a general representation of a service – grid, network, etc.), Storage Elements (attributes and objects related to storage systems in the original schema, now enhanced with a complex protocol (SRM Website, 2009) to manage large-scale Grid-enabled storage) and Computing Elements (defined to map a queue in a batching system enhanced with grouping capabilities as the VOView).

GLUE schema is highly used by the MDS information model, which organizes information into well-defined collections – entries, each representing an instance of a type of object. There are several projects that are participating in the GLUE schema activity: EGEE, LCG, OSG, Globus, NorduGrid, GridICE. The latter is the monitoring service for the European Data Grid (EDG) currently deployed on EDG's testbed. While its main advantages are the collection of all GLUE information, plotted in a useful way and giving both a detailed and a general overview of the Grid, the notification service and the support for custom graphs, a significant drawback is close relation to the schema as statistics not present in the GLUE schema are not analyzed by GridIce. However, the experience of the schema with other Grids has proven that evolution of the Grid technology itself also implies changes in the schema. The current release is 1.2 and 1.3 the working version but current efforts are now underway towards a major upgrade of the GLUE schema (2.0 specification in planning), which should unify all relevant modeling efforts in the Grid context and provide a firm foundation for Grid interoperability.

The Common Information Model (CIM). As the GLUE schema, CIM (CIM Website, 2009) is also an object-oriented information model. However, CIM is more complex aiming at a standardization for publication IT environment information and specification for all available components. It was proposed by the Distributed Management Task Force (DMTF) as a management standard and has the advantage of being user-extensible. CIM models both physical attributes and logical abstractions as users, dependencies, administration policies and hardware capabilities all useful to monitoring processes. As the GLUE schema CIM has different format implementations, including xmlCIM, the representation in XML format used by the DMTF. The widespread of CIM is mainly caused by its possibility to express relations such as inheritance or other dependencies as opposed to flat information models expressed for instance in Management Information Base (MIBs). Indeed, relevant CIM information is hold by classes organized in a hierarchy based on inheritance. Instances can relate through an association model, containing regular and referential properties. Hence, the key innovations of CIM compared to other information models, as shown by (Wesner, 2008) are: reduced complexity of the models based on the performed abstraction and classification of the problem domain defining high level and fundamental concepts, common characteristics and their relationships as baseline for the specific objects; utilization of object oriented concepts such as object inheritance or the use of associations to

depict relationships between the objects; use of semantic annotations of the associations allowing to express common characteristics and features; definition of abstract behavior independent of the underlying hardware; common model across the whole management environment and potentially custom defined other problem spaces.

These features motivate the current research (Diaz. 2008) on making CIM even more accessible and providing it a query service for resource management information in Grid systems and thus integrating the CIM with MDS4. This involves publishing the CIM information on the MDS4 and the development of a query engine that supports queries with arbitrary navigation depth on a CIM instance tree. This approach benefits applications needing structured and interrelated information models as the one ensured by CIM. It also makes possible the specification of complex expressions through the query implementation, which couldn't be formulate on other information models, like GLUE, without ad-hoc code, as authors observe.

Flexible Schemas. Some monitoring applications prefer using particular schemas having the advantages of easy extensibility and flexibility in mapping to specific application constrains. Nagios (Velt, 2008) is a system and network monitoring application built around a central core providing scheduling and using plugins to access resources. It is designed to be extensible and easy customizable hence plugins can be used to create user-defined metrics (using virtually any language available). The Simple Network Management Protocol (SNMP) monitors and manages the network components. It maintains a set of management information following the specific format described in a Management Information Base (MIB). The information is hold in a hierarchical manner with unique identifiers. However for very large MIBs performance quickly degrades. In MonALISA, the system has the ability to transport and store different types of monitoring data; this data is user-definable so any service user can easily implement its own data type, extending a base object: MLData. The new defined data only has to be self-describing so that the database engine can store it in transparent manner.

VISUALIZATION OF MONITORING INFORMATION

The highest level of the monitoring layered model is the presentation level at which the monitoring information is visualized by users in formats that meet their application requirements. Such an interface should be able to cope with the high rate of data updates involved by a real-time monitoring system, the large amounts of data produced and with the various levels of abstraction needed for both global and particular detailed views. The main techniques for displaying monitoring information have been identified in (Mansouri et al. 1993): textual data presentation (which involves simple text with special format rendering the monitored information), time series diagrams (the most commonly used in web interfaces) and animations. Recently, new chart types emerged with higher expressivity: pies, multiple axes charts, spider graphs, bars for real time information, geo map monitoring information (monitoring data rendered on maps to highlight the locations of the captured data), flash views. However, no single view is always sufficient for monitoring purposes so combinations of these presentation techniques are often used.

In Ganglia for instance, the web interface is built around Apache HTTPD server in PHP and uses presentation templates so the interface can be easily customized. It presents an overview of all nodes within the grid or cluster, and also detailed individual charts both in textual and graphical views. The interface uses RRDTool – Round Robin Database Tool (RRDTool Website, 2009), a storage and trend graphing tool. It defines fixed size databases that hold data of various configurable granularity. Thus, it enables high performance data logging and graphing systems

for time series data due to the constant and predictable data storage size and the automatic data consolidation over time. This is achieved through the use of various Round Robin Archives (RRA) which hold data points at decreasing levels of granularity. Multiple data points from a more granular RRA are automatically consolidated and added to a courser RRA.

A similar technique is used by the MonALISA Repository – the special type of client responsible for collection of data from all the distributed services and presentation through a web interface. In this case, data is written in the database only at the end of an aggregation interval, using asynchronous operations, to minimize the impact of IO over the main monitoring tasks. Upon request the system will automatically select the most appropriate storage structure, depending on the time interval and the number of data points that are requested. For instance, a yearly report generated by the repository will take data from the structure with the lowest resolution, while looking in detail over a few hours around the time of an event that happened a week ago will use the highest resolution structure. If a single structure cannot cover the entire request length then data from multiple structures can be aggregated to form the response. A data reduction scheme like the one above has the advantage of conserving disk space while providing enough detail for recent events. Concerning the data visualization, MonALISA relies on a servlet engine which translates the user requests from the interface to statistics tables, geo maps, history and real-time charts rendered using JFreeChart (JFreeChart Webpage, 2009).

In GridIce the highest layer of the architecture is the Presentation Service, a web-based interface designed according to a role-based strategy which renders different views depending on the type of consumer: GOC view, targeting at the whole set of Grid resources managed by a Grid Operations Center; the Site view, whose target is the set of resources belonging to a certain site; and the Virtual Organization view, whose target is the whole set of Grid resources that can be accessed by users of a certain VO.

USING THE MONITORING TOOLS FOR CONTROL AND OPTIMIZATION

The main purpose of a distributed monitoring infrastructure is the ability to invest the system with control capabilities and some degree of automated management, as the large amounts of data and vast resources harnessed by these applications make the task of administration only through user interaction not a trivial one. The goal is to develop new building blocks based on the existing infrastructure and using the collected monitoring information to control remote resources and applications in a standardized way. The Resource Management Systems are the most likely to use monitoring information to perform their functionalities, but the application field is not limited to them: anomaly detection, diagnosis, pattern detection, predictions, automated actions and alarms use the information from monitoring services to perform a distributed control.

Resource Management

The general requirements of Resource Management Systems have been presented and evaluated in the dedicated Chapter of this book. In this section we are interested by the functionalities required from these systems with respect to monitoring information. The job execution and the provisioning of the resources need additional input from monitoring data providers since access to resources may be different and generic execution and provisioning functions are not supported by current middleware. Moreover, Service Level Agreement Management relies on efficient monitoring and ensures agreement –based resource planning. A flexible and automatic brokering and scheduling system uses critical data from monitoring producers to take its decisions. Being an essen-

tial component of every Resource Management System it needs more complex monitoring traces as it should support scheduling of both simple jobs and complex ones expressed as workflows, which require co-allocation of several resources in parallel with corresponding dependencies.

In MonALISA interaction with RM Systems is well supported through the Monitoring Modules which are dynamically loadable and execute some data collection procedure with a certain frequency, then sending back the desired results the Monitoring Service. Even simpler, using ApMon – a dedicated client API – users can send any type of customized information for resource management purposes into the MonALISA system. In contrast, the NWS (Wolski, 2003) system is not well suited for resource management as it doesn't cope reliably with fast changing data sets. Evens systems like R-GMA or MDS are too resource-demanding and induce important delays to be effective in such an environment.

Diagnosis and Accounting

Once the monitoring data is collected for longer periods one can use it to determine certain patterns in selected parameters traces to identify and troubleshoot problems. This is achieved using several detection methods as the statistical models (e.g. window averaging) or using Fourier transform for capturing normal periodic behavior. The goal is to further detect anomalies and diagnose their possible causes. There is a continuous research effort (Yang et al., 2007) to extend the traditional window-based strategies by using signal-processing techniques to filter out recurring, background fluctuations in resource behavior. The authors also developed a diagnosis technique that uses standard monitoring data to determine which related changes in behavior may cause anomalies. Evaluation showed that these techniques detects more anomalies while reducing the false positives rate compared to traditional window averaging strategies.

Monitoring information is also vital for accounting purposes. A Grid accounting system has the main role of recording the resource consumption for each user, and may have other functionalities like enabling the administration of the storage of this information, and interacting with other related services. The accounting information is usually obtained with the aid of a monitoring system deployed over the Grid. One of the functions of the accounting system is to enable an economically self-sustaining Grid, as shown in (Ainsworth et al., 2005): if so far most of the Grids have been used for academic and research applications, and have been supported by different types of grants, in the future they should be able to function without external support. For this purpose, in a Grid there should exist the possibility to charge the users for the resources consumed, or at least the possibility to trade resources among organizations. As the importance of Grid accounting has been recognized, several projects have been initiated in this domain, but there are some significant challenges in developing an accounting system (most of them related to the complexity and heterogeneity of Grid environments). We distinguish between accounting systems and monitoring systems that include accounting features (Gaido et al., 2007): while an accounting system stores detailed information about single jobs/users and can provide the usage record for a particular job, a monitoring system usually collects statistical information like the total number of jobs run by each user, or per-VO resource consumption In fact, the Global Grid Forum introduced a standard for accounting, named Usage Record, intended to facilitate the sharing of usage information among Grid sites (Mach et al., 2006). A usage record is specified in the XML format and may contain two types of properties: base properties (that are considered critical for accurate usage recording), and differentiated properties (representing additional metrics that may be used for certain jobs). The specification for the usage record format can also be extended as long as all the involved resources agree upon the format of the extension.

APEL (Byrom et al., 2005) is an accounting application, which analyzes batch system and gatekeeper logs and produces accounting records and publishes them into R-GMA. DGAS (Gaido et al., 2007), which stands for Distributed Grid Accounting System, is developed within the EGEE and OMII-Europe projects. Its purpose is to implement a complete accounting system (usage metering, accounting, resource pricing) for Grid environments. The system is designed as a multi-layered one, having usage metering and accounting as the lower layers, and the accounting balancing / resource pricing as an upper, optional layer. In GridICE various accounting statistics are provided, like the number of jobs and the CPU usage for each VO; GridIce also records the availability of each Grid site and the amount of free resources.

Predictions

To make the best use of the resources in a shared distributed environment, an application scheduler should make some predictions of available performance on each resource. Some solutions to develop algorithms based on prediction methods using monitoring information exist in the current literature. In (Yang et.al., 2003) the authors propose a conservative scheduling technique based on a predictor component to help in making scheduling. The component is able to adjust the scheduling decisions based on a feedback mechanism. The authors compare the prediction accuracy of their method against the ones obtained by using another prediction instrument, Network Weather Service (NWS). In (Spooner et al., 2003) the architecture proposed uses Globus as an underlying middleware to provide scheduling based on performance predictions. One weakness of both approaches is that, for the most part, they don't consider the local characteristics of individual cluster sites and allow the selection of jobs that can lead to the increase of job queuing time.

In (Sugaya et al., 2008), the authors are proposing a set of long-term load prediction methods which reference the properties of processes and the runtime predictions. These methods are used by a prediction module selector that is able to select an appropriate prediction method, based on actual situation and according to a state of dynamically changing CPU load. This solution is also based on the use of a neural network. However, the scheduling decisions are strictly based on CPU load predictions hence new and more efficient solutions should make use of a wider range of performance parameters. Previous attempts to develop scheduling solutions based on predictions faced the difficulty of installing monitors to record the performance of the Grid components and feed a predictor component, a problem that now can easily be overcame by using one of the widely used monitoring frameworks. Another problem faced by schedulers is the difficulty in accurately predicting the hosts' characteristics (such as CPU computational power, CPU load, etc). Some of them have proposed techniques to predict the values regarding hosts and tasks by using the Network Weather Service (Wolski et al., 2003), a distributed system that periodically monitors and dynamically forecasts the performance of various network and computational resources. The NWS operates a set of forecasting methods that it can invoke dynamically, passing as parameters the CPU load measurements it has taken from each resource. Conversely, the availability prediction is based on a nonparametric method called Binomial Method (Brevik et al., 2004). This method is able to make future availability prediction (with provable confidence bounds) with as few as 20 measurements of the previous availability values.

Scheduling is not the only field benefiting from monitoring based predictions. In fact, these are used at a high scale for optimization of large file transfers. GridFTP (part of Globus Toolkit) is the defacto standard for grid file transfers and is widely used to analyze and predict the behavior of file transfers. The processing is based on GridFTP's log files, identifying patterns and using standard statistical predictions with means, medians and autoregressive techniques.

CONCLUSION

In this chapter we presented a set of models and requirements that describe the monitoring process in large scale distributed environments. We identified a set of core components (production, processing, dissemination, presentation of monitoring information) and discussed their implementations and the issues raised. These components may describe a layered model with data production as the lowest level and the presentation on top of other layers. However, as we have seen, current monitoring systems may perform these activities with some restrictions or additional features, in different places and various interactions in order to meet specific monitoring requirements.

REFERENCES

Aiftimiei, C., Andreozzi, S., Cuscela, G., Donvito, G., Dudhalkar, V., Fantinel, S., et al. (2007). Recent evolutions of GridICE: a monitoring tool for grid systems. In *Proceedings of the 2007 Workshop on Grid Monitoring* (Monterey, California, USA, June 25 - 25, 2007) (pp. 1-8). New York: ACM.

Ainsworth, J. D., & Brooker, J. M. (2005). Testing for scalability in a grid resource usage service. In *Proceedings of the UK e-Science All Hands Meeting 2005*, 19-22 September 2005.

ALICE Website (n.d.). Retrieved April 20, 2009, from http://aliceinfo.cern.ch/

Al-Shaer, E., Abdel-Wahab, H., & Maly, K. (1997). High-performance Monitoring Architecture for Large-scale Distributed Systems Using Event Filtering. In *The 3rd International Conference on Computer Science and Informatica*, North Carolina, USA.

Aydt R., Smith, W., Swany, M., Taylor, V., Tierney, B., & Wolski, R. (2001). *A Grid Monitoring Architecture*.

Baker M., G. Smith, JINI Meets the Grid, 2009

Brevik, J., Nurmi, D., & Wolski, R. (2004). Automatic Methods for Predicting Machine Availability in Desktop Grid and Peer-to-peer Systems. In *Proc. of 4th Int. Workshop on Global and Peer-to-Peer Computing*, Chicago, Illinois, April 19-22.

Burke, S., Andreozzi, S., & Field, L. (2008). Experiences with the GLUE Information Schema in the LCG/EGEE Produc-tion Grid International Conference on Computing in High Energy and Nuclear Physics (CHEP'07). *Journal of Physics: Conference Series, 119*.

Byrom, R., Cordenonsib, R., Cornwall, L., Craig, M., Djaoui, A., & Duncan, A. (2005). An implementation of Grid ac-counting using R- GMA. In *UK e-Nottingham*. APEL.

Chu, K., Labonte, K., & Levine, B. N. (2002 July). Availability and Locality Measurements of Peer-to-Peer File Systems. In *Proc. ITCom Conference* (Vol. 4868, pp. 310–321).

CIM Website Distributed Management Task Force, Inc. (2008). *Common Information Model (CIM) standards* [online]. Retrieved April 20, 2009, from http://www.dmtf.org/standards/cim

Clifford, B. (2004). *Globus Monitoring and Discovery*.

Condor. (n.d.). *Project homepage*. Retrieved April 20, 2009, from http://www.cs.wisc.edu/condor/

Czajkowski, K., Kesselman, C., Fitzgerald, S., & Foster, I. (2001). Grid information services for distributed resource sharing. In *HPDC '01: Proceedings of the 10th IEEE International Symposium on High Performance Distributed Computing*. Washington, DC: IEEE Computer Society.

Diaz, I., Fernandez, G., Martin, M. J., Gonzalez, P., & Tourino, J. (2008). *Integrating the Common Information Model with MDS4*. Poster presented at Grid2008.

Dunn, R., Zahorjan, J., Gribble, S. D., & Levy, H. M. (2005 August). Presence-Based Availability and P2P Systems. In *Proc. IEEE International Conference on Peer-to-Peer Computing* (pp. 209–216).

Feng, H., Misra, V., & Rubenstein, D. (2007). PBS: a unified priority-based scheduler. In *Proceedings of the 2007 ACM SIGMETRICS international Conference on Measurement and Modeling of Computer Systems* (San Diego, California, USA, June 12 - 16, 2007) (pp. 203-214). New York: ACM.

Gaido, L., Guarise, A., Patania, G., Piro, R., Rosso, F., & Werbrouck, A. (2007). *The Distributed Grid Accounting System (DGAS)*. Retrieved April 20, 2009, from http://www.to.infn.it/grid/accounting/main.html

Glue Schema Website. (n.d.). Retrieved April 20, 2009, from http://www.globus.org/toolkit/mds/glueschemalink.html

Harren, M., & Hellerstein, J. M. Huebsch, R., Loo, B.T., Shenker, S., & Stoica, I. (2002 March). Complex queries in dht based peer-to-peer networks. In *Proceedings of the 1st International Workshop on Peer-to-peer Systems*.

Hawkeye Website. (n.d.). Retrieved April 20, 2009, from http://www.cs.wisc.edu/condor/hawkeye/

Hui, L. (2007 May). Performance Evaluation in Grid Computing: A Modeling and Prediction Perspective. In *Cluster Computing and the Grid, 2007 (CCGRID 2007)* (pp. 869-874).

JFreeChart Website. (n.d.). Retrieved April 20, 2009, from http://www.jfree.org/jfreechart/

JINI Website. (n.d.). Retrieved April 20, 2009, from http://www.jini.org/

Kandaswamy, G., Mandal, A., & Reed, D. A. (2008). Fault Tolerance and Recovery of Scientific Workflows. In Computational Grids, Cluster Computing and the Grid, 19-22 May 2008.

Liang, J., Kumar, R., & Ross, K. W. (2006). The FastTrack Overlay: A Measurement Study. *Computer Networks*, *50*(6), 842–858. doi:10.1016/j.comnet.2005.07.014

Lumb, I., & Smith, C. (2004). Scheduling attributes and platform LSF. In Nabrzyski, J., Schopf, J. M., & Weglarz, J. (Eds.), *Grid Resource Management: State of the Art and Future Trends* (pp. 171–182). Norwell, MA: Kluwer Academic Publishers.

Mach, R., Lepro-Metz, R., Jackson, S., & McGinnis, L. (2006). *Usage Record – Format Recommendation*. Retrieved April 20, 2009, from https://forge.gridforum.org/sf/projects/ur-wg

Mansouri-Samani, M., & Sloman, M. (1993). Monitoring distributed systems. *IEEE Network*, *7*(6), 20–30. doi:10.1109/65.244791

Massie, M., Chun, B. N., & Culler, D. E. (2004). The Ganglia distributed monitoring system: design, implementation, and experience. *Parallel Computing*, *30*, 817–840. doi:10.1016/j.parco.2004.04.001

MDS4 The GT4 Monitoring and Discovery System. (n.d.). Retrieved April 20, 2009, from http://www.globus.org/toolkit/mds

MonALISA Website. (n.d.). Retrieved April 20, 2009, from http://monalisa.caltech.edu/

Ratnasamy, S., Francis, P., Handley, M., Karp, R., & Schenker, S. (2001). A scalable content-addressable network. In *Proceedings of the 2001 Conference on Applications, Technologies, Architectures, and Protocols For Computer Communications* (San Diego, California, United States) (pp. 161-172). New York: ACM.

Reilly, C. F., & Naughton, J. F. (2009). Transparently gathering provenance with provenance aware condor. In *First Workshop on theory and Practice of Provenance* (San Francisco, CA) (pp. 1-10). Berkeley, CA: USENIX Association.

Renesse, R., Birman, K. P., & Vogels, W. (2003). *Astrolabe: a robust and scalable technology for distributed system monitoring management and data mining*. ACM Transactions on Computer Systems.

RRD Tool Website. (n.d.). Retrieved April 20, 2009, from http://oss.oetiker.ch/rrdtool/

Saroiu, S., Gummadi, P. K., & Gribble, S. D. (2002). A Measurement Study of Peer-to-Peer File Sharing Systems. In *Proc. SPIE/ACM Multimedia Computing and Networking* (Vol. 4673, pp. 156–170).

Schopf J., Pearlman, L., Miller, N., Kesselman, C., Foster, I., d'Arcy, M., & Chervenak, A. (2004). *Monitoring the Grid with the Globus Toolkit MDS*.

Sen, S., & Wang, J. (2004). Analyzing Peer-to-Peer Traffic Across Large Networks. *IEEE/ACM Trans. Netw.*, *12*(2), 219–232.

SGE Website. (n.d.). Retrieved April 20, 2009, from http://www.sun.com/software/sge/

Spooner D., Jarvis, S., Cao, J., Saini, S., & Nudd, G. (2003). Local grid scheduling techniques using performance prediction. *IEEE proceedings: Computer Digest Tech.*, *150*(2).

SRM. *Storage Resource Manager Website*. (n.d.). Retrieved April 20, 2009, from http://sdm.lbl.gov/srm-wg/documents.html

Stefano, A. D., Morana, G., & Zito, D. (2008). Advanced Reservation in Grid Using PBS. In *Proceedings of the 2008 IEEE 17th Workshop on Enabling Technologies: infrastructure For Collaborative Enterprises - Volume 00* (June 23 - 25, 2008) (pp. 216-221). Washington, DC: IEEE Computer Society.

Stosser, J., Bodenbenner, P., See, S., & Neumann, D. (2008). A Discriminatory Pay-as-Bid Mechanism for Efficient Scheduling in the Sun N1 Grid Engine. In *Proceedings of the Proceedings of the 41st Annual Hawaii international Conference on System Sciences* (January 07 - 10, 2008) (HICSS). Washington, DC: IEEE Computer Society.

Stutzbach, D., & Rejaie, R. (2006). Understanding Churn in Peer-to-Peer Networks. In *Proc. ACM IMC* (pp. 189–202).

Stutzbach, D., Rejaie, R., & Sen, S. (2005). Characterizing Unstructured Overlay Topologies in Modern P2P File-Sharing Systems. In *Proc. ACM IMC* (pp. 49–62).

Sugaya, Y., Tatsumi, H., Kobayashi, M., & Aso, H. (2008). Long Term CPU Load Prediction System for Scheduling of Distributed Processes and its Implementation. In *Proc. of the 22nd International Conference on Advanced Information Networking and Applications* (pp. 971-977).

Tierney, B., Aydt, R., Gunter, D., Smith, W., Swany, M., Taylor, V., & Wolski, R. (2002 August). A Grid Monitoring Architecture. In GWDPerf 16–3. Global Grid Forum.

Velt, S. (2008). Neues vom schutzheiligen: Nagios in version 3.0 freigegeben. *Technical Report, 9*.

Wang, X., Yao, Z., & Loguinov, D. (2009). Residual-based estimation of peer and link lifetimes in P2P networks. *IEEE/ACM Trans. Netw., 17*(3), 726–739.

Wesner, S. (2008 December). *Integrated Management Framework for Dynamic Virtual Organizations*. Höchstleistungsre-chenzentrum, Universität Stuttgart.

Wolski, R. (2003). Experiences with predicting resource performance on-line in computational grid settings. *ACM SIGMETRICS Performance Evaluation Review, 30*(4), 41–49. doi:10.1145/773056.773064

Yang, L., Liu, C., Schopf, J. M., & Foster, I. (2007). Anomaly detection and diagnosis in grid environments. In *Proceedings of the 2007 ACM/IEEE Conference on Supercomputing,* Reno, Nevada.

Yang, L., Schopf, J., & Foster, I. (2003). Conservative Scheduling: Using Predicted Variance to improve Scheduling Deci-sions in Dynamic Environments. *ACM/IEEE SC2003 Conference (SC '03)*.

Zhang, X., Freschl, J., & Schopf, J. (2003). A performance study of monitoring and information services for distributed systems. In *Proceedings of the 12th IEEE High Performance* [Seattle, WA: IEEE Computer Society Press.]. *Distributed Computing, HPDC-12*, 270–282.

Zhang, X., Freschl, J. L., & Schopf, J. M. (2007). Scalability analysis of three monitoring and information systems: MDS2, R-GMA, and Hawkeye. *Journal of Parallel and Distributed Computing, 67*(8), 883–902. doi:10.1016/j.jpdc.2007.03.006

Zhou, J., & Zeng, G. (2007). Validity Checking On Grid Service Composition. In *31st Annual International Computer Software and Applications Conference*.

Chapter 8
Fault Tolerance

ABSTRACT

The domains of usage of large scale distributed systems have been extending during the past years from scientific to commercial applications. Together with the extension of the application domains, new requirements have emerged for large scale distributed systems. Among these requirements, fault tolerance is needed by more and more modern distributed applications, not only by the critical ones. In this chapter we analyze current existing work in enabling fault tolerance in case of large scale distributed systems, presenting specific problem, existing solution, as well as several future trends. The characteristics of these systems pose problems to ensuring fault tolerance especially because of their complexity, involving many resources and users geographically distributed, because of the volatility of resources that are available only for limited amounts of time, and because of the constraints imposed by the applications and resource owners. A general fault tolerant architecture should, at a minimum, be comprised of at least a mechanism to detect failures and a component capable to recover and handle the detected failures, usually using some form of a replication mechanism. In this chapter we analyzed existing fault tolerance implementations, as well as solutions adopted in real world large scale distributed systems. We analyzed the fault tolerance architectures being proposed for particular distributed architectures, such as Grid or P2P systems.

INTRODUCTION

Large scale distributed systems are hardly ever "perfect". Due to their complexity, it is extremely difficult to produce flawless designed distributed systems. **Fault tolerance** is the ability of a large scale distributed system to perform its function correctly even in the presence of faults occurring in various components. In this chapter we present fault tolerance solutions designed to cope with the inability to produce perfect distributed solutions.

DOI: 10.4018/978-1-61520-703-9.ch008

Today, both in the academic and industrial environments there is an increasingly growing interest in large scale distributed systems, which currently represent the preferred instruments for developing a wide range of new applications. The Grid computing domain has especially progressed during the last years due to the technological opportunities that it offers. While until recently the research in the distributed systems domain has mainly targeted the development of functional infrastructures, today researchers understand that many applications, especially the commercial ones, have some complementary necessities that the „traditional" distributed systems do not satisfy. Today current application requirements include the need to tolerate well faults. Traditional approaches for high availability (high resilience to faults occurrences) are based on the combination of redundancy and 24/7 operations support. This involves the presence of human operators that can detect and repair failures and restore redundancy before or short after the service provided by the system is compromised. However, both redundancy and 24/7 operations support are expensive, and this cost may be prohibitive for many application domains. Therefore, automated recovery of failed hardware and software components (especially through restart) has been gaining attention since the mid 1990s. Activity in this area has recently increased thanks to the IBM autonomic computing initiative (Kephart & Chess, 2003), recent work on recursive restartability (Candea, et al, 2002), and recovery-oriented computing (Oppenheimer, et al, 2002).

Although the importance of fault tolerance is today widely recognized and many research projects have been initiated recently in this domain, the existing systems often offer only partial solutions that follow a particular underlying distributed architecture. The characteristics of large scale distributed systems make fault tolerance a difficult problem from several points of view. A first aspect is the geographical distribution of resources and users that implies frequent remote operations and data transfers. These lead to a decrease in the system's capability to detect faults and handle recovery mechanisms, even to manage correct simple mechanisms needed for consensus for example. Another problem is the volatility of the resources, which are usually available only for limited periods of time. The system must ensure the correct and complete execution of the applications even in situations when the resources are introduced and removed dynamically, or when they are damaged. Solving such issues still represents a research domain. In this we present problems and innovative solutions that aim to solving the many requirements involved in obtaining fault tolerant large scale distributed systems.

In the rest of this chapter we present an analysis of the challenges, directions and solutions to the problem of preserving the good functionality of a large scale distributed system in the presence of faults occurrences. The chapter is organized as follows. We first present an analysis of the existing work in designing appropriate models for fault tolerance solution design in case of large scale distributed systems. We continue describing issues concerning the detection of failures, analyzing current proposed solutions. We then describe the existing solutions to recovering from failures in large scale distributed systems. We continue analyzing several techniques designed to ensure fault tolerance. Next we present several future identified future trend about fault tolerance and, in the end, we give several conclusions.

BACKGROUND

The term **fault tolerance** first appeared in 1965, as a concept to unify the previous proposed theories of masking redundancy. Fault tolerance is currently envisioned as a solution to continue delivering correct services in the presence of faults. A delivered service is widely recognized as the behavior of the system as perceived by its users. A failure represents an event that occurs when the delivered service deviates from correct service. The causes of a system failure are diverse, ranging from faulty software implementations to hardware malfunctions or users performing chaotic actions. A transition from incorrect service to correct service is service restoration or fault recovery. The time interval during which the system delivers incorrect service is known as a service outage. An error is that part of the system that may cause a subsequent failure: a failure occurs when an error reaches the service interface and alters the service. A fault is the root cause of error.

Faults are inherent to large scale distributed systems because of their complexity. However faults are considered to be threats only when they produce errors, or their status change from being dormant to being active. The importance of fault tolerance in the context of large scale distributed system is best summarized in the following definition of such a system that is attributed to Leslie Lamport (Schroeder, 1993):

"You know you have one when the crash of a computer you've never heard of stops you from getting any work done."

This definition illustrates one of the main issues in distributed systems: detecting and handling failures. Unfortunately, fault-tolerant computing is extremely hard, involving intricate algorithms for coping with the inherent complexity of the distributed systems. As it turns out, in practice it is extremely difficult, if not impossible, to devise absolutely foolproof, 100% fault tolerance distributed systems. No matter how hard we try, there is always a possibility that something can go wrong. The best we can do is to reduce the probability of failure to an "acceptable" level. Unfortunately, the more we strive to reduce this probability, the higher the cost.

Of course, fault tolerance is a recursive concept. Generally the mechanisms implementing fault tolerance should also be protected, in some way, against possible faults that might affect them.

Several techniques for this include voter replication, self-checking checkers, stable memory for recovery programs and data, etc.

According to Jean-Claude Laprie (Laprie, et al, 2002), some of the most frequent faults occurring in daily used large networked computer systems are human activity, co-design of human activity and system, as the absence of exploitation of findings (faulty components for example) and the diversity of large scale systems, generated by the decreasing natural robustness of hardware and software. In the same year, the study conducted in (Oppenheimer, et al, 2002) analyzed the causes of failures in case of three large-scale Internet services, together with the effectiveness of various techniques for preventing and mitigating service failures. The authors found that operator errors is one of the largest causes of failures, configuration errors are the largest category of operator errors, and that failures in custom-written front-end software and lack of thoroughly online testing for exposing and detecting component failures are significant. Errors are therefore largely human-made and are inevitable to happen, especially in case of large scale distributed systems, involving many components and distributed software.

A general architecture of a fault tolerance architecture designed for large scale distributed systems consists of the components presented in Figure 1.

FAULT TOLERANCE MODELS

The design and verification of fault-tolerant distributed applications is widely viewed as a complex endeavor. Distributed systems in general are hard to design and understand. Because of their complexity and the large number of incorporated components they exhibit with a high probability failures at different levels. In order to understand the behavior of such systems in the presence of faults, researchers devised various simplified **fault tolerance models**.

Figure 1. Components of a generic fault-tolerance mechanism for LSDS

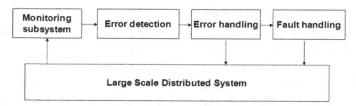

The traditional formalism being used to describe fault tolerance issues in large scale distributed systems is represented by the asynchronous (or time-free) model. The distributed asynchronous model assumes no bounds on message delays, clock drifts, or the time necessary to execute a step. In this model the functional requirements of a fault-tolerant distributed system are represented by two properties: safety and liveness. The safety property describes what is not allowed to happen, the most used definition in literature for this being "no message is received unless it was sent". The liveness property demand what eventually must happen, as in "every message which is sent is eventually received". The foundations of these two properties were constructed in 1985, when Apern and Schneider came up with a decomposition theorem, proving that every fault tolerance property could be written as the intersection of a safety and a liveness property.

Currently the asynchronous model is the preferred way to express properties of fault tolerant distributed systems. Over time, several attempts were made to improve the original model. For example, the system model being proposed by Chen et al. (2002) considers a simple asynchronous model that consists of only two processes, p and q. The processes are subject to crash failures only and, in addition, crashes are considered to be permanent. The processes in the model are connected by two unidirectional channels that cannot create, duplicate or corrupt messages. The channels are also considered to be fair-lossy, meaning that if a process, say p, sends an infinite number of messages to process q and q is correct, then q eventually receives an infinite number of messages from p. This resembles the communication between two services using a best-effort lossy communication protocol, such as UDP. In addition, processes have access to some local physical clock, giving them the ability to measure time. The model does not assume anything regarding the synchronization of these clocks. Other models were further designed to reflect more accurately the properties of modern distributed systems approaches (Chandra, 1996), or to correct several weak properties of the original model (Defago, et al., 2003).

The asynchronous model is weak in the sense that it provides no guarantees on the timing behavior of the system (unlike end-to-end real-time communication systems). For example, the asynchronous model suffers from the inherent difficulty of determining whether a process has actually crashed or it is only very slow. In fact, several distributed agreement paradigms cannot be solved deterministically in asynchronous systems if even a single process might crash. Examples of such paradigms are Consensus, Atomic Broadcast, Total Order Broadcast (Defago, et al, 2004), Leader Election, Group Membership and Atomic Commit.

As a result, several attempts were made to define partially synchronous models to cope with the real-world constraints of the communication delays (Dwork, et al, 1988). Such models assume a global stabilization time that enforces guarantees on the timing behavior of the system. Outside this time, the model assumes no time bounds. In such models, the synchrony assumptions are at best probabilistic. Compared with the asynchronous model, any synchronous or semi-synchronous model has a more complex semantics. The applications being programmed based on the asynchronous model are easier to port.

The asynchronous model also models better the properties of large scale distributed systems. In such systems communication is prone to changing networking conditions. Beside, heterogeneity and unpredictable system loads imply that the speeds of the processes are not homogeneous and cannot be predicted accurately. Because of these reasons the asynchronous model proves more adequate to study the behavior of fault tolerance in case of large scale distributed systems. But, in order to be widely adopted, the researchers had to designed solutions to the deterministic impossibility of the distributed agreement paradigms.

The impossibility deterministic result no longer holds if the system is augmented with some unreliable failure detector oracle. This means that the hardware and software properties of the system, aspects that influence the detection of faults, are considered in a separated detection layer. Over the years many detection mechanisms were developed starting from this observation, the most frequently cited being the unreliable failure detection mechanism (Chandra & Toueg, 1996), detailed in the next section.

A more modern approach to define formal models for describing fault tolerance in the context of distributed systems tries to integrate into an unifying theory all the dependability aspects, meaning linking together the fault tolerance aspects with security issues. Although several attempts were made in this direction, today they continue to remain two distinct views with different communities. A first attempt to define a dependable model was made in (Avizienis, et al, 2004). The work was then further continued in (Benenson, et al, 2006). The formal framework being described in the second work is in fact based on the specification of three identified fundamental properties (classes) that are needed to support the definition of fault-tolerance and security within a uniform system model: safety, liveness and information flow. The first two properties are the basis of the asynchronous model. In addition the authors also identified a third property that best expresses the security issues. The proposed model represents a step forward in the direction of specification of complete dependability requirements of a distributed system, alleviating the definition of fault detection and handling together with security issues. However, the model is still incomplete, as it lacks one important aspect: the formalism to describe complexity and probabilities. For this cause the model cannot describe for example reliability (or express the mean time to failure) and work is still needed in this direction.

These models are well designed to study the behavior of the distributed system itself. However, in order to be adequate for fault tolerance studies, they must consider appropriate model(s) to represent the possible types of encountered failures. Several **failure models** have been proposed, all being based on the idea of assigning responsibility for faulty behavior to the system's components: processes and communications channels. In contrast to the classic work on fault-tolerant computing systems, the failure models for distributed systems consider the number of faulty components, and not the occurrences of faulty behavior. For example, a t-fault tolerant system is a system that continues functioning correctly provided that no more than t of its components are faulty. Some care, however, is generally required in defining failure models. For example, consider a fault that leads to a message fault. The fault in this case could be attributed to the sender, the receiver or the channel. Due to this diversity in faulty behavior, failure models commonly found in the distributed systems literature include:

- *Failstop*. A process fails by halting. Once it halts, the processor remains in that state. The fact that a processor has failed is assumed to be detectable by other processors.
- *Crash*. A processor fails by halting. Once it halts, the processor remains in that state.

The fact that a processor has failed may not be detectable by other processors.

- *Crash+Link*. A processor fails by halting. Once it halts, the processor remains in that state. A link fails by losing some messages, but does not delay, duplicate, or corrupt messages.
- *Receive-Omission*. A processor fails by receiving only a subset of the messages that have been sent to it or by halting and remaining halted.
- *Send-Omission*. A processor fails by transmitting only a subset of the messages that is actually attempts to send or by halting and remaining halted.
- *General Omission*. A processor fails by receiving only a subset of the messages that have been sent to it, by transmitting only a subset of the messages that it actually was supposed to send, or by halting and remaining halted.
- *Byzantine Failures*. A processor fails by exhibiting arbitrary behavior.

These classes of failures range from the least disruptive (failstop failures are detectable, so processes can safely perform recovery actions) to the most disruptive (a system that can tolerate Byzantine failures can tolerate anything). Their use depends on the purpose of the fault tolerance system model being considered.

FAILURE DETECTION

Failure detection is an essential property of any fault tolerant distributed application that needs to react in some way in the presence of failures. A failure detector is widely recognized as an oracle that can intelligently suspect processes to have failed (Chandra & Toueg, 1996). In distributed applications, failure detection is generally implemented through the use of directly invoked local services (local failure detectors), or through the use of a group membership service or other group communication primitives (such as consensus or total order broadcast).

One traditional approach for failure detection, for either hard or transient types of failures, is the use of **replicating actions**. The two approaches to detecting failures using replicating actions are: replication in space and replication in time. Replication in space means performing the same actions using different isolated components. Replication in time means performing the same actions using a single set of components repeatedly. The choice is in favor of the first approach, as the second one works only for the transient type of failures. Both these approaches are based on observing the set of replicated actions and, if the observer sees disagreement, conclude that a fault occurred. However, if the results do agree, we cannot assert that no component is faulty; this is because if there are enough faulty components, all might be corrupted and still agree. For example, for Byzantine failures, $t+1$ replicated actions permit t-fault tolerant failure detection, but not masking (one cannot assume the majority value is correct). In order to implement t-fault tolerant masking, $2t+1$ replicated actions are needed, since then t faulty components cannot mislead the majority vote.

The major drawback of the replicating actions solution is that faults are detected very slow. A transient failure being triggered as a result of a first action is detected only when all other actions in its set are completed. Also, a crashed component is detected only when needed, as a result of a costly timeout operation that can result in slowing down the entire flow of a distributed application.

A more appropriate solution to detect mainly hard (crash) failures consists in attaching to each processes of a distributed application a **failure detection module** (see Figure 2). The failure detection module works asynchronous and independent on the application flow and is responsible with monitoring a subset of the processes in the system and maintaining a list of those it currently

Figure 2. Federation of unreliable failure detector modules

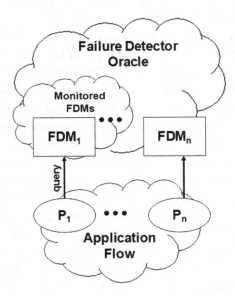

Table 1. Classes of failure detectors

Accuracy	Strong	Weak
Perpetual	P (Perfect)	S (Strong)
Eventual	$\lozenge P$ (Eventually Perfect)	$\lozenge S$ (Eventually Strong)

suspects to have crashed. A process can query its local failure detector module at any time. Internally, the failure detector module maintains a list of suspect processes that he suspects are crashed. The suspect processes list is permanently updated such that, at any time, new processes can be added and old ones removed. For example, a process suspected to have crashed at time t can be removed from the list at time $t+1$ (it is no longer suspected). The failure detector is considered unreliable (Chandra & Toueg, 1996) because is allowed to make mistakes, to a certain degree. A module can erroneously suspect some correct process (wrong suspicion) or can fail to detect processes that are already crashed. At any given time two failure detector modules may have different lists of processes.

Failure detectors are classified into several classes according to the types of mistakes that they are allowed to make. Table 1 presents the classification of the binary failure detectors. Such a class is specified by means of two important properties, completeness and accuracy, that failure detectors must satisfy. The table is based on the

classes of failure detectors presented in (Chandra, 1998). However, as the authors demonstrate, any failure detector presenting weak completeness can be easily transformed into a corresponding (in terms of accuracy specifications) failure detector presenting strong completeness. For this reason, in opposition with the original classification, here we consider as distinctive categories only the classes of failure detectors presenting different accuracy properties.

Other classes of failure detectors were later proposed for the special case of accrual detectors (Defago, et al, 2005). However, as the authors demonstrate, there is a relation of equivalence between accrual and binary types of detectors, one being easily transformed into another. For this reason we do not considerate the accrual classes of failure detectors to be distinctive from the original unary classes.

The four classes of failure detectors are characterized by their completeness and accuracy properties, aspects which detail the levels of mistakes that the detectors are allowed to make. As an example, a failure detector of class $\lozenge S$, which is one of the weakest failure detectors to solve Consensus (to be exactly, the weakest detectors, according to (Chandra & Toueg, 1996), are of class $\lozenge W$, however any $\lozenge W$ failure detector can be transformed into a $\lozenge S$ failure detector), must meet the following two properties:

- **Strong Completeness.** *Eventually every process that crashes is permanently suspected by every correct process.*
- **Eventual Weak Accuracy.** *There is a time after which some correct process is never suspected by any correct process.*

The strongest failure detectors are those of class $\Diamond P$ that, in addition to the Strong completeness property, must meet the following property:

- **Eventual Strong Accuracy.** *There is a time after which correct processes are not suspected by any correct process.*

A failure detector plays two important roles: detecting when monitored processes fail and mitigating their information to the monitoring process. For scalability reasons, it is generally assumed that in large scale distributed systems these two aspects are distinctive. The detection of failures remains a local mechanism, whereas the distributed of failure suspicions being left to some notification mechanism. The notification mechanisms come in the form of a push or pull model. In the pull model the monitoring system periodically pulls information from the local detectors. In the push model the local detectors convey their information on updates to the monitoring system.

The most common implementation of local failure detection is based on the heartbeat strategy. In this strategy every failure detector module periodically sends a heartbeat message to the other modules, to inform them that it is still alive. When a module fails to receive a heartbeat from another process for a predetermined amount of time (timeout) it concludes the remote process crashed. There is a tradeoff to consider, however, for the timeout values being considered. If the timeout is short then crashes are detected quickly, but there is a high chance of suspecting of being crashed processes that takes a longer time to respond (due to a possible high load for example). Conversely, if the timeout is long, the chance of wrong suspicions if low, but the detection time is deteriorated. This approach does not consider also the heterogeneity of distributed systems. The fact that the timeout is fixed means that the failure detection mechanism is unable to adapt to changing conditions. A long timeout in some

systems can turn out to be very short in a different environment.

In the last years there have been many proposals to address some of the problems of ensuring scalable failure detection. Some relate to scalability. In a large scale distributed system, letting a failure detector module monitor the entire set of other modules is unfeasible. Several solutions proposed (hierarchical protocols, gossip-style protocols, and adaptive protocols) limit the number of processes that are monitored by a detector module to only a subset of the entire distributed failure oracle. These solutions also raise the problem of mitigating a detected failure to the entire distributed system. Other solutions, such as the accrual failure detectors (Defago, et al, 2003)(Defago, et al, 2005), address the problem of meting the quality of service requirements of the distributed applications.

In a large scale distributed system, consisting of many nodes, it is impractical to let the failure detection modules monitor each others. An alternative to this consists in arranging processes into an hierarchical structure (such as tree, forest, etc.) along which traffic is channeled. In this approach a failure detector module is responsible with monitoring only a partial subset of nodes. In the event of a failure the information is then propagated and aggregated into upper levels. In general, the hierarchy is assumed to closely match the physical topology of the underlying network, for increased benefit. There have been several propositions of hierarchical failure detection schemes. For example, one such solutions being proposed relies on the use of a two-level hierarchy and is specifically designed for the Globus toolkit (Stelling, et al, 1998). However, being a detection scheme based on only a two-level hierarchy, the proposed solution fails to take full advantage of the hierarchical approach and, consequently, do not scale well for large scale distributed systems. (Felber, 1999) also proposed an architecture for a CORBA failure detection service. Although the paper focuses on a hierarchical architecture, the first-class CORBA objects acting as failure detectors can easily be adapted to a gossip-like or adaptive architecture.

An alternative technique for implementing failure detectors comes in the form of gossip-like protocols. In this approach processes randomly pick partners with whom they exchange their information. The idea is that, with high probability, eventually all processes obtain any piece of information. Protocols implementing this approach are also sometimes called epidemic protocols. One of the advantages of gossip-style protocols, beside their capability to efficiently propagate failure suspicions, is that they are completely oblivious to underlying topology changes.

One of the pioneering works in implementing gossip-style failure detectors is (van Renesse, et al, 1998). In their work the authors identify a variant specifically designed for large scale distributed systems: the multilevel gossiping. The idea is to define a multilevel hierarchy using the structure of Internet domains and subdomains as defined by comparing IP addresses. In the failure detector protocol, most gossip messages are sent using the basic protocol only within a subnet. Then the gossiping information is further propagated between subnets and finally across different domains. There is, however, a price to pay for this. The protocol does not work well when a large number of components crash or become partitioned away.

Another gossip-based failure detection solution was further developed in the context of SWIM group membership protocol (Gupta, et al, 2001). The approach considers that the detector modules do not communicate randomly. Instead, they inquire failure detector modules located in their neighborhood. The failure detector can be tuned to ensure a given detection time, with an accuracy that depends on several parameters such as network conditions. The detection protocol however can only handle a fixed set of monitored processes. This disadvantage comes from the fact that, in the proposed architecture, the join and leave operations are left to be handled by the membership protocol.

An alternative approach to implementing failure detectors comes in the form of adaptive protocols (Defago, et al, 2003). These protocols are designed to adapt dynamically to their environmental and, in particular, adapt their behavior to changing network conditions. Failure detectors can also be made to adapt to changing application behavior. Unlike in the case of the heartbeat detector, the main idea behind an adaptive failure detector is that the timeout in this case is modified dynamically according to environmental conditions.

A protocol that adjusts the timeout by using the maximum arrival interval of heartbeat messages was proposed in (Fetzer, et al, 2001). The protocol assumes a partially synchronous system model, being based on the assumption of a bound on message delays. Chen et al. (2002) proposed a different approach based on a probabilistic analysis of network traffic. Their protocol uses arrival times sampled in the recent past to compute an estimation of the arrival of the next heartbeat. The timeout is set according to the estimation and a safety margin, based on application QoS requirements (e.g. upper bound on detection time) and network characteristics (e.g., network load). One of the strongest contributions of the paper is the definition of a set of metrics to evaluate the QoS of failure detectors. The metrics relates to the two fundamental properties of failure detectors, completeness and accuracy. For example, assuming the asynchronous model consisting of only two processes, p and q, the defined metrics are:

- *Detection Time T_D* is the time that elapses since the crash of p and until q begins to suspect p permanently.
- *Mistake Recurrence Time T_{MR}* measures the time elapsed between two consecutives mistakes.
- *Mistake Duration T_M* measures the time it takes for the detector to correct a mistake.

- *Average Mistake Rate λ_M* measures the rate at which a failure detector makes mistakes.
- *Query Accuracy Probability P_A* is the probability that the failure detector's output is correct at a random time.
- *Good Period Duration T_G* measures the length of a good period, in which a process is not suspected.

An alternative estimation that was further proposed (Bertier, et al, 2002) provides a shorter detection time than the Chen's, but also leads to more wrong suspicions. However, the resulting failure detector is shown to belong to class $\Diamond P$ when executed in a partially synchronous system model.

Another adaptive detector (Sotoma & Madeira, 2001), proposed for the use with CORBA, computes a dynamic timeout value based on the average time arrivals of heartbeat messages, plus a ratio between arrival intervals.

In addition to adapting to changing network conditions, failure detectors can also adapt to changing behavioral patterns of the application. For example, if a failure detector is not monitored by any of the other modules it could stop, at least temporary, to send heartbeat messages, and thus improving the performance of the entire distributed application. Sergent et al. (2001) analyzed several failure detector implementations, among which they proposed a more specific approach, called the "ad hoc heartbeat" strategy. It requires the application developer to identify critical messages in the protocol. For example, in this approach, a process p starts monitoring a process q until, for example, some result is returned back from q to p. Until the results are returned back q sends heartbeat to p. When the result is sent back, q stops sending heartbeats to p. The authors illustrated and analyzed the ad hoc failure detector with a consensus protocol, but the principle can be easily applied to other protocols as well. In case of consensus, they show that the proposed approach can significantly reduce the overhead of the failure detector.

A distinctive category of detectors is represented by the accrual failure detectors (Defago, et al, 2005). The family of accrual failure detectors consists of detector modules that associate, to each of the monitored processes, a real number value that changes over time. The value represents the suspicion level, where zero means the process is not suspected at all, and the larger the value the stronger the suspicion. The accrual failure detectors were proposed as an alternative to the limited binary model, where detectors could only output two possible values: a process is suspicious or not. In this new approach the interpretation of the suspicion level is left to the distributed application using it. In this way multiple applications, having different QoS requirements, use the same failure detectors in different ways. The application could take either conservative (slow and accurate) or aggressive (fast, but inaccurate) decisions. One example of an implementation of an accrual failure detector is the φ-failure detector (Defago, et al, 2003). The φ-failure detector samples the arrival time of heartbeats and maintains a sliding window of the most recent samples. The window is used to estimate the arrival time of the next heartbeat. In addition, the distribution of past samples is used as an approximation for the probabilistic distribution of future heartbeat messages. With this information, the detector computes a value φ with a scale that changes dynamically to match recent network conditions. For the global failure notification mechanism the authors proposed the use of a hierarchical approach. A similar approach was also proposed in (Bertier, et al, 2002). However, the proposed failure detectors are poorly adapted to very conservative failure detection because of their vulnerability to message losses. In practice message losses tend to be strongly correlated (i.e., losses tend to occur in bursts). A proposed accrual detector designed to handle this problem is the k-failure detector (Hayashibara, et al, 2004). The k-failure detector takes into account both messages losses and short-lived network partitions, each missed heartbeat contributing to raising the level of defined suspicion according to a predetermined scheme. An alternative implementation was also proposed in (de Araujo Macedo, et al, 2004), in the form of a neural network based failure detector. In this case the neural network uses information extracted from network equipments as one of its inputs.

The detection of failure is far from being a trivial task. All previously proposed detectors had issues. Some work better in WANs, while other in LANs. Some account for the lost of messages, some for the transient types of failures (although, in our opinion, this problem still remains an issue to be solved). Wiesman et al. (2006) proposed an alternative standard approach, such that any distributed application could use the failure detection capabilities of some failure detector proposed implementation as a service. The proposed architecture is based on a two level model. First, the authors considered that the failure detection itself could be left to some previously defined detector module. The failure detection information is further aggregates using SNMP. In this way, the detection notification can be correlated to hardware and software monitored parameters to possible correctly detect the source of failure. This way, the failure detector can identify between process failures, link crash failures, host failures or network failures. Another advantage of such an approach is the better interoperability. Failure detectors components can use a variety of strategies to detect failures and report such failures with different quality of service parameters and formal properties. In turn, because of the standardized proposed MIBs, the failure detector services can be used directly by applications, or be used for building distributed systems protocols, such as consensus, total order broadcast, or atomic commitment.

An important issue with failure detectors is their scalability. In case of large scale distributed systems, where data is exchanged at high rate, the failure detection could sometimes lead to exhaustion and poor detection rates. One solu-tion to this problem was proposed, for example, in (Krishnamurthy, et al, 2003). The authors proposed an approach based on Sketch. Sketch is a set of hash tables which provide probabilistic guarantees. The authors build a forecast model for the streams based on the observed data in the Sketch. Differences in the forecasted values and actual streams of data are reported as errors. The idea is to obtain a statistical model of the stream. This idea is further extended in (Schweller, et al, 2006). In this, authors provide an efficient reversible-hashing scheme to quickly identify the streams which have significantly changed. In this also the new incoming values of the streams are matched against a statistical model to find errors.

An alternative approach that focuses on the scalability of failure detection was proposed in (Bertier, et al, 2003). However, the proposed system assumes simpler failure semantics such as crash failures. Khanna, et al, (2007) proposed a different approach to failure detection, based on stateful identification of the application state. The advantage of such a system is its scalability, as the system is specifically designed for high data rate scenarios. Their proposed failure detection system aggregates exchanged application messages in order to deduce the application state and match it against anomaly-based rules. In this system the messages are sampled using an optimization approach to reduce the rate of incoming packets to be examined. The authors also demonstrate improved results of their proposal in terms of detecting failures in high-speed data communication links.

RECOVERY

Recovery represents the set of actions that are activated as a result of the detection of failures and/or errors in the system state. Recovery consists of error handling and fault handling. **Error handling** represents the set of actions that are made in order to eliminate the errors from the system state. It takes two forms: rollback and rollforward. Backward recovery (rollback) is the state transformation of returning the system back to a saved state that existed prior to error detection. Forward recovery (rollforward) takes the system into a new state without the detected errors. This technique is difficult to implement because it requires knowing in advance which errors might occur. An alternative recovery technique that, given sufficient redundancy, allows recovery without explicit error detection is fault masking.

The second component of recovery, **fault handling**, is the set of preventing actions designed to make faults not being activated again. Fault handling is generally used after the system is taken to an error-free state. Fault handling involves four steps: first the cause of error is identified and possible recorded (fault diagnosis), then the faulty previously identified components are physically or logically isolated from the rest of the system, so that not to influence any more the state of the system (fault isolation), a set of reconfiguration actions takes place so that the possible reassign tasks among non-failed components (system reconfiguration) and, finally, the system state is updated to reflect the result of the corrective set of actions (system reinitialization). Usually, fault handling is followed by fault maintenance – the intervention of an external agent to remove the faults isolated by fault handling.

Rollback recovery is a simple technique that consists for example in the repeated execution of some function in order to overcome a transient or intermittent fault. Instead of executing the same function again, it can be also useful to use some other function or to execute the function on other processing unit. However, other approaches for rollback recovery also exist. Such approaches are, in their vast majority, based on the use of two widely used techniques: checkpointing and logging. **Checkpointing** is the method of periodically recording the state of the system in stable storage. A checkpoint is a complete record of the state of the application. The global state is a set of individual process states. In case of failures,

the processes of the distributed applications are revived and their state is rolled forward to the last checkpointed state saved on hard stores. The existing checkpointing algorithms are divided into several classes: consistent, independent and coordinated checkpointing.

In order to compare the different checkpointing algorithms being proposed, several key metrics are generally used: snapshot time, commit time and recovery time are among the most commonly used. Snapshot time represents how long it takes to identify and copy (to intermediate storage) all required program state. Commit time is how long it takes to copy snapshots into non-volatile storage. Finally, recovery time represents how long it takes to restore state to a failed process. All the checkpointing techniques must implement one condition: the rolled back state that is generated after a failure must be consistent, without any orphans. The consistency requirement is usually expressed in terms of orphan processes, which are surviving processes whose states are inconsistent with the recovered state of a crashed process. An example is one process that moves to a state after receiving a message, while another one is rolled back to a state where it didn't even sent that particular message.

Consistent checkpointing is a technique designed to simplify failure recovery and eliminate the domino effects in case of failures by preserving a consistent global checkpoint state. The domino effects are caused by algorithms trying to reach a consistent state across the local states of all processes, when the rollback to a previous state generates inconsistence in the state of another process, which must be rolled back to an even earlier state, which in turn generates inconsistencies in state for other processes, and so on. In case of consistent checkpointing a global checkpoint is taken periodically and the processes have to synchronize themselves to assure that their set of local checkpoints corresponds to a consistent state of the application. This approach suffers from the high overhead associated with the checkpointing process.

In case of independent checkpointing the application processes are allowed to establish checkpoints in an independent way and no synchronization is enforced between their checkpoint operations. In case of a failure the system searches a set of local checkpoints that together correspond to a consistent state of the application. In this case, in order to guarantee with high probability the existence of a consistent state, each process must keep several checkpoints in stable storage. This technique is appealing because there is no need to exchange any protocol messages during a checkpoint operation (the application runs faster) and, because each process can decide on its own when to checkpoint, the checkpoint consumes less bandwidth required to access the possible remote stable storage on which the state is saved. However, its main drawback is that it suffers from the domino effect. The probability of occurrence of the domino-effect can be reduced if checkpoints are taken very often, at the expense of an increased overhead. An alternative way to avoid the domino effect is the use of an additional message-logging scheme.

Coordinated checkpointing tries to combine both the advantages of consistent and independent checkpointing. In this case the checkpointing behave as in the independent case, however, in order to reduce the number of messages necessary to produce a consistent state in case of a failure the coordinated checkpointing requires the use of a global coordinator. The coordinated checkpointing is an attractive recovery technique for large scale systems and can be easily implemented for example using vector timestamps (Jinno, et al, 2006).

An alternative checkpointing solution consists in the use of a global time synchronization mechanism. In this case, the global state is checkpointed based on a global time and using a synchronization layer that already is assumed to exist in the system and that is used for the synchronization of the individual clocks. When processes decide to asynchronous synchronize their state, the synchronization layer is used for example to carry also state synchronization messages piggybacked in the time synchronization messages (Neogy, et al, 2001).

The other approach to rollback recovery consists in the use of **message logging**. The message logging protocols require that each process periodically record its local state and log the messages it received after having recorded that state. Based on the way that these protocols ensure the consistency requirement, they are classified into pessimistic, optimistic, and causal (Alvisi, et al, 1998). Pessimistic protocols avoid at all costs the creation of orphans during an execution, while optimistic protocols take appropriate actions during recovery to eliminate all orphans. The causal message logging protocols neither create orphans when there are failures, nor do they ever block a process when there are no failures. Such protocols can be constructed using for example piggybacking.

The choice between checkpointing and message logging depends on the distributed system. For example, in case of a large cluster having one fault every hour and applications running with large datasets logging can be considered a more adequate solution (Bouteiller, et al, 2003).

Typical mechanisms for Grids consist of retrying failed executions, perhaps starting at a recent checkpoint. One mechanisms, identified in (Zhang, et al, 2004), consists in the use of two or more replicas of the same services, using a primary-backup approach. In this case a client sends request to a primary designed replica, which receives and replies to the client. The problems related to this approach are: Grid services are stateless and, as a result, replicas of the same service should continuously also synchronize the current state of the primary service; Grid systems behave in nondeterministic ways and, as a result, without proper consistency protocols, two replicas executing the same sequence could become inconsistent; a Grid recovery service should be provided as a high-level functionality and, if not properly

Figure 3. The difference between proactive and a reactive recovery solution

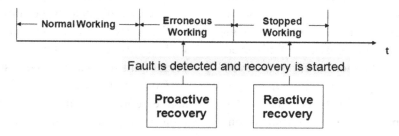

implemented, it could result in the performance degradation of the entire system. Typically, the primary does not reply to the client until all its backup replicas are state-updated. This is done to ensure that the backups are always consistent with the client. In case of a failure of the primary backup one of the backup service instances is designed as a primary. This is usually accomplished using a voting protocol. After a failure of the primary, the backups agree on a new primary and ensure that all future requests are directed to it.

Several fault handling techniques have also been proposed in literature. Given the set of possible repair actions, as defined by the application behavior or given as input by the user, one idea is to learn the effectiveness of a repair action by trying it out and then observing its effect in the system (Littman, et al, 2004). Such a learning algorithm for the construction of a repair policy can specify the test and repair actions to be taken based on the outputs (true or false) of the previous test and repair actions. An alternative approach, based on dynamic decisions, was further proposed in (Joshi, et al, 2005).

However, when faults propagate faster than traditional reactive mechanisms (which typically wait to detect a fault before reacting to recover from it) are able to recover the system, then, the availability of the system may ultimately be compromised. This could lead to an epidemic situation in which the system is, as a consequence of faults, no longer able to recover. To curtail propagating faults, a system can instead employ proactive recovery mechanisms. The difference

between the proactive based recovery systems and reactive based recovery systems is that the former may act to increase resistance, to initiate recovery, or to adapt: before or concurrently with the recognition of a problem in the system. Figure 3 illustrated this difference.

Reactive fault tolerant system keeps a continuous check on the performance of various devices in the system. They poll the device for its failure status. If a failure is detected during the run of the system, it then informs the fault monitoring system and does the related recovery process.

Predictive (proactive) systems assume that faults, which are inherently unpredictable, do show some disruptive effect on the performance of the system (Dumitras, et al, 2005). Research studies show that faults do show a pattern of occurrence. Predictive fault tolerant systems exploit these patterns to predict a fault.

An example of a solution to implement proactive recovery is based on the use of a hypervizor that provides isolation between applications subject to Byzantine failures and secure components that are not affected by faults (Reiser, et al, 2007). The hypervizor is able to shut down and reboot any operating system instance of a service replica, and thus can be used for proactive recoveries.

FAULT TOLERANCE TECHNIQUES

One widely used technique to guarantee the availability and good performance large scale distributed systems in the presence of faults is replication. **Replication** implies the use of more services or components performing the same function. Whenever a replicated entity encounters a failure (a crash is the most commonly used scenario, but some replication solutions are even adapted to deal with Byzantine failures) another replica is switched on and takes its place.

One of the simplest forms of replication, still widely used, is to perform computations using multiple channels, either sequentially or concurrently. The channels may be of identical design or separate designs and implementations. The former choice is adequate for elusive design faults, via rollback, while the latter, also known as design diversity, is more appropriate for solid design faults.

The current replication techniques can be classified in two classes: active and passive replication. In case of active replication each request is processed by all replicas. The technique ensures a fast reaction to failures. However, active replication uses processing resources heavily and requires the processing of requests to be deterministic. This last point is a very strong limitation since, in a distributed application, there are many potential sources of non-determinism. With passive replication (also called primary-backup), only one replica (primary) processes the request, and sends update messages to the other replicas (backups). The technique uses fewer resources than active replication does, without the requirement of operation determinism. On the other hand, the replicated service usually has a slow reaction to failures. For instance, when the primary crashes, the failure must be detected by the other replicas, and the request may have to be reprocessed by a new primary. This may result in a significantly higher response time for the request being processed.

At local level, passive replication can rely on dedicated hardware devices. However, in large scale distributed systems the detection of failures is not certain. In such systems, all implementations of passive replication are based on a group membership service and must exclude the primary whenever it is suspected to have crashed. In practice, this is a strong limitation of passive replication since this means that a mere suspicion will be turned into a failure, thus reducing the actual fault-tolerance of the system.

Conversely, there exist implementations of active replication that neither require a group membership service nor need to kill suspected processes (e.g., active replication based on the Atomic Broadcast algorithm proposed in (Chandra & Toueg, 1996)).

An alternative approach to replication combines the power of these two classes. The new class, called semi-passive replication (Defago, et al, 2002), retains the essential characteristics of passive replication while avoiding the necessity to force the crash of suspected processes.

A widely used term in replication is Byzantine fault tolerance (or BFT). This is a replication technique designed to protect against arbitrary problems, ranging from crash faults to software bugs and security violations. A BFT service can function correctly even if a number of its replicas being to act arbitrary instead of according to specification. For large scale distributed systems, BFTs require a higher degree of replication than techniques that tolerate only crash faults (BFT requires a minimum of $3f + 1$ replicas to tolerate f arbitrary faults), making it an expensive solution. A great deal of work has been done on Byzantine fault tolerance and making it efficient. Also, tradition approaches to BFT (e.g. state-machine-replication) assumed a client-server model. These solutions do not provide support for multi-tiered computing in which a replicated BFT service must act as a client of a second service, as in Grid service operations.

A solution to these problems considers the use of multi-tier BFT systems, in which every tier is BFT replicated. This can be implemented in the forms of BFT quorums that act as listeners (Fry, 2004) or multi-tiered BFT DNS systems (Ahmed, 2001). The use of Web service programming models has been also previously explored as an alternative to building BFT systems. For example, the ITDOS project (Sames, et al, 2002) aims to providing a framework for building heterogeneous BFT distributed object CORBA systems on top of CLBFT (Castro & Liskov, 1999), a popular state-machine-replication protocol.

The modern approaches aim to reduce the number of required BFT replicas to $2f + 1$ in order to tolerate f Byzantine faults, to allow the insertion of a privacy firewall, and to increase throughput (Yin, et al., 2003)(Kotla & Dahlin, 2004). Thema (Merideth, et al, 2005), a BFT middleware system, provides a structured way to build Byzantine-fault-tolerant, survivable Web Services. It consists of a client library, a BFT service library and an external service library. Each component is designed to support the standard multi-tier Web Service programming model and SOAP communication.

Steward (Amir, et al, 2006) is another BFT protocol that is suitable for systems that span multiple wide area sites, each consisting of several server replicas. Steward assumes no trusted component in the entire system, other than a valid mechanism to pre-distribute private/public keys. The hierarchical replication architecture can scale well for large scale distributed systems, assuming a lightweight communication protocol among replicas.

Zyzzyva (Kotla & Dahlin, 2004) is another BFT protocol that uses speculation to reduce the cost and simplify the design of the state machine replication. In Zyzzyva, replicas respond to a client's request by optimistically adopting the order proposed by the primary. This approach has the advantage of reduced the time needed for the client to receive a response. However, replicas can become temporarily inconsistent with one another, but clients detect inconsistencies, help correct replicas converge on a single total ordering of requests, and only rely on responses that are consistent with this total order. This approach allows Zyzzyva to reduce replication overheads to near their theoretical minima.

Another approach used to implement replication consists in the use of architectures based on logical machines. In such an architecture, the state machine is used to transform the physical machines in each site into a logical machine, and the logical machines run a wide-area protocol. Using the state machine approach to build logical machines is a well-known technique for cleanly separating the protocol used to implement the logical machine from the protocol running on top of it. Representative systems include BASE (Rodrigues, et al, 2001) or Starfish (Kihlstrom & Narasimhan, 2003).

Other fault tolerance techniques address the problem of **reliable broadcast**. Such solutions aim at ensuring that all correct participants receive all broadcast messages, even in the presence of network omissions or node failures. The traditional solutions to implement reliable broadcast are based on gossip protocols or hierarchical protocols. The problem with gossip protocols is that, in steady state, they exhibit an excessive overhead in order to ensure reliability with high probability. The hierarchical protocols, such as tree-based, on the other hand, are very fragile in the presence of faults. For these reason, the more modern approaches to implement resilient broadcast algorithms rely on a combination of both.

Bimodal multicast (Birman, et al, 1999) was among the first works that combined the tree-based and epidemic protocols. The binomial multicast involves two phases: first the message is disseminated using multicast; then participants involve in gossip exchanges in order to mask omissions that could occur during the first phase. The approach involves the use of two distinctive protocols, making it difficult to implement in practice. On the other hand, the IP multicast is not widely deployed in large-scale.

Narada (Chu, et al, 2002) is a protocol designed to replace the use of IP multicast with some application-level multicast protocol. Narada employs a random overlay network that is used to build a spanning tree, and a routing algorithm that is executed on top of the overlay. Scribe (Castro, et al, 2002) is also a scalable application-level multicast infrastructure that supports multicast groups with multiple senders. In Scribe the infrastructure is divided into a hierarchy of groups. Each group has a node that serves as a rendezvous point and as a root for the spanning tree being considered by the algorithm.

GoCast (Voulgaris, et al, 2005) is a protocol that embeds a spanning tree in an unstructured overlay network for efficient message dissemination. It involves the creation of a broadcast tree embedded on a gossip-based overlay. Broadcast is achieved mainly by using push gossip on the tree branches, while the remaining links are used to propagate the message using a lazy-push approach. A similar approach is presented by Plumtree (Leitao, et al, 2007). The solution is based on the use of a low cost scheme to build and maintain broadcast trees embedded on a low cost gossip-based random overlay networking. The protocol disseminates payload messages via tree branches and uses the remaining links of the random overlay for fast recovery and tree healing.

In case of large scale distributed systems, a novel problem is catching up the interest of researchers. Today most developers of large scale distributed systems seem to favor the use of model-based development frameworks. This is because developers of such systems are generally domain experts with less background in programming fault-tolerant solutions. However, the model-based approach suffers from the non-existence of appropriate automatic tools to develop safety-critical applications. The solution widely used so far is the use of dedicated developers to cope with this problem. However, the solution, apart from being time-consuming, is very expensive and, for these reasons, many large scale distributed systems are implemented without appropriate fault-tolerant mechanisms. One reason for the non-existence of automatic code generation tools for fault-tolerance mechanisms is the strict requirements on the application, like replica determinism (Poledna, et al, 2000).

One approach to cope with the need for replica determinism consists in the use of logical execution time (Kopetz & Bauer, 2002) concept, which is defined as an approach based on a time-triggered architecture. The approach ensures the system behaves deterministic, due to the absence of race conditions. The time-triggered architecture is appealing and was already used for example in the development of the time-triggered protocol (TTTech Computertechnik AG, 2003). The protocol is dedicated to realizing fault-tolerance mechanisms for the communication layer of any distributed architecture. The time-triggered protocol provides different services like predictable communication with small latency, clock synchronization and even a membership service.

A solution for automatic generation of fault-tolerance mechanisms (Buckl, et al, 2007) in model-based development (at system level) is based on the use of logical execution time. In the proposed framework the developer can specify the fault-tolerance mechanisms that should be applied. Besides fault-tolerance mechanisms, the code generation tool allows also the generation of other system level code, like communication or process management.

Several fault tolerance solutions designed to address the Grid computing challenges were also proposed in literature. For example, (Zhang, et al, 2004) presents a fault tolerant service designed for Grids designed using a primary-backup approach. The proposed solution addresses the problem of building highly available Grid services by replicating a service on two or ore hosts. The authors tested three different alternatives for implementing the primary-backup replication approach: one that makes heavy use of the notification interface defined in OGSI, one that uses standard Globus Grid service requests, and one that uses low-level socket primitives. Their overall conclusion is that the OGSI notification model is suitable for building highly-available services, aspect which makes the task of engineering such services easier than when adopting a low-level approach.

However, one problem that is not considered is the existence of software errors. Such "bugs" can lead to completely correlated failures, such as the primary and backups simultaneously crashing.

(Jin, et al, 2006) introduces an adaptive system for fault detection in Grids and a policy-based recovery mechanism. Fault detection is achieved by monitoring the system, and for recovery several mechanisms are available, among which task replication and checkpointing. A reputation based classification of Grid services, similar to the one in peer-to-peer systems, designed to handle the good behaved replicas is described in (Sonnek & Weissman, 2005). Also, a Grid operating system architecture, with self-healing properties, is presented in (Rilling, 2006).

(Neocleous, et al, 2006) carries out a detailed study on defects in Grid systems, providing case-studies from the EGEE (Enabling Grids for E-Science) European project. The authors identify several classes of failures occurring at different levels in the Grid: at Resource Broker level, in some Computing Elements, or even a Storage Element could get corrupted. An interesting observation is that, while there are solutions for the detection and automatic action in case of failures, in real-world situations the most used solution consists in the human intervention. The described experiences show that currently manual failure management in large-scale infrastructures in a tedious and cumbersome process. As the author notice, the current middleware systems do not provide adequate support for handling failures.

(Grimshaw, et al, 2005) emphasizes on the idea of survivability, which consists in providing, in case of a defect, an alternative service, even if the latter doesn't fully satisfy the initial user requirements. For requirements specification, the authors propose DESL (Dependability Exchange and Specification Language), an XML based language; DESL isn't fully specified yet.

Other fault-tolerance solutions designed specifically for web services have also been proposed in literature. In one solution, based on the implementation of a fault-tolerant container (Sommerville, et al, 2005), the fault-tolerant containers manage a set of replicated services, which can be offered by external providers as well. The containers can be configured for various fault tolerance strategies (either an equivalent service is invoked when a service fails, or multiple equivalent services are invoked from the beginning and a voting mechanism is applied etc.).

Another problem with the fault tolerance mechanisms designed for web services is the inadequate recovery of in-progress requests. These are the requests that were not processed due to a possible failure. With most replication mechanisms simply detect failures and route future requests to backup servers. An approach to address this limitation consists in the use of a hot standby backup server that maintains logs of requests and replies (Aghdaie & Tamir, 2002).

FUTURE TRENDS

Contemporary large scale distributed systems handles fault tolerance in different ways. In peer-to-peer systems the fault tolerance solutions are mature, although work still needs to be done. In contrary, the current middleware (Grid) systems do not provide adequate support for handling failures and for supporting Grid dependability. Therefore, there is a need to develop tools to replace the human based failure tolerance, a costly solution, with automatic instruments that are able to identify failures of Grid components and to investigate their route causes. The fault-tolerance tools should provide a higher-level representation of failures, integrating information from a variety of error-information sources. Furthermore, they should ease the troubleshooting process undergone by Grid system administrators by automating diagnostic and corrective functions, and helping them cope with the complexity of error-information provided by underlying monitoring systems through proper abstractions and uniform user-interfaces. Also, there is a need to develop systems and algorithms for processing the information collected by the various failure-information sources in order to support the automatic identification and prediction of failures, in order to improve the dependability of the Grid's operation.

Several solutions were proposed in the last years; however, they are purely theoretical, and not so much implemented in real-world scenarios. We believe this to be a scenario that will change in the next years. This observation is based on the importance large scale distributed systems gained also outside scientific communities, in enterprises for whom fault-tolerance is must property to achieve.

One approach that we believe will be further researched is the integration of P2P system with Grid computing (Foster, 2002). This approach could combine the power of fault-tolerance solutions currently adopted in P2P systems with the computational advantages of Grid systems under a single umbrella.

Another future trend relates to the combining of fault tolerance approaches with security solutions designed for large scale distributed systems. In this context more and more people are talking about dependable distributed systems, instead of just fault tolerant distributed systems. Dependability introduces under the same concept several properties: reliability, availability, security and maintainability. In this context security breaches are envisioned as particular cases of faults, as they usual result in the disturbance of the normal accepted behavior of the distributed system. However, in large scale distributed systems fault tolerance and security were long seen as two different domains, having their own directions of research. The bridge between these two domains has recently been introduced and work to combine their solutions is still in its early stage. However, it should be expected that in the near future we will have various proposed intrusion tolerant architectures. Such architecture would integrate various defense-in-depth layers to achieve intrusion-tolerance

(meaning having all the components required to ensure avoidance, prevention, detection followed by diagnosis, isolation, recovery, reconfiguration and response).

For dependability we also need adequate models. As seen before, research in this direction was already started; however work still needs to be done. We expect in the near future to see some interesting new models that consider both security and fault tolerance. We believe that such models will be based on fault tolerance models, which will be augmented with security submodels.

Several trends were already also established for implementing automatic detection of failures. However, work still needs to be done to design appropriate failure detector solutions. The important problem with today's failure detectors is their incapacity to scale well, an important aspect when designing large distributed architectures. There are two important aspects to consider. First, the local failure detectors are limited by the resources they have at their disposal. This influences the number of nodes that they are able to monitor. Also, at a larger level, the problem of communicating fast the known faults to the entire system is still a problem even today. Adequate grouping solutions of the failure detectors and improved communication scheme could lead to performances that would be acceptable for Internet scale distributed systems, however we are not there yet and work still needs to be done in this direction too.

Today service-based development is widely used for large scale applications. However, they manifest specific properties that are not completely researched. The vast majority of fault tolerance solutions were designed to be generic, for use in a majority of large scale distributed architectures. However, one possible future trend could be the development of specific solutions for different cases of scenarios. For example, in case of Grid services, their stateful property was not very well exploited in terms of fault tolerance. In this case instead of looking into single packets for failures we could consider an entire data stream and compare its behavior against predefined failure patterns.

Also, failure patterns are not very well investigated. Large scale distributed systems are complex by their nature, so providing automatic sets of patterns for all possible types of failures is a tremendous effort. However, another possible future trend would be to exploit monitoring data to identify automatic pattern for particular types of faults. For example, the monitoring of the data streams could result in the identification of several useful patterns that could be further exploited by automatic failure recovery instruments.

Adaptive failure detectors are fast catching up the interest of researchers. An identified future trend consists in the proposal of various new algorithms that accurately and faster adapt to changing environment conditions. Also, accrual failure detectors represent a promising solution that combines fault detection with QoS requirements coming from the applications. In the future we expect to see new ideas on how such detectors are designed and possible their adoption by the large scale distributed systems communities.

Byzantine types of failures are the most difficult to cope with. Recovery in the presence of such failures represents an issue. Most of the current research in fault tolerance concentrates on the problem of detecting fail-stop crash failures. Detecting Byzantine failures in distributed systems is a difficult problem that did not yet yield a general solution. In the particular case of local components of the distributed system there are results in detecting and correcting Byzantine failures using special mechanisms such as redundancy and retransmission, which are covered in greater depth in the next pages. However, the Byzantine failures handling at the generic distributed system level generally require detailed knowledge about the underlying components and this, coupled with the aspect that such failures are most often masked at the component level, complicates even further the research in founding a general solution to this problem. One solution is represented by the use of a primary-backup design. However, two backups

that use the same code could results in simultaneous errors, so work still needs to be done in this direction also.

An alternative approach, one that is catching up really fast, is represented by the self-healing systems. Such solutions start from the premise that faults are imminent, and, just like the humans do handle viruses by learning to defend against them in time, so such systems could dynamically learn to bypass faults. We consider this to be an interesting approach that, in the future, could catch the attention of more and more researchers. Such systems should be able to restore the system capabilities to full functionality following an event, should automatically reassess success and failure of all actions before, during and after an event and, in the end, should autonomously incorporate the lessons learned into the systems layers. Several immune algorithms were already proposed on smaller scale. They are though characterized by highly decentralized local optimization strategies that achieve some complex desirable global behavior. What is needed are solutions to use such algorithms in complex systems such as the Internet.

Today there are many solutions being proposed when it comes to detecting or handling faults. Several new efforts were started towards standardization. We expect in the near future to see several standards being adapted by the vast majority of fault tolerance communities, as a result of mature fault tolerance solutions being developed around the world. The challenge for the fault-tolerance community is to define "best practice" solutions for building fault tolerant large scale distributed systems, but to also provide supporting evidence to sustain this.

CONCLUSION

In this chapter we presented an analysis of current existing solutions to ensure fault tolerance in large scale distributed systems. The characteristics of these systems pose problems to ensuring fault tolerance especially because of their complexity, involving many resources and users geographically distributed, because of the volatility of resources that are available only for limited amounts of time, and because of the constraints imposed by the applications and resource owners. The problem of ensuring fault tolerance in such systems represents a hot research subject today and, despite the fact that many projects obtained valuable results in this domain, no acceptable general solution was yet found that could integrate all the requirements for designing a fault tolerant large scale distributed system and that could exploit and account for all the capabilities of modern systems.

Failures could be encountered at different levels in a large scale distributed system. The messages could be lost or disrupted in the communication layer, the components could crash, the middleware could insert transient failures, and the application running on top could result in abnormal behavior due to different "bugs". A fault tolerance solution designed for such systems should consider all these layers. However, designing a generic fault tolerance solution is a complex endeavor and we believe that it is generally preferred to use instead decentralized solutions. For example, the components could be permanently monitored for crash failures and a redundancy mechanism be used to reinstate the functionality of such a component to another one still working. But on the same type at application level another approach could be used, one that uses N-programming for example, running the same application on multiple nodes and testing in the end the obtained results.

A general fault tolerant architecture should, at a minimum, be comprised of at least a mechanism to detect failures and a component capable to recover and handle the detected failures, usually using some form of a replication mechanism. Thus, there are several components that are currently researched. The problem of detecting faults is more complex that would seem. This is because of the hetero-geneity of the environments composing a large scale distributed system. The traditional heartbeat approach of detecting failed components could not be generically applied to such systems. Based on this observation several works obtained more appropriate results, such as the ones presented in this chapter, that adapt more appropriate to the heterogeneity of the underlying infrastructure.

Also, the problem of scalability is important when considering fault detection implementations. Currently several proposals consider different approach to minimize the costs involved in the detection scheme, from bandwidth to the number of updates needed to obtained a complete dissemination of the detected faults to the entire system. Such solutions are based on hierarchical or gossip schemes, but new approaches to combine and exploit the advantages of each of these main classes are also being considered.

The recovery from faults is another important aspect to consider in a fault-tolerant architecture designed for large scale distributed systems. General approaches consist in continuously recording the state of the system (checkpointing and logging) and, in the event of a failure, reconstitute the last known good state. In the chapter we presented an analysis of existing recovery solutions that are designed for large scale distributed systems.

One of the most common techniques to achieve fault tolerance is the use of replication. We presented several approaches to using replication, ranging from Byzantine fault replication to solutions designed to handle faults in communication using replication techniques. The Byzantine fault replication architectures for example consider the use of several replicas that can be used to handle transient faults. We presented several solutions that try to minimize the number of needed replicas or that minimize the costs involved using various techniques, such as machine learning.

In this chapter we analyzed existing fault tolerance implementations, as well as solutions adopted in real world large scale distributed systems. We analyzed the fault tolerance architectures being proposed for particular distributed architectures, such as Grids or web services.

In the end we presented several future trends in designing fault tolerant solutions for large scale distributed systems. We identify several open issues that still need to be address in this domain, indicating several possible research directions.

We believe fault tolerant to be an important and active research domain in today's large scale distributed systems being deployed all around the world. The solutions being analyzed are in their vast majority theoretical and work still needs to be done in deploying the proposed solutions into real world scenarios. We believe this to be happen, as large scale distributed systems gain more and more attention from user communities that pose requirements such as fault tolerance. Fault tolerance is today a property that is needed by more and more large scale distributed applications, not only by the critical ones.

REFERENCES

Aghdaie, N., & Tamir, Y. (2002). Implementation and Evaluation of Transparent Fault-Tolerant Web Service with Kernel-Level Support. In *Proceedings of Eleventh International Conference on Computer Communications and Networks* (pp. 63–68). Los Angeles, CA: IEEE Computer Society.

Ahmed, S. (January 2001). *A scalable Byzantine fault tolerant secure domain name system.* Unpublished Master's thesis, MIT, USA.

Alvisi, L. (1998). Message Logging: Pessimistic, Optimistic, Causal and Optimal. *IEEE Transactions on Software Engineering, 24*(2), 149–159. doi:10.1109/32.666828

Amir, Y., Danilov, C., Dolev, D., Kirsch, J., Lane, J., Nita-Rotaru, C., et al. (2006). Scaling Byzantine Fault-Tolerant Replication to Wide Area Networks. In Proc. of the Intl. Conf. on Dependable Systems and Networks, DSN 2006 (pp. 105–114). Baltimore, MD: IEEE Computer Society.

Avizienis, A., Laprie, J.-C., Randell, B., & Landwehr, C. E. (2004). Basic Concepts and Taxonomy of Dependable and Secure Computing. *IEEE Transactions on Dependable and Secure Computing, 1*(1), 11–33. doi:10.1109/TDSC.2004.2

Benenson, Z., Freiling, F. C., Holz, T., Kesdogan, D., & Penso, L. D. (March 2006). Safety, Liveness, and Information Flow: Dependability Revisited. In E. Maehle (Ed.), *Proc. of the ARCS 2006 - 19th International Conference on Architecture of Computing Systems, Dependability and Fault Tolerance* (pp. 56–65). Frankfurt am Main, Germany: IEEE Computer Society.

Bertier, M., Marin, O., & Sens, P. (2002, June). Implementation and performance evaluation of an adaptable failure detector. *Proc. of the Intl. Conf. on Dependable Systems and Networks* [Bethesda, MD: IEEE Computer Society.]. *DSN, 02,* 354–363.

Bertier, M., Marin, O., & Sens, P. (2003). Performance analysis of a hierarchical failure detector. In *Proc. of the 2003 Intl. Conf. on Dependable Systems and Networks, DSN 2003* (pp. 635–644), San Francisco, CA: IEEE Computer Society.

Birman, K., Hayden, M., Ozkasap, O., Xiao, Z., & Budiu, M. (1999). Bimodal multicast. *ACM Transactions on Computer Systems, 17*(2), 41–88. doi:10.1145/312203.312207

Bouteiller, A., Lemarinier, P., Krawezik, G., & Cappello, F. (2003). Coordinated checkpoint versus message log for fault tolerant MPI. In *Proc. of the IEEE Intl. Conf. on Cluster Computing, CLUSTER'03* (pp. 242–250). Hong Kong, China: IEEE Computer Society.

Buckl, C., Regensburger, M., Knoll, A., & Schrott, G. (2007). Generic Fault-Tolerance Mechanisms Using the Concept of Logical Execution Time. In *Proc. of the 13th IEEE Intl. Symp. on Pacific Rim Dependable Computing* (pp. 3–10). Melbourne, Australia: IEEE Computer Society.

Candea, G., Cutler, J., Fox, A., Doshi, R., Gang, P., & Gowda, R. (2002). Reducing recovery time in a small recursively restartable system. In *Proc. of the 2002 International Conference on Dependable Systems and Networks* (pp. 605 – 614). Bethesda, MD: IEEE Computer Society.

Castro, M., Druschel, P., Kermarrec, A., & Rowstron, A. (2002). SCRIBE: A large-scale and decentralized application-level multicast infrastructure. [JSAC]. *IEEE Journal on Selected Areas in Communications, 20*(8), 1489–1499. doi:10.1109/JSAC.2002.803069

Castro, M., & Liskov, B. (1999). Practical Byzantine fault tolerance. In *Proceedings of the third symposium on Operating systems design and implementation* (pp. 173 – 186). Berkeley, CA: USENIX Association.

Chandra, T. D., & Toueg, S. (1996). Unreliable failure detectors for reliable distributed systems. *Journal of the ACM, 43*(2), 225–267. doi:10.1145/226643.226647

Chen, W., Toueg, S., & Aguilera, M. K. (2002). On the quality of service failure detectors. *IEEE Transactions on Computers, 51*(2), 13–32. doi:10.1109/12.980014

Chu, Y.-H., Rao, S., Seshan, S., & Zhang, H. (2002). A case for end system multicast. *IEEE Journal on Selected Areas in Communications, 20*(8), 1456–1471. doi:10.1109/JSAC.2002.803066

Cox, A., Mohanram, K., & Rixner, S. (2006). Dependable ≠ Unaffordable. In *Proc. of the 1st workshop on Architectural and system support for improving software dependability* (pp. 58-62). San Jose, CA: ACM Press.

de Araujo Macedo, R., & Ramon Lima e Lima, F. (2004). Improving the quality of service of failure detectors with SNMP and artificial neural networks. In Annais do 22o. Simposio Brasileiro de Redes de Computadores (pp. 583-586). Washington, DC: IEEE Computer Society.

Defago, X., Hayashibara, N., & Katayama, T. (2003). On the Design of a Failure Detection Service for Large-Scale Distributed Systems. *Intl. Symp. Towards Peta-bit Ultra Networks* [Ishikawa, Japan: IEEE Computer Society.]. *PBit, 2003*, 88–95.

Defago, X., & Schiper, A. (2002). *Specification of Replication Techniques, Semi-Passive Replication, and Lazy Consensus*. Japan: Report for School of Knowledge Science, Japan Advanced Institute of Science and Technology.

Defago, X., Schiper, A., & Urban, P. (2004). Total Order Broadcast and Multicast Algorithms: Taxonomy and Survey. *ACM Computing Surveys, 36*(4), 372–421. doi:10.1145/1041680.1041682

Defago, X., Urban, P., Hayashibara, N., & Katayama, T. (2005). Definition and Specification of Accrual Failure Detectors. In *Proc. of the 2005 International Conference on Dependable Systems and Networks, DSN'05* (pp. 206–215). Yokohama, Japan: IEEE Computer Society.

Dwork, C., Lynch, N., & Stockmeyer, L. (1988). Consensus in the presence of partial synchrony. *Journal of the ACM, 35*(2), 288–323. doi:10.1145/42282.42283

Felber, P., Defago, X., Guerraoui, R., & Oser, P. (1999). Failure detectors as first class objects. In *Proc. of the 9th IEEE Intl. Symp. on Distributed Objects and Applications, DOA'99* (pp. 132 – 141). Edinburgh, UK: IEEE Computer Society.

Fetzer, C., Raynal, M., & Tronel, F. (2001). An adaptive failure detection protocol. In *Proc. of the 8th IEEE Pacific Rim Symp. on Dependable Computing, PRDC-8* (pp. 146 – 153). Seoul, Korea: IEEE Computer Society.

Foster, I. (2002). Peer to Peer & Grid Computing. Talk at Internet2 Peer to Peer Workshop, Tempe, USA.

Fry, C. P., & Reiter, M. K. (2004). Nested objects in Byzantine quorum-replicated systems. In *Proceedings of the 23rd IEEE International Symposium on Reliable Distributed Systems* (pp. 77 – 89). Washington, DC: IEEE Computer Society.

Grimshaw, A., Humphrey, M., Knight, J. C., Nguyen-Tuong, A., Rowanhill, J., Wasson, G., & Basney, J. (2005). The Development of Dependable and Survivable Grids. In J. Dongarra (Ed.). *Proc. of the 2005 Workshop on Dynamic Data Driven Applications* (Vol. 3515, pp. 729 – 737). Berlin: Springer.

Gupta, I., Chandra, T. D., & Goldszmidt, G. S. (2001 August). On scalable and efficient distributed failure detectors. In 20th Annual ACM Symp. on Principles of Distributed Computing, PODC-20 (pp. 170–179). Las Vegas, NV: ACM Press.

Hayashibara, N., Defago, X., & Katayama, T. (2004). *Flexible Failure Detection with K-FD*. Research Report IS-RR-2004-006, Japan Advanced Institute of Science and Technology.

Jin, H., Shi, X., Qinag, W., & Zou, D. (2006, February). DRIC: Dependable Grid Computing Framework. *Oxford Journals, IEICE - Transactions on Information and Systems. E (Norwalk, Conn.)*, 89-D(2), 612–623.

Jinno, T., Kamiya, T., & Nagata, M. (2006). Coordinated Checkpointing using Vector Timestamp in Grid Computing. In *The 2006 International Conference on Parallel and Distributed Processing Techniques and Applications, PDPTA 2006* (pp. 710 – 716). Las Vegas, Nevada: IEEE Computer Society.

Joshi, K. R., Hiltunen, M. A., Sanders, W. H., & Schlichting, R. D. (2005). Automatic Model-Driven Recovery in Distributed Systems. In *Proc. of the 2005 24th IEEE Symp. on Reliable Distributed Systems, SRDS'05* (pp. 25 – 38). Orlando, FL: IEEE Computer Society.

Kephart, J., & Chess, D. (2003, January). The vision of autonomic computing. *IEEE Computing*, 36(1), 41–50.

Khanna, G., Laguna, I., Arshad, F. A., & Bagchi, S. (2007). Stateful Detection in High Throughput Distributed Systems. *Proc. of the 26th IEEE Intl. Symp. on Reliable Distributed Systems* (pp. 275-287). Beijing, China: IEEE Computer Society.

Kihlstrom, K. P., & Narasimhan, P. (2003). The Starfish system: Providing intrusion detection and intrusion tolerance for middleware systems. *Proc. of the 8th International Workshop on Object-Oriented Real-Time Dependable Systems, WORDS '03* (pp. 191–199). Guadalajara, Mexico: IEEE Computer Society.

Kopetz, H., & Bauer, G. (October 2002). The Time-Triggered Architecture. *Proceedings of the IEEE Special Issue on Modeling and Design of Embedded Software* (pp. 112 – 126), IEEE Computer Society.

Kotla, R., & Dahlin, M. (2004). *High throughput Byzantine fault tolerance. Proc. of the Intl. Conf. on Dependable Systems and Networks* (p. 575). San Francisco, CA: IEEE Computer Society.

Krishnamurthy, B., Sen, S., Zhang, Y., & Chen, Y. (2003). Sketch-based Change Detection. *Proc. of the 3rd ACM SIGCOMM conf. on Internet measurement* (pp. 234 – 247). New York: ACM Press.

Laprie, J.-C. (2002, January). *(Some remarks about) Dependability of large networked computer systems*. Paper presented at the 41st meeting of IFP 10.4, St. John, USVI.

Leitao, J., Pereira, J., & Rodrigues, L. (2007). Epidemic Broadcast Trees. *Proc. of the 26th IEEE Intl. Symp. On Reliable and Distributed Systems* (pp. 301 – 310). Beijing, China: IEEE Computer Society.

Littman, M., Ravi, N., Fenson, E., & Howard, R. (July 2004). An instance-based state representation for network repair. *Proc. of the 19th National Conference on Artificial Intelligence, AAAI 2004* (pp. 287 – 292). San Jose, California: American Association for Artificial Intelligence.

Merideth, M. G., Iyengar, A., Mikalsen, T., Tai, S., Rouvellou, I., & Narasimhan, P. (2005). Thema: Byzantine-fault-tolerant middleware for web-service applications. *Proc. of the 24th IEEE Symposium on Reliable Distributed Systems, SRDS'05* (pp. 131 – 142). Orlando, FL: IEEE Computer Society.

Mostefaoui, A., Raynal, M., Travers, C., Patterson, S., Agraval, D., & Ebbadi, A. L. (2005). From Static Distributed Systems to Dynamic Systems. *Proc. of the 2005 24th IEEE Symposium on Reliable Distributed Systems, SRDS'05* (pp. 109 – 119). Orlando, FL: IEEE Computer Society.

Neocleous, K., Dikaiakos, M. D., Fragopoulou, P., & Markatos, E. (October 2006). Grid Reliability: A study of Failures on the EGEE Infrastructure. In S. Gorlatch, M. Bubak, & T. Prior (Eds.), Proc. of the CoreGRID Integration Workshop (pp. 165–176). Crete, Greece: Academic Computer Centre CYFRONET AGH.

Neogy, S., Sinha, A., & Das, P. K. (2001). Checkpoint Processing in Distributed Systems Software Using Synchronized Clocks. In Information Technology: Coding and Computing (pp. 555 – 559). Las Vegas, NV: IEEE Computer Society.

Oppenheimer, D., Brown, A., Beck, J., Hettena, D., Kuroda, J., & Treuhaft, N. (2002, February). Roc-1: Hardware support for recovery-oriented computing. *IEEE Transactions on Computers, 51*(2), 100–107. doi:10.1109/12.980002

Oppenheimer, D., Ganapathi, A., & Patterson, D. A. (2003). Why do Internet Services fail, and what can be done about it? In *Proc. of the 4th conference on USENIX Symposium on Internet Technologies and Systems* (Vol. 4 (pp. 1-10). Berkeley, CA: USENIX Association.

Poledna, S., Burns, A., Wellings, A., & Barrett, P. (2000, February). Replica determinism and flexible scheduling in hard real-time dependable systems. *IEEE Transactions on Computers, 49*(1), 100–110. doi:10.1109/12.833107

Reiser, H. P., & Kapitza, R. (2007). Hypervisor-Based Efficient Proactive Recovery. In *Proc. of the 26th IEEE Intl. Symp. on Reliable Distributed Systems* (pp. 83-92). Beijing, China: IEEE Computer Society.

Rilling, L. (August 2006). Vigne: Towards a Self-Healing Grid Operating System. In Proc. of Euro-Par 2006 (LNCS 4128, (pp. 437 – 447). Dresden, Germany: Lecture Notes in Computer Science, Springer.

Rodrigues, R., Castro, M., & Liskov, B. (2001). BASE: using abstraction to improve fault tolerance. In *Proc. of the 18th ACM symposium on Operating systems principles, SOSP '01* (pp. 15 – 28). Alberta, Canada: ACM Press.

Sames, D., Matt, B., Niebuhr, B., Tally, G., Whitmore, B., & Bakken, D. (2002). Developing a heterogeneous intrusion tolerant CORBA system. In Proc. of the Intl. Conf. on Dependable Systems and Networks (pp. 239 – 248). Bethesda, MD: IEEE Computer Society.

Schroeder, M. D. (1993). A State-of-the-Art Distributed System: Computing with BOB. In Mullender, S. (Ed.), *Distributed Systems* (2nd ed., pp. 1–16). Reading, MA: ACM Press Frontier Series, Addison-Wesley.

Schweller, R., Chen, Y., Parsons, E., Gupta, A., Memik, G., & Zhang, Y. (2006 April). Reverse Hashing for Sketch-based Change Detection on High-speed Networks. In *Proc. of INFOCOM 2006* (pp. 1 – 12). Barcelona, Spain: IEEE Computer Society.

Sergent, N., Defago, X., & Schiper, A. (2001 Dec.). Impact of a failure detection mechanism on the performance of consensus. In *Proc. of the 8th IEEE Pacific Rim Symp. on Dependable Computing, PRDC-8* (pp. 137 – 145). Japan: IEEE Computer Society.

Sommerville, I., Hall, S., & Dobson, G. (2005). Dependable Service Engineering: A Fault-tolerance based Approach. UK: Lancaster University. Retrieved March 20, 2009, from http://digs.sourceforge.net/papers/2005_tosem_ftc.pdf.

Sonnek, J. D., & Weissman, J. B. (2005). A Quantitative Comparison of Reputation Systems in the Grid. In *Proc. of the 6th IEEE/ACM International Workshop on Grid Computing* (pp. 242 – 249). Seattle, WA: IEEE Computer Society.

Sotoma, I., & Madeira, E. R. M. (2001). Adaptation – algorithms to adaptive fault monitoring and their implementation on corba. In *Proc. of the 3rd Intl. Symp. on Distributed-Objects and Applications, DOA'01* (pp. 219 – 228). Rome, Italy: IEEE Computer Society.

Stelling, P., Foster, I., Kesselman, C., Lee, C., & von Laszewski, G. (1998). A fault detection service for wide area distributed computations. In *Proc. of the 7th IEEE Symp. on High Performance Distributed Computing* (pp. 268 – 278). San Jose, CA: IEEE Computer Society.

TTTech Computertechnik AG. (2003). *Time Triggered Protocol TTP/C. High-Level Specification Document, Internal Document Report.* TTA-Group.

van Renesse, R., Minsky, Y., & Hayden, M. (1998). A gossip-style failure detection service. In Davies, N., Raymond, K., & Seitz, J. (Eds.), *Proc. of Middleware '98* (pp. 55–70). Lake District, UK: IEEE Computer Society.

Voulgaris, S., Gavidia, D., & Steen, M. (2005). Cyclon: Inexpensive membership management for unstructured p2p overlays. *Journal of Network and Systems Management, 13*(2), 197–217. doi:10.1007/s10922-005-4441-x

Wiesman, M., Urban, P., & Defago, X. (2006). An SNMP based failure detection service. In *25th IEEE Symposium on Reliable Distributed Systems, SRDS '06* (pp. 365 – 376). Leeds, UK: IEEE Computer Society

Yin, J., Martin, J.-P., Venkataraman, A., Alvisi, L., & Dahlin, M. (2003). Separating agreement from execution for Byzantine fault tolerant services. In *Proceedings of the 19th ACM Symposium on Operating Systems* (pp. 253-267). Bolton Landing, NY, USA: IEEE Computer Society.

Zhang, X., Zagorodnov, D., Hitunen, M., Marzullo, K., & Schlichting, R. D. (2004). Fault-tolerant Grid Services Using Primary-Backup: Feasibility and Performance. In *Proc. of CLUSTER 2004* (pp. 105-114). San Diego, CA: IEEE Computer Society.

Chapter 9
Security

INTRODUCTION

Security in distributed systems is a combination of confidentiality, integrity and availability of their components. It mainly targets the communication channels between users and/or processes located in different computers, the access control of users / processes to resources and services, and the management of keys, users and user groups. Distributed systems are more vulnerable to security threats due to several characteristics such as their large scale, the distributed nature of the control, and the remote nature of the access. In addition, an increasing number of distributed applications (such as Internet banking) manipulate sensitive information and have special security requirements. After discussing important security concepts in the Background section, this chapter addresses several important problems that are at the aim of current research in the security of large scale distributed systems: security models (which represent the theoretical foundation for solving security problems), access control (more specific the access control in

DOI: 10.4018/978-1-61520-703-9.ch009

distributed multi-organizational platforms), secure communication (with emphasis on the secure group communication, which is a hot topic in security research today), security management (especially key management for collaborative environments), secure distributed architectures (which are the blueprints for designing and building security systems), and security environments / frameworks.

BACKGROUND

Organizations and individuals expect the information held by distributed systems be available when needed, be disclosed exclusively in controlled ways, and be modified only by authorized entities. In other words, the systems must preserve the information security, which is characterized by three main attributes: availability, confidentiality, and integrity. These attributes apply not only to the information, but also to other **assets** that have value for the organization or individual users, such as computers, networks, software, databases, services, etc. **Confidentiality** refers to the concealment of information (Bishop, 2003) to be disclosed only to authorized entities (individuals or processes). Unauthorized entities will be unable, for example, to read the content of transferred messages or the data held in distributed files. **Integrity** means preventing improper or unauthorized change (Bishop, 2003). Assets can be modified only by authorized parties or in authorized ways. Unauthorized entities cannot, for example, modify a message in transfer or change the data in a distributed file. Integrity refers both to information (data integrity) and to the origin of the information (origin integrity, also called **authentication**). **Availability** is the ability to use the information or resource desired (Bishop, 2003). An asset is available if it can be accessed and used by the authorized entities. A message is not available to the legitimate receiver if its transfer is interrupted. Also, a file record is not available to the authorized user if the corresponding file service is denied.

The security of a distributed system can be violated. A **threat** is a potential event that breaches the security and can cause loss or harm to the system. Threats can be classified as malicious (such as virus, worm, Trojan horse, logic bomb, spoof, scan, snoop, scam, and spam), unintentional (hardware or software malfunction, human error), and physical (fire or water damage, power loss, vandalism, and theft or loss of computers). Some security threats that need particular attention are the spam (in particular the bandwidth-eating image spam), bots (computer programs that perform automated tasks), and viruses (Bernard, 2006).

Threats could be favored by **vulnerabilities**, which are weaknesses in the security system's procedures, design or implementation. An example is a vulnerability of Web application frameworks known as Cross Site Scripting (or XSS). The flow occurs when an application takes data from the user, don't validate the content, and sends it to a Web browser. This allows an attacker to execute a script in the browser and determine worms insertion, phishing attacks, etc. (OWASP, 2007). Security developers aim to identify the vulnerabilities and find solutions to eliminate them. Sev-

eral organizations, foundations, and specialized companies (OWASP, SANS) publish information about the most important vulnerabilities and the areas where the organizations need to improve the security processes. Attackers are also interested to know the vulnerabilities and exploit them in preparing the attacks on the system.

While common threats that manifest in distributed systems can be studied globally, and general security solutions to eliminate them can be found, each security system developer confront with specific requirements, which differ from one case to another. For example, the requirements of a secure distributed system used in the banking sector will be different from those found in a system that belongs to the academic environment. A good starting point for the developer is the **security policy**, which specifies the "set of rules, practices, and procedures dictating how sensitive information is managed, protected, and distributed." (Bhaiji, 2008). The security policy is a general "statement of what is and what is not allowed" (Bishop, 2003) and is intended to a large audience that includes the users, managers, security officers, information system administrators, etc.

A more useful instrument for the security developers is the **security model** that incorporates, in a formal representation, the security policy that must be enforced. The security model is more detailed and precise than the security policy, and supports the implementation of a security policy. It includes elements that make easier the mapping of the security policy into system's requirements, and the selection of the appropriate **mechanisms** (methods, procedures, and tools) that will be used in building the system. For example, if the security policy states that each user can access the assets according to his/her position in the organization, the security model might lay out a **role based access control** that can be specified in more precise terms and serve as a basis for implementation. The design of the security system can identify several components that control different vulnerabilities and act in cooperation to enforce the security policy. This leads to a specific **security architecture**, which describes the roles of the components and their inter-relations. Different concepts, such as **security in depth** or **multi-layered security**, are used in the design of the security architecture.

The security model can also be used as a baseline in systems' evaluation. A **trusted** system is one that is believed to enforce the security policy, in other words to correctly respond to the security requirements. The evaluation is performed by specialists not involved in the development process, which increases the confidence in the evaluation results. The evaluation is based on specific standards that refer to the features of the security system (i.e. to the functionalities provided) and to the quality of the implementation process (the methodology used for system development ensures the effective enforcement of the security policy).

SECURITY MODELS

Formal **security models** are at the aim of developing high assurance security systems (Hashii, 2004). They provide a formal reference specification to be used not only in the design and implementation phases but also in proofing that "a model, design, and implementation are correct" (Pfleeger, 2007), in other words the evaluated system is trusted. Hashii (2004) identifies three main benefits of using a formal specification: (a) the model helps the designer to concentrate on the important issues and ignore details that are not relevant in the first phase of the development; (b) the model allows developers to identify critical problems and adopt proper solutions before the implementation phase, avoiding the waste of time and resources; (c) the ability to proof the correctness of the specification increases the chance to obtain a system that responds to the requirements.

The evaluation itself is performed by independent experts and is based on standard criteria such as those specified in the Trusted Computer System Evaluation Criteria (TCSEC), the Information Technology Security Evaluation Criteria (ITSEC) or in the more recent Common Criteria for Information Technology Security Evaluation (CC) standards (Pfleeger, 2007). These standards are used to evaluate the security system functionality and the quality of the procedures used in its development, and to assign a rank to the system. For example, the Common Criteria standard defines seven Evaluation Assurance Levels with specific assurance requirements concerning design documentation, design analysis, functional testing, or penetration testing (Common Criteria, 2008):

- EAL1: Functionally Tested
- EAL2: Structurally Tested
- EAL3: Methodically Tested and Checked
- EAL4: Methodically Designed, Tested, and Reviewed
- EAL5: Semiformally Designed and Tested
- EAL6: Semiformally Verified Design and Tested
- EAL7: Formally Verified Design and Tested

The higher EALs require more systematic and complete analysis and verification procedures than the lower levels. Obviously, high assurance levels claim for formal specification and for semiformal or formal verification of the design and test.

A formal security model is based on a finite state machine (FSM) model of the system (Gutmann, 2003) that specifies an initial state known to be secure and a set of states that are reachable from the initial state. Model analysis aims at checking that all reachable states are also secure, more specific satisfy the security policy expressed as a set of mathematical formulae. The analysis process has two important drawbacks. First, elaborating the formal description of a security policy is not trivial. Second, FSM models suffer from the explosion of states, in other words they are not scalable. This is why the research related to the formal analysis of security models targets the simplification of the verification process by defining easier to use specification languages and developing higher performance associated analysis tools. Hashii (2004) presents the use of the Alloy language and of the Alloy Analyzer tool for the formal specification and analysis of a solution to the Multi Level Security (MLS) problem developed on the Polymorphous Computing Architecture (PCA) of the Defense Advanced Research Projects Agency (DARPA). The Alloy language is based on a state-transition model which includes states (specified as sets) and relationships among states. An operation modifies the sets and thus determines a transition to a new state. In order to check a specification, one can specify invariants that describe the correct behavior and use the Alloy Analyzer to demonstrate that all reachable states are legal, i.e. conform to the invariants. Hashii presents these aspects for the MLS-PCA model, and highlights the capability of the formal model and analysis method to identify design errors and simplify the design.

As stated before, preserving the information security means that information is disclosed and / or modified exclusively in controlled ways. Consequently, it is not surprising that formal security models refer to the access control of users to different assets. An **access control model** must allow one to determine if a **subject** *s* has the **access right** *a* to a specified **object** *o*. The access control may be represented by a function f(s, o, a) that returns *true* or *false* and may be implemented as a **reference monitor**, *RM* which is interposed between the subject *s* and the protected object *o*. Since an access right is equivalent to an operation (read, write, execute, etc.) that can be executed by subject *s* on object *o*, RM can be viewed as a controller, which either transforms *a* into an authorized request or rejects it (Tanenbaum & van Steen, 2007).

There are two broad classes of access control models: discretionary and mandatory. The models have some common characteristics. For a system, both models specify the sets of subjects, objects, and rights. In addition, they highlight the **autho-**

rization rules for each <subject, object> pair. The difference between the two classes is related to how rights are attributed to subjects. In **Mandatory Access Control** (MAC) model, subjects cannot grant their rights to other subjects. In protection systems that use these models, the rights are usually allocated by system administrators and remain unchanged until a new manual intervention. By contrast, in a **Discretionary Access Control** (DAC) model, subjects can transfer some of their rights to other subjects at their discretion. For example, if *s* is the owner of an object *o* then *s* can grant or revoke an access right *a* on *o* to other subjects. In the sequel we highlight the problems posed by DAC models due to this flexibility offered to subjects, and discuss several possible solutions. We'll address the important issue of protection system safety, meaning that a certain right is not given to unsafe subjects.

DAC models can be defined in terms of states and transitions as described in (Bishop, 2003). If

- $S = \{s1, s2, ..., sn\}$ is the ordered set of subjects,
- $O = \{o1, o2, ..., om\}$ is the ordered set of objects, and
- $R = \{r1, r2, ..., rk\}$ is the set of access rights (actions),

then a **state** is represented by a matrix A: S x O U S -> 2^R. Each element A[s,o] specifies the rights subject s has on object o (s can execute the actions A[s,o] on object o); similarly, each element A[s,s'] specifies the rights subject s has on another subject s'. A **transition** is described by an action in R. For example, the action *"grant access right r to s on o"* leads from a state in which *s* doesn't have the right *r* to one in which s has this right. Other possible actions can be: create or delete a subject, create or delete an object, delete an access right or transfer an access right from one subject to another.

Harrison, Ruzzo and Ullman (1976) defined a new model (HRU) by introducing more complicated actions, in the form of commands that may include several primitive operations like the ones mentioned above. The authors used their model to study the **safety problem**, which is expressed as follows: a state M in a protection system is safe relative to a right r if no sequence of commands permits the leakage of r to another subject that didn't have it before. The authors demonstrate that the safety problem is undecidable in the HRU model for the general case of an "arbitrary configuration of an arbitrary protection system" (Harrison et al, 1976). Instead, the problem is decidable (i.e. there is an algorithm to determine if a system is safe) in some particular cases, such as the mono-operational commands (each command represents one primitive operation).

A different approach is taken by Lipton and Snyder (1977), who defined the **take-grant** model based on operations such as: create an object and add a right on it, remove the right on an object, grant a right to a subject, and take a right from a subject. The authors demonstrate that, with this model, it is possible to determine if the rights may leak for a specified protection model. Other models have been developed with the aim of making the safety problem decidable. Sandhu (1988) defined the **Schematic Protection Model** (SPM), which introduces the notion of protection type. The rights set associated with a subject has two parts: the static part, which is determined by a protection scheme according to the type of the subject (each subject is created with a specific type that cannot be changed); the dynamic part, which is based on tickets. The authors demonstrate that the safety problem is decidable for a large class of SPM specifications. The model is more general than take-grant, which can be described as a specific SPM scheme. Another model defined by Sandhu (1992) in the **Typed Access Matrix** (TAM) model. The author demonstrates that Monotonic TAM (MTAM) has properties similar to SPM and is NP-hard for safety decidability. Instead, ternary MTAM has polynomial complexity, which makes it useful for the analysis of monotonic security

policies. The same approach of typing is taken by Tidswell and Potter (1998) in the definition of the **Dynamically Typed Access Control** (DTAC) model. In this model, both the types and the rights can change. Obviously, this complicated the safety problem and obliged the authors to adopt a change in the safety approach. The innovation is to change the problem itself (safety decidability) for a simpler one, namely the dynamic preservation of a safety invariant.

DAC models are flexible and are frequently used in distributed systems, in which resources are shared among users. Unfortunately, the flexibility is associated with possible leakage of access rights. An example related to a Web-based system is given in (Joshi et al, 2001). Since the model makes it possible to copy data from one object to another, a user may read the copy of data while not having access to the original. DAC models has been traditionally used in the development of operating systems, and were adopted in systems that fall within the security class C, as defined in the DoD TCSEC or, equivalently are ranked at the Evaluation Assurance Level 4 (EAL4) as specified by the Common Criteria standard.

A second classification of security models is based on their definition of security. Two main model categories can be distinguished. **Information-flow models** organize the subjects and objects on several levels of sensitivity, and are concerned with the information flows between different levels. **Direct access control models** cope with different operations that subjects can apply on objects (read, write, execute, append, etc.) and are concerned with their authorization.

The most known multilevel confidentiality model is **Bell - La Padula** (Pfleeger, 2007). In this model, each object has a sensitivity level or rank (from unclassified, restricted, confidential, secret, and top secret), and is associated with one or more projects or compartments. Together, the rank and the compartments form the object's access class, C(o). Similarly, each subject has a clearance C(s), expressed as an access class

<rank, compartments> that represents the rank at which the subject has access and the projects he is involved in. The model specifies two rules that must be respected to preserve the confidentiality:

- (no read-up rule) the subject s has read access to the object o only if his clearance dominates the object's access class, i.e. $C(s) \geq C(o)$;
- (no write-down rule) the subject s, which has read access to an object p, can have write access to another object o only when the access class of o dominates the access class of p, i.e. $C(o) \geq C(p)$.

Here, Ci dominates Ck, written $Ci \geq Ck$, means that:

- rank $(Ci) \geq$ rank (Ck) and
- compartments (Ci) include compartments (Ck).

The model is closer to policies used in military systems, but it has been also adopted in several non-military kernel-based systems (Landvehr, 1981). The idea that a small module of a system (the kernel) should be responsible for the security of the entire system was based on three principles: the kernel must be correct (the formal verification is made possible by the small size of the kernel); it would monitor all access requests (program references), in other words it would act as a reference monitor for the rest of the system; and it would be highly protected so that possible attacks could not change its functionality. The model has been used, for the first time, in a specific practical solution in the Multics operating system (Bell, 2005) and then in other operating systems, but the use for application systems proved to be difficult.

The interest for finding solutions to the information-flow problem led to several extensions of the Bell – La Padulla model. One significant proposal is **Biba**, which introduced the concepts and formalism for representing and maintaining the integrity in security systems (Pfleeger, 2007). The model defines integrity classes (similar to confidentiality classes of the Bell – La Padulla model), and specifies two rules that must be respected to preserve the integrity:

- a subject s can modify an object o that has a lower integrity, i.e. $I(s) \geq I(o)$
- if the subject s has read access to the object p then he can have write access to the object o only if $I(p) > I(o)$.

Biba was thought to be used in conjunction with Bell – La Padulla, for defining a combined model that captures both the confidentiality and the integrity properties of security systems. Nevertheless, since malicious integrity attacks were solved by using detection techniques, the interest for the integrity models was much lower than for confidentiality models. A more comprehensive discussion of this subject and of other issues related to information-flow security models can be found in (Landwehr, 1981).

ACCESS CONTROL

Distributed systems security has two main concerns: one is the access control, which ensures that resources are used in the right way, only by authorized entities; the other is the secure communication between entities (users, processes, clients, servers, peers, resources, and services), which protects against interception, modification, and fabrication of messages (Tanenbaum & van Steen, 2007). In this section we discuss the access control issues; communication security is presented in the next section.

Concerning the **access control**, we mention here the "classical" models:

- **Access Matrix**, which was discussed in a previous section; each entry corresponds to a (subject, object) pair and specifies the access rights the subject has on the corresponding object;

- **Access Control List**; there is one list for each object; each entry corresponds to a subject and specifies the access rights the subject has on that object;
- **Capability**; there is a list of capabilities for each subject; each entry corresponds to an object and specifies the access rights the subject has on that object.

These models have several drawbacks (Tolone, 2005). First, they don't support dynamic changes. For example, changing the rights of a subject claims for modifications in the ACLs associated with all system's objects. Also, finding the subjects that have access to a specific object claims for visiting the Capability lists associated with all system's subjects. Second, the models cannot represent more complex policies (for example access rules based on competencies, least privileges or conflicts of interests). Third, they cannot manage access rights determined by objects' content or attributes, or by context. Finally, they cannot register and manage rights that are granted for a specific period of time or the usage-based access. In the sequel, we present several access control solutions that brought improvements to these important issues. Their development still continues as result of the ongoing research. We first present the Role Based Access Control (RBAC) model; we then discuss its extensions for controlling the access in collaborative systems.

The most important and largely studied model, RBAC (Ferraiolo et al, 2001) is based on the notion of role. The **role** is a grouping mechanism of subjects having a common attribute such as: the function in the enterprise, the tasks to be accomplished, the qualification or the responsibilities. Access rights (or permissions) are associated to roles and one or several roles can be associated with each subject. This indirect association of permissions, through roles, to subjects simplifies the security administration. Since the enterprise

organization is relatively stable, it is possible to define relatively persistent roles, in other words more stable relationships between roles and permissions. In this way, the administration of the access control can be guided by the function or responsibilities a subject has in the organization; assigning roles to a subject is much easier than assigning permissions.

The RBAC standard has two parts: the **RBAC Reference Model** and the **RBAC Requirements Specification**. They refer separately to four components: Core RBAC, Hierarchical RBAC, Static Separation of Duty Relations, and Dynamic Separation of Duty Relations. The Reference Model (see Figure 1) is described in terms of sets of basic **element sets**, a set of **relations** among them, and a set of **mapping functions** that relate one member in a basic element set to members in another element set.

For **Core RBAC**, the element sets represent users, roles, objects, operations, permissions (access rights), and also sessions. A relation is defined as a subset of the cartesian product of element sets. For example, the User Assignment (UA) relation is defined as: $UA \subseteq USERS \times ROLES$, meaning that a user can have several roles and a role can be assigned to several users. An example mapping function is *assigned_users*, which is defined as $assigned\_users(r:ROLES) = \{u \in USERS \,|\, (u, r) \in UA\}$, and yields the set of users that have the role r.

The relations and mapping functions, which are similarly defined, form a complete, unambiguous, and consistent specification of the Core RBAC reference model. We briefly mention here the main characteristics of the model. The UA relation specifies the roles assigned to each user. Only part of them can be activated in a session. To describe this, the model introduces the sessions set and two mapping functions: *user_sessions* gives the subset of sessions associated with a user, while *session_roles* yields the roles that can be activated in a specific session. A user can be involved in one session or in several sessions at the same time. Also, there are two activation policies, namely

Figure 1. RBAC reference model

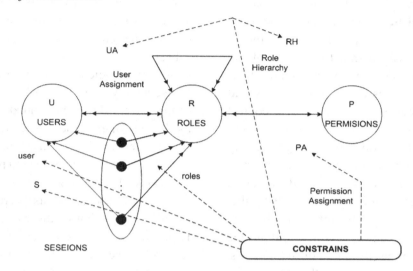

single-role activation and multiple-role activation. In addition, two roles cannot be active at the same time if they conflict. For example, a user cannot have the roles of instructor and student in the same class. In fact, this subject is approached by the **Static Separation of Duty Relations**, and **Dynamic Separation of Duty Relations** RBAC components. In the "Static" case, two conflicting roles cannot be assigned both to the same user while, in the "Dynamic" case, two conflicting roles cannot be activated at the same time for the same user.

The other component, **hierarchical RBAC** defines role hierarchies. A role can **include** another role; for example, an instructor has all the permissions of a student and additional permissions. Otherwise, we can say that the instructor role **inherits** the permissions from the student role, and that role hierarchies define an inheritance relation among roles. Hierarchies can be limited to a tree structure or can be more general (lattice) and allow the multiple inheritance.

The RBAC Requirements Specification refers to administrative functions (creation and maintenance of element sets and relations), support system functions (session creation, addition of an active role, check the access permission), and review functions (find the set of users assigned to a role, find the set of active roles associated with a session, etc.).

The RBAC model is actually used in many distributed systems. Examples are the Web-based applications (Joshi et al, 2001), in which traditional and emerging access control models are used. Ferraiolo et al (1999) describe a RBAC system for Web environments (RBAC/Web), which implements the RBAC model by organizing the authorization data in a single database that is closer to the business process of an enterprise. A role is associated with each user when logging into the system, which controls the permissions assigned in the current session. A visualization and management tool is also offered to the administrator, and facilitates the implementation of different access control policies.

Another example, presented in (Yao et al, 2007), refers to the use of RBAC for the decentralized authorization and data security in **Content Delivery Networks** (CDNs). CDNs not only support information delivery, but also they support content modifications such as aggregation and transcoding to adapt to users' requirements. Proxies can be used to take over these operations and fasten the delivery process by distributed execution of different transformations. The configuration can include the **publisher** (content delivery server), a lot of users, and several proxies (trusted by the publisher) that perform transformations of the content before its delivery. Content modification by several proxies claims for integrity and confidentiality preservation. The access control approach is adopted to ensure that proxies perform only those transformations that are granted by their authorizations, which correspond to their specific roles. The solution proposed by Yao et al (2007) includes several extensions RBAC that make the solution flexible and robust. Each proxy maintains a role lookup table, which contains the role information about its neighbouring proxies, and uses it to coordinate with other proxies for transforming or delivering the information without centralized server's intervention. The lookup table is also used to select an alternative solution to forward the content when some proxies failed. A final control can be applied when the content is delivered to the end user, which is able to check its integrity.

While RBAC has been widely adopted in many products for controlling users' access to computer resources and services, the model was not exempted from critics and debates. In a recent paper (Ninghui et al, 2007), the authors claim, among other things, that the notion of session should be removed from the core RBAC, the standard should also model systems in which only one role can be activated in a session, the semantics of the role inheritance should be clearly specified, etc. In their answer (Ferraiolo et al, 2007), the authors of the standard present the rationales behind their decisions in the standard elaboration and encourage the work on changes of the RBAC standard to make it more responsive to new requirements.

Several access models have been proposed for extending and adapting RBAC to the requirements of the collaborative systems (Tolone, 2005). In this respect, **Task Based Access Control** (TBAC) adds a context to the role based access control. In this model (Thomas & Sandhu, 1997), each

workflow (set of tasks) has an associated role and, consequently, a set of associated permissions. On the other hand, each task is associated with a subset of these permissions (the Protection state), which are sufficient for supporting its execution. Consequently, the subset of active permissions changes according to the context, represented here by the task in execution. A similar secure workflow model is presented in (Hung & Karlapalem, 2003). A workflow consists of a partially ordered set of tasks that are coordinated by a set of events. There are two special events that represent the start and the completion of the workflow. Each task is performed by an agent and has an associated temporal access control, which is a set of document / privilege pairs. According to this model, there are several possible legitimate paths for a workflow. A secure workflow management system must ensure that workflows follow only legitimate paths. The authors propose a multi-layered state machine model that is used to describe the flow of authorizations and is synchronized with the workflow to ensure its secure execution. Three layers are defined for a secure state, namely: Workflow, Data, and Control. Also, three security requirements are imposed (and transformed into three invariants) two of them ensure the integrity, authorization and availability in the workflow layer, while a third requirement is for the integrity and authorization in the data layer. The three invariants state the followings (Hung & Karlapalem, 2003):

"For every task there must be at least one agent who is able to execute the task."

"An agent can only execute the assigned task if and only if the privilege "execute" is granted. The secure workflow has to revoke the privilege from an agent if the task has completed execution."

"An agent can only access a document with a specific privilege if and only if the document access privilege is granted to the agent and also it is

needed to access the document with the privilege during the task execution. The secure workflow has to revoke the document access privilege from an agent if the document access privilege is no longer needed."

The **TeaM based Access Control** (TMAC) introduces the notion of team, which represent a group of users, which have different roles but work together towards the same goal (Thomas, 1997). For each subject, permissions depend on its role, but also on the team the user belongs to. Permissions can be activated and deactivated collectively, for all team members.

The **Context-Aware Access Control** model (Covington et al, 2001) extends RBAC with environment roles that are automatically activated / deactivated according to the environmental conditions. For this model, a permission request by a subject, expressed as a triple <p, r, e-set>, can be granted if: the permission p is in the permissions set associated with the role r; the role r is among the active roles of the subject; the set of active enabling environment roles include the roles in e-set.

COMMUNICATION SECURITY

Secure channels are built based on cryptographic algorithms, and are operated according to security protocols, which usually support the authentication of the communicating entities, the selection of the encryption methods, keys and of other security parameters (for example, the initialization vector), and the actual encryption and signing of messages. The standard protocol that provides these operations over the Internet is the **Secure Sockets Layer** (SSL) or its successor the **Transport Layer Security** (TLS). TLS is used to offer security to several other protocols of the application layer. For example, **Hypertext Transfer Protocol Secure** (HTTPS) is nothing more than the Hypertext Transfer Protocol that uses TLS as

transport protocol for securely transmitting HTTP methods (such as GET, POST and others) and responses. It is also possible to use Java Remote Invocations with SSL / TLS. In addition, **Java Secure Sockets Extension** (JSSE) is a package that offers a Java implementation of the SSL and TLS protocols. Similarly, **Secure Remote procedure Call** (Secure RPC) library is designed to use SSL/TLS for remote procedure calls.

Web Service messages sent over SOAP (**Simple Object Access Protocol**) can also be secured by using security tokens, such as X.509 certificates, for authentication and encryption. These facilities are included in **WS-Security**, an OASIS standard (OASIS, 2006) that provides elementary end-to-end security mechanisms for individual messages. To extend security from one message to multiple message exchanges, **Web Services Secure Conversation Language** (WS-SecureConversation) and **Web Services Trust Language** (WS-Trust) have been defined (OASIS, 2007). WS-Trust copes with token request and issuance, while WS-SecureConversation refers to the use of security context tokens to ensure a secure conversation between two parties. In a simple scenario, a client can contact a security token server to ask for a security context token. In its request, the client specifies its identity and the identity of the target service (it intends to use). The security token server creates a context (which it shares with the target service) and sends it in a response to the client. The client and the target service will then establish a conversation secured by the key derived from the common context. A formal model derived from these standards (and expressed in a formal scripting language for security protocols, TulaFale), has been developed (Bhargavan et al, 2007) with the aim of studying security properties, identify potential limitations and vulnerabilities, and suggest corrections to standards.

Large Scale Distributed Sensor Networks have specific security requirements, which depend on the types of packets that are exchanged in these networks. Consequently, several keying mechanisms must be used. Zhu et al (2004) identify four key types to be used in LEAP, a key management protocol for sensor networks. Node individual key is used in the communication with the base station. A pairwise shared key serves to communicate with each of the immediate neighbors. A cluster key is used to secure the broadcast communication with all the neighbors. A group key is used in the global communication of the base station with all group nodes. LEAP is designed to reduce the communication, energy consumed and the participation of the base station in establishing and updating these different keys. LEAP is robust against security attacks like HELLO Flood, Sybil and Wormhole attacks.

An important issue is securing the existing IP communication infrastructure against security threats such as **Denial of Service** (DoS) attacks. There are two main approaches to protect resources from DoS attacks. In the reactive approach, protection mechanisms are activated when an attack is detected. There is a delay in the application of protective measures, which can lat the target to be affected. Also, attackers can change the method of attack when the protection mechanism is activated. In the proactive approach, a target destination is protected by continuously performing specific actions. It can be applied for very high sensitive information that cannot be replicated due to specific technical reasons. Keromytis et al (2002) propose SOS – Secure Overlay Services, an architecture that proactively protects specific targets by performing intensive filtering near the specific resource and "introducing randomness and anonymity into the architecture". It has the advantage of making use of actual software and protocols for filtering, authentication and authorization of sources, and tunneling used in an overlay that includes routers and high-speed end systems.

DoS attacks can target the application as well, for example the Web applications. Srivatsa et al (2008) propose to protect the target by combining the limiting the number of concurrent clients with congestion control on admitted clients. The first control is based on hiding the port at which the service can be reached for unauthorized users. The second control associates a priority with each client and updates it based on the evaluation of each request. The priority decreases in case of DoS attackers, whose requests are of low utility and high resource consumption.

KEY MANAGEMENT

Key management is an important topic of any security system that uses cryptographic techniques. It must obey to general requirements such as the followings:

- encryption and decryption must be efficient for all keys;
- the system must be easy to use, more specific, key generation should not be a complicated process;
- security must depend on keys, not on algorithms.

Traditionally, key generation is delegated to a third party, a **Key Distribution Center** (KDC), which has also the task of distributing the generated keys to users of a security system. An alternative is to use specific protocols, such as Diffie-Hellman (Tanenbaum & van Steen, 2007) that performs key generation and distribution at the same time. For **Public Keys Infrastructures** (PKIs), the keys are generated and distributed by a **Certificate Authority** (CA). Key management is an active research field. New key generation methods are required by distributed applications that are now emerging. In the sequel, we refer to research trends in group key management, key management in mobile networks, identity based encryption, and threshold cryptography.

Many large scale applications are collaborative and require the participation of users that form a specific group. Usually, the groups are very dynamic, users joining and leaving the group frequently. Also, applications must ensure the security at the group level. Consequently, there must be group keys that are used by all group participants for securely exchange and access data. A new group key must be generated and distributed each time a member leaves the group (it shouldn't be able to understand the messages exchanged after leaving the group) or joins the group (it shouldn't be able to understand the messages exchanged before joining the group). The role of key management is to identify and authenticate the members, validate the joining of a new member (validate the access to the group), generate, validate, and install the new group keys, which must be independent from the old ones (to not create vulnerabilities in the security system). We refer in the sequel to key generation and distribution.

These operations are simple when a new member joins the group (Rafaeli & David, 2003). Supposing that a KDC is used, which has a secret key with each member, KDC can generate a new group key and multicast it encrypted with the old group key to group members, and with the secret key to the new member. This method can't be used when a member leaves the group. In this case, KDC should generate a new group key, encrypt it separately with the secret keys shared with members remaining in the group, gather the results in a message and send multicast the message to group members. Each member extracts its part from the message and decrypts it with its secret key to find the new group key. The solution is not efficient since the KDC is overcharged with many encryptions (which take time) and the multicast message is long (consuming transmission capacity).

Several solutions have been proposed to improve the efficiency of key distribution. They fall into three categories (Rafaeli & David, 2003): centralized protocols (that use a central KDC controlling the whole group) – an example is the Logical Key Hierarchy (LKH) proposed by Wong et al (2000), decentralized protocols (that split

the group in several sub-groups and use several controllers) – an example is the dual encryption protocol by Dondeti et all (1999), and distributed protocols (group members generate and distribute the new keys). We describe here the distributed protocol proposed by Steiner et al (1996), which generalizes the Diffie-Helmann protocol. It is supposed that the group has n members and each member has a secret number xi. The group establishes two prime numbers, q and a, and starts calculating several intermediate values. The protocol has n rounds. The first member calculates a^{x1} and passes it to the next member. The second member calculates a^{x2} and a^{x1*x2} and sends the set $\{a^{x1}, a^{x2}, a^{x1*x2}\}$ to the third member. The first two terms of this set are named intermediate values, while the third term is named cardinal value. Similar operations are performed by each member m_i, which receives a set of i-1 terms and calculates a set of i terms with i-1 intermediate values and one cardinal value. The last member, xn calculates a new set, retains the cardinal value $a^{x1*x2*...*xn}$ and sends multicast the intermediate values. It then calculates the group key $k = a^{x1*x2*...*xn} \mod q$. Each other member extracts one intermediate value from the last set and obtains the group key with the same formula $k = a^{x1*x2*...*xn} \mod q$.

Different key management solutions are adopted in distributed systems based on mobile networks. Recent research results for the key management in **Vehicular Ad-hoc Networks** (VANETs) are reported in (van der Merwe, 2007). Both fully self-organized and authority based VANETs are considered and the role of secure routing protocols is highlighted. Secure key management is at the aim of these protocols. It must ensure the establishment (agreement and transport) of keying materials (keys, certificates, and initialization vectors) needed to establish and maintain cryptographic keying relationships among the mobile nodes. Key management protocols use the public key cryptography and can be grouped in several categories. In partially distributed certificate authority protocols, a distributed certificate authority consists of a group of n server nodes (not all the nodes in the VANET) that have together a public/private key pair. Each server has a partial private key (secret). The Combiner (which can be any server node) obtains a number (over a specific threshold) of partial signatures and uses them to produce the threshold group signature. In fully distributed certificate authority protocols the secret is shared among all nodes of the network. Other key management protocols are based on user identities, certificate chains between entities, offline authorities, node mobility or combinations of the above.

The identity based encryption and threshold cryptography, which were mentioned above, have been used for securing the communication in other large scale distributed systems. These are built on untrusted, public networks and claim for the use of public / private keys in security protocols like SSL and TLS. Due to the large number of nodes with a dynamic behavior (nodes frequently join and leave the network), the use of the traditional PKI infrastructure is not efficient. To improve the performance, Stading (2003) proposed Scribe, a key management method that uses, as public keys, the unique identities of public resources. Scribe offers a service that authenticates resources based on their identities, and generates the corresponding private key. Scribe has been proposed for Chord (Stoica et al, 2001) but its use can be extended to other distributed systems as well.

SECURE DISTRIBUTED ARCHITECTURE

The **security architecture** describes the functionality of- and inter-relations between- components of a security system. Traditionally, it is described as a hierarchical multi-layered ensemble, which includes physical, technical, organizational / user, and policy security controls. Some example controls are: guidelines and procedures for the policy layer; authentication/authorization for the user layer; Web Service security, identity management, anti-virus, anti-spyware, VPN, and firewalls for the technical layer; locks and biometrics for the physical layer.

The idea of layering is not new. It was used in structuring the operating systems (OSs), which are the most critical software since it supports the execution of the applications and the management of the information stored in a computer system. Protecting this information against unauthorized use is one of the main goals of the OS. Several protection models are known such as the hierarchical protection domains or protection rings that protect data and functionality from faults (fault tolerance) and malicious behavior (computer security). Rings are arranged in a hierarchy from the most privileged (most trusted, Ring 0) to least privileged. Each process or resource belongs to a specific ring. Processes can use resources or call other processes that belong to the same or higher level rings. The use of resources and calls to processes in higher level rings are restricted and performed in a controlled way.

Hardware supported rings were introduced in the **Multics** operating system (Corbato, 2009). Each program has a specific level, and each memory segment has a level as well. Attempts to access data at a lower level are not permitted and cause traps. Also, calls to procedures at a lower level rings are strictly controlled by **call gates**, which ensure that calls are performed in a restricted way.

Unix has also a layered architecture, which is at the base of the Unix security (Fernandez & Sorgente, 2009). At the lowest level, closest to the hardware, there are the basic hardware interface modules. The next level provides the kernel functions. The uppermost layer consists of user processes running Shells, Unix commands, utility programs and user application programs. Protection is ensured by two "rings of protection". The inner protected ring is known as **kernel space**, while the outer ring is called **user space**. Kernel space is a privileged area. The kernel has access

Figure 2. Layering in operating systems

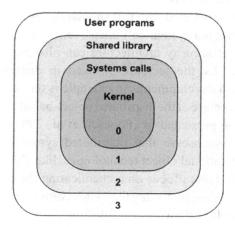

to all machine instructions and devices. Also, a kernel process can modify the memory map, an operation frequently required to perform process scheduling.

This protection layered architecture used for OSs has been extended to distributed systems as well. A **Trusted Computing Base** (TCB) is "a small amount of software and hardware that security depends on" (Lampson et al, 1992) and that is used to implement a security policy. It is called trusted since it has been evaluated and found to comply with specific criteria. The second attribute, which refers to the small volume, facilitates the use of formal methods for the evaluation, and the assignment of a higher rank to the evaluated TCB. Similar to the kernel space approach, it is possible to build a privileged zone for hosting the components of the TCB and isolate them from the rest of the components in a distributed system. The **Reduced Interfaces for Secure System Components**, RISSC (Neumann, 1995) architecture constructs this zone on separate secured machines, which are protected from the rest by access control devices that filter all the access requests.

The security architecture derives from the security policy but is also influenced by the characteristics of the systems or platforms to which it applies. A first separation can be made between the two large categories of distributed systems:

client-server based systems and derivatives on one side, and peer-to-peer on the other. The main difference is in the trust management approach. While in the client-server systems the trust is managed by a central third party authority, in peer-to-peer systems trust management is distributed. Also, in client-server systems the security is handled by a central server, while in peer-to-peer systems security is handled by each peer. For a very good presentation of trust models in distributed system you can see (Li and Singhal, 2007).

In large scale client-server based distributed systems we find common characteristics that are not present in other kinds of systems, such as (Foster et al, 1998): large and dynamic number of users and resources; large applications composed of dynamic processes that run on different resources, which are distributed in different administrative domains; authentication and authorization mechanisms might differ from one resource to the other; one user could access different sites, and have separate accounts and specific credentials on these sites. These similar characteristics give rise to special requirements and stimulate new research for finding efficient technical solutions. An obvious requirement is that the user should be allowed to authenticate once, at login, and this authentication remains valid during the entire user session (single sign-on). To do this, the authenticated user (called also principal) has a global name (identity) by which the principal is recognized in any domain. Since the access control is governed by local security policies (it is impractical to change the domain's security policy when a system joins temporarily a large distributed platform), principal's global name is mapped to a local name, and the control is applied to the local subject. In addition, some proxy processes, can act on behalf of a principal and be delegated a part of its rights. Also, some applications run as a collection of processes for which the secure group communication should be facilitated. These requirements address mainly the distributed system architecture to which we dedicate this section of the book and present some of the known solutions. New solutions are expected to come as result of the ongoing research.

A general security architecture is defined by Foster et al (1998) that responds to above specified requirements. The authors define several entities, namely: user, process, user proxy, and resource proxy. A user proxy acts on behalf of a user for a limited period of time (the user doesn't need to be online during the entire computation). A resource proxy serves to translate the interdomain security operations into local ones, which are adapted to local security mechanisms. Also, four protocols are identified to allow the user proxy creation, resource allocation, resource allocation from a process, and mapping from the global name to a local name. This architecture was adopted in the **Globus Security Infrastructure** as part of the Globus project (Foster et al, 1998), which supports the basic security services: message protection, authentication, authorization, and delegation. The **Globus Toolkit** Version 4 (GT4) contains Web Service and non-Web Service Grid components (Welch, 2005) that are based on standards from the Global Grid Forum (GGF), Internet Engineering Task Force (IETF), The World Wide Web Consortium (W3C), and the Organization for the Advancement of Structured Information Standards (OASIS).

The above mentioned mapping of global to local identities complicates identity administration and restricts data sharing possibilities. To avoid these problems, Thain (2005) proposes a different technique, named identity boxing, in which only global identities are attached to processes and resources and are used to validate the access invocations. The idea is similar to the sandbox, in which untrusted programs are executed in a controlled environment. Similarly, visiting processes run in a controlled domain, which protects the owners and users from each other and allows the data sharing. The author implemented the new solution using Parrot (Thain & Livny, 2003) and demonstrated that the performance overhead is

reasonably good, namely 0.7 to 6.5 percent for a group of selected scientific simulation applications that are not system-call intensive.

The security architecture can also be influenced by the technology used in distributed system development. An example is the security architecture of the distributed object-based system **Globe** presented in (Popescu et al, 2002). The authors observe that distributed systems built on traditional object technologies, like CORBA, DCOM, etc., focus on authenticating the clients and servers, protecting their inter-communication, controlling the access, and delegating rights. They allow object sharing but not object replication. Instead, object replication is present in Globe and gives raise to new security problems (in addition to consistency ones), which are grouped in three categories: secure binding (the client installs the right object and securely associate an object identifier – OID with an individual or a company), platform security (protecting hosts against threats posed by the mobile code and protecting the mobile code against malicious hosts), and secure method invocation (the reverse access control facilitates finding the replica that is trustworthy enough to execute specific user requests). The solution used in Globe is based on public keys. Unique public / private key pairs are associated with objects, replica, and users. They are used in three types of certificates: a user certificate specifies the methods that user can invoke; a replica certificate indicates what methods the replica is allowed to execute; an administrative certificate can be used by an authorized entity to generate certificates of the other two types. With this approach, each entity can be identified through its public key and permissions are granted based on certificates. The above mentioned problems are solved base on the following mechanisms: for secure binding, the object's public key is included in object's ID; protecting hosts against malicious code is based on sandboxing combined with code signing; protecting against malicious hosts uses the reverse access control mechanism; a secure method invocation is performed in several steps, which authenticate the client and the replica, and checks that the invocation is authorized.

A large category of distributed systems are based on the per-to-peer architecture. Security issues related to peer-to-peer (P2P) systems for content delivery are presented, along with other topics, in (Androutsellis-Theotokis & Spinellis, 2004). The authors define P2P systems in this category as systems "consisting of interconnected nodes able to self-organize into network topologies with the purpose of sharing resources such as content, CPU cycles, storage and bandwidth, capable of adapting to failures and accommodating transient populations of nodes while maintaining acceptable connectivity and performance, without requiring the intermediation or support of a global centralized server or authority." The definition highlights the composition of P2P systems (nodes and overlay network), their purpose (sharing resources), and their attributes (adapting to failures,). The architecture of P2P systems can be decentralized (all nodes act both as clients and servers), partially centralized (several supernodes act as local indexes for files shared by peers), and hybrid decentralized (a central server acts as directory and lookup server). The **overlay network** can be unstructured (the placement of content is not related to the topology) or structured (content is placed at specific locations). Representative examples of unstructured P2P systems are Napster, Gnutella, and Edutella; among structured P2P systems we can cite Chord, CAN and Tapestry (see Androutsellis-Theotokis & Spinellis, 2004).

P2P systems are special cases for security since their nodes are considered untrusted parties. Consequently, special techniques must be used to ensure content's security. For example, self-certifying data is used to allow checks by the node retrieving it. Secure routing is used against malicious nodes that try to modify or fabricate copies of objects transferred between nodes. An important issue in content distribution P2P systems is the provision for anonymity, which can refer to the publisher, the node storing the content, the content itself, and the query for content retrieval. For example, in **Freenet** (Clarke et al, 2002), a user can store a file by sending a message that contains the file and a globally unique identifier (GUID) calculated as a SHA-1 hash. The file is stored on several nodes. When a file is retrieved, it is not moved directly to the recipient. Instead, the file is transmitted along a chain. On each link of the chain, the file is individually encrypted, which makes impossible the identification of the file source. A similar solution is used by Freedman and Morris (2002) in Tarzan, a peer-to-peer network overlay that ensures the anonymity of clients and servers, based on layered encryption and multihop routing.

Trust management in P2P systems is a hot research topic (Singh and Liu, 2003). Each peer has an associated trust value, which is calculated based on peer reputation. Peers with high trust values offer high quality services. The trust values are continuously updated by a peer-reviewing process (each peer that received a service rates the quality of the service provider) and are stored by peers in a distributed way. The solution for securely store and access the trust values must satisfy several requirements (Singh and Liu, 2003): ensure protection of the trust hosting peers against security attacks, offer always the true trust values even in presence of malicious peers, identify malicious peers that try to modify the trust values. In order to achieve these requirements, Singh and Liu (3003) propose TrustMe, a "secure and anonymous underlying protocol for trust management". It is based on Public Key cryptography and provides the protection of peers that host the trust values and of the peers that access them. The solution is based on ensuring the mutual anonymity of both peers.

Another interesting use of P2P architectures is presented in (Vlachos et al, 2004). The authors propose the NetBiotic application to enforce network security against malicious attacks. The application is based on two components that act as independent daemons for UNIX systems, namely the Notifier and the Handler. The Notifier monitors the hosting node and collects information about probable security attacks from the log files of firewalls, antivirus software and Intrusion Detection Systems. Then it calculates some statistics on the collected values, detects recent security attacks on its host, and notifies the other nodes about the identified attacks. The Handler receives the notifications from other nodes and takes decisions on the security policy, such as increase of the security level of the node.

SECURITY ENVIRONMENTS / FRAMEWORKS

Many security environments and frameworks developed recently refer to collaborative systems, in general, and Grid systems, in particular. We describe in the sequel the salient features of some frameworks.

An extension of the Reference Monitor model to the Grid environments is presented in (Zhao et al, 2005). The authors propose SVGrid, a Secure Virtual Grid computing Environment to separate the applications from the filesystem and network resources. Each application runs on a separate **Grid Virtual Machines** (GVMs). A separate Monitor Virtual Machine offers filesystem and network services for all the GVMs. Any service request is checked for compliance with the security policies enforced by the Monitor. In this way, the sensitive system files and networks are protected against possible malicious applications.

In (Zhang et al, 2008), the authors propose a security framework, called PEI (the acronym comes from the Policy, Enforcement, and Implementation model layers on which the framework is based), for collaborative systems. Users are organized in groups (**Virtual Organizations**, VO) and share resources offered by resource providers. The platform must ensure not only the user access to resources according to their privileges, but also the availability of resources according to policies agreed by resource providers. It aims to provide a flexible and fine-grained access control that takes into account that user needs variable usage quota on a specific resource, context-based permissions (not fixed, pre-assigned ones), usage constraints on resources, and other aspects. This is why, in the policy model layer, security policies defined by VOs and constraints specified by resource owners are supported. In the enforcement layer, attributes are stored in VOs' repositories and managed by monitors in each resource provider. A prototype system has been implemented and experiments for performance evaluation have been done.

After a critical analysis of the single sign-on facility in several Grid middleware platforms (Globus, Condor, UNICORE), Kolano (2007) proposes Mesh (Middleware using Existing SSH Hosts), a lightweight Grid middleware, which is based on existing SSH infrastructure to which the single sign-on capability is added. The author highlights the drawbacks of former solutions that make them more vulnerable, such as the use of special clients and addition of protocols over SSH to retrieve security certificates, or centralized design based on a key distribution center or certificate authority. His solution is entirely based on the standard SSH and uses private keys loaded into an SSH agent (Kolano, 2007). To create a grid environment, several services have been integrated in Mesh: resource discovery, high performance file transfer, and job management.

A solution to support the execution of large applications on remote resources that fit clients' requirements is the use of virtual machine (VM) technology (Keahey, 2007). Several virtual machines can be deployed on a single physical machine and share its physical resources. Each VM can run its own operating system (OS), which may be different from the OSs of the other VMs that share the same physical system. The VM idea is captured in Grid platforms in the form of workspaces, and the Virtual Workspace Service (VWSS) has been developed in GT4. The security model originally associated with VWSS considers the computing platform is trusted. To cope with users' special security requirements, Demchenko et al (2007) propose a solution for building a user-controlled secure virtual workspace environment (VWSS-UC) that is based on a combination of the VWSS with the Trusted Computing Group (TCG) platform, and with tools for security management at user application level AuthZ of the GAAA authorization framework.

Collaboration can span several domains, each one having its own administration and access control policy. Inter-domain operations require mapping between different access control policies and may be achieved with or without a trusted mediator. Shehab et al (2008) propose a mediator-free distributed environment to support secure collaboration. They use the RBAC model for access control in each domain and define the user's access path as a sequence of roles, in different domains, acquired by the user during a session. Two other techniques are associated with an access path. One is used for path authentication and is based on a signature generated by all the domains included in the access path. The second is an ensemble of algorithms that are executed, in the collaboration environment, for on-demand path discovery. The authors demonstrate the effectiveness of their solution against several categories of attacks and the high performance of the proposed path discovery algorithms.

The framework designed by Blanc at al (2006) approaches a similar problem with a different solution that is based on combining a meta-policy with intrusion detection. A meta-policy is a global security policy that contains an initial protection policy for each host in a distributed system, and a set of modification rules. The initial protection policy is used by each host to tailor a local access control. Each host is able to modify the local policy as it needs but obeying to the constraints imposed by the set of modification rules. The enforcement of the meta-policy is done by an **Intrusion Detection System** (IDS), at two levels:

at one level, illegal modifications of the policy are detected; at the second level copes with detecting illegal interaction sequences between entity pairs of the distributed system. The framework implementation is based on a set of Control Agents that manage the meta-policy (expressed in XML) and local protection policies. The framework has been experimented on SELinux and grsecurity systems.

Several other frameworks and environments have been developed and reported in the literature. We shortly mention here some of the most relevant ones. The work in (Cavalcanti et al, 2006) describes OurGrid, which uses virtualization to build security in a Grid system. Lin et al (2007) present a Grid based virtual collaborative environment based on distributed mobile agent to ensure the security and integrity of data and systems. Lee at al (2008) discuss Traust, an authorization service that can be integrated with existing or legacy applications. Traust allows entities to negotiate resource access policies and then issues access tokens to be used in resource utilization. Koshutanski and Massacci (2003) describe a framework for the access control of business processes for web Services.

CONCLUSION

The chapter presented a selection of research challenges in the area of large scale distributed systems. The focus was on research topics like security models, secure distributed architectures, secure communication, security environments, access control, and security management. We mentioned the most important problems, and analyzed the works that tailored the research in the field or have a high potential to influence the research in the future. Many contributions refer to security models and architectures, which represent the "key" to build solutions for systems that are complex by scale, by their large scale, and by their heterogeneity. The actual problems and the relevant methods of investigation have been presented together with performance results, which give to the user a comprehensive image of the actual research in the domain.

REFERENCES

Androutsellis-Theotokis, S., & Spinellis, D. (2004). A survey of peer-to-peer content distribution technologies. *ACM Computing Surveys*, *36*(4), 335–371. doi:10.1145/1041680.1041681

Bell, D. E. (2005). Looking Back at the Bell-La Padula Model. In *Proceedings of the 21st Annual Computer Security Applications Conference* (pp. 337 – 351). Washington, DC: IEEE Computer Society.

Bernard, A. (2006). *McAfee's Top Ten Security Threats for 2007*. Retrieved September 2009, http://www.cioupdate.com/trends/article.php/3646826/McAfees-Top-Ten-Security-Threats-for-2007

Bhaiji, Y. (2008). Overview of Network Security. *Network World*. Retrieved February 2009, from http://www.networkworld.com/subnets/cisco/072508-ch1-net-security-technologies.html

Bhargavan, K., Corin, R., Fournet, C., & Gordon, A. D. (2007). Secure Sessions for Web Services. *ACM Transactions on Information and System Security*, *10*(2), 332–351. doi:10.1145/1237500.1237504

Bishop, M. (2003). *Computer Security: Art and Science*. Reading, MA: Addison-Wesley.

Blanc, M., Briffaut, J., Lalande, J. F., & Toinard, C. (2006). Distributed Control Enabling Consistent MAC Policies and IDS based on a Meta-Policy approach. In *Proceedings of the Seventh IEEE International Workshop on Policies for Distributed Systems and Networks* (pp. 153-156). Washington, DC: IEEE Computer Society.

Cavalcanti, E., Assis, L., Gaudencio, M., Cirne, W., Brasileiro, F., & Novaes, R. (2006). Sandboxing for a free-to-join grid with support for secure site-wide storage area. In *Proceedings of the Second International Workshop on Virtualization Technology in Distributed Computing* Tampa, FL (pp. 11-11).

Clarke, I., Miller, S., Hong, T., Sandberg, O., & Wiley, B. (2002). Protecting free expression online with Freenet. *IEEE Internet Computing*, *6*(1), 40–49. doi:10.1109/4236.978368

Common Criteria. (2008). *The Common Criteria for Information Technology Security Evaluation portal*. Retrieved February 2009, from http://www.commoncriteriaportal.org/

Corbato, F. J., Saltzer, J. H., & Clingen, C. T. (2009). *Multics--The first seven years*. Retrieved February 12, 2009, from web http://www.multicians.org/f7y.html

Covington, M., Long, W., Srinivasan, S., Dey, A., Ahmad, M., & Abowd, G. D. (2001). Securing context-aware applications using environment roles. In *ACM Symposium on Access Control Model and Technology*, Chantilly, VA (pp. 10-20).

Demchenko, Y., Gommans, L., Siebenlist, F., de Laat, C., Groep, D., & Koeroo, O. (2007). Security and Dynamics in Customer Controlled Virtual Workspace Organisation. In *Proceedings of the 16th international symposium on High performance distributed computing*, Monterey, CA (pp. 231-232).

Dondeti, L., Mukherjee, S., & Samal, A. (1999). *A distributed group key management scheme for secure many-to-many communication*. Tech. Rep. PINTL-TR-207-99, Department of Computer Science, University of Maryland.

Fernandez, E., & Sorgente, T. (2009). *Ideas for Operating Systems Patterns*. Retrieved March 2009, from http://www.cse.fau.edu/~security/public/docs/3OS_security_patternsIdeas.ppt

Ferraiolo, D., Kuhn, R., & Sandhu, R. (2007). RBAC Standard Rationale: Comments on A Critique of the ANSI Standard on Role-Based Access Control. *IEEE Security & Privacy, 5*(6), 51-53.

Ferraiolo, D. F., Barkley, J. F., & Kuhn, D. R. (1999). A role-based access control model and reference implementation within a corporate intranet. [TISSEC]. *ACM Transactions on Information and System Security, 2*(1), 34–64. doi:10.1145/300830.300834

Ferraiolo, D. F., Sandhu, R., Gavrila, S., Kuhn, D. R., & Chandramouli, R. (2001). Proposed NIST Standard for Role-Based Access Control. *ACM Transactions on Information and System Security, 4*(3), 224–274. doi:10.1145/501978.501980

Foster, I., Kesselman, C., Tsudik, G., & Tuecke, S. (1998). A Security Architecture for Computational Grids. In *Proc. Fifth Conf. Computer and Communications Security* (pp. 83 – 92). New York: ACM.

Freedman, M. J., & Morris, R. (2002). Tarzan: A peer-to-peer anonymizing network layer. In *Proceedings of the 9th ACM conference on Computer and communications security* (pp. 193-206). New York: ACM.

Gutmann, P. (2003). *Cryptographic Security Architecture: Design and Verification*. New York: Springer-Verlag.

Harrison, M. A., Ruzzo, W. L., & Ullman, J. D. (1976). Protection in Operating Systems. *Communications of the ACM, 19*(8), 461–471. doi:10.1145/360303.360333

Hashii, B. (2004). Lessons Learned Using Alloy to Formally Specify MLSPCA Trusted Security Architecture. In *Proceedings of the 2004 ACM workshop on Formal methods in security engineering* (pp. 86-95). New York: ACM.

Hung, P. C. K., & Karlapalem, K. (2003). A secure workflow model. In C. Johnson, P. Montague, & C. Steketee (Eds.), *ACSW Frontiers 2003. Proceedings of the Australasian Information Security Workshop AISW 2003* (pp. 33-41). Adelaide, Australia: ACS.

Joshi, J. B. D., Aref, W. G., Ghafoor, A., & Spafford, E. H. (2001). Security Models for Web-Based Applications. *Communications of the ACM, 44*(2), 38–44. doi:10.1145/359205.359224

Keahey, K., Freeman, T., Lauret, J., & Olson, D. (2009). *Virtual Workspaces for Scientific Applications*. Presented at SciDAC 2007 Conference, Boston, MA, June 2007. Retrieved February 2009, from workspace.globus.org/papers/SciDAC_STAR_POC.pdf

Keromytis, A. D., Misra, V., & Rubenstein, D. (2002). SOS: Secure Overlay Services. In *Proceedings of ACM SIGCOMM, 2002* (pp. 61-72).

Kolano, P. Z. (2007). Mesh: Secure, Lightweight Grid Middleware Using Existing SSH Infrastructure. In *Proceedings of the 12th ACM symposium on Access control models and technologies, SACMAT'07* (pp. 111-120). New York: ACM.

Koshutanski, H., & Massacci, F. (2003). An Access Control Framework for Business Processes for Web Services. In *Proceedings of the 2003 ACM Workshop on XML Security* (pp. 15 – 24). New York: ACM.

Lampson, B., Abadi, M., Burrows, M., & Wobber, E. (1992). Authentication in Distributed Systems: Theory and Practice. *ACM Transactions on Computer Systems, 10*(4), 265–310. doi:10.1145/138873.138874

Landwehr, C. E. (1981). Formal Models for Computer Security. *Computing Surveys, 13*(3), 247–278. doi:10.1145/356850.356852

Lee, A. J., Winslett, M., Basney, J., & Welch, V. (2008). The Traust Authorization Service. *ACM Transactions on Information and System Security, 11*(1). doi:10.1145/1330295.1330297

Li, H., & Singhal, M. (2007). Trust Management in Distributed Systems. *IEEE Computer, 40*(2), 45–53.

Li, N., Byun, J.-W., & Bertino, E. (2007). A Critique of the ANSI Standard on Role-Based Access Control. *IEEE Security & Privacy, 5*(6), 41-49.

Lin, Q., Neo, H. K., Zhang, L., Huang, G., & Gay, R. (2007). Grid-Based Large-scale Web3D Collaborative Virtual Environment. In *Proceedings of the twelfth international conference on 3D web technology*, Web3D 2007, Perugia, Italy, April 15–18, 2007 (pp. 123 - 132).

Lipton, R. J., & Snyder, L. (1997). A Linear Time Algorithm for Deciding Subject Security. *Journal of the ACM, 24*(3), 455–464. doi:10.1145/322017.322025

Neumann, P. (1995). *Architectures and Formal Representations for Secure Systems. Technical report, Computer Science Laboratory*. Menlo Park, CA: SRI International.

OASIS. (2006). *Web Services Security: SOAP Message Security 1.1*. OASIS Standard Specification. Retrieved February 2009, from http://docs.oasis-open.org/wss/v1.1/

OASIS. (2007). *WS-Trust 1.3, OASIS Standard, 19 March 2007*. Retrieved February 2009, from http://docs.oasis-open.org/ws-sx/ws-trust/200512/ws-trust-1.3-os.doc

OASIS. (2007). *WS-SecureConversation 1.3, OASIS Standard, 1 March 2007*. Retrieved February 2009, from http://docs.oasis-open.org/ws-sx/ws-secureconversation/200512/ws-secureconversation-1.3-os.doc

OWASP. (2007). *The Ten Most Critical Web Applications Security Vulnerabilities*. Retrieved August 2008, from http://www.owasp.org/images/e/e8/OWASP_Top_10_2007.pdf

Pfleeger, C. P., & Pfleeger, S. L. (2007). *Security in computing* (4th ed.). Upper Saddle River, NJ: Prentice Hall.

Popescu, B., Van Steen, M., & Tanenbaum, A. (2002). A Security Architecture for Object-Based Distributed Systems. In *Proc. 18th Ann. Computer Security Application Conference* (pp. 161-171). Washington, DC: IEEE Computer Society.

Rafaeli, S., & David, H. (2003). A survey of key management for secure group communication. *ACM Computing Surveys, 35*(3), 309–329. doi:10.1145/937503.937506

Sandhu, R. S. (1988). The Schematic Protection Model: Its Definition and Analysis for Acyclic Attenuating Schemes. *Journal of the ACM, 35*(2), 404–432. doi:10.1145/42282.42286

Sandhu, R. S. (1992). The Typed Access Matrix Model. In *Proceedings of the 1992 IEEE Symposium on Security and Privacy* (pp.122-136). Washington, DC: IEEE Computer Society.

SANS. (2007). *SANS Top-20 2007 Security Risks (2007 Annual Update)*. Retrieved March 2009, from http://www.sans.org/top20/

Shehab, M., Ghafoor, A., & Bertino, E. (2008). Secure Collaboration in a Mediator-Free Distributed Environment. *IEEE Transactions on Parallel and Distributed Systems, 19*(10), 1338–1351. doi:10.1109/TPDS.2008.26

Singh, A., & Liu, L. (2003). TrustMe: Anonymous Management of Trust Relationships in Decentralized P2P networks. In *Proceedings of the third IEEE Conference on Peer-to-Peer Computing*, Linkoping, Sweden (pp. 142-149).

Srivatsa, M., Iyengar, A., Yin J., & Liu, L. (2008). Mitigating Application Level Denial of Service Attacks on Web Servers: A Client Transparent Approach. *ACM Transactions on the Web (TWEB), 2*(3).

Stading, T. (2003). Secure Communication in a Distributed System Using Identity Based Encryption. In *Proceedings of the 3rd IEEE/ACM International Symposium on Cluster Computing and the Grid* (pp. 414 – 420). Washington, DC: IEEE Computer Society.

Steiner, M., Tsudik, G., & Waidner, M. (1996). Diffie-Hellman key distribution extended to group communication. In *SIGSAC Proceedings of the 3rd ACM Conference on Computer and Communications Security* (pp. 31–37). New York: ACM.

Stoica, I., Morris, R., Karger, D., Kaashoek, M. F., & Balakrishnan, H. (2001). Chord: A scalable peer-to-peer lookup service for Internet applications. In. *Proceedings of SIGCOMM, 31*, 149–160. doi:10.1145/964723.383071

Tanenbaum, A. S., & van Steen, M. (2007). *Distributed Systems. Principles and paradigms* (2nd ed.). Upper Saddle River, NJ: Prentice Hall.

Thain, D. (2005). Identity boxing: secure user-level containment for the grid. In *Proceedings of the ACM/IEEE Conference on Supercomputing, SC05* (pp. 51). Washington, DC: IEEE Computer Society.

Thain, D., & Livny, M. (2003). Parrot: Transparent user-level middleware for data-intensive computing. In *Workshop on Adaptive Grid Middleware 2003*. Retrieved September 2009, from http://pages.cs.wisc.edu/~thain/library/parrot-agm2003.pdf

Thomas, R. (1997). Team-based access control (TMAC). In *Proceedings of 2nd ACM Workshop on Role-Based Access Control* (pp. 13-19). New York: ACM.

Thomas, R. K., & Sandhu, R. S. (1997). Task-based Authorization Controls (TBAC), A Family of Models for Active and Enterprise-oriented Authorization Management. In *Proceedings of the IFIP WG11.3 Workshop on Database Security*. Retrieved August 2009, from http://www.list.gmu.edu/confrnc/ifip/i97tbac.pdf

Tidswell, J. E., & Potter, J. M. (1998). A Dynamically Typed Access Control Model. In *Information Security and Privacy, Third Australasian Conference, ACISP '98, Brisbane, Australia* (LNCS 1438, pp. 308-319). Berlin/Heidelberg: Springer.

Tolone, W., Aahn, G. J., Pai, T., & Hong, S. P. (2005). Access Control in Collaborative Systems. *ACM Computing Surveys, 37*(1), 29–41. doi:10.1145/1057977.1057979

van der Merwe, J., Dawoud, D., & McDonald, S. (2007). A Survey on Peer-to-Peer Key Management for Mobile Ad Hoc Networks. *ACM Computing Surveys, 39*(1).

Vlachos, V., Androutsellis-theotokis, S., & Spinellis, D. (2004). Security applications of peer-to-peer networks. *Computer Networks, 45*(2), 195–205. doi:10.1016/j.comnet.2004.01.002

Welch, V. (Ed.). (2005). *The Globus Security Team: Globus Toolkit Version 4 Grid Security Infrastructure: A Standards Perspective*. Version 4 updated September 12, 2005. Retrieved September 2009, from www.globus.org/toolkit/docs/4.0/security/GT4-GSI-Overview.pdf

Wong, C. K., Gouda, M. G., & Lam, S. S. (2000). Secure group communications using key graphs. *IEEE/ACM Trans. Netw., 8*(1), 16–30.

Yao, D., Koglin, Y., Bertino, E., & Tamassia, R. (2007). Decentralized authorization and data security in web content delivery. In *Proceedings of the 2007 ACM symposium on Applied computing*, Seoul, Korea (pp. 1654 - 1661).

Zhang, X., Nakae, M., Covington, M. J., & Sandhu, R. (2008). Toward a Usage-Based Security Framework for Collaborative Computing Systems. *ACM Transactions on Information and System Security, 11*(1). doi:10.1145/1330295.1330298

Zhao, X., Borders, K., & Prakash, A. (2005). SVGrid A Secure Virtual Environment for Untrusted Grid Applications. In *Proceedings of the 3rd International Workshop on Middleware For Grid Computing, MGC '05* (pp. 1-6). New York: ACM.

Zhu, S., Setia, S., & Jajodia, S. (2004). LEAP Efficient Security Mechanisms for LargeScale Distributed Sensor Networks. In *Proceedings of the 10th ACM conference on Computer and communications security* (pp. 62 – 72). Washington, DC: IEEE.

Chapter 10
Application Development Tools and Frameworks

INTRODUCTION

Large scale distributed systems are used for executing a wide variety of applications; while the first distributed applications were from the scientific area, today many of them are dedicated to businesses or even to home users. The constantly increasing demand for large scale distributed applications has brought on a need for tools and frameworks that ease their development. The main role of these tools and frameworks is to assist the developer in implementing some common functionalities and patterns that are specific to distributed applications – for example, dividing a large computational task into smaller subtasks to be executed on multiple machines, or sending e-mails automatically, or managing the access to resources in a secure way.

One of the most important issues that the application development frameworks have to address is the abstraction of the underlying middleware: their main objective is to relieve the application programmer from the effort of dealing with lower-level components. Another important aspect is the

performance of the communication among the application components; hence, some development tools are specifically targeted to optimizing the communication performance. We also observe an increasing interest in the interoperability among applications developed with different platforms, which has led to many standardization initiatives.

This chapter discusses the issues introduced above, and makes an overview of the current tools and frameworks for developing various types of distributed applications. We start with web applications, which are the most frequently used nowadays; we introduce some general design issues, and present tools for server-side and client-side programming. Then, we discuss about developing applications in grids, clouds and peer-to-peer systems; we present the specific aspects of programming applications in these types of systems and introduce some of the most widely used tools and frameworks. The last section is dedicated to distributed workflows – complex applications that are composed of multiple smaller applications or services; the development and execution of workflows poses more challenges compared to traditional applications, requiring specific tools and runtime environments.

DOI: 10.4018/978-1-61520-703-9.ch010

WEB APPLICATION DEVELOPMENT

Web applications are applications that are accessed over a network, with the aid of a web browser, and use the Hypertext Transfer Protocol (HTTP) for communication. A special case are the web services, applications that also use HTTP and standardized messages for communication, but their results are intended to be used by other applications rather than by humans. The popularity of Web applications is constantly increasing as they are beginning to cover more and more domains – online commerce and banking, webmail, e-government, wikis, weblogs and others.

The World Wide Web has undergone a significant evolution since its invention by Tim Berners-Lee at the beginning of the 1990s. The scientist from CERN had the initiative of putting together hypertext and Internet technologies, to create a collection of hyperlinked documents accessible to anyone who had an Internet connection. Since then, multiple changes have occurred in the networking hardware, in the development technologies, in the structure of the users community and in many other aspects. These changes had an important impact on the philosophy behind the World Wide Web, and in order to mark their occurrence the community has added "version numbers" to the Web concept. Thus, at the moment of writing this book most of the current applications follow the Web 2.0 principles, while the Web as it was originally created has been retroactively tagged as "1.0".

Researchers are already looking ahead at Web 3.0, which will evolve in the next decade.

Although the version numbers may suggest the change of a technology, the differences among 1.0, 2.0 and 3.0 are rather in the principles that stand behind Web applications: how the content is generated, how the information is processed and interpreted, how the users interact with (and possibly participate to) the application, how the application is designed etc. It is difficult to make a clear distinction between the versions – precisely because they are not actual versions but terms adopted by the community; for example, many of the current applications have both Web 2.0 and Web 1.0 features. Table 1 summarizes the principles on which Web 1.0, 2.0 and 3.0 are based; Lassila & Hendler (2007) and Cho (2008) provide a more in-depth discussion on this topic and also some historical facts.

The Structure of Web Applications

Due to the evolution of the technologies and of the users' demands, web applications are becoming more and more complex. Most of them are structured on multiple tiers, the most popular model being the 3-tiered one; this model consists of the following components:

- *Presentation Tier:* this tier is responsible with the user interface, generating the content that will be ultimately provided to the user

Table 1. The evolution of Web applications

Web 1.0 (1990)	Web 2.0 (2004)	Web 3.0 (2006)
static pages one-way publishing not interactive proprietary applications content management tools directories	dynamic content content comes from multiple sources (mashup) community contribution (users are co-developers) democracy loosely coupled components tagging	semantic web data mining intelligent applications distributed databases ubiquitous connectivity 3D vision

- *Application Tier*, also known as *business logic tier*: contains the code that receives users' requests, processes them and possibly looks up for the needed information in a database with the aid of the data tier; the results are passed to the presentation tier which will generate the user-readable content
- *Data Tier:* handles the storage and retrieval of the information from a database; there are many types of information that need to be stored, from product catalogs to user-related data.

Besides these three tiers, there can be another one at the client side – when the web application has parts that are executed directly on the client's machine (most often, within the web browser).

Structuring the applications on multiple tiers have several advantages, like achieving a separation of concerns (the three tiers have different roles and should be developed by persons with different technical backgrounds), the possibility to replace or update separately any of the tiers, and an improvement in performance and in scalability. However, the multi-tier model may not be the best choice in all the cases, especially for small

applications, as it requires multiple technologies and often involves much development overhead. There are a wide variety of technologies that address the particular aspects of each tier, and that can be used for application development; some of them are listed in Figure 1.

Server-Side Programming

Currently, the most widely used platforms for programming server applications are Java Platform Enterprise Edition and Microsoft.NET.

Java Platform, Enterprise Edition - also known as Java EE - is a standard for developing web applications, based on the Java programming language (Sun Microsystems, 1999). Java EE offers APIs for web services, e-mail, accessing databases, XML processing, naming services and many others. It also introduced some specific components for building web applications – like servlets, Java Server Pages and Enterprise Java Beans. The servlets are Java objects that are used for generating dynamic web pages, and that are run within a servlet container (which in turn runs within a web server); the container manages the servlets' lifecycle and intermediates their interactions with the clients. Java Server Pages provide support for web page scripting, by allowing fragments of code to be embedded in the HTML content; they can be either interpreted or compiled into servlets. Enterprise Java Beans are, like the servlets, presentation tier components. They are meant to implement the back-end business logic of an application, while the servlets usually implement the front-end code that generates the user interface.

The Java EE specifications have been implemented by many vendors and also by some open source projects. Among the current open source implementations we mention the JBoss application server, Apache Geronimo and GlassFish. Some popular commercial Java EE servers are Sun Java System Application Server (based on GlassFish), IBM WebSphere Application Server, Oracle Con-

Figure 1. Tools and frameworks for developing web applications

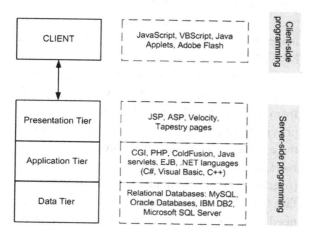

tainers for Java EE, BEA WebLogic Application Server and SAP NetWeaver Application Server.

The Microsoft.NET platform has a broader usage area, being designed to support application development for the Windows operating system, and also providing extensive functionalities for web applications. Like the Java platform, .NET is based on a virtual runtime environment – the Common Language Runtime (CLR). However, a significant difference (which is one of the most important. NET features and an advantage in comparison with Java EE) is that CLR is able to support multiple programming languages. Microsoft has designed a specification for programming languages, named Common Language Specification, and any language that implements it can be run on a.NET platform; some well-known compliant languages are C#, Visual Basic and Visual J#. The program compilation is a two-step process, in which the programs are first translated to an intermediate language (Microsoft Intermediate Language), and then, within the CLR, they are compiled into native machine code. Another important feature of.NET is language interoperability – due to a common data type specification (Common Type System) for the.NET languages, the platform supports the exchange of object instances among programs written in different languages. Through the Base Class Library, the framework provides a large number of utility classes – covering collections, network communication, security, threading, data access, user interfaces etc. We also mention that there have been efforts to port the.NET framework on other platforms than Windows – one example is the Mono project, presented in (Bergman-Terrell, 2008).

ASP.NET is a framework dedicated to web applications development, integrated in the.NET platform. It brings several improvements in comparison with ASP, the previous technology for web applications provided by Microsoft (Moroney, 2006). One of the most important improvements is regarding the performance, as the ASP.NET applications are compiled (in the same way with

the other.NET applications), and not interpreted. Other advantages are the support for multiple programming languages, the ease in handling multiple types of browsers, and the management functionalities provided by the Common Language Runtime (which to some extent are similar with the ones provided by the Java Enterprise Edition platform).

In the competition between the Java EE and. NET platforms, it is difficult to find a clear winner, and the opinions are very diverse. We note that they were designed with different philosophies in mind: the goal of Java EE was the possibility to run Java programs on any kind of platform ("write once, run everywhere"), while.NET is mainly used on a single operating system, but provides support for multiple programming languages. The compatibility with multiple platforms used to be a strong advantage of Java EE, but currently, as we have mentioned, there are projects that enable running.NET applications on non-Windows platforms as well. The Java EE platform is still more open to the community than.NET, as through the Java Community Process, the interested users are able to propose changes in the technologies and to influence their evolution.

Among the other solutions for developing web applications we mention PHP, a scripting language that can be used to generate dynamic HTML pages. Its popularity comes from the simplicity, and also from the compatibility with many web servers and operating systems. It has been widely used for developing web applications, especially in the open source communities, together with the MySQL database management system.

The current research in the domain of web application frameworks targets various aspects, from improving the development process to providing higher performance and scalability at the execution time. Yu (2007) proposes a framework for automatically integrating presentation (user interface) components, motivated by the fact that currently, the web mash-up developers need to integrate application and presentation components manually – which takes a significant amount of effort. The framework is event-driven and uses an XML-based language for describing components and compositions. Yang et al. (2007) addressed another time-consuming part of the web application development process – the partitioning among the application tiers. Although, as we showed above, this partitioning into tiers leads to a well-structured design and provides separation of concerns, it also has some drawbacks: the necessity to learn multiple programming tools and the difficulty of moving content from one tier to another. The solution proposed by Yang et al. is to use a single programming language for all the tiers (specifically, Hilda – a high-level declarative programming language) and to partition the application automatically, in order to achieve load balancing among the clients and the server; as this optimization problem is NP-complete, the authors have developed an approximation heuristic that takes into account the characteristics of the client machines.

For improving the web applications' performance, one of the most important techniques is replication. Perez-Sorrosal et al. (2007) introduced an approach for replicating multiple application tiers in a coordinated way. The proposed protocol replicates the application tier and the data tier in a vertical way, considering the pair of application and database server as the replication unit; this approach provides a more elegant solution for consistency, and also improves the scalability of the application framework.

Client-Side Programming

Placing the functionalities of a web application at the client (that is, executing a part of the application within the user's browser) has the benefit of reducing the load on the server, which will be able to respond to a greater number of clients. However, this approach adds more load on the clients' machines, and this might not be acceptable in some situations - for example, if the

user's machine is not powerful enough or if s/he executes computing intensive applications in the same time with the browsing. Another important drawback of using client-side applications is the security risk – if the user's browser is enabled to execute scripts, it is exposed to malicious code coming from the visited sites.

There are two main possibilities for executing client-side web applications: scripts (that are embedded in HTML pages, or placed in separate files that are referenced from the HTML pages) and compiled applications (that are downloaded by the browser as bytecode and then executed).

Three of the most well-known client side scripting languages are:

- *JavaScript* – scripting language designed to have a similar syntax with Java, although besides the syntax the two languages are quite different. Java script is an object-based language, supports dynamic typing and treats functions as first-class objects;
- *VBScript* – this language, whose full name is Visual Basic Scripting Edition, is a limited version of the Visual Basic programming language. VBScript is also an object-based language, and is included in the ASP. NET framework;
- *ActionScript* – this scripting language is mainly used for developing applications that are run using Adobe Flash Player. It is an object-oriented programming language, with data types that are similar with the ones from Java.

For compiled applications, the two main technologies are Java applets and Microsoft Silverlight. Java applets are bytecodes executed by the web browser through a Java Virtual Machine, in a sandbox that prevents them from accessing local data – although the user can configure the level of access an applet has to the local machine. As they are based on Java, the applets have the advantage of cross-platform compatibility. They can be executed by most of the browsers through a specific plug-in. A similar technology with the Java applets is made available by Microsoft Silverlight, a browser plug-in that can execute.NET applications. Silverlight fully implements the Common Language Runtime and can be used to execute programs written in any.NET language; it also includes a subset of the Base Class Library. Currently there is a limited support for Silverlight on other operating systems than Linux.

A newer alternative to executing bytecode within the browser is to run Internet applications outside the browser, thus overcoming the browser compatibility problems. The most widely used technologies for launching web applications on the user's machine are Java Web Start (which uses a protocol named Java Network Launching Protocol) and ClickOnce (a Microsoft technology available in the.NET platform).

A relatively recent technique related to client-side programming is AJAX (Asynchronous JavaScript + XML); this technique is used for acquiring data from the web server asynchronously, in the background, which improves the application's responsiveness. Although it has become well known under this name, the technique does not actually require JavaScript for implementation or XML for representing the data – practically it can be realized with any programming language and data representation standard.

ENVIRONMENTS FOR DEVELOPING AND EXECUTING GRID APPLICATIONS

Grid environments have been chosen as execution platforms for a wide range of computing and data intensive applications, from many domains like physics, astronomy, economy, chemistry or biology. By providing access to various types of resources distributed in large geographical areas and by establishing a base for collaboration among remote partners through the concept of virtual or-

ganizations, grids have contributed to computing the solutions for many complex problems.

However, the users come across various difficulties when developing and executing applications in grids – from the heterogeneity of the resources (different hardware platforms, operating systems or middleware) to the dynamism of the environment (resources fail, come alive or just have software updates very often). Taking into account the fact that most of the Grid users have various scientific backgrounds but are not computer specialists, the necessity of some tools that simplify the development of Grid applications becomes clear. Specifically, programming environments are needed that abstract the complexity of the Grid middleware, maximize the communication performance and possibly even provide a high-level model for developing applications. Several projects have been building instruments that perform these functions, and we shall discuss them in the following sections; Figure 2 presents an overview of some of the existing instruments.

Abstracting the Grid Middleware

The most important function of an environment for developing Grid applications is to provide an abstraction of the middleware, hiding the complexity of the underlying system from the user. This involves satisfying a set of requirements that are summarized by Nieuwpoort et al. (2007):

- Provide a high-level programming interface, as opposed to the low-level interfaces offered by middleware platforms like the Globus toolkit
- Hide the heterogeneity of the Grid – by interoperating with multiple types and versions of middleware platforms, and offering to the users a unique interface
- Identify and handle errors that occur in the middleware components

Figure 2. Functionalities provided by Grid application frameworks

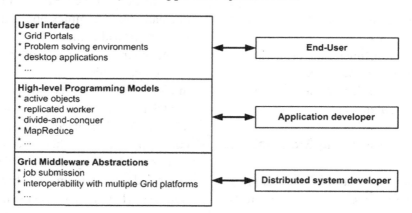

One of the frameworks that satisfies these requirements is JavaGAT (Nieuwpoort et al., 2007), which is an implementation of the GAT API. In order to support multiple types of middleware, JavaGAT uses a plugin-based architecture, in which a plugin (also named adaptor) performs the binding to a specific middleware platform. The plugins form the lowest layer of the JavaGAT system; above it there are three other layers: the plugin interface, the JavaGAT engine that delegates the operations to the correct middleware, and the high-level user API. JavaGAT has an intelligent dispatching mechanism that can select at runtime a suitable middleware platform to which an API call should be forwarded, and is also able to handle faults – if an operation does not succeed on the selected middleware platform, it is re-tried on other platforms. Another fault handling feature is the concept of nested exceptions, whose purpose is to provide the user with meaningful error messages from all the components where faults have occurred.

Java CoG Kit (Laszewski & Hategan, 2005) has the similar purpose of providing a high-level interface to the Grid middleware. It offers access to the user a set of functionalities, named abstractions, among which are job execution, file transfer, workflow abstractions and job queues; the set of abstractions is extensible and the users can include their own abstractions as well. Like JavaGAT, CoG Kit allows interoperability with multiple middleware platforms, through a set of providers, which have a similar role with the JavaGAT adaptors; providers are available for all the versions of the Globus Toolkit. A specific feature of the Java CoG Kit is that it provides access to Grid functionalities through multiple means – either standalone applications, web portals or a desktop utility. It also introduces the workflow abstraction, which helps the users organize complex tasks that consist of multiple applications; we shall discuss more about workflows in a further section.

Another research direction in this context is related to establishing a standardized programming model for the Grid. This is the purpose of the Grid Component Model (INRIA, 2007), which aims to provide definitions for Grid components, to describe the way they interact and also to specify their semantics and to build performance models. This standardized description is useful both for developing applications and for building programming environments. The GCM specification has evolved from the Fractal model, which is based on the following concepts:

- Encapsulation (the components are considered "black boxes")
- Composition (the model is hierarchical)
- Sharing

- Life-cycle (a component passes through different phases during its life)
- Activities
- Control (the non-functional properties of the components can be managed)
- Dynamicity (this refers to the ability to re-configure the component)

High-Level Programming Models

From the point of view of a distributed application architect, the first question that needs to be answered when designing the application is how to divide its functionality into components that can be executed separately, on different machines. There is no single best solution for this aspect, as the most efficient way to parallelize the application depends both on the problem that it solves and on the distributed system's characteristics (the number of machines, their computational power, the communication performance, the amount of storage space etc.).

However, most of the applications suit to one of a few well-known distributed programming models, and in many cases the task of the software architect can be reduced to choosing one of these models which is appropriate for his or her application and for the execution platform. We present in the following paragraphs a few representative high-level programming models.

ProActive (Baduel et al., 2005) is based on the active objects model, using remote method invocation rather than message passing for communication; this approach has the benefit of an object-oriented structuring for the application, and also of reusing the code. The entities that compose the application, active objects, have their own control thread and also the ability to choose the order in which they respond to incoming method calls. The method calls are asynchronous, and another important facilities are: the remote creation of remotely accessible objects, the possibility to migrate objects from one virtual machine to another, group communications. By combining

the active objects according to the Fractal model, one can obtain complex applications that can be viewed as Grid components.

Another popular approach in parallel and distributed applications is the *replicated-workers* model, also known as *master-workers*. In this model, a process that has the master's role creates a set of tasks and places their descriptions into a common space; the other processes, which act as workers, repeatedly take tasks from the common space and process them, possibly producing other new tasks. This model is very simple to implement and suits to a large class of problems, however it has a major drawback – the necessity of having a shared memory among the processes, that will act as the "common space". Shared memory is available physically on multiprocessor machines, but in distributed systems the middleware has to simulate it (this functionality is named "distributed shared memory"). Another disadvantage of the shared memory paradigm is the lack of scalability – the memory access will become a bottleneck when a large number of processes attempt to work with it simultaneously. Many distributed shared memory implementations are available, one of the most widely used being JavaSpaces (Freeman et al., 1999), which provides common "spaces" in a distributed system where objects are stored based on an associative memory model. The ComputeFarm project (ComputeFarm, 2009) is a framework for developing replicated-workers applications, whose implementation is based on JavaSpaces.

The *divide-and-conquer* model is more general than replicated-workers, and involves the recursive division of the problem into sub-problems, the sub-problems being assigned to worker nodes in the system. Divide-and-conquer applications have been proved to run efficiently on heterogeneous distributed systems with high communication latency, and a well known framework for developing distributed divide-and-conquer programs is Satin (Wrzesinska et al., 2006). Satin is based on Java, extending the language with two specific primitives, spawn and sync. It is implemented on top of the Ibis communication library, presented above, and includes a bytecode rewriter that generates communication, load-balancing and fault-tolerance code. By considering the data sharing issue, Satin has been extended to implement a new model, *divide-and-share*, which adds the idea of shared objects to the divide-and-conquer model. The new paradigm allows data sharing among a task and its subtasks through replicated shared objects; in order to improve the applications' performance, a relaxed consistency model (guard consistency) was introduced.

Communication Performance

While complex applications clearly benefit from the large number of resources provided by grids, these environments also have a number of drawbacks; the most notable one is the decrease in communication performance. When an application is distributed on the resources from a single cluster, a high speed network is usually available among the stations and communication does not represent an issue. However, when the application is deployed on multiple clusters interconnected by a wide area network, the standard TCP protocol introduces a significant communication delay. The environments for Grid application development must handle this problem and provide solutions for efficient communication in multi-cluster systems.

One of the most well known frameworks for optimizing communication performance is Grid-MPI (Takano et al., 2007), an implementation of the MPI standard that enables applications deployment over multiple geographically distributed clusters. GridMPI optimizes the communication on inter-cluster links by controlling the traffic, so that the available bandwidth not be exceeded; thus, TCP congestions that cause severe performance degradation can be avoided. A specialized software for packet pacing is used in order to limit the transmissions done over the network links. By employing this optimization mechanism,

GridMPI hides from the users the details of the network topology, and also the heterogeneity of the links (which usually have various bandwidths and latencies).

The Ibis project (Nieuwpoort et al., 2005) comes with another approach to communication optimization, by providing a communication library named IPL (Ibis Portability Layer). IPL is able to use multiple types of networks, including fast ones like Myrinet, and has a mechanism for selecting the best network when several are available. The library was used for implementing an optimized RMI version on top of Ibis, which reduces the serialization overhead through customized methods that avoid reflection, and has an improved wire protocol that makes use of caching object type information in order to avoid sending it multiple times.

ENVIRONMENTS AND TOOLS FOR CLOUD APPLICATIONS

The cloud computing model has proven to be suitable for many types of distributed applications, ranging from web content management and web indexing to data mining and document processing. There are two levels at which vendors provide support for developing cloud applications (Jones, 2008):

- *Platform-as-a-Service (PaaS):* this refers to a virtualized platform that serves as a base for developing cloud applications. Besides the operating system, the platform contains additional software components like web and application servers, databases or application development sandboxes.
- *Software-as-a-Service (SaaS):* the vendors provide access to software over the Internet, charging the customers for the usage of the software. The software can be executed either on the client's machine (in this case the client "leases" the software),

or on a server owned by the vendor. The later alternative, of providing access to applications executed remotely, is more specific to cloud systems and is currently the predominant way of using "software as a service". Google Apps and Microsoft Live Services are two of the most well known implementations of this model.

Platform-as-a-Service (PaaS)

The purpose of the PaaS products is to provide a complete environment for cloud application development. Besides the bare virtual machine (which is provided through "Infrastructure-as-a-Service"), PaaS also offers a software stack whose role is to simplify the development and deployment of the applications. While in some cases the users have to select from a set of available software components, in other cases they have the freedom to install their own components in the virtual machine.

Among the main targets of the PaaS solutions are web applications, data management, and also distributed computations.

A widely used approach to supporting the development of the cloud applications is to provide a set of core components as web services; some typical examples are Microsoft.NET Services and Amazon Web Services..NET Services aim to support the developers in creating the infrastructure needed for cloud applications. Specifically, there are three types of.NET services:

- *Access Control* – this service provides functionalities for managing the users in a cloud system; it implements identity federation, allowing the users to access resources from multiple companies (organization) through a single security token. This idea is similar with the "single sign on" concept from Grid systems;
- *Service Bus* – allows applications to expose their functionalities as web service

endpoints that can be accessed by other applications;
- *Workflow* – service for running composite applications (workflows) in a cloud; it is based on Windows Workflow Foundation.

Amazon Web Services is a more diverse set of services, in which some of the components have the role of providing infrastructure, while the others offer various functionalities that can be used in cloud applications. The main infrastructure services are Amazon Elastic Compute Cloud, which provides scalable sets of virtual machines, and Amazon Simple Storage Service, which provides storage space. Some of the services that can be used by application developers are:

- *Amazon Simple Queue Service* – a queue messaging service that can be used for communication among web applications;
- *Amazon Associates Web Service* – a web service that allows searching and browsing through Amazon's product catalog;
- *Alexa Web Service*s – provides web traffic information.

For web applications, a popular PaaS solution is represented by "sandboxes" that provide APIs for common tasks like managing data and users or sending e-mail. One of the most well-known sandboxes is Google AppEngine, which provides a Python-based environment for web applications. AppEngine includes APIs for HTTP requests, sending e-mail, manipulating images, caching, storing and retrieving data. However, it imposes a significant number of limitations, due to security and performance constraints. For example, the only way to store persistent data is through a BigTable database (writing to the file system or using a relational database is not possible). This follows the general philosophy of the current cloud frameworks, which is to provide less functionality but with better performance. Heroku provides another application sandbox, based on the Ruby on Rails language.

As some of the cloud applications are computing intensive, PaaS also needs to offer mechanisms for efficiently distributing computation tasks in a large scale system. Currently the most widely used mechanism is MapReduce (Dean & Ghemawat, 2004), a model created at Google and inspired by functional programming (specifically, by the map and reduce primitives from the Lisp language). In MapReduce, the computation is done in two steps: firstly, the "map" operation passes through the input data and produces a set of (key, value) pairs; secondly, the "reduce" operation involves combining the previously produced pairs to obtain the final results. For example, if we consider the problem of counting the occurrences of each word in a set of documents, the "map" function would generate pairs that have a word as the key and 1 as the value; the "reduce" function would produce the final result by summing the values from all the pairs that have the same key. These steps can be both distributed across multiple machines: the map operation is distributed by partitioning the input data into a set of "splits", and the reduce operation – by partitioning the key space according to a problem-specific function; but the optimal way to choose the partitioning method and the number of workers depends on the execution environment as well.. The model can be applied for various other problems, like inverted indexing, sorting or "grep"-ing a large number of documents. Open source frameworks are also available, for example Hadoop (http://hadoop. apache.org/core) - a Java-based implementation of MapReduce that supports several types of distributed file systems for data storage.

Software-as-a-Service (SaaS)

The idea of providing software as a service is not new, and has been implemented for many years by various vendors. However, the popularity of this model has increased significantly after the introduction of the cloud computing model, and nowadays most of the major IT companies are providing software services.

We mention here Google Apps (Conner, 2008), a collection of products and services that Google provides to companies and to individual users. Among the most popular applications from this set are Google Docs (used for creating and sharing online documents), Gmail (web-based e-mail with powerful search features), Google Talk (instant messaging service), Google Calendar (time management instrument) and Page Creator (used for designing and publishing web pages). The standard edition of Google Apps is free and is targeted to home users, while the premier edition, intended to be used by companies, offers an extended set of features in exchange of a price. Google also provides an educational version, which contains many of the premier edition's features and is available for free to educational institutions.

Microsoft has also adopted the SaaS model and provides a set applications grouped under the name "Windows Live". Besides webmail (Windows Live Hotmail) and instant messaging (Windows Live Messenger), the group also includes Windows Live Spaces – an application for social networking, blogging and photo sharing. Microsoft Office Live is an online service for storing and sharing documents, and for designing and hosting web sites; the difference from Google Documents is that the documents need to be edited with Microsoft Office tools (rather than online, through a web browser). Xbox Live is a service for online multiplayer gaming and digital media delivery, only available in exchange of a fee. Microsoft has also customized some Live services for mobile devices, providing them as "Windows Live for mobiles".

PEER-TO-PEER APPLICATION FRAMEWORKS

The peer-to-peer models are being adopted in more and more types of distributed applications, among which we mention content distribution (including media streaming), data storage, monitoring, and even e-mail and social networks. However, at this moment there are only few generic frameworks or tools for developing peer-to-peer applications; this is due to the variety of peer-to-peer architectures (structured or unstructured, pure or hybrid etc.), and to the fact that many applications are designed for a specific architecture.

Some of the existing frameworks aim to provide low-level support for developing any type of application; this is the case of JXTA (https://jxta.dev.java.net), and also of the generic APIs proposed by Dabek (2003), Ciaccio (2007) and Chan (2007). Other frameworks are designed at a higher level and targeted to specific types of applications.

JXTA, the most well known peer-to-peer programming platforms, provides a set of basic protocols upon which peer-to-peer applications can be built. The protocols cover communication, advertisement and discovery, self-organizing into groups, and also monitoring. They are independent of the programming language or of transport protocols, and interoperability is maintained among peers that use different implementations. The JXTA software architecture comprises three layers:

- JXTA Core – a set of essential mechanisms that enable peer-to-peer networking, like communication supported even in the presence of firewalls and NAT, discovery, security, and creation of peer groups;
- Services Layer – includes a set of services that are commonly used in P2P applications, but that are not absolutely necessary for the system's operations; some examples are distributed file systems, searching and indexing, file sharing, directory and authentication services;
- Application Layer – this is the level where integrated P2P applications are implemented.

We note that there isn't meant to be a clear distinction between the services and application layers, as the framework allows applications to act as services for other applications; this modular design eases the development of complex P2P software.

JXTA is based on a hybrid peer-to-peer model, in which some of the nodes (super-peers) have special functionalities: *relay* (storing and forwarding messages between peers that are behind firewalls or NAT), *rendezvous* (keeping advertisement indexes, performing search operations and message broadcasting) and *proxy* (providing support for the peers that only support a minimal set of JXTA services). In order to support the indexing and searching of content, the super-peers are organized in a structured overlay. The regular peers can be of two types – *minimal-edge* (implement only the core set of services, and need support from proxy super-peers) and *full-edge* (can participate in all the JXTA protocols). Typically, the minimal-edge peers are sensor devices or home automation devices, while the full-edge peers are regular PCs or phones.

Although JXTA provides a powerful and well designed framework that has been successfully used in a number of applications, its popularity in the P2P community is still rather limited. One cause for this is the fact that JXTA is built upon a specific overlay architecture, described above; the APIs cannot be used in other types of structured overlays, or in unstructured overlays. This approach puts a significant limit on JXTA's usability, since the research in the past years has resulted in a wide variety of structured overlay architectures. In order to overcome these limitations, there have been some initiatives to create generic APIs for structured overlays.

One of the first proposals for a generic structured overlay API is presented by Dabek (2003). Aiming to identify the fundamental abstractions that characterize structured overlays, this work proposes a three-layer architecture for classifying the functionalities of P2P services, following a similar approach as the JXTA software architecture. The proposed architectural levels are:

- *Tier 0:* represents the basic capability of a structured overlay – key based routing (KBR). This functionality is implemented by all the existing structured overlay protocols, and can be used to build higher level services and applications;
- *Tier 1:* higher level abstractions that can be built upon key based routing; the authors have identified three abstractions: distributed hash tables (DHT), group anycast and multicast (CAST), and decentralized object location and routing (DLR);
- *Tier 2:* this level corresponds to applications, that can use services from Tier 1 or even the Tier 0 functionality.

The API introduced in this work contains a set of primitives grouped into two categories; the first one includes functions for routing messages, and the second one has functions for accessing the nodes' states.

Ciaccio (2007) proposes another generic API for structured overlays, taking (Dabek, 2003) as a starting point. This more recent work proposes a set of extensions to the API introduced by Dabek et al. – such as primitives for request-response communication, or mechanisms to support peer arrival and departure. The newer API also aims to make some simplifications from the programmer's point of view. For example, it eliminates the possibility of the application programmer to alter the overlay routing mechanism; the author argues that this facility would be used in a very small number of applications, and adds too much complexity to the API.

Another generic framework for developing peer-to-peer applications is CAESAR (Chan, 2007), which aims to introduce Service Oriented Architecture concepts into the pee-to-peer systems. In CAESAR, the peers can provide specific services, and all the peers that provide the same service are grouped in an overlay. This approach increases the system's efficiency and fault tolerance, as it allows a service provider to delegate the processing to other peers from the group. A plug-in mechanism allows the addition of new services and protocols, and the services can be dynamically bound to various protocols in order to be able to offer different quality levels. CAESAR is implemented in C++, and the base implementation provides plug-ins for the Chord and FLOC protocols; it has been used to develop applications such as massively multiplayer online games.

Although we have seen several initiatives to create generic frameworks for P2P overlays, they have not reached maturity yet (some of them were not even implemented); there is still a lot of work to be done in this direction, especially since we expect the number of P2P applications to increase during the following years.

DISTRIBUTED WORKFLOWS

Most of the current distributed applications, both in the academic and enterprise environments, comprise multiple components (programs or services). These components are aggregated together into workflows, and workflow management systems are built in order to assist the user in developing and executing such applications. Workflow management systems allow the developer to organize the components and to specify the dependencies among them.

Workflow Languages

Workflow languages allow higher level programming than the usual programming languages, which deal with lower level issues; Leymann (2003) presents this type of programming as "programming in the large". Being used only for orchestrating application components, workflow languages often have a much simpler structure than programming languages.

There are several aspects to be considered when attempting to classify the existing workflow languages:

- The programming paradigm – declarative or imperative
- The types of components that are orchestrated – can be services or plain executable programs
- The standardization of the language

From the programming paradigm point of view, we distinguish languages that have adopted the declarative model, usually representing the flow of activities as an oriented acyclic graph; Condor DAGMan, for example, goes into this category. Oppositely, there are imperative languages (for example, SwiftScript), which represent the workflow as an instruction sequence, also providing more complex structures(decisions, cycles, etc.). We note here that some languages (WS-BPEL, Karajan) implement both programming styles.

Regarding the type of components (activities), there are languages in which components are plain executables (usually batch jobs), like DAGMan Condor or Karajan, and languages used to orchestrate web services (WS-BPEL). The web service orchestration languages can also be used to run Grid jobs, by invoking "submit" services - if they are available at the middleware level. There are also, although relatively rare, languages that support the composition of both types of components - services and executable programs; an example is the XScufl language used in Taverna workflow engine (Hull, 2006).

From the standardization point of view, the most substantial effort has been done in the enterprise applications domain, the WS-BPEL standard being supported by a large number of major companies. In the scientific area, most workflow engine developers prefer to introduce

a proprietary language that meets the requirements of specific applications – rather than use a standard. However WS-BPEL has recently started to gain popularity among scientists as well – so it is expected that in the near future it will be used as a standard in a wide range of scientific applications. We also mention the JSDL language (JSDL, 2008), whose specification is undertaken by the Global Grid Forum. Although JSDL is not a workflow language, but a language used for describing individual jobs, the next version (2.0) is intended to introduce support for specifying the dependencies between jobs.

Workflow Engines Overview

A workflow management system, or workflow engine, has the role of interpreting and executing the users' workflows, and this involves multiple aspects, among which the most important are:

- Interpreting (compiling) the workflow scripts
- Workflow scheduling
- Data management
- Fault handling

We briefly discuss as follows a few of these aspects, and for a more thorough presentation we direct the reader to (Yu, 2005).

Scheduling represents assigning the workflow's tasks to computational resources, and in many cases it involves collaboration with a resource management system; from this point of view, we can see the workflow engine as an additional layer on top of the resource management system, to which it transmits job execution requests. The architecture of a workflow scheduling system can be either centralized, meaning that a single entity takes the scheduling decisions for all the workflow components, or decentralized, in which multiple schedulers exist, each one being in charge with a part of the workflow. Another type of scheduling architecture is the hierarchical one, where there is a central scheduling component that coordinates the other lower-level ones. While the centralized model has the advantages of producing efficient schedules, the other two models achieve a better scalability and also fault tolerance. Although most of the currently available workflow engines follow the centralized model, there are projects that have adopted a decentralized scheduling architecture (Triana) or a hierarchical one (GridFlow). We also note here that in the case of service orchestration workflows, the scheduling component is practically inexistent, as the activities in the workflow are service invocations rather than batch jobs.

A major challenge in today's applications is the physical management of data in the distributed environments. In a workflow execution there are several operations in which data has a central role: discovering the input data and the workflow components, staging-in and staging-out the data of the computational resources, and possibly archiving the produced data and generating metadata and provenance information so that they can be later interpreted. Discovery of data sets, application codes, workflow templates, etc., is often done by querying various catalogs. Metadata catalogs store attributes that describe the contents of data sets. Provenance catalogs (Miles, 2007) store information about computations and workflows to provide a detailed record of how analyzes are run, including information about inputs to computations, application parameters used, calibration values for equipment, versions of workflow and analysis software used, etc. Based on knowledge of the state of resources (the latency, bandwidth and load of storage systems, network bandwidth among nodes, etc.) that may be provided by information services, the workflow planner selects among available data replicas. In particular, the planner may try to select copies of the data that are close to the computational resources where workflow tasks will run, with respect to network latency or other metrics. It may be advantageous for workflow planning and execution services to

coordinate with data placement services, whose role is to move data asynchronously with respect to workflow execution with the goal of improving the execution time of workflows.

In order to have a good fault handling strategy for workflows, it is important to identify first the levels at which the faults can occur. Plankensteiner et al. (2007) introduced a level-based classification for workflow faults, which we summarize below:

- *Low-level faults:* can occur at hardware, operating system or middleware level (for example, machine crashes, exceeding quotas, job submission failures)
- *Task-level faults:* these are faults directly related to individual workflow tasks, like missing libraries, deadlocks or memory leaks
- *Workflow-level faults:* failures that occur from incorrect input data in a workflow, infinite loops, data movement errors etc.
- *User-level faults:* either user-defined exceptions, or assertions that can cause errors

After surveying some workflow engines that are most widely used in distributed systems, Plankensteiner et al. show that while most of the engines are able to handle hardware, middleware and workflow level faults, task and user level faults are much rarely detected and recovered from.

CONCLUSION

As this chapter has shown, the tools and frameworks for developing large scale distributed applications are very diverse. This is due to the variety of the application types, of the underlying middleware platforms and of the communities of users. At this moment, choosing the right framework for developing a new distributed application requires a careful study of the existing solutions, also taking into account the available middleware platforms.

One of the aspects that needs further study is achieving interoperability among different applications. This problem has been partially solved for grids (with platforms like CogKit and JavaGAT) and for web applications (by introducing standards like SOAP/WSDL). But for cloud and peer-to-peer applications, the efforts in this direction are in an incipient phase and will take a significant amount of further work.

REFERENCES

Anjomshoaa, A., Brisard, F., Drescher, M., Fellows, D., Ly, A., McGough, S., et al. (2005). *Job Submission Description Language*. Retrieved April 14, 2009, from http://www.gridforum.org/documents/GFD.56.pdf

Baduel, L., Baude, F., Ranaldo, N., & Zimeo, E. (2005). Effective and Efficient Communication in Grid Computing with an Extension of ProActive Groups. In *Proceedings of the 19th International Parallel and Distributed Processing Symposium (IPDPS 2005)*, Denver, CO, USA (pp. 183b). Washington, DC: IEEE Computer Society.

Bergman-Terrell, E. (2008). *NET Development on Linux*. Retrieved April 25, 2009, from http://www.ddj.com/windows/212201484.

Chan, L., Karunasekera, S., Harwood, A., & Tanin, E. (2007). CAESAR: Middleware for Complex Service-Oriented Peer-to-Peer Applications. In *Proceedings of the Workshop on Middleware for Service Oriented Computing*. New York: ACM Press.

Cho, A. (2008). *What is Web 3.0? The Next Generation Web: Search Context for Online Information*. Retrieved April 30, 2009 from: http://internet.suite101.com/article.cfm/what_is_web_30

Ciaccio, G. (2007). A Pretty Flexible API for Generic Peer-to-Peer Programming. In *Proceedings of the Parallel and Distributed Processing Symposium (IPDPS 2007)*, Long Beach, CA, USA (pp. 1-8). Washington, DC: IEEE Computer Society.

ComputeFarm. (2009). Retrieved April 30, 2009, from https://computefarm.dev.java.net

Conner, N. (2008). *Google Apps: The Missing Manual*. New York: Pogue Press.

Dabek, F., Zhao, B., Druschel, P., Kubiatowicz, J., & Stoica, I. (2003). Towards a Common API for Structured Peer-to-Peer Overlays. In M.F. Kaashoek & I. Stoica (Eds.), *Proceedings. of the 2nd International Workshop on Peer-to-Peer Systems (IPTPS03)*, Berkeley, CA (pp. 33-44). Berlin, Germany: Springer.

Dean, J., & Ghemawat, S. (2004). MapReduce: Simplified Data Processing on Large Clusters. In *OSDI'04: Sixth Symposium on Operating System Design and Implementation*, San Francisco, CA (pp.137-150).

Freeman, E., Hupfer, S., & Arnold, K. (1999). *JavaSpaces(TM) Principles, Patterns, and Practice (Jini Series)*. Upper Saddle River, NJ: Pearson Education.

Hull, D., Wolstencroft, K., Stevens, R., Goble, C.A., Pocock, M.R., Li, P., & Oinn, T. (2006). Taverna: a tool for building and running workflows of services. *Nucleic Acids Research, 34*(Web-Server-Issue), 729–732.

INRIA. (2007). *Basic Features of the Grid Component Model*. CoreGRID deliverable D.PM.04.

Kanazawa, H., Yamada, M., Miyahara, Y., Hayase, Y., Kawata, S., & Usami, H. (2005). Problem Solving Environment Based on Grid Services: NAREGI-PSE. In *Proceedings of the First International Conference on e-Science and Grid Computing*, Melbourne, Australia (pp. 456–463).

Lassila, O., & Hendler, J. (2007). Embracing Web 3.0. *IEEE Internet Computing, 11*(3), 90–93. doi:10.1109/MIC.2007.52

Laszewski, G., & Hategan, M. (2005). Java CoG Kit Workflow Concepts. *Journal of Grid Computing, 3*(3-4), 239–258. doi:10.1007/s10723-005-9013-5

Leymann, F. (2003). Web services: Distributed applications without limits. In G. Weikum, H. Schoning & E. Rahm (Eds.), *Proceedings of the BTW 2003 Conference,* Leipzig, Germany (pp. 2–23).

Miles, S., Groth, P. T., Branco, M., & Moreau, L. (2007). The requirements of using provenance in e-science experiments. *Journal of Grid Computing, 5*(1), 1–25. doi:10.1007/s10723-006-9055-3

Moroney, L., & MacDonald, M. (2006). *Pro ASP.NET 2.0 in VB 2005*. Berkeley, CA: Apress. doi:10.1007/978-1-4302-0118-2

Perez-Sorrosal, F., Patino-Martinez, M., Jimenez-Peris, R., & Kemme, B. (2007). Consistent and Scalable Cache Replication for Multi-tier J2EE Applications. In R. Cerqueir & R.H. Campbell (Eds.), *Proceedings of ACM/IFIP/USENIX 8th International Middleware Conference,* Newport Beach, CA, USA (pp. 328-347). New York: Springer.

Plankensteiner, P., Prodan, R., Fahringer, T., Kertesz, A., & Kacsuk, P. (2007). *Fault-tolerant behavior in state-of-the-art Grid Worklow Management Systems*. Technical report, TR-0091, Institute on Grid Information, Resource and Worklow Monitoring Services, CoreGRID - Network of Excellence.

Schuchardt, K., Didier, B. T., & Black, G. (2002). Ecce - a problem-solving environment's evolution toward Grid services and a Web architecture. *Concurrency and Computation, 14*(13-15), 1221–1239. doi:10.1002/cpe.673

Sun Microsystems. (1999). *Simplified Guide to the Java 2 Platform, Enterprise Ed*. Retrieved April 20, 2009, from http://java.sun.com/javaee/overview/whitepapers

Takano, R., Matsuda, M., Kudoh, T., Kodama, Y., Okazaki, F., & Ishikawa, Y. (2007). Effects of Packet Pacing for MPI Programs in a Grid Environment. In *Proceedings of the 2007 IEEE International Conference on Cluster Computing, Austin, Texas, USA* (pp. 382-391). Washington, DC: IEEE Computer Society.

van Nieuwpoort, R., Kielmann, T., & Bal, H. E. (2007). User-Friendly and Reliable Grid Computing Based on Imperfect Middleware. In B. Verastegui (Ed.), *Proceedings of the ACM/IEEE Conference on Supercomputing (SC'07),* Reno, NV, USA (pp. 34). New York: ACM Press.

van Nieuwpoort, R. V., Maassen, J., Wrzesinska, G., Hofman, R., Jacobs, C., Kielmann, T., & Bal, H. E. (2005). Ibis: a flexible and efficient Java based grid programming environment. *Concurrency and Computation, 17*(7-8), 1079–1107. doi:10.1002/cpe.860

Wrzesinska, G., Maassen, J., Verstoep, K., & Bal, H. E. (2006). Satin++: Divide-and-share on the grid. In *Second IEEE International Conference on e-Science and Grid Computing (e-Science '06), Amsterdam, The Netherlands* (pp. 61). Washington, DC: IEEE Computer Society.

Yang, F., Gupta, N., Gerner, N., Qi, X., Demers, A., Gehrke, J., & Shanmugasundaram, J. (2007). A Unified Platform for Data Driven Web Applictions with Automatic Client-Server Partitioning. In C.L. Williamson, M.E. Zurko, P.F. Patel-Schneider & P.J. Shenoy (Eds.), *Proceedings of the 16th International World Wide Web Conference* (pp. 341-350). New York: ACM Press.

Yu, J., Benatallah, B., Saint-Paul, R., Casati, F., Daniel, F., & Matera, M. (2007). A Framework for Rapid Integration of Presentation Components. In C.L. Williamson, M.E. Zurko, P.F. Patel-Schneider & P.J. Shenoy (Eds.), *Proceedings of the 16th International World Wide Web Conference* (pp. 924-932). New York: ACM Press.

Yu, J., & Buyya, R. (2005). Taxonomy of Workflow Management Systems for Grid Computing. *Journal of Grid Computing*, *3*(3-4), 171–200. doi:10.1007/s10723-005-9010-8

Chapter 11
Applications

INTRODUCTION

This chapter covers the subject of application in LSDS. The chapter is organized in two parts. The chapter parts present two aspect of application in LSDS: the overview of applications in entire world and the method of applications development. It is also presented a description of current projects and applications in large scale distributed systems, like applications from OSG projects in USA, EGEE and SEE-GRID applications in Europe and Asia, DEISA initiative (Distributed European Infrastructure for Supercomputing Applications). This part also presents the relevant applications in LSDS, like Grids, P2P systems.

A **distributed application** is made up of distinct components (stand alone programs, web services) in separate runtime environments, usually on different platforms (geographically distributed) connected via a network. Typical distributed applications are two-tier (client-server), three-tier (client-middleware-server), and multitier.

In a two tier application, the client process runs on a workstation or personal computer that interacts with a server process which runs on a shared device that is accessed through a network. In a three tier application the client process runs on a client workstation that interacts with a server process which runs on a server device. The server device is connected to a host that provides services to the server device. In an N-tier application the client process runs on any workstation; the server process runs on one or more distributed server devices. The middleware mediates all interactions between the various processes. Components and integration adapters allow access to various information sources.

According with this distributes applications model, a variety of important projects has grown up in recent years, especially in biology, earth science, physics and astronomy, mathematics, artificial intelligence. Many applications were started running on a volunteer basis, and involve users or corporations donating their unused computational power to work on interesting computational problems. Examples of such projects include the Stanford University Chemistry Department Folding@home project,

DOI: 10.4018/978-1-61520-703-9.ch011

which is focused on simulations of protein folding to find disease cures and to understand biophysical systems; World Community Grid, an effort to create the world's largest public computing grid to tackle scientific research projects that benefit humanity, run and funded by IBM; SETI@home, which is focused on analyzing radio-telescope data to find evidence of intelligent signals from space, hosted by the Space Sciences Laboratory at the University of California, Berkeley (the Berkeley Open Infrastructure for Network Computing (BOINC), was originally developed to support this project); OurGrid, which is a free-to-join peer-to-peer grid provided by the idle resources of all participants; LHC@home, which is used to help design and tune the Large Hadrons Collider, hosted by CERN in Geneva; and distributed.net, which is focused on finding optimal Golomb rulers and breaking various cryptographic ciphers.

Now, the **cloud computing** offer new possibility to develop, deploy and run a complex application in a distributed environment (Buyya et al., 2009). For example, Amazon Web Services (AWS) are a collection of remote computing services that offer: Amazon Elastic Compute Cloud (EC2) for scalable virtual private servers using Xen, Amazon Elastic Block Store (EBS) for persistent block level storage volumes for EC2, Amazon Simple Storage Service (S3) for Web Service based storage for applications and many other services (Robinson, 2008). Another example, Azure Services Platform is an application platform in the cloud that allows applications to be hosted and run at Microsoft datacenters. It provides a cloud operating system called Windows Azure that serves as a runtime for the applications and provides a set of services that allows development, management and hosting of managed applications off-premises. The platform includes five services: Live Services, SQL Services, .NET Services, SharePoint Services and Dynamics CRM Services. These services can be used by the developers to build the applications that will run in the cloud (Windows Azure, 2009).

GRID APPLICATIONS

This section is aimed at creating a directory of existing grid applications. The presented applications do not include the Grid tools. The detailed categorization enables finding relevant domains of applicability of Grid computing. We shall start with an introduction about Grid applications design and about the strategies for Grid applications development. Then we shall present some important applications from international projects.

A **grid application** can use registered services and tools (query, monitoring, discovery, factory, notification, security, registration, management, scheduling) along with grid infrastructure. We can define a grid application like a collection of work items or jobs that carry out a complex computing task by using grid resources.

So, according with this definition, designing an application for grid computing is much easier if you know what to expect and which are the main work items. You should plan to use a development environment or toolkit specifically designed for grid applications, such as the **Globus** Toolkit and **MonALISA** or **Ganglia**.

Designing a grid application must consider three aspects:

- *Jobs*: flow, type of job, number of difficult jobs, depth of sub-jobs, redundant jobs execution, scavenging grid and job topology.
- *Data*: topology, data type – character sets and multimedia formats, amount of data, data separable per jobs, job data I/O, shared data access, temporary data space, time-sensitive data, data encryption.
- *Environment*: dependence of the OS, memory needed per job, compiler settings, library needed, runtime environment, application server, external application, hardware dependency, network bandwidth and scalability, security policy, single user interface, time constrains.

A running application in a grid system is called grid-enabled. For making an application grid-enabled, there are six strategies, according to (Kra, 2009). These strategies are:

- *Batch Anywhere*. In this strategy only the grid (not the application, the client, the user, or anything else) decides which node to use for the job.
- *Independent Concurrent Batch*. This supports multiple independent instances of the same application running concurrently.
- *Parallel Batch*. In this case takes each user's batch work, subdivides it, disperses it out to multiple nodes, collects it, and then aggregates the results.
- *Service*. Service is follow-on to Independent Concurrent Batch, not follow-on to Parallel Batch. Service, it is not assumed that each client subdivides its work and spreads it over multiple service instances.
- *Parallel Service*. This strategy combines the service-oriented architecture of Service with the subdivided work model of Parallel Batch.

- *Tightly Coupled Parallel Programs*. This is the domain of specialized applications in engineering, physics, and biological modeling, such as finite state analysis.

It is important in this generation of grid applications to establish what type of strategies to use in the design process. For example, the run stage for your job must consider the first three strategies. The adapt process for job consider parallel batch, service and parallel service to be important and the last aspect; exploit the cluster infrastructure considered the last one strategy.

One of the most used layered architecture for Grid application development is **Java Commodity Kit** (CoG). The Java CoG Kit layered architecture provides a framework for developing Grid clients and servers (see Figure 1).

Hence, you will be able to access classes and methods not only including a convenient API focusing on elementary Grid functionality, but also the ability to formulate workflow through XML specifications, command line tools, and graphical user interfaces. The Java CoG Kit layers are conceptually organized as follows: providers,

Figure 1. View of the layered architecture of the Java CoG Kit

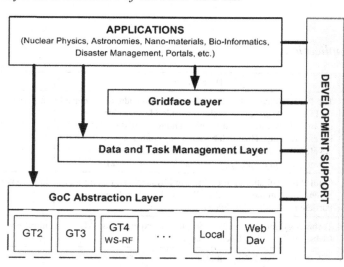

basic abstractions, data and task management abstractions and Grid faces (Amin et al., 2006).

We shall present in the following paragraphs some examples of Grid applications and of related research projects. It is difficult to select a small set of relevant Grid applications because there is a large number of universities and research centers developing such applications.

DEISA (Distributed European Infrastructure for Supercomputing Applications) describes some examples of application profiles and "use cases" that are well adapted to the present status of the supercomputing Grid, and that can benefit from the computational resources made available by the Extreme Computing Initiative (Soddemann, 2007):

- International collaborations involving scientific teams that access the nodes of the AIX super-cluster in different countries
- Extreme computing demands for challenging projects requiring a dominant fraction of a single supercomputer.
- Work flow applications involving at least two platforms.
- Coupled applications involving more than one platform.

Another consortium, **SEE-GRID**, intends to provide specific support actions to pave the way towards the participation of the SE European countries to the Pan-European and worldwide Grid initiatives.

This will be accomplished through dissemination conferences and training material including cookbooks, pilot and demonstration test-beds for hands-on experience, applications' adaptations to be able to use the Grid, operational and support centre schemes and organization, and finally feasibility studies and road maps for the integration of the SEE to the European Research Area (ERA) via an extended Pan-European Grid infrastructure.

Statistically, more than a thousand scientists from all over the world have submitted around two million jobs in the first ten months of 2005. These jobs vary from very short batches to large single computations, and their results are relating to any one of the scientific areas already mentioned. For example, many jobs run using the **EGEE** Grid Infrastructure today.

Two of the most important classes of grid applications are: High Energy Physics Applications (HEP) and Biomedical Applications. In Table 1 are presented some Physics applications.

Biomedical and Bioinformatics applications are another class of grid applications. Some

Table 1. High energy applications

Name	Description	Web site
Particle Physics DataGrid (PPDG)	The Particle Physics Data Grid collaboration addresses the need for Data Grid services to enable a worldwide distributed computing model for current and future high-energy and nuclear physics experiments. This collaboration has contributed to the early development of the Data Grid architecture as well as evaluating prototype Grid middleware (Alexandrov et al., 2002).	http://www.ppdg.net/
GridPP	GridPP is a collaboration of Particle Physicists and Computing Scientists from the UK and CERN, who are building a Grid for Particle Physics (Coles, 2005).	http://www.gridpp.ac.uk/
Grid Physics Network (GriPhyN)	Technology for data analysis in physics experiments: ATLAS, CMS, LIGO, SDSS (Deelman et al., 2004).	http://www.griphyn.org
Southern California Earthquake Centre 2	Full geophysics modeling using Grids and knowledge-based systems	http://www.scec.org

relevant applications from this class are shown in Table 2. For example the HealthGRID cluster gathers grid-related projects with the following goals: acquire and share experience in deploying biomedical applications using the existing middleware, promote the grid concept in the biomedical community and identify the specific biomedical requirements on the middleware (Solomonides, 2008).

Earth science applications are another type of grid applications. We could consider it like a part form physics applications. European DataGrid project support some of this applications and is to enable next generation of scientific exploration.

To develop some of these applications it is necessary to have an API, a programming language and protocol to interact with grid resources.

An important tool for grid application is **GridMPI**. It is an implementation of the MPI (Message Passing Interface) standard designed for high performance computing in the Grid. It establishes a synthesized cluster environment by efficiently binding multiple cluster computers from geographically distributed sites. It enables users to seamlessly deploy their application programs from a local system to the Grid environment for processing very large data sets, where the programs can be coded and tested in a usual manner.

GridLab proposes PAPI that aims to provide the tool designer and application engineer with a consistent interface and methodology for use of the performance counter hardware found in most major microprocessors (Kurowski et al., 2004).

Java is another standard for grid applications. Ibis is a programming environment for development of grid applications in Java. Some theoretical problems were implemented in Ibis (IBIS, 2009). For example: a cellular automata simulator, o solution for satisfiability problem, a grammar-based text analysis. Java GRID Component - The Java GRID Component can be used in Java applets and in Java applications another tool is Java GRID Component that can be used in Java applets and in Java applications including Swing applications. The grid component is highly configurable and it has a very developer friendly API.

Grid portals are defined as a "class of www application servers that provide a secure online environment for gathering information about grid services and resources as well as provide tools for utilizing these grid services and resources to perform useful tasks" (Cactus, 2009). The Grid Computing Environment Research Group (GCE,

Table 2. Biomedical and bioinformatics applications

Name	Description	Web site
AMBER	AMBER is the collective name for a suite of programs that allow users to carry out molecular dynamics simulations, particularly on biomolecules (Doake & Duncan, 1998).	http://www.amber.ucsf.edu/amber http://asdp.bio.bnl.gov/asda/LSD/Modeling/AMBER7.html
EMBOSS	EMBOSS is a free Open Source software analysis package specially developed for the needs of the molecular biology (e.g. EMBnet) user community. EMBOSS integrates a range of currently available packages and tools for sequence analysis into a seamless whole (Gordon et al., 2007).	http://www.hgmp.mrc.ac.uk/Software/EMBOSS/
BBSRC	This UK initiative aims to support the development and use of algorithms, software and analytical methods to solve defined biological problems by encouraging the interaction between the biological sciences, Bioinformatics, IT, computer science, mathematics, statistics, physics and other related disciplines (Sinnott, 2007).	http://www.bbsrc.ac.uk/science/initiatives/bep.html
BIRN	BIRN represents a first attempt to develop a "protocol" for distributed collaborative research amongst neuro and medical scientists. It depends on the new computational and networking technologies that have been developed to bring researchers together over the Internet. BIRN is testing this new way of undertaking large-scale medical science (Gupta et al., 2003).	http://birn.ncrr.nih.gov

Table 3. Earth science applications

Name	Description	Web Site
Earth System Grid (ESG)	Delivery and analysis of large climate model datasets for the climate research community.	http://www.earthsystemgrid.org
Information Power Grid	Create and apply a production Grid for aero sciences and other NASA missions	http://www.ipg.nasa.gov
Network for Earthquake Eng. Simulation Grid	Create and apply a production Grid for earthquake engineering.	http://www.neesgrid.org
National Virtual Observatory (NVO)	Create and apply production Grids for data analysis in astronomy.	http://www.srl.caltech.edu/nvo
BOINC	BOINC lets you donate computing power to scientific research projects such as: • Climateprediction.net: study climate change • Einstein@home: search for gravitational signals emitted by pulsars • LHC@home: improve the design of the CERN LHC particle accelerator • Predictor@home: investigate protein-related diseases • Rosetta@home: help researchers develop cures for human diseases • SETI@home: Look for radio evidence of extraterrestrial life • SIMAP: calculate protein similarity data for use by many biological research projects. • World Community Grid: advance our knowledge of human disease. • Cell Computing biomedical research (Japanese; requires nonstandard client software)	http://boinc.berkeley.edu/

2009) divides grid portals into user portals and application portals (Haili et al., 2005). User portals provide grid services such as single sign-on, job submission and status tracking for a Virtual Organization (VO). Application portals are interfaces for users mostly from scientific research who are using in their work the computational power on the grid, to execute complex tasks in a problem solving environment (PSE).

In a business context, multiple computing resources are needed both by scientific enterprises and business. The scales and types of these resources are various. As a target, enabling simplified access to distributed data, more efficient scheduling of work, aggregation of multiple resources for large tasks, and orchestration of multiple tasks into automated workflows they all represent grid computing technologies that integrate these resources. As it might seem, grid technologies are sometimes difficult to use and learn and an easy web portal interface it's a solu-

tion for the user to better manage the resources and grid technologies he works with. An interface offers the user a familiar and consistent way to interact with all the jobs and technologies he works with.

A web graphical interface usually enables actions like monitoring, creation and execution of workflows in grid environments. "The Grid Portals usually hide the low-level details of Grid access mechanisms by providing a high-level Grid user interface that can be used for any Grid." (Kacsuk et al., 2009).

An important feature of Grid Portals is their portability between different grids. The user is encouraged this way to work with various Grid systems without any re-learning of the features for a new grid. Another important fact about Grid Portals is that access can be made through certificates for every Grid if the user has valid certificates for several Grids. The user can work simultaneously on these Grids.

The goal of Grid Portals is to develop common applications that can be used to build a portal where developers are securely authenticated to resources remotely, that can permit users to schedule different jobs, to view information about available or working resources and obtain this information stored in databases, to create profiles of the users for them to monitor and track jobs submitted, it view results of executions.

Below are some links regarding Grid Portals (toolkits for building grid portals, collections of links to grid portals) that can be very useful for implementing a Grid Portal:

- **Grid Portal Development Kit (GPDK)** - The Grid Portal Development Kit offers two types of applications: a portal development environment for the creation of new portals and a collection of Grid service beans used to accomplish basic operations. These operations can be: job submission, file transfer, querying of information services. The goal is to develop common components that can be used by portal developers to build a website that can securely authenticate users to remote resources and help them make better decisions for scheduling jobs by allowing them to view pertinent resource information obtained and stored on a remote database. In addition, profiles are created and stored for portal users allowing them to track and monitor jobs submitted and view results. (Alameda et al., 2007) (http://doesciencegrid.org/projects/GPDK).
- **Open Grid Portals** – a collection of links to Grid Portals or toolkits providers like: OGCE - Open Grid Computing Environments Collaboratory, GridSphere, NPACI – Hotpage Grid Portal(all this portals are also suggested by CERN) (OGP, 2009) (http://www.opengridportals.org/space/start)
- **P-GRADE Grid Portal** - The P-GRADE Grid Portal is a portal oriented on workflow, enabling the creation, execution and monitoring workflows in grid environments using a graphical Web interface. P-GRADE Grid Portal offers a lot of features like: cooperation with a variety of the various Grid systems, developing and creating new Grid applications, portability of applications between Grid systems, executing Grid applications, monitoring application execution in the Grid, transparency of executions of Grid application.

WEB-BASED APPLICATIONS

A **web-based application** is accessed via web browser over a network such as the Internet. It could be a computer software application that is coded in a browser-supported language (such as HTML, JavaScript, Java, etc.). The structure of a Web application is divided into several tiers that correspond to the logical services provided by the application (Zheng, 2006). Also, the tiers represent logical divisions of an application's services, and not necessarily physical divisions between hardware or software components. In some cases, a single machine running a single WebLogic Server instance can provide all of the tiers (Di Lucca & Fasolino, 2006).

- *Web Tier*. The web tier provides static content (for example, simple HTML pages) to clients of a Web application. The web tier is generally the first point of contact between external clients and the Web application. A simple Web application may have a web tier that consists of one or more machines running WebLogic Express, Apache, Sun One Web Server, or Microsoft Internet Information Server.
- *Presentation Tier*. The presentation tier provides dynamic content (for example, servlets or Java Server Pages) to clients of a Web application. A cluster of WebLogic

Server instances that hosts servlets and/or JSPs comprises the presentation tier of a web application. If the cluster also serves static HTML pages for your application, it encompasses both the web tier and the presentation tier.

- *Object Tier*. The object tier provides Java objects (for example, Enterprise JavaBeans or RMI classes) and their associated business logic to a Web application. A WebLogic Server cluster that hosts EJBs provides an object tier.

One of the important classes of web based applications is represented by Rich Internet applications (RIAs). RIAs have some of the characteristics of desktop applications, typically delivered by way of a proprietary web browser plug-ins or independently via sandboxes or virtual machines. The used framework for this type of applications is based on **Adobe Flex**/AIR, Java/JavaFX and **Microsoft Silverlight** (Bozzon et al., 2006). The keys characteristic for RIAs are: accessibility, complexity, consistency, performance, richness, advance communications, security, management, and maintenance. *Accessibility* of data to search engines and web accessibility can be impaired. For example it took over a decade from release for Adobe Flash to be universally searchable (Hickson & Hyatt, 2008). *Complexity* of advanced solutions can make them more difficult to design, develop, deploy and debug than traditional web applications (but typically less so than application software). *Consistency* of user interface and experience can be controlled across operating systems. Performance monitoring and fault diagnosis can be particularly difficult. *Security* can improve over that of application software (for example through use of sandboxes and automatic updates) but the extensions themselves are subject to vulnerabilities and access possible is often much greater than that of native web applications. *Performance* can improve depending on the application and network characteristics. In particular, applications which can avoid the latency of round-trips to the server by processing locally on the client are often a lot faster. Offloading work to the clients can also improve server performance. Conversely the resource requirements can be prohibitive for small, embedded and mobile devices (Stamos et al., 2008).

Based on this concept, **Google** offer a set of applications named Google Apps. The main characteristics of Google Apps refers to proven cost saving, 99.9% uptime reliability guarantee, 50 times more storage than the industry average (25 GB for email storage), mobile email, calendar and IM access, information security and compliance, full administrative and data control, helpful 24/7 customer support (Dewsbury, 2007).

The main principle for Google Apps is "*Software-as-a-service for business email, information sharing and security*". Here are the 10 Google apps that we find the most intriguing, whether for their sheer usefulness or for the controversy they attract, according with CNET Reviews (http://reviews.cnet.com) in 2009: 1) Gmail is a star among the Web's top e-mail tools, especially for its inventive message-organizing methods. Gmail offers a natural-language abilities for many business or personal activities, for example, detecting when someone sends you an event invitation; 2) Google Calendar is enables to manage appointments and discover events from assorted sources that other users have made public; 3) Google Talk is an instant-messaging tool loaded with expressive emoticons, as well as links to news stories and streaming music sites. Using Google talk it is possible to run this no-frills chatting client either within a floating window or embedded within Gmail; 4) Google Writely is a free document processor that is able to compose and edit basic text files; 5) Google Spreadsheets offers the possibility to make calculations on the fly from anywhere, as long as you're online; 6) Google Maps is serving up free satellite views to the public. Since then, enthusiasts have been shaping this dynamic mapping tool to pinpoint the locations of hot dog stands, celebrity sightings, and visits from outer space. This application is integrated with different mobile equipments and offers multiple possibilities for itinerary establishment; 7) Google Earth 4 presents the entire globe and offers the possibility to explore its nooks and crannies. This application contains many possibility and facility for advance search and offers a mechanism for custom views; 8) Google SketchUp offers a possibility to build a dream house in 3D detail without a lick of CAD or architectural expertise; 9) Picasa Web Albums is one of the finest freebie apps for tweaking digital pictures in albums to the Web. Picasa has many features for editing, tagging, and sharing photos online. 10. Google Desktop 4 installs a top-notch search tool to find files on your computer, and it stacks fun Gadgets on your desktop. This desktop application is also integrated with many Google online applications.

Another class of web-based applications is represented by social network applications. Nowadays, social applications became a very popular instrument for virtual group's interactions. They allow the association of a set of user defined keywords, named tags, when publishing these objects, in order to allow searching for them later using a subset of these tags. Commercial systems and recent research community proposals preclude a wide Internet deployment due to the emergence of scalability and hot spot problems in the nodes. One of the efficient solutions capable to o cope with these high demanding requirements, in a fully scalable, distributed and balanced way is based on **T-DHT**, an innovative hybrid unstructured-structured DHT based approach (Mozo & Salvachua, 2008). The search process is based on DHT typical search combined with an unstructured search algorithm using the tag information previously stored into bloom filters of node links.

Tomiyasu et al. (2005) describe the design and implementation of a query propagation mechanism and its applications to realize a social network composed of mobile users. The in this case, the social network consists of multiple mobile phones and a server with the query propagation mechanism. But people use different systems, social network services and technologies to interact, communicate, and inform themselves and others within their community. Menkens et al. (2007) identify that it is necessary to use different systems and technologies like bulletin boards, cell phones, pagers, instant messaging, E-Mail, social network services for advance and custom interaction and offer an IMS social network application that can be used to do all these tasks using IMS enabled cell phones.

The tools based on web application for online collaboration in a virtual community considers instant messaging, text chat, internet forums, blogs, wikis, collaborative real-time editor, prediction markets, social network search engines, deliberative social networks, commercial social networks, social guides, social bookmarking, social cataloging, social libraries, social online storage, virtual worlds, **Massively Multiplayer Online Games** (MMOGs). A hybrid of web-based social networks, instant messaging technologies and peer-to-peer connectivity and file sharing, peer-to-peer social networks generally allow users to share blogs, files (especially photographs) and instant messages. Some examples are imeem, SpinXpress, Bouillon, Wirehog, and Soulseek. Also, Groove, Collanos, WiredReach and Kerika have similar functionality.

Some examples for social network web-based applications consider **Facebook, LinkedIn**, MySpace, Hi5, Ning, Orkut, etc. **MySpace** and YouTube have affected election campaigns in simple, but significant, ways. MySpace have also posed a new set of challenges to campaign staff, the most important of which is the reduced level of control that campaigns have over the image and message of the candidate (Gueorguieva, 2008). Another important application that offer support for personal and professional profile is LinkedIn (Neville, 2008). LinkedIn combine a various set of web applications like TripIt, SribDB, and offer support for professional groups and forums.

These social networking websites offer many additional features like blogs and forums, where members can express themselves by designing their profile page to reflect their personality. The most popular extra features include music and video sections.

For client-server based systems some important distributed applications refers to web crawler (especially parallel crawling of the web) and search engine, such as Google, Yahoo. One of the most important uses of crawling the web is for indexing purposes and keeping web pages up-to-date, later used by search engine to serve the end user queries (Yadav et al., 2008). An example of this type of applications is WebCrawler. This web application integrate different web search engines and offer in a distributed way facilities for web pages, images, videos, news, yellow pages (like business, peoples, maps, mobile) and white pages (ZIP code lookup, phone and address lookup).

The **web crawling** is very difficult because of large volume of date available on the web and its rate of change, as there is a huge amount of pages being added, changed and removed every day. These aspects are considered in the presented application. Also, network speed has improved less than current processing speeds and storage capacities. The large volume implies that the crawler can only download a fraction of the Web pages within a given time, so it needs to prioritize it's downloads. The high rate of change implies that by the time the crawler is downloading the last pages from a site, it is very likely that new pages have been added to the site, or that pages that have already been updated or even deleted (Baeza-Yates & Poblete, 2003).

A **web search engine** consists of three parts: a crawler that retrieves web pages to be put into the engine's collection of web pages, an indexer that builds the inverted index and a query handler that answers user queries using the index. The most important issues for web search engines, according with the presented structure, refer to uniformly sampling of web pages, modeling the web graph, finding duplicate hosts, finding top gainers and losers in data streams, finding large dense bipartite graphs and understanding how eigenvectors partition the web. Another important aspect is page refreshment. Baeza-Yates & Poblete (2003) used a three-step algorithm for page refreshment, method used in many actually web search engine. This checks for whether the structure of a web page has been changed or not, the text content has been altered or whether an image is changed.

For a web user, it is difficult enough tracking down relevant and useful sites. Keeping up with changes to the pages is an important issue for monitoring changes on the web. For example **WebCQ** application can monitor and track various types of changes to static and dynamic web pages, personalize delivery of change notifications, summarization and prioritization of Web page changes, and web page structure analysis (Liu et al., 2000). The main principle behind WebCQ require object extraction algorithms are explored to locate, identify objects of interest in web pages, change detection algorithms are used to detect changes to arbitrary objects in the web pages of interest (Liu et al., 2002). There are used different algorithms to compute how a page is changed and what are the types of changes, mechanisms to provide richer and pleasant display of changes. The application also uses Proxy cache service for minimization of access latency and reduces the workload of remote information servers. For this application, a suite of efficient and scalable solutions to large scale information monitoring over structured or semi-structured data sources is considered (Tang, 2003).

PEER-TO-PEER APPLICATIONS

A peer-to-peer application runs on your machine, allowing you to connect directly to other users' machines and giving other users the ability to connect to your machine, in order to transfer

Figure 2. JXTA software architecture

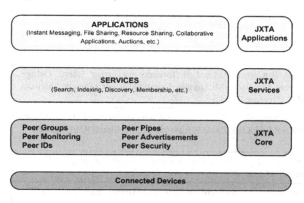

files back and forth between the machines. A peer-to-peer application is closer to peer-to-peer network structure that can be classified by what they can be used for: file sharing, telephony, media streaming (audio, video), discussion forums, etc. There are three key characteristics defining a P2P application: the ability to discover other peers, the ability to query other peers and the ability to share content with other peers. Kelaskar et al. in 2002 evaluate four discovery mechanisms (flooding and the forward routing algorithms CHORD, Pastry and CAN) against the requirements of three prevalent classes of peer-to-peer applications, and investigate the suitability of these mechanisms for the applications. So, to improve all described ability, especially discovery mechanisms, the solutions based on DHTs is considered. DHTs have been widely used for file sharing, but recent research and standardization efforts are exploring their use for interpersonal communication as well (Hautakorpi, 2007).

For **peer-to-peer application** it was investigated the architecture for decoupling the client server model prevalent in all of today's implementations of Linda Spaces (Fleckenstein, 1989). This is useful to make them applicable in P2P systems. Tentative suggestions of how this approach can be used in the real world application domain of telecoms management are illustrated and empirical

results of framework performance presented and discussed in (Parker & Cleary, 2005).

Like web-based applications, typical P2P software can be stack into three layers. The core layer that deals with peer establishment, communication management such as routing. The middle layer is a service layer that deals with higher-level concepts, such as indexing, searching, and file sharing. The top layer is for applications, such as emailing, auctioning, and storage systems. JXTA technology is designed to provide a framework for peer-to-peer application development based on these three layers (see Figure 2).

At the highest abstraction level, JXTA technology is a set of protocols. The defined protocols are: Peer Discovery Protocol, Peer Resolver Protocol, Peer Information Protocol, Peer Membership Protocol, Pipe Binding Protocol, Endpoint Routing Protocol, Networks and protocols. Each of these protocols is defined by one or more messages exchanged among participants of the protocol. **JXTA** technology is transport independent and can utilize TCP/IP as well as other transport standards (Boukerche et al., 2008). The JXTA Services developed using these protocols are: search, indexing, discovery and membership. The applications are developed based on these services.

One of the applications developed based on JXTA is Collanos Workplace (Teamwork software). It entails countless emails, messages, documents, tasks, comments, versions, revisions, approvals, etc, having a single space to share, interact and collaborate with your team. Other example is Sixearch. It is a collaborative peer network application, which aims to address the scalability and context limitations of centralized search engines and also provides a complementary way for Web search (Wu et al., 2009).

Table 4 presents an example of protocols and its' usage and some represented applications (Abbes & Dubacq, 2009).

Table 4.

Network or Protocol	Usage	Applications
Ares	File sharing	Ares Galaxy, Warez P2P, KCeasy
BitTorrent	File sharing / Software distribution / Media distribution	AllPeers, Vuze (formerly Azureus), BitComet, BitLord, BitTornado, BitTorrent, Burst!, Deluge, FlashGet, G3 Torrent, Halite, KTorrent, LimeWire, MLDonkey, Opera, QTorrent, rTorrent, Shareaza, TorrentFlux, Transmission, Tribler, µTorrent, Xunlei
Direct Connect	File sharing, chat	DC++, NeoModus Direct Connect, SababaDC, BCDC++, RevConnect, fulDC, LDC++, CzDC, McDC++, DCDM++, DDC++, iDC++, IceDC++, Zion++, R2++, rmDC++, LinuxDC++, LanDC++, ApexDC++, StrongDC++.
eDonkey	File sharing	aMule, eDonkey2000 (discontinued), eMule, eMule Plus, FlashGet, iMesh, Jubster, lMule, MLDonkey, Morpheus, Pruna, Shareaza, xMule
FastTrack	File sharing	giFT, Grokster, iMesh (and its variants stripped of adware including iMesh Light), Kazaa (and its variants stripped of adware such as Kazaa Lite), KCeasy, Mammoth, MLDonkey, Poisoned
Gnutella	File sharing	Acquisition, BearShare, Cabos, FilesWire, Gnucleus, Grokster, gtk-gnutella, iMesh, Kiwi Alpha, LimeWire, MLDonkey, Morpheus, MP3 Rocket, Poisoned, Shareaza, Swapper, XoloX
JXTA	Peer applications	Collanos Workplace (Teamwork software), Sixearch
Napster	File sharing	Napigator, Napster
OpenNap	File sharing	WinMX, Utatane, XNap, Napster
P2PTV	Video stream or file	TVUPlayer, Joost, CoolStreaming, Cybersky-TV, TVants, PPLive, LiveStation
Peer casting	Multicasting streams	PeerCast, IceShare, FreeCast, Rawflow
Usenet	Distributed discussion	See list of news clients
Windows Peer-to-Peer	Distributed peer application development, collaboration	Shipped with Advanced Networking Pack for Windows XP, Windows XP SP2, Windows Vista.

MOBILE APPLICATIONS

In the context of Internet evolution the mobile applications appeared as a people's necessity. An important challenge for **mobile applications** is represented by the running environment, which is in rapid and significant fluctuations in the context of Quality of Service. In the last years the mobile applications became very popular in the context of people's virtual connectivity.

A number of mobile applications have emerged that allow users to locate one another. An example of this type of applications is represented by PeopleFinder described by Sadeh et al. (2009), This application enables cell phone and laptop users to selectively share their locations with others (e.g. friends, family, and colleagues). **People-Finder** offers capability to find people by name, address, telephone number, age, birth, marriage etc. Another application that fall in this category is Tracesmart. It have revolutionized traditional people search techniques, replacing poor search engine tools with a fresh multi-source database providing instant access to tracing tools including official Electoral Rolls, both past and present, to help you find lost friends and family. Tracesmart have only a handful of people finder websites offering to find people instantly.

An important application that reclaims security issue in for a public environment is **MobileCampus**. It offers a wireless information query and messaging solution that complements radio system and gives campus security. For the administration, the tool shares information quickly and respond effectively to any on-campus incident. Closely to this application, in the educational field, the mobile applications based on communication environment allows students to access registrar records, enter enrollment information, obtain grades, etc (Wuthrich et al., 2003). An example of such application is Wateen – NOON (developed by WateenTech Inc.) The application helps university and students in their university life to follow and save data about semesters, courses, grades, schedule, etc. The application is free and runs on every mobile phone that supports Java applications.

Mobile social networking, such as crowdsourcing or twittering is another important category of mobile application. The category of mobile social networking also includes P2P concepts (Tsai et al., 2009). The convergence of mobile and P2P networking have generated increasing interest in the **mobile peer-to-peer** (MP2P) community. A very good example of such application is MoSoSo, that is a class of mobile applications whose scope is to support social interaction among interconnected mobile users. MoSoSo is to overlay a location and time element to the idea of digital networking. It enables users to find one another, in a particular vicinity and time, for social or business networking. The twittering applications are based on Twitter, which is a free social networking and micro-blogging service that enables its users to send and read messages. Twitter is also a popular micro-blogging tool (Java et al., 2007). Using this tool, peoples can restrict delivery to those in their circle of friends or, by default, allow open access and can send and receive tweets (message of up to 140 characters) via the Twitter website, SMS or external mobile applications.

Healthcare, such as emergency notification or body monitoring systems, is an important challenge for mobile devices and mobile applications. The healthcare applications have benefited from advances of wireless systems and the Ra-

dio Frequency Identification (**RFID**) tags are increasingly used in healthcare applications (Tu et al., 2009). So, with an increasing of healthcare services, providing a high degree of privacy to patients is becoming a major challenge due to: an increased number device, access points, switches and database, more threats to privacy and a higher expectation from society. A list of software packages and applications that correspond with described requirements are: Community Health Information Tracking System (CHITS), Electronic Medical Record (EMR) software, Veterans Administrations, Care2x - Hospital information system/practice management system/HER, district health management information system and data warehouse (DHIS), platform for management of human resources for health developed by Intra-Health International (iHRIS Suite).

Mobile Web and mobile web application frameworks (such as Mobile Ajax, Mobile Flash, J2ME, and others) refer to browser-based web services available on mobile devices (WAP or i-Mode in Japan). An example Web 2.0 technology used on the mobile web is the blog, resulting in the term moblog. Critics point to the difficulties of transferring Web 2.0 concepts such as open standards to the mobile web. An important aspect for mobile web browsers is emerging which try to solve the interaction problems that occur when small-screen devices are used to access web pages designed for large screen viewing (Shrestha, 2007). The problem is accentuated by the performance that was poor on mobile browser as users expected similar experience as on desktop.

A large set of mobile applications are included in **Google Mobile Platform**. The platform offers full of Google: search, e-mail, maps, talk, single sign-in for fast and easy access to your applications, automatically back up for contacts and emails, real-time synchronizing (contacts, emails, and calendar).

Another areas covered by mobile applications are: transportation, such as nav-sat systems or traffic congestion management, nnline mobile targeted advertising, m-commerce, mobile ticketing, m-retailing, mobile entertainment, mobile multimedia, mobile and context-aware games. On the other hand, the mobile applications could be used for personalization and context-aware applications.

For all type of described categories of mobile applications the behind services are very important. They refer to application lifecycle management, smartphone platforms (e.g. Windows Mobile, iPhone, Symbian, Android), adaptive, self-configuring applications, support for large-scale, scalable messaging and event processing, context-modeling and ontologies, middleware and distributed systems in support of mobile applications.

CONCLUSION

In one of his papers, Ian Foster, the parent of the Grid, said: "*I lead computer science projects developing advanced distributed computing (Grid) technologies, computational science efforts applying these tools to problems in areas ranging from the analysis of data from physics experiments to remote access to earthquake engineering facilities, and the Globus open source Grid software project*". We can affirm that the future of LSDS is the future of LSDS applications. Many universities and research centers support the LSDS, and are currently developing more applications for these systems.

Traditional applications based on standard model like web-based or Grid are used in LSDS represented the support for migration to P2P or mobile environment. The implications of LSDS computing on market depend on the risks and opportunities that this technology provides. Large-scale compute applications and also data intensive computing are solved using a single and unified resource. So Grid computing provides consistent, inexpensive access to computational resources (supercomputers, storage systems, data sources, instruments, and people) regardless of their physical location or access point.

REFERENCES

Abbes, H., & Dubacq, J. (2009). Analysis of Peer-to-Peer Protocols Performance for Establishing a Decentralized Desktop Grid Middleware. In E. César, M. Alexander, A. Streit, J. L. Träff, C. Cérin, A. Knüpfer, D. Kranzlmüller, & S. Jha (Eds.), Euro-Par 2008 Workshops - Parallel Processing: VHPC 2008, UNICORE 2008, HPPC 2008, SGS 2008, PROPER 2008, ROIA 2008, and DPA 2008, Las Palmas De Gran Canaria, Spain, August 25-26, 2008, Revised Selected Papers, Lecture Notes In Computer Science (pp. 235-246). Berlin, Heidelberg: Springer-Verlag.

Alameda, J., Christie, M., Fox, G., Futrelle, J., Gannon, D., & Hategan, M. (2007). The Open Grid Computing Environments collaboration: portlets and services for science gateways: Research Articles. *Concurr. Comput.: Pract. Exper*, *19*(6), 921–942. doi:10.1002/cpe.1078

Alexandrov, I., Amorim, A., Badescu, E., Barczyk, M., Burckhart-Chromek, D., Caprini, M., et al. (2002). OBK: an online high energy physics' meta-data repository. In *Proceedings of the 28th international Conference on Very Large Data Bases* (pp. 920-927). Hong Kong, China: VLDB Endowment.

Amin, K., von Laszewski, G., Hategan, M., Al-Ali, R., Rana, O., & Walker, D. (2006). An abstraction model for a Grid execution framework. *Journal of Systems Architecture*, *52*(2), 73–87. doi:10.1016/j.sysarc.2004.10.007

Baeza-Yates, R., & Poblete, B. (2003). Evolution of the Chilean Web structure composition, In *Proceedings of Latin American Web Conference* (pp. 11–13). Santiago, Chile: IEEE CS Press.

Boukerche, A., Zhang, M., & Xie, H. (2008). An Efficient Time Management Scheme for Large-Scale Distributed Simulation Based on JXTA Peer-to-Peer Network. In *Proceedings of the 2008 12th IEEE/ACM international Symposium on Distributed Simulation and Real-Time Applications 00(1)* (pp. 167-172). Washington, DC: IEEE Computer Society.

Bozzon, A., Comai, S., Fraternali, P., & Carughi, G. T. (2006). Conceptual modeling and code generation for rich internet applications. In *Proceedings of the 6th international Conference on Web Engineering, ICWE '06, 263*(1) (pp. 353-360). New York: ACM Press.

Buyya, R., Yeo, C. S., Venugopal, S., Broberg, J., & Brandic, I. (2009). Cloud computing and emerging IT platforms: Vision, hype, and reality for delivering computing as the 5th utility. *Future Generation Computer Systems, 25*(6), 599–616. doi:10.1016/j.future.2008.12.001

Cactus Project. (2009). *Open source problem solving environment*. Retrieved March 12, 2009, from http://www.cactuscode.org

Coles, J. (2005). The Evolving Grid Deployment and Operations Model within EGEE, LCG and GridPP. In *Proceedings of the First international Conference on E-Science and Grid Computing* (pp. 90-97). Washington, DC: IEEE Computer Society.

Deelman, E., Blythe, J., Gil, Y., & Kesselman, C. (2004). Workflow management in GriPhyN. In Nabrzyski, J., Schopf, J. M., & Weglarz, J. (Eds.), *Grid Resource Management: State of the Art and Future Trends* (pp. 99–116). Norwell, MA: Kluwer Academic Publishers.

Dewsbury, R. (2007). *Google Web Toolkit Applications* (1st ed.). Reading, MA: Addison-Wesley Professional.

Di Lucca, G. A., & Fasolino, A. R. (2006). Testing Web-based applications: The state of the art and future trends. *Information and Software Technology, 48*(12), 1172–1186. doi:10.1016/j.infsof.2006.06.006

Doake, J., & Duncan, I. (1998). Amber Metrics for the Testing and Maintenance of Object-Oriented Designs. In *Proceedings of the 2nd Euromicro Conference on Software Maintenance and Reengineering, Csmr '98* (pp. 205-208). Washington, DC: IEEE Computer Society.

Fleckenstein, C. J., & Hemmendinger, D. (February 1989). A parallel `make' utility based on Linda's tuple-space. In *Proceedings of the 17th Conference on ACM Annual Computer Science Conference, CSC '89* (pp. 216-220). New York: ACM Press.

GCE. (2009). *Grid Compute Environment (GCE) Research Group-Global Grid Forum*. Retrieved February 12, 2009, from http://www.computing-portals.org

Gordon, P. M., Kawas, E., Wilkinson, M., & Sensen, C. W. (November 2007). Using a Novel Data Transformation Technique to Provide the EMBOSS Software Suite as Semantic Web Services. In *Proceedings of the 2007 IEEE international Conference on Bioinformatics and Biomedicine, BIBM* (pp. 117-124). Washington, DC: IEEE Computer Society.

Gueorguieva, V. (2008). Voters, MySpace, and YouTube. *Social Science Computer Review, 26*(3), 288–300. doi:10.1177/0894439307305636

Gupta, A., Ludäscher, B., & Martone, M. E. (June 2003). BIRN-M: a semantic mediator for solving real-world neuroscience problems. In *Proceedings of the 2003 ACM SIGMOD international Conference on Management of Data, SIGMOD '03* (pp. 678-678). New York: ACM Press.

Haili, X., Hong, W., Xuebin, C., Sungen, D., & Honghai, Z. (2005). An implementation of interactive jobs submission for grid computing portals. In R. Buyya, P. Coddington, P. Montague, R. Safavi-Naini, N. Sheppard & A. Wendelborn (Eds.), *Proceedings of the 2005 Australasian Workshop on Grid Computing and E-Research* (pp. 67-70). Darlinghurst, Australia: Conferences in Research and Practice in Information Technology Series, Australian Computer Society.

Hautakorpi, J., & Camarillo, G. (December 2007). Evaluation of DHTs from the viewpoint of interpersonal communications. In *Proceedings of the 6th international Conference on Mobile and Ubiquitous Multimedia, MUM '07* (pp. 74-83). New York: ACM Press.

Hickson, I., & Hyatt, D. (2008). *A vocabulary and associated APIs for HTML and XHTML.* Retrieved February 21, 2009, from http://www.w3.org/html/wg/html5

IBIS. (2009). *IBIS project homepage.* Retrieved March 12, 2009, from http://www.cs.vu.nl/ibis

Java, A., Song, X., Finin, T., & Tseng, B. (August 2007). Why we twitter: understanding microblogging usage and communities. In *Proceedings of the 9th WebKDD and 1st SNA-KDD 2007 Workshop on Web Mining and Social Network Analysis, WebKDD/SNA-KDD '07* (pp. 56-65). New York: ACM Press.

Kacsuk, P., Kiss, T., & Sipos, G. (2008). Solving the grid interoperability problem by P-GRADE portal at workflow level. *Future Generation Computer Systems, 24*(7), 744–751. doi:10.1016/j.future.2008.02.008

Kelaskar, M., Matossian, V., Mehra, P., Paul, D., & Parashar, M. (May 2002). A Study of Discovery Mechanisms for Peer-to-Peer Applications. In *Proceedings of the 2nd IEEE/ACM international Symposium on Cluster Computing and the Grid, CCGRID* (pp. 444). Washington, DC: IEEE Computer Society.

Kra, D. (2006). *Six strategies for grid application enablement.* Retrieved February 18, 2009, from http://www.ibm.com

Kurowski, K., Ludwiczak, B., Nabrzyski, J., Oleksiak, A., & Pukacki, J. (2004). Dynamic grid scheduling with job migration and rescheduling in the GridLab resource management system. *Sci. Program., 12*(4), 263–273.

Liu, L., Pu, C., & Tang, W. (2000 November). WebCQ-detecting and delivering information changes on the web. In *Proceedings of the Ninth international Conference on information and Knowledge Management, CIKM '00* (pp. 512-519). New York: ACM Press.

Liu, L., Tang, W., Buttler, D., & Pu, C. (2002). Information Monitoring on the Web: A Scalable Solution. *World Wide Web (Bussum), 5*(4), 263–304. doi:10.1023/A:1021028509335

Menkens, C., Kjellin, N., & Davoust, A. (September 2007). IMS Social Network Application with J2ME compatible Push-To-Talk Service. In *Proceedings of the the 2007 international Conference on Next Generation Mobile Applications, Services and Technologies, NGMAST* (pp. 70-75). Washington, DC: IEEE Computer Society.

Mozo, A., & Salvachúa, J. (2008). Scalable tag search in social network applications. *Computer Communications, 31*(3), 423–436. doi:10.1016/j.comcom.2007.08.035

Neville, P. (2008). *Linkedin Top Success Secrets and Best Practices: Linkedin Experts Share the World's Greatest Tips.* London: Emereo Pty Ltd.

OGP. (2009). *Open Grid Portals.* Retrieved February 17, 2009, from http://www.opengridportals.org/space/start

Parker, D., & Cleary, D. (2005 January). Building Richer JXTA Applications with Collaborative Spaces in a Peer-2-Peer Environment. In *Proceedings of the Proceedings of the 38th Annual Hawaii international Conference on System Sciences, HICSS, Vol. 09* (pp. 301.2). Washington, DC: IEEE Computer Society.

Robinson, D. (2008). *Amazon Web Services Made Simple: Learn how Amazon Ec2, S3, SimpleDB and SQS Web Services Enables You to Reach Business Goals Faster*. London: Emereo Pty Ltd.

Sadeh, N., Hong, J., Cranor, L., Fette, I., Kelley, P., Prabaker, M., & Rao, J. (2009). Understanding and capturing people's privacy policies in a mobile social networking application. *Personal and Ubiquitous Computing, 13*(6), 401–412. doi:10.1007/s00779-008-0214-3

Shrestha, S. (2007 September). Mobile web browsing: usability study. In *Proceedings of the 4th international Conference on Mobile Technology, Applications, and Systems and the 1st international Symposium on Computer Human interaction in Mobile Technology, Mobility '07* (pp. 187-194). New York: ACM Press.

Sinnot, R. (2007). From access and integration to mining of secure genomic data sets across the Grid. *Future Generation Computer Systems, 23*(3), 447–456. doi:10.1016/j.future.2006.07.007

Soddemann, T. (2007). Science gateways to DEISA: user requirements, technologies, and the material sciences and plasma physics gateway. *Research Articles. Concurr. Comput.: Pract. Exper., 19*(6), 839–850. doi:10.1002/cpe.1082

Solomonides, T. (June 2008). Review of HealthGrid 2008: Global HealthGrid: eScience meets Biomedical Informatics. In *Proceedings of the 2008 21st IEEE international Symposium on Computer-Based Medical Systems* (pp. 342). Washington, DC: IEEE Computer Society.

Stamos, A., Thiel, D., & Osborne, J. (2008). Living in the RIA World: Blurring the Line between Web and Desktop Security. *iSEC Partners series.* Retrieved March 12, 2009, from http://www.isecpartners.com/files/RIA_World_BH_2008.pdf

Tang, W. (2003). *Internet-Scale Information Monitoring: a Continual Query Approach*. Doctoral Thesis. UMI Order Number: AAI3117949., Georgia Institute of Technology, US.

Tomiyasu, H., Maekawa, T., Hara, T., & Nishio, S. (April 2005). Social Network Applications using Cellular Phones with E-mail Function. *Proceedings of the 21st international Conference on Data Engineering Workshops, ICDEW* (pp. 1253). Washington, DC: IEEE Computer Society.

Tsai, F. S., Han, W., Xu, J., & Chua, H. C. (2009). Design and development of a mobile peer-to-peer social networking application. *Expert Systems with Applications, 36*(8), 11077–11087. doi:10.1016/j.eswa.2009.02.093

Tu, Y., Zhou, W., & Piramuthu, S. (2009). Identifying RFID-embedded objects in pervasive healthcare applications. *Decision Support Systems, 46*(2), 586–593. doi:10.1016/j.dss.2008.10.001

Windows Azure. (2009). *Windows Azure*. Retrieved February 07, 2009, from http://www.microsoft.com/azure

Wu, L., & Menczer, F. (2009). Diverse peer selection in collaborative web search. *Proceedings of the 2009 ACM Symposium on Applied Computing, SAC '09* (pp. 1709-1713). New York, NY: ACM Press.

Wuthrich, C., Kalbfleisch, G., Griffin, T., & Passos, N. (2003). On-line instructional testing in a mobile environment. *J. Comput. Small Coll., 18*(4), 23–29.

Yadav, D., Sharma, A. K., & Gupta, J. P. (2008). Parallel crawler architecture and web page change detection. *W. Trans. on Comp., 7*(7), 929–940.

Zheng, X. (2006). *Modeling Multi-Tier Web Applications for Testing and Maintenance*. Doctoral Thesis. UMI Order Number: AAI3222286. State University of New York at Albany.

About the Authors

Valentin Cristea (author and coordinator) is a professor of the Computer Science and Engineering Department of the University Politehnica of Bucharest (UPB). He teaches several courses on Distributed Systems and Algorithms. The course Distributed Computing in Internet delivered to master degree students is close to the subject of the proposed book. Also, as a PhD supervisor he directs several thesis on Grids and Distributed Computing. The co-authors of this proposal are among his former or actual PhD students. Valentin Cristea is Director of the National Center for Information Technology of UPB and leads the laboratories of Collaborative High Performance Computing and eBusiness. He is an IT Expert of the World Bank, Coordinator of national and international projects in IT, member of program committees of several IT Conferences (IWCC, ISDAS, ICT, etc), reviewer of ACM. He directs R&D projects in collaboration with multinational IT Companies (IBM, Oracle, Microsoft, Sun) and national companies (RomSys, UTI).

Ciprian Dobre, PhD, is assistant professor of the Computer Science and Engineering Department of the University Politehnica of Bucharest (UPB). The main fields of expertise are Grid Computing, Monitoring and Control of Distributed Systems, Modeling and Simulation, Networking, Parallel and Distributed Algorithms. He is involved in a number of national projects (CNCSIS, GridMOSI, MedioGRID, PEGAF) and international projects (MonALISA, MONARC, VINCI, VNSim, EGEE, SEE-GRID, EU-NCIT). He is actively collaborating with Oracle from which he received a PhD grant of excellence. His PhD thesis was oriented on Large Scale Distributed System Simulation. His research activities were awarded with the Innovations in Networking Award for Experimental Applications in 2008 by the Corporation for Education Network Initiatives (CENIC).

Corina Stratan, PhD, is a postdoctoral researcher in the Computer Systems Group at Vrije Universiteit Amsterdam, working on resource selection in large scale distributed systems. In 2008 she obtained a PhD in Computer Science from the University Politehnica of Bucharest, Romania; her PhD research was focused on monitoring and performance analysis in distributed systems. During the PhD studies she contributed to several national and international projects, and was a teaching assistant for courses like Parallel/Distributed Algorithms and Communication Protocols. She received IBM PhD Fellowship awards in 2006 and 2007 and worked as a summer intern at the IBM T.J. Watson Research Center.

Florin Pop, PhD, is assistant professor of the Computer Science and Engineering Department of the University Politehnica of Bucharest. His research interests are oriented to: scheduling in Grid environments (his PhD research), distributed system, parallel computation, communication protocols and numerical methods. He received his PhD in Computer Science in 2008 with "Magna cum laudae" distinction. He is member of RoGrid consortium and participates in several research projects in these domains, in collaboration with other universities and research centers from Romania and from abroad developer (in the national projects like CNCSIS, GridMOSI, MedioGRID and international project like EGEE, SEE-GRID, EU-NCIT). He has received an IBM PhD Assistantship in 2006 (top ranked 1st in CEMA out from 17 awarded students) and a PhD Excellency grant from Oracle in 2006-2008.

Alexandru Costan is a PhD student and Teaching Assistant at the Computer Science department of the University Politehnica of Bucharest. His research interests include: Grid Computing, Data Storage and Modeling, P2P systems. He is actively involved in several research projects related to these domains, both national and international, from which it worth mentioning MonALISA (in collaboration with Caltech and CERN), MedioGRID, EGEE, P2P-NEXT. His PhD thesis is oriented on Data Storage, Representation and Interpretation in Grid Environments. He has received a PhD Excellency grant from Oracle in 2006 and was awarded an IBM PhD Fellowship in 2009.

Index